Shojo Beat

# Natsume's BOOK of FRIENDS

**STORY** and **ART** by
**Yuki Midorikawa**

VOLUME **7**

Natsume's
# BOOK of FRIENDS

## VOLUME 7 CONTENTS



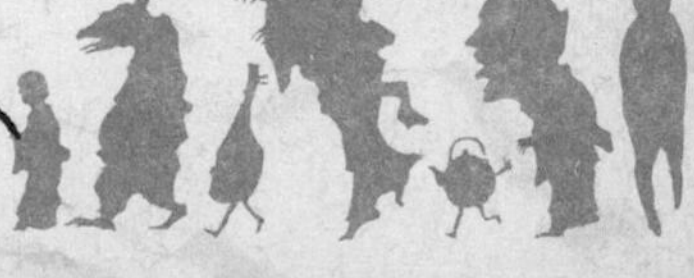

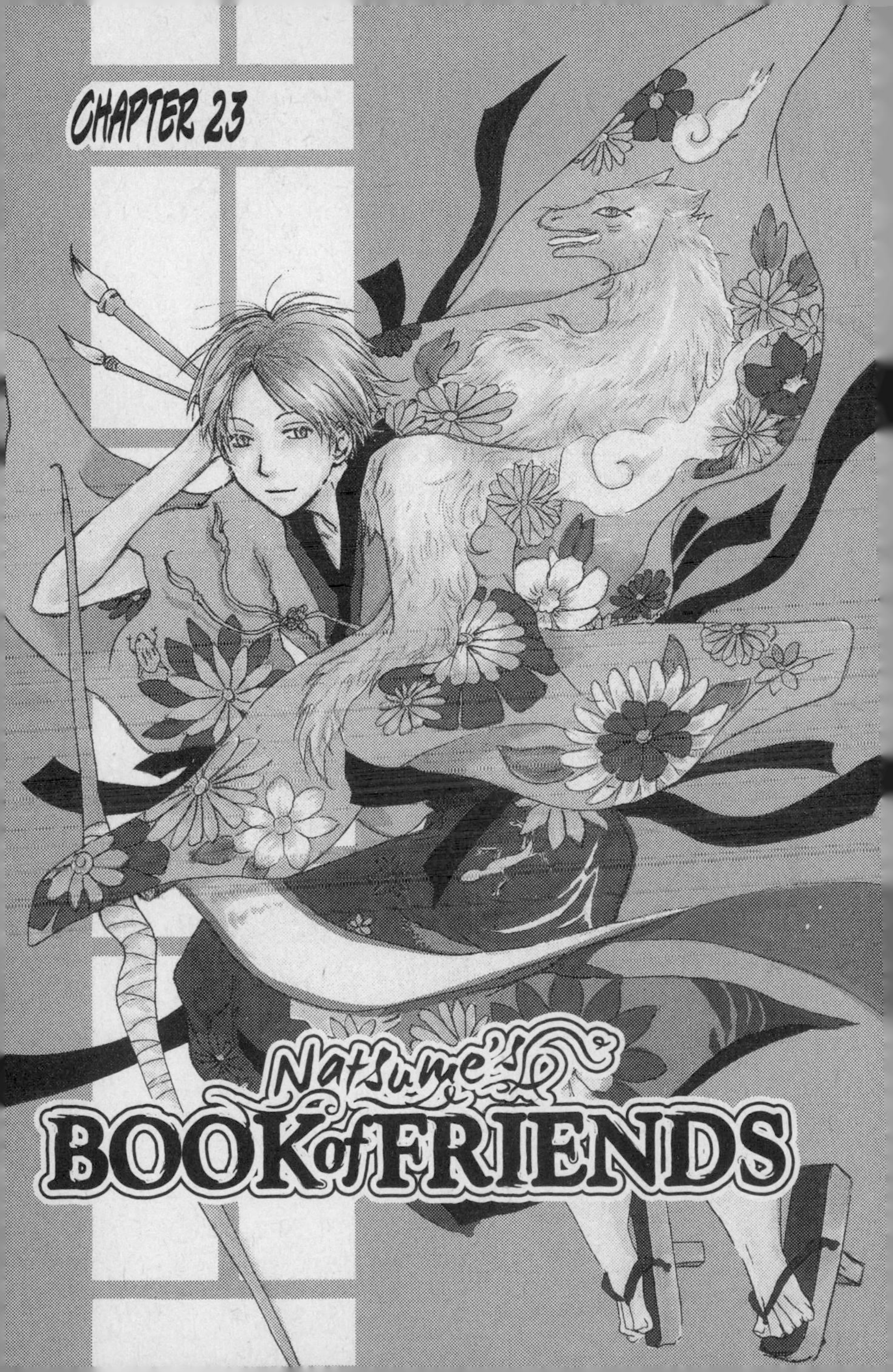
CHAPTER 23
Natsume's
BOOK of FRIENDS

Natsume's
# BOOK of FRIENDS
## CHARACTER GUIDE

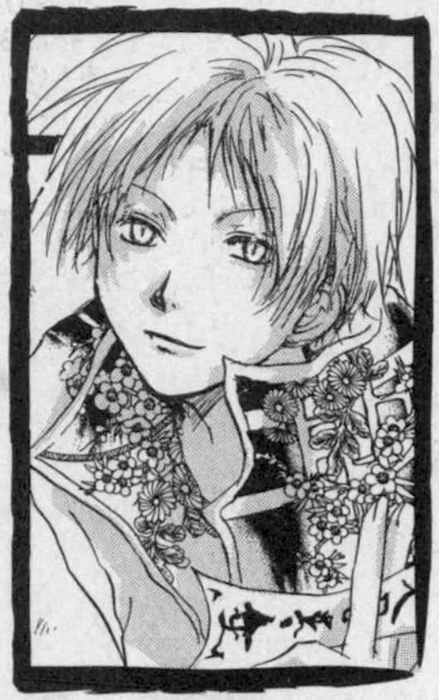

### Takashi Natsume
A lonely orphan with the ability to see the supernatural. He inherited the *Book of Friends* from his grandmother and currently lives with the Fujiwaras, to whom he is distantly related. Like his grandmother, he's powerful enough to subdue yokai with a single punch.

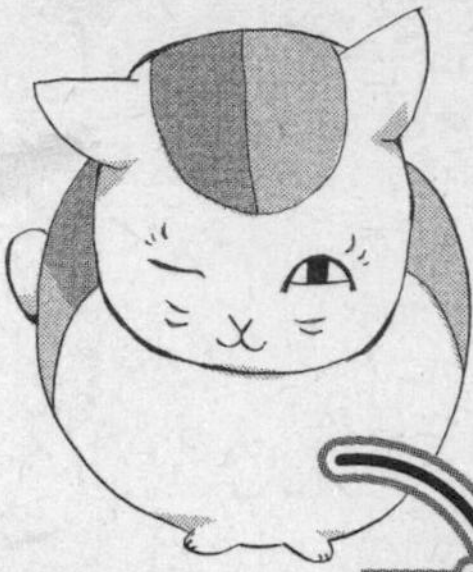

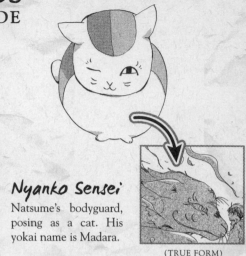

### Nyanko Sensei
Natsume's bodyguard, posing as a cat. His yokai name is Madara.

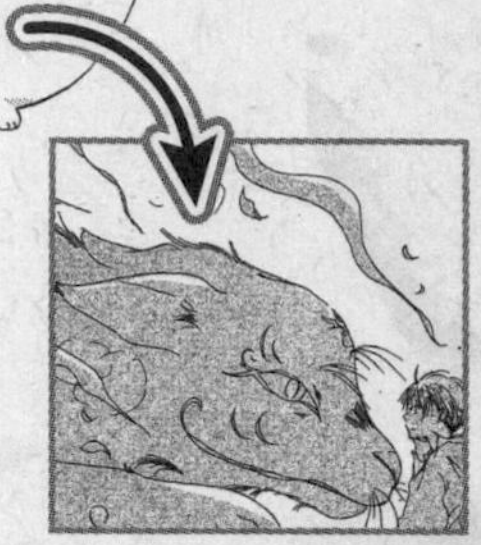

(TRUE FORM)

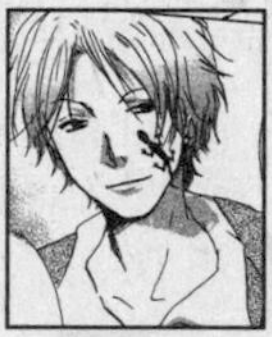

### Shuichi Natori
An exorcist and an actor. His gecko tattoo is actually a yokai that lives on his body.

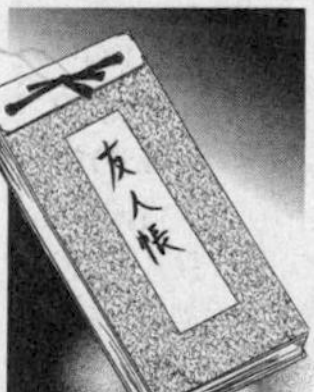

**The Book of Friends**
A collection of contracts put together by Reiko, Takashi's grandmother, that grants her mastery over the yokai who sign.

## THE STORY
Takashi Natsume has a secret sixth sense—he can see supernatural creatures called yokai. And ever since he inherited the *Book of Friends* from his grandmother, the local yokai have been coming after him. Takashi frees Nyanko Sensei from imprisonment and promises he will get the *Book* when Takashi dies. With his new bodyguard, Takashi leads a busy life returning names to yokai.

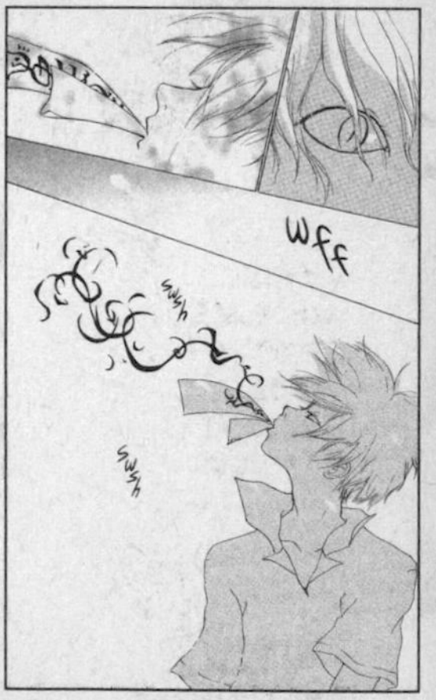
wff

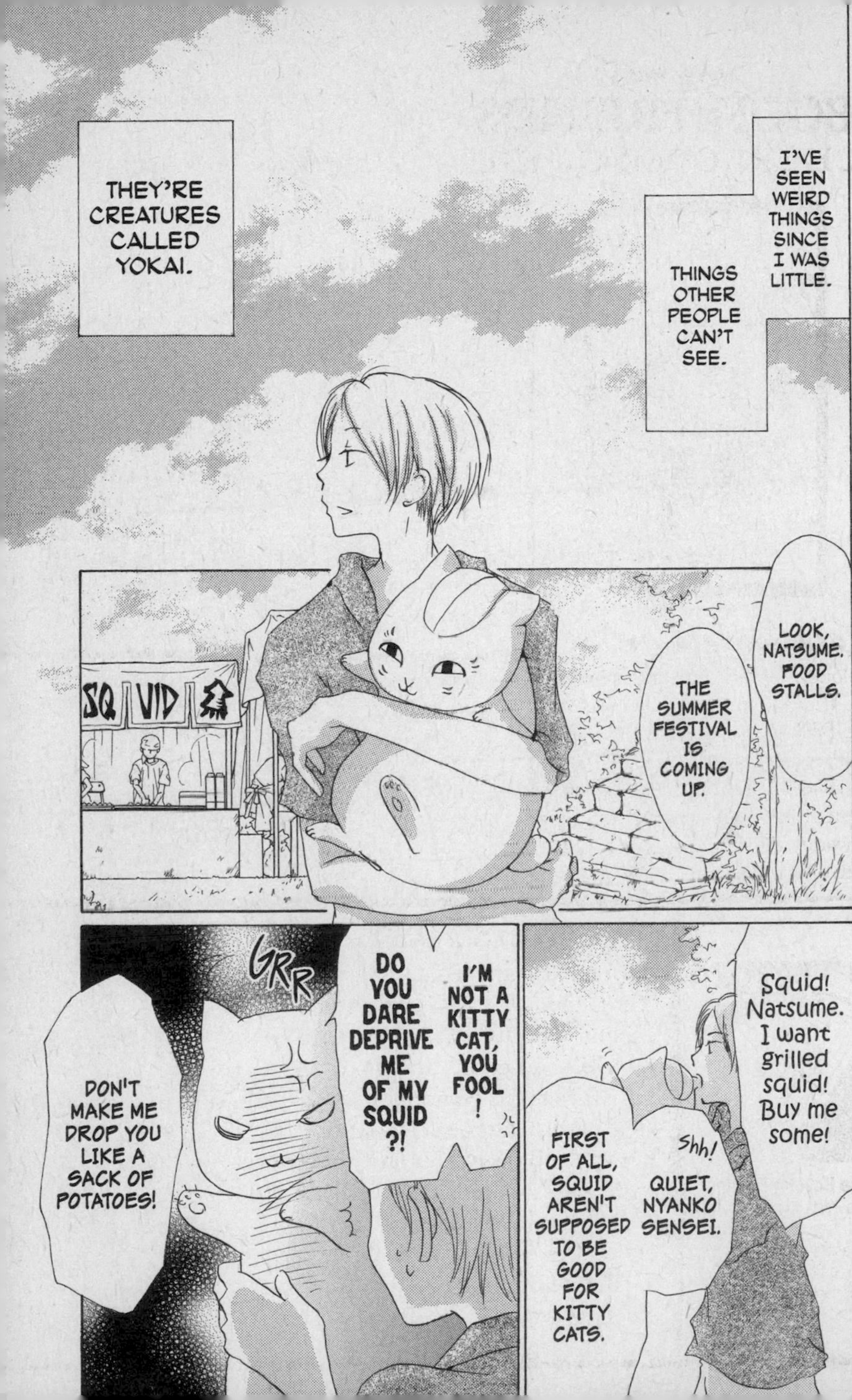
I'VE SEEN WEIRD THINGS SINCE I WAS LITTLE.
THINGS OTHER PEOPLE CAN'T SEE.
THEY'RE CREATURES CALLED YOKAI.
LOOK, NATSUME. FOOD STALLS.
THE SUMMER FESTIVAL IS COMING UP.
SQ VID
Squid! Natsume. I want grilled squid! Buy me some!
Shh!
QUIET, NYANKO SENSEI.
FIRST OF ALL, SQUID AREN'T SUPPOSED TO BE GOOD FOR KITTY CATS.
GRR
I'M NOT A KITTY CAT, YOU FOOL!
DO YOU DARE DEPRIVE ME OF MY SQUID?!
DON'T MAKE ME DROP YOU LIKE A SACK OF POTATOES!

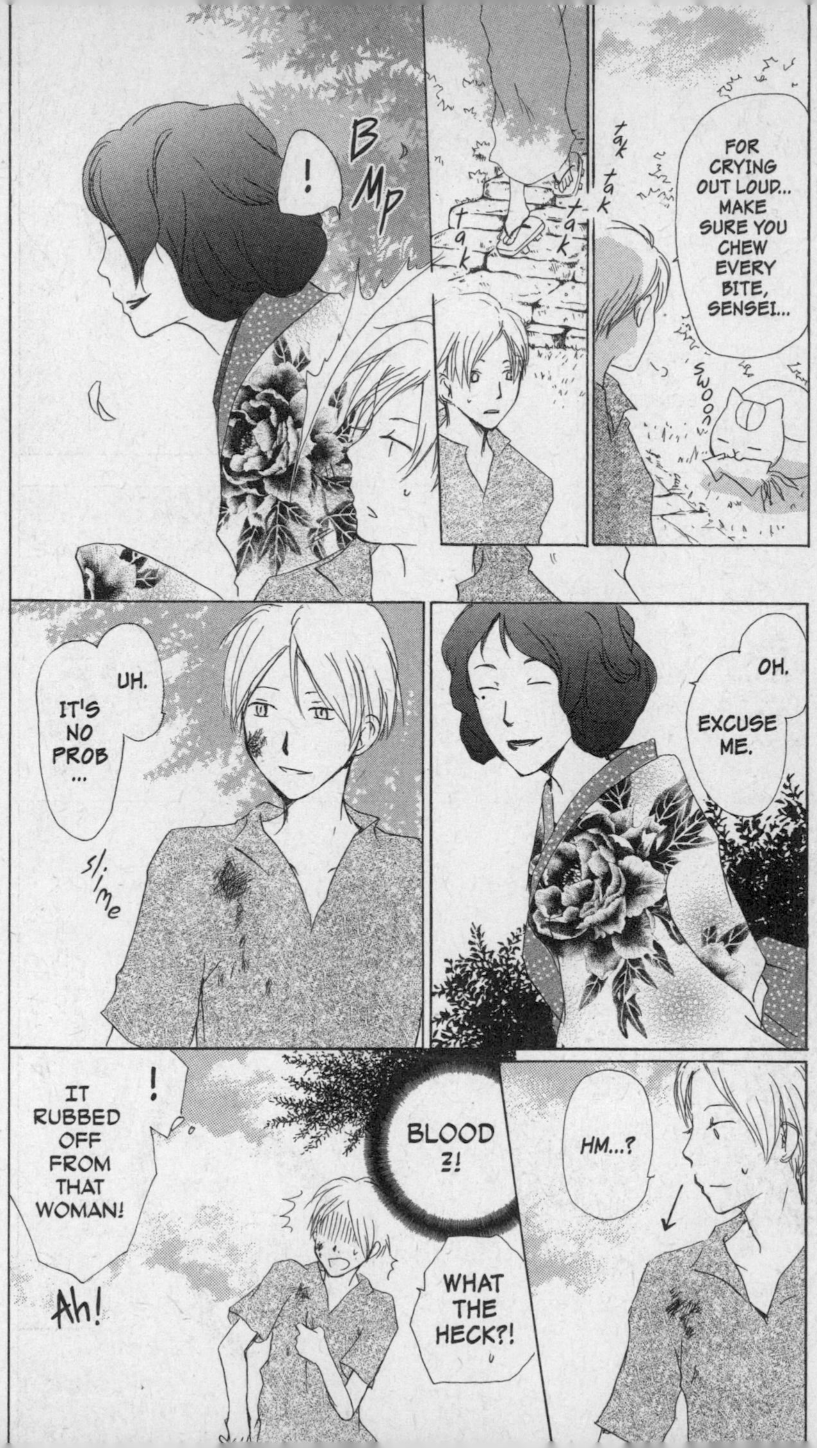
FOR CRYING OUT LOUD... MAKE SURE YOU CHEW EVERY BITE, SENSEI...
swoon
tak tak
tak tak
BMp
!
OH.
EXCUSE ME.
UH.
IT'S NO PROB ...
slime
HM...?
BLOOD?!
WHAT THE HECK?!
!
IT RUBBED OFF FROM THAT WOMAN!
Ah!

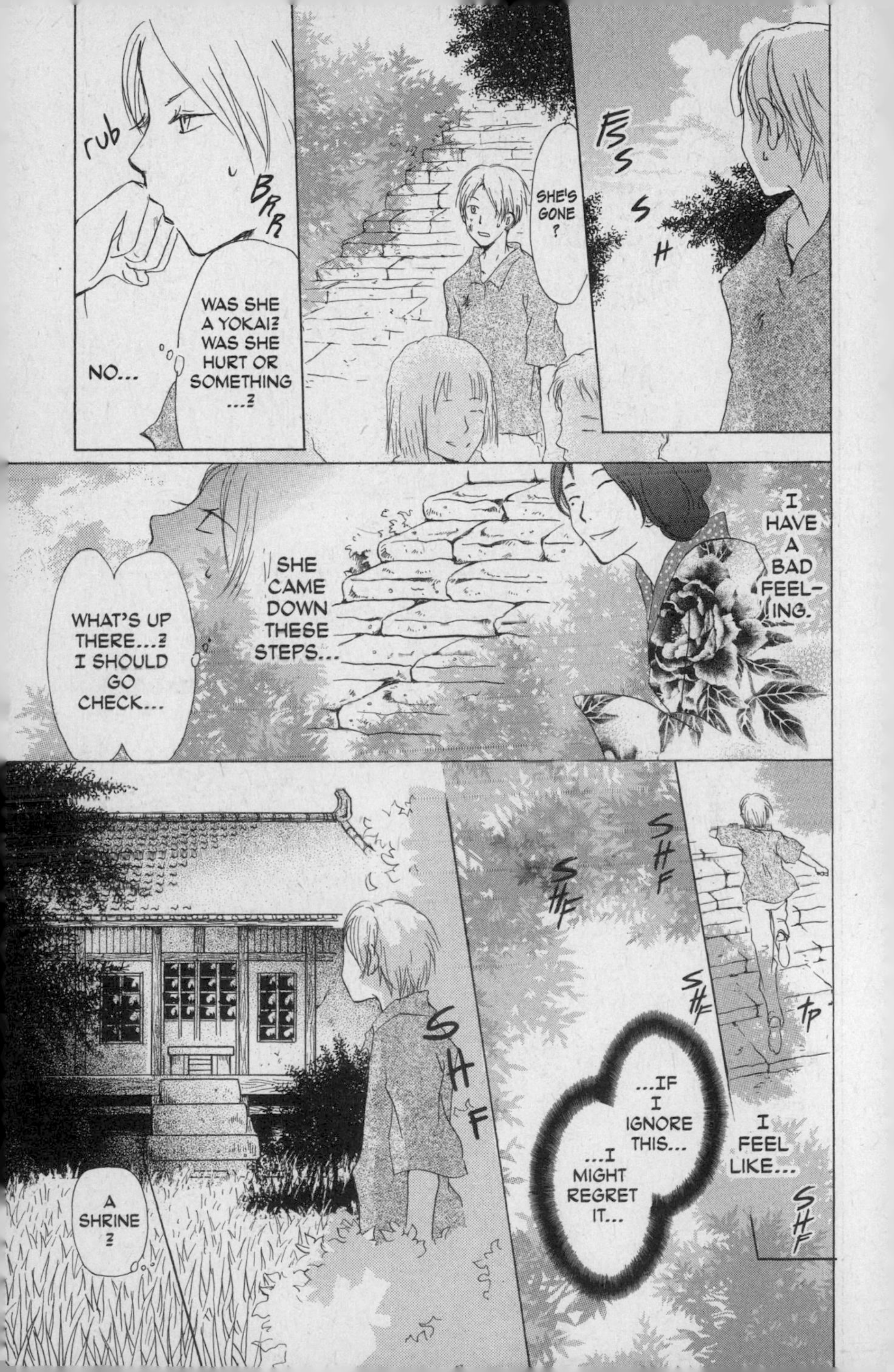
FSS
SH
SHE'S GONE?
rub
BRR
WAS SHE A YOKAI? WAS SHE HURT OR SOMETHING...?
NO...
I HAVE A BAD FEEL-ING.
SHE CAME DOWN THESE STEPS...
WHAT'S UP THERE...? I SHOULD GO CHECK...
SHF
SHF
SHF
tp
I FEEL LIKE...
...IF I IGNORE THIS...
...I MIGHT REGRET IT...
SHF
SHF
A SHRINE?

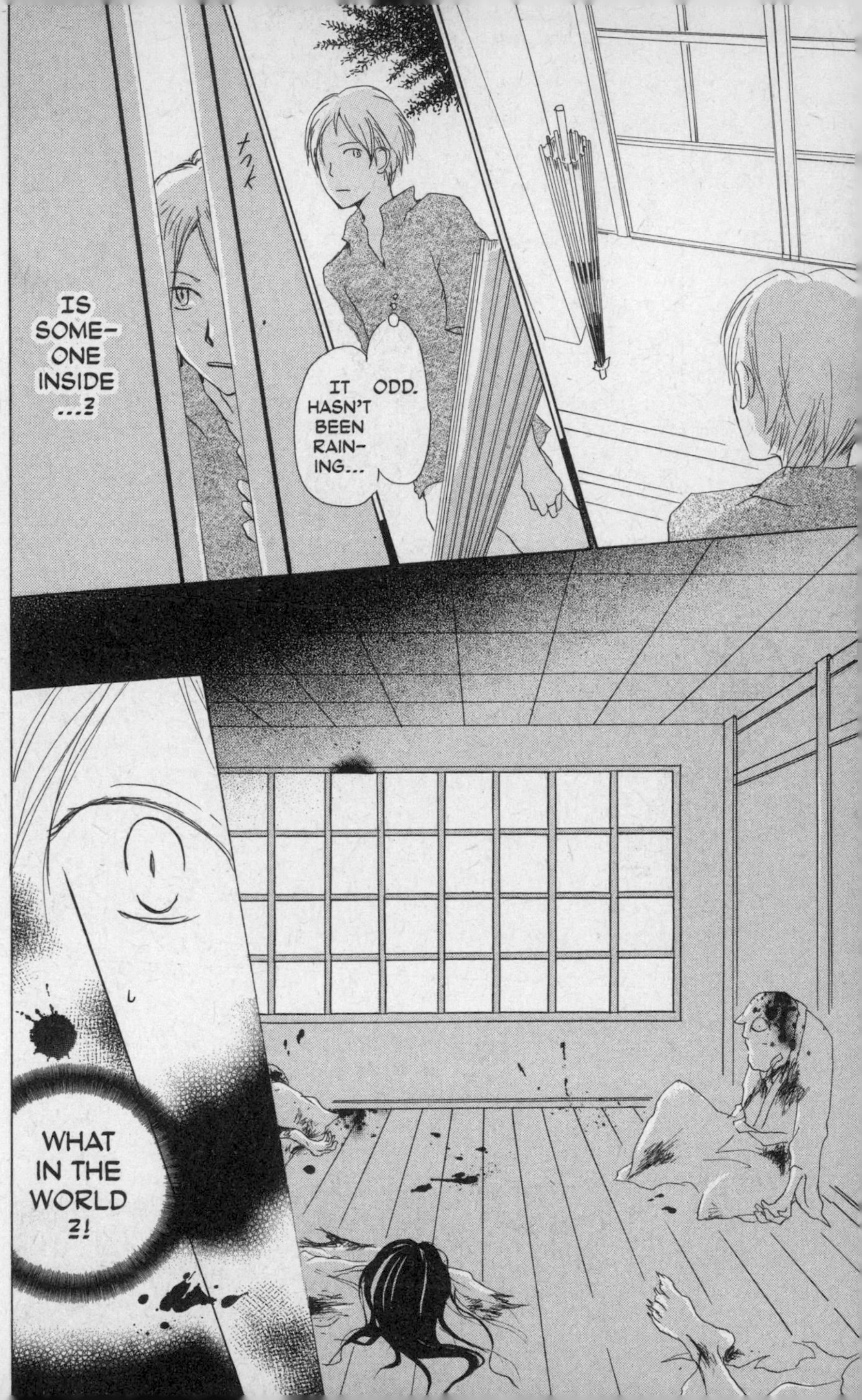
ODD.
IT HASN'T BEEN RAIN-ING...
IS SOME-ONE INSIDE ...?
WHAT IN THE WORLD ?!

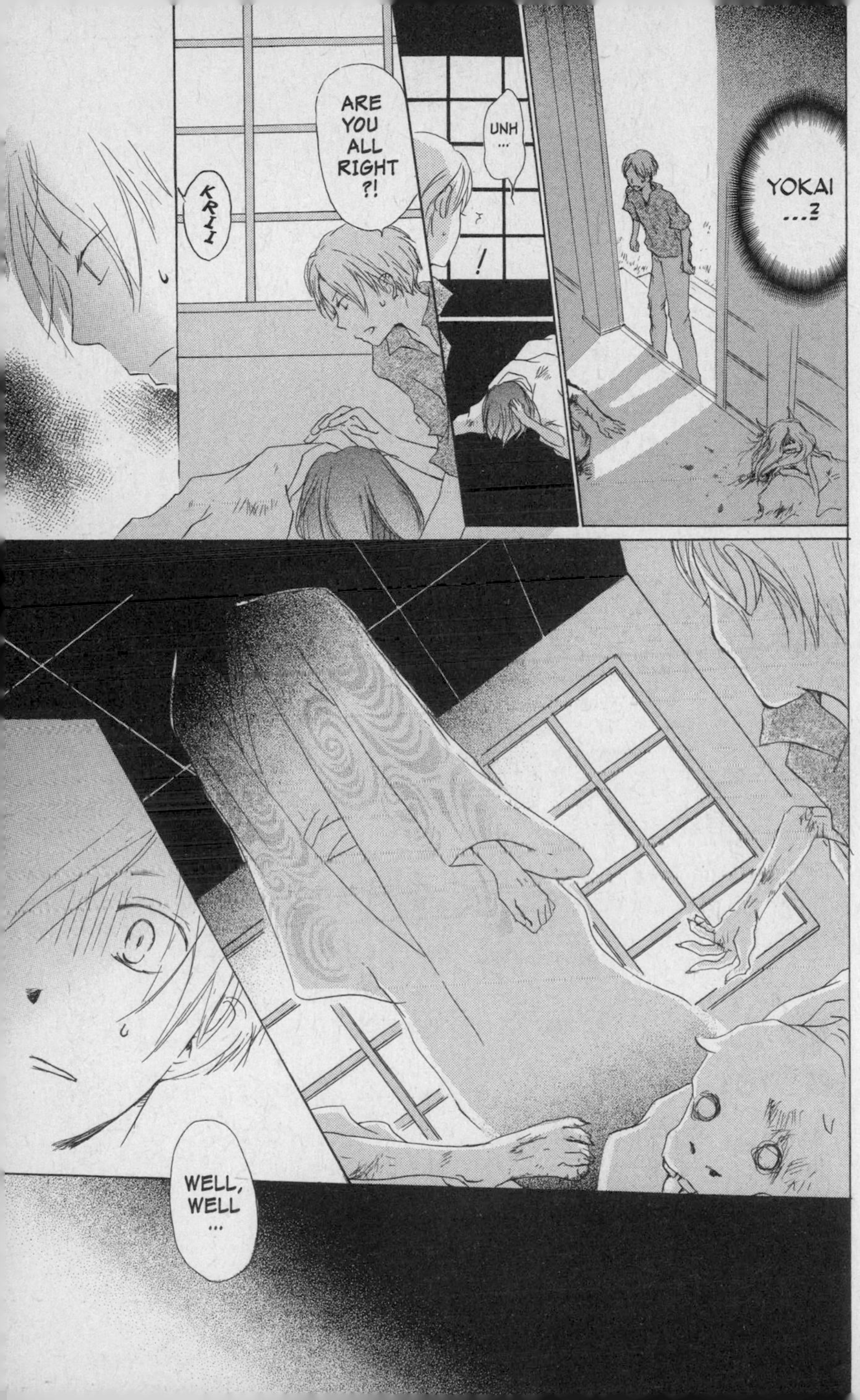
YOKAI ...?
UNH ...
!
ARE YOU ALL RIGHT ?!
KRII
WELL, WELL ...

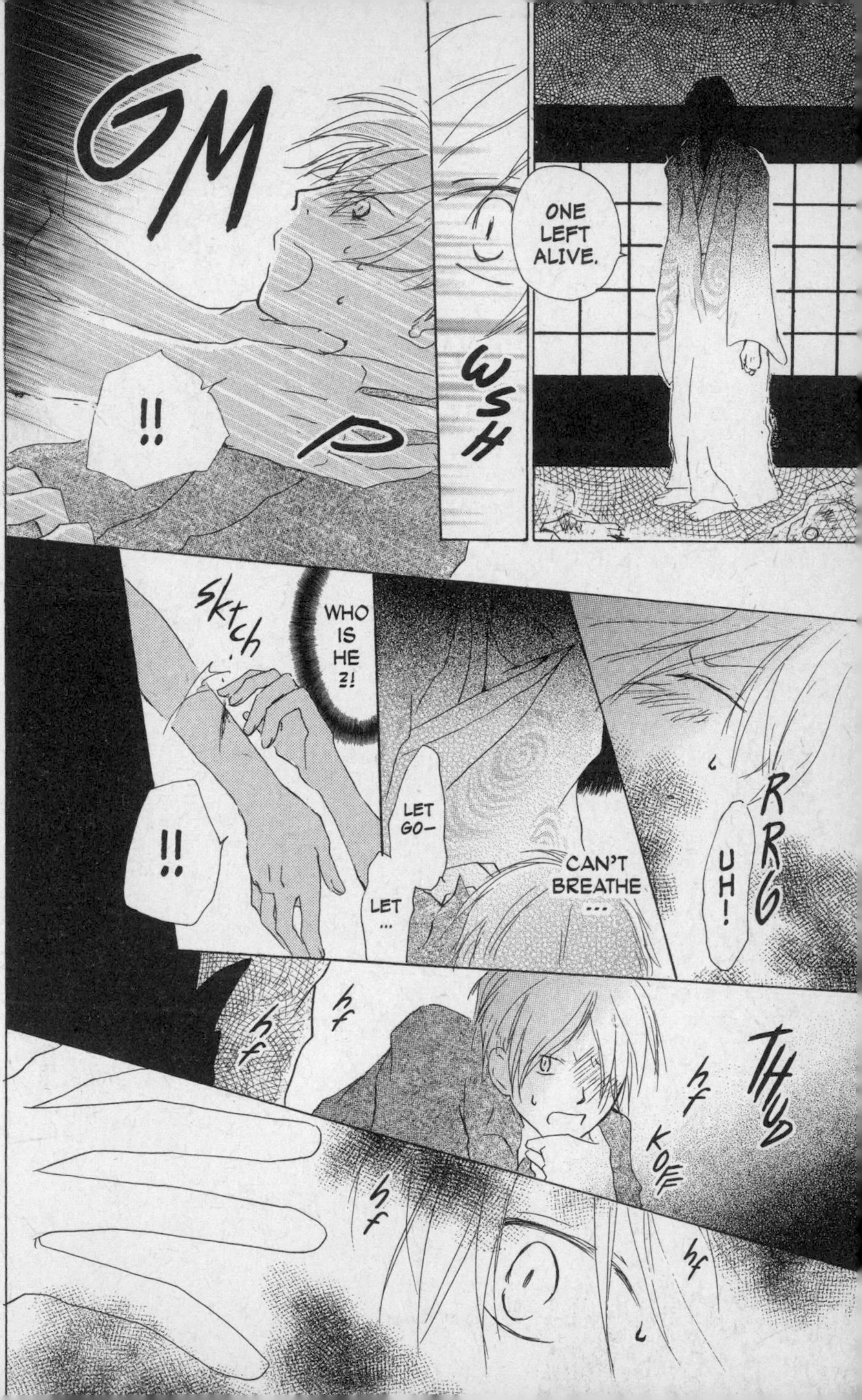

ONE LEFT ALIVE.
WSH
GM
P
!!
RRG
UH!
CAN'T BREATHE...
LET GO—
LET...
WHO IS HE?!
sktch
!!
THUD
hf
KOFF
hf
hf
hf
hf

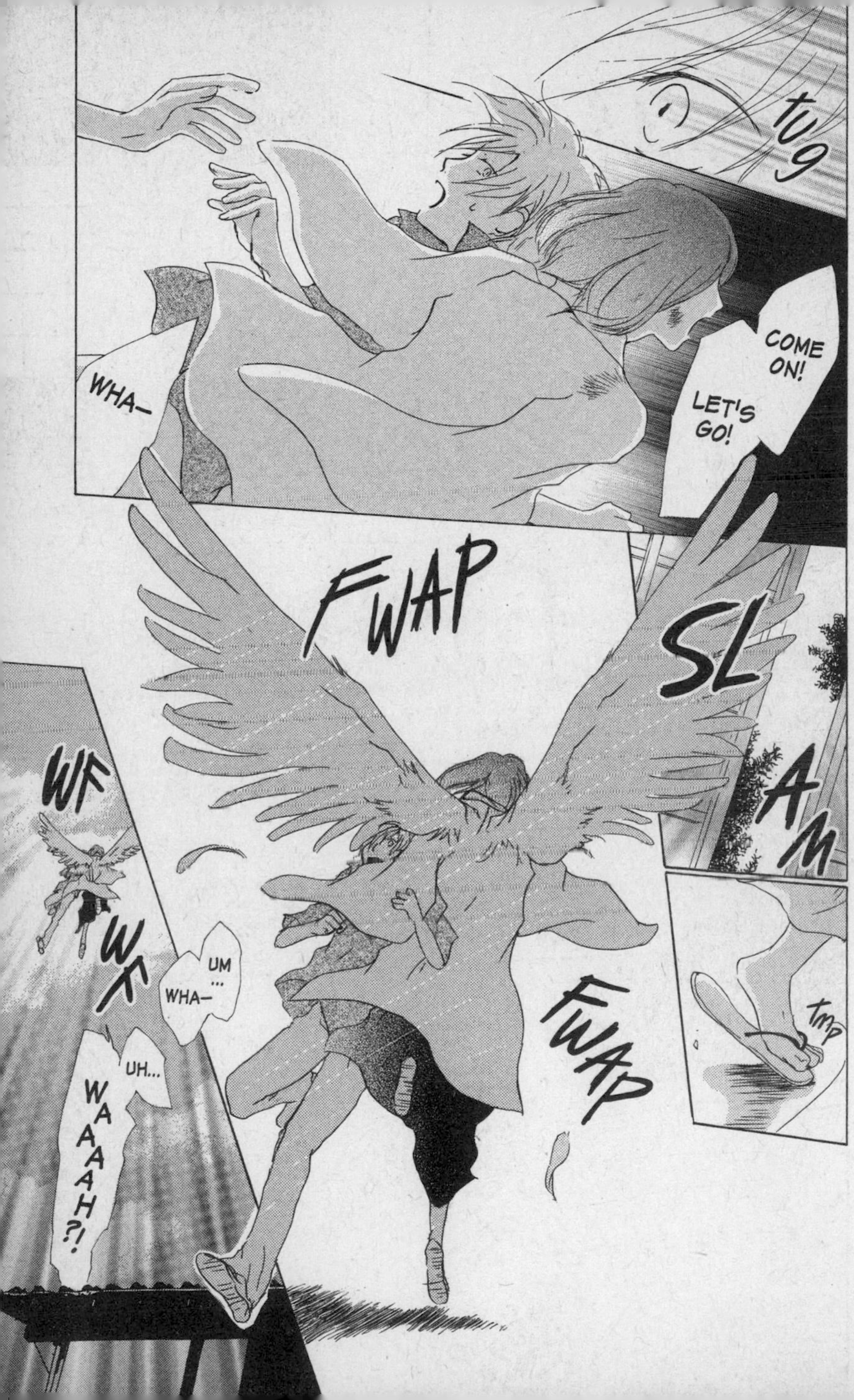
TUG
COME ON!
LET'S GO!
WHA-
SLAM
tmp
FWAP
FWAP
WF
WF
UM... WHA-
UH...
WAAAAH?!

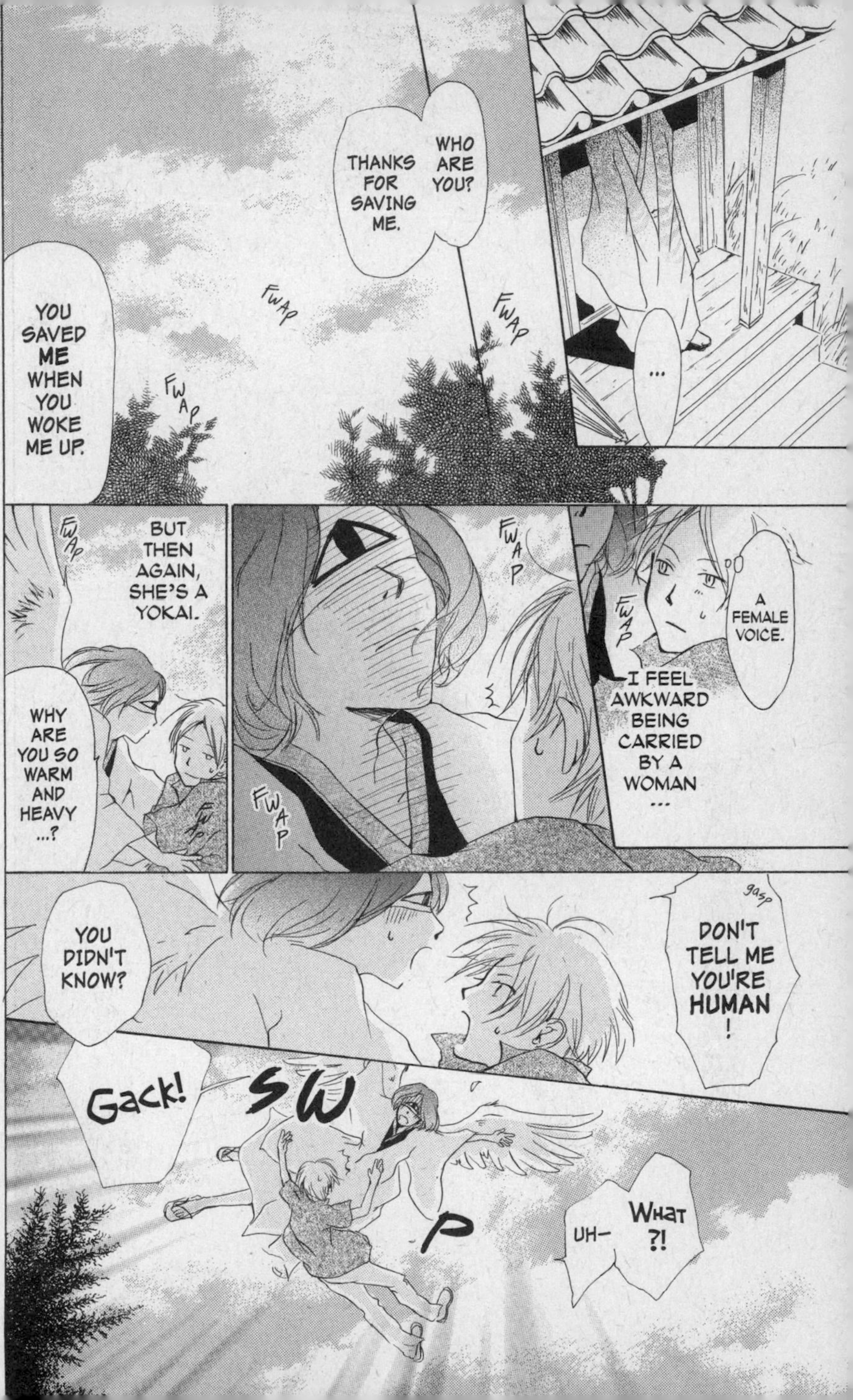
...
WHO ARE YOU?
THANKS FOR SAVING ME.
FWAP
FWAP
YOU SAVED ME WHEN YOU WOKE ME UP.
FWAP
A FEMALE VOICE.
FWAP
I FEEL AWKWARD BEING CARRIED BY A WOMAN...
FWAP
FWAP
BUT THEN AGAIN, SHE'S A YOKAI.
FWAP
WHY ARE YOU SO WARM AND HEAVY...?
FWAP
gasp
DON'T TELL ME YOU'RE HUMAN!
YOU DIDN'T KNOW?
WHAT?!
UH-
SWP
Gack!

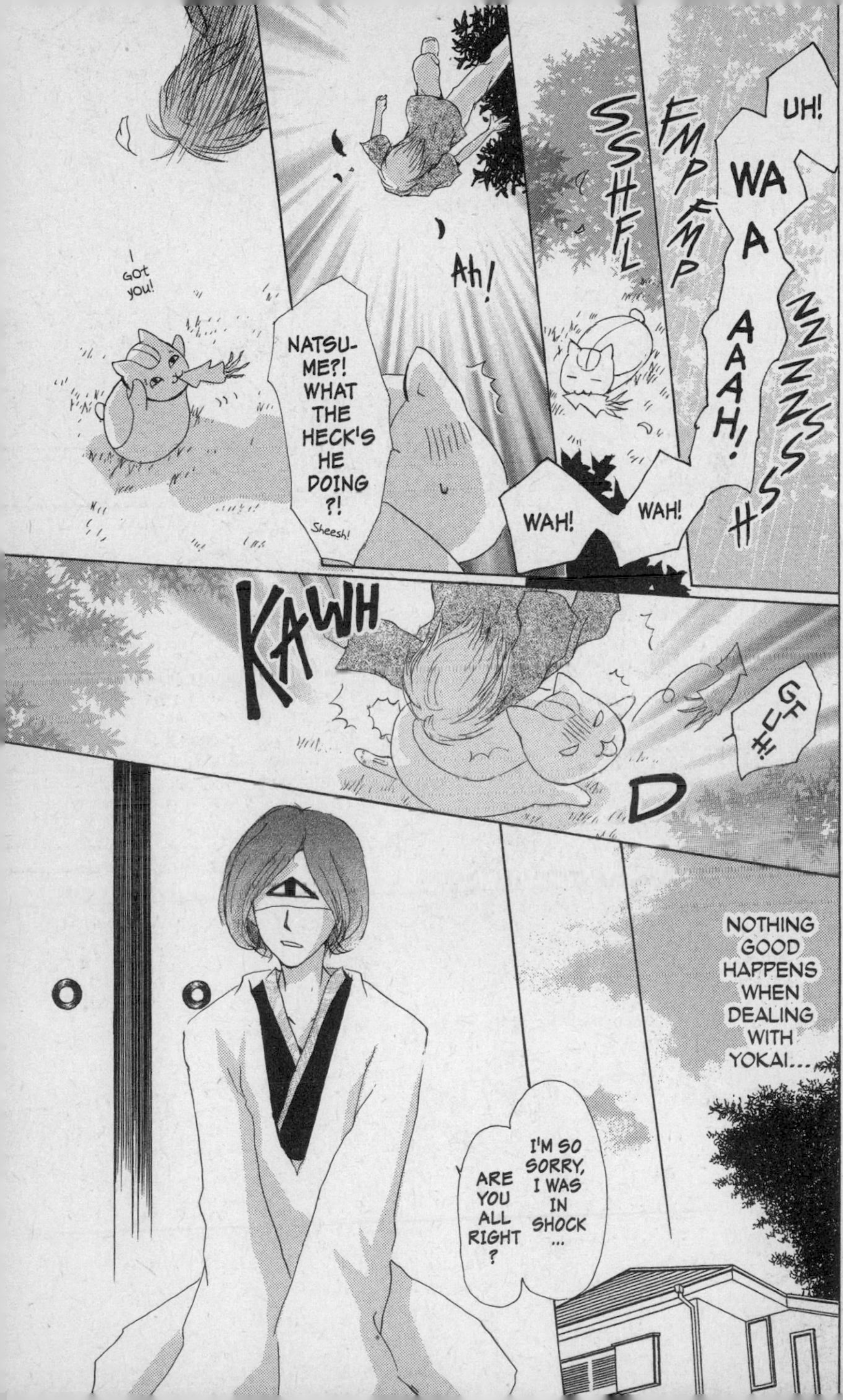
UH!
WAAAAAH!
ZZZZSSSH
FMP FMP FMP
SSHFL
Ah!
WAH!
WAH!
NATSUME?! WHAT THE HECK'S HE DOING?!
Sheesh!
I got you!
KAWH
GFUH!
D
NOTHING GOOD HAPPENS WHEN DEALING WITH YOKAI...
I'M SO SORRY, I WAS IN SHOCK...
ARE YOU ALL RIGHT?

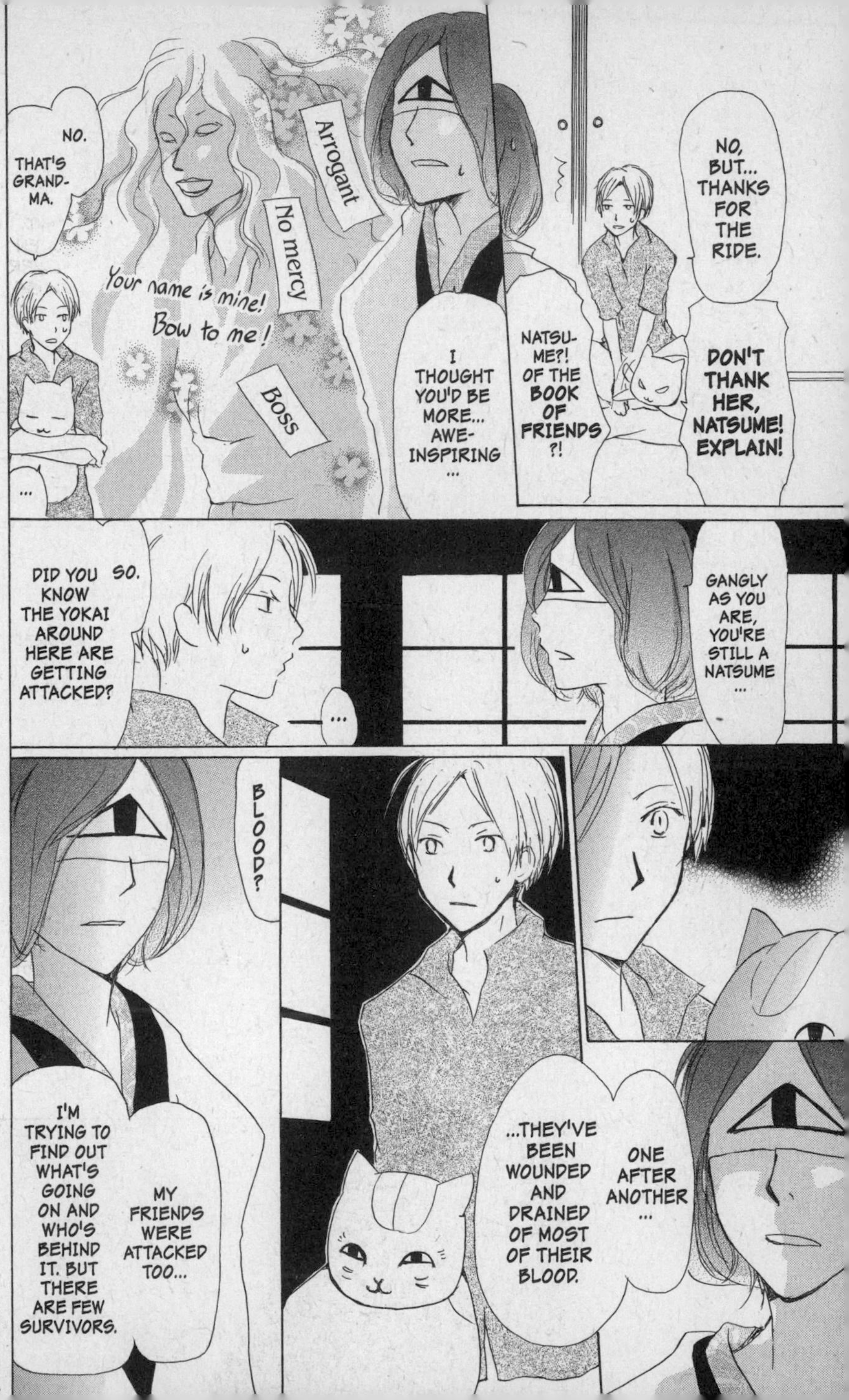
NO, BUT... THANKS FOR THE RIDE.
DON'T THANK HER, NATSUME! EXPLAIN!
NATSUME?! OF THE BOOK OF FRIENDS?!
I THOUGHT YOU'D BE MORE... AWE-INSPIRING...
Arrogant
No mercy
Your name is mine! Bow to me!
Boss
NO. THAT'S GRAND-MA.
...
GANGLY AS YOU ARE, YOU'RE STILL A NATSUME...
...
SO.
DID YOU KNOW THE YOKAI AROUND HERE ARE GETTING ATTACKED?
ONE AFTER ANOTHER...
...THEY'VE BEEN WOUNDED AND DRAINED OF MOST OF THEIR BLOOD.
BLOOD?
MY FRIENDS WERE ATTACKED TOO...
I'M TRYING TO FIND OUT WHAT'S GOING ON AND WHO'S BEHIND IT. BUT THERE ARE FEW SURVIVORS.

## 01

Hello, I'm Midorikawa. This is my 15th total graphic novel, and the seventh for Natsume.

I get so overwhelmed with emotion every time I write in this space. I don't even know how to thank everyone. I thought I'd get less nervous as I got older, but it looks like this is how I'm going to be for life. As usual, I might gush so much that my topics jump all over the place, but I hope you'll be patient with me.

I'd like to thank all my readers, editors, and the people in the editorial department for supporting me and making this possible.

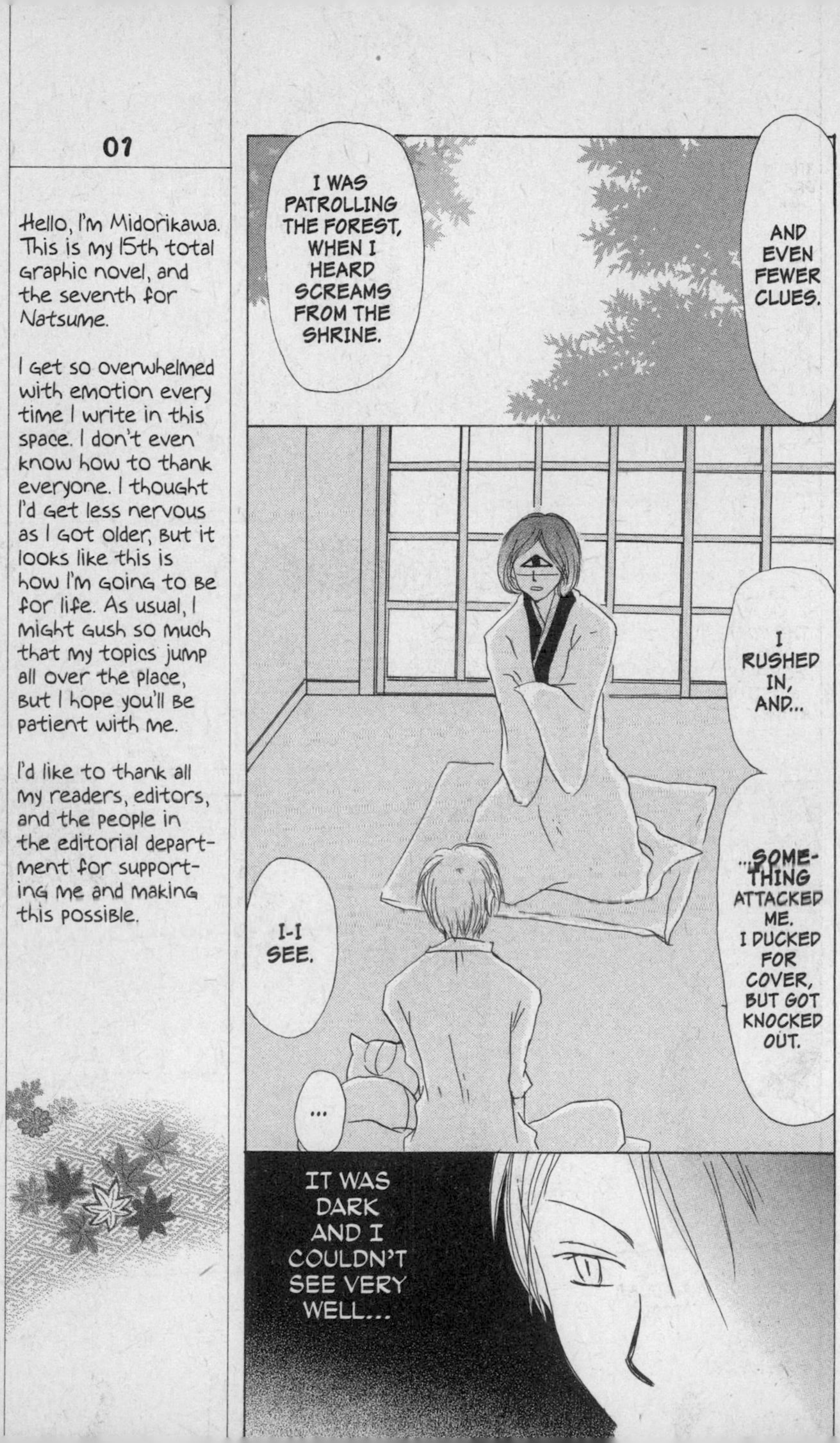
AND EVEN FEWER CLUES.
I WAS PATROLLING THE FOREST, WHEN I HEARD SCREAMS FROM THE SHRINE.
I RUSHED IN, AND...
...SOMETHING ATTACKED ME. I DUCKED FOR COVER, BUT GOT KNOCKED OUT.
I-I SEE.
...
IT WAS DARK AND I COULDN'T SEE VERY WELL...

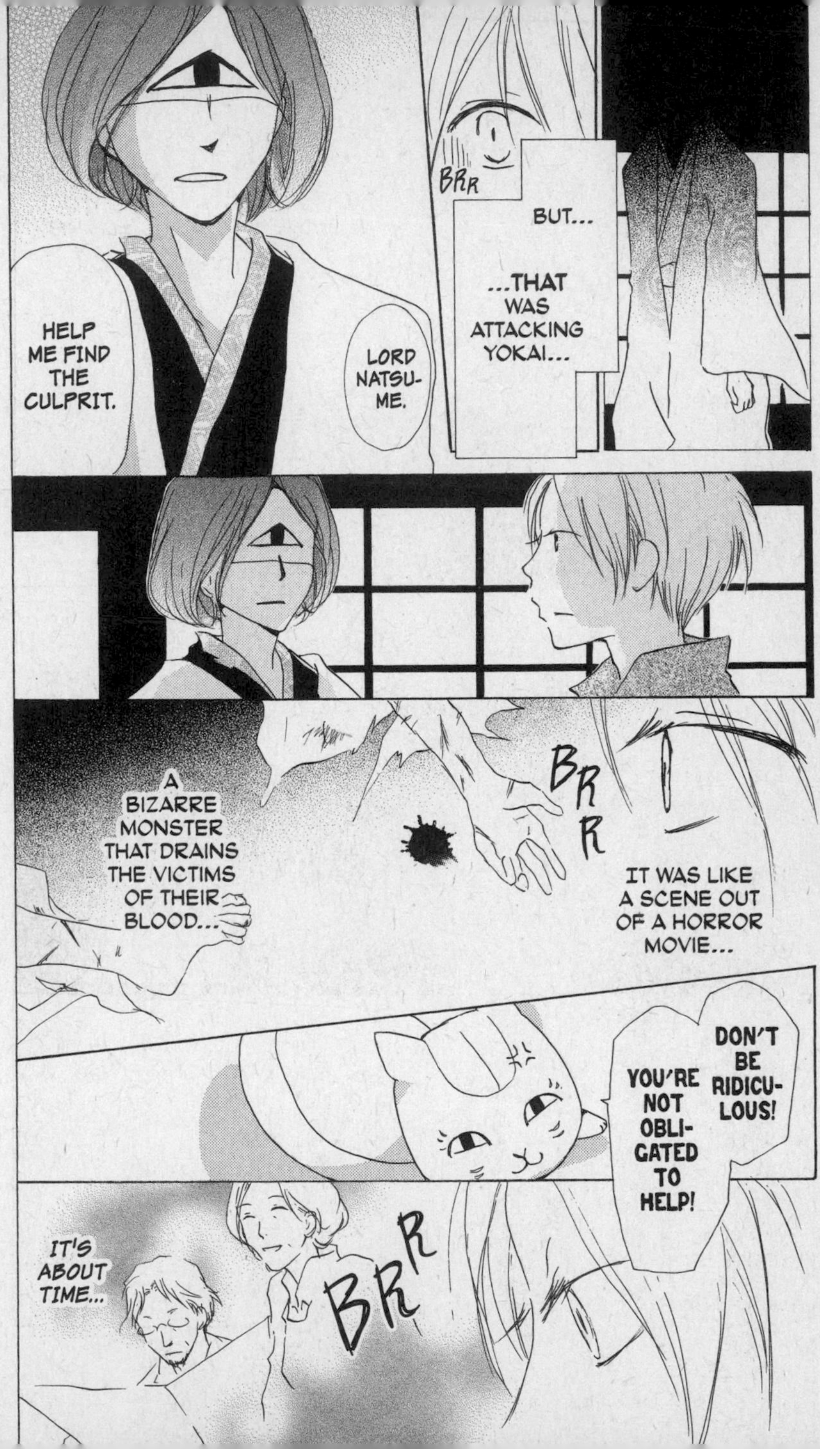
BRR
BUT...
...THAT WAS ATTACKING YOKAI...
LORD NATSUME.
HELP ME FIND THE CULPRIT.
BRR
IT WAS LIKE A SCENE OUT OF A HORROR MOVIE...
A BIZARRE MONSTER THAT DRAINS THE VICTIMS OF THEIR BLOOD...
DON'T BE RIDICULOUS!
YOU'RE NOT OBLIGATED TO HELP!
BRR
IT'S ABOUT TIME...

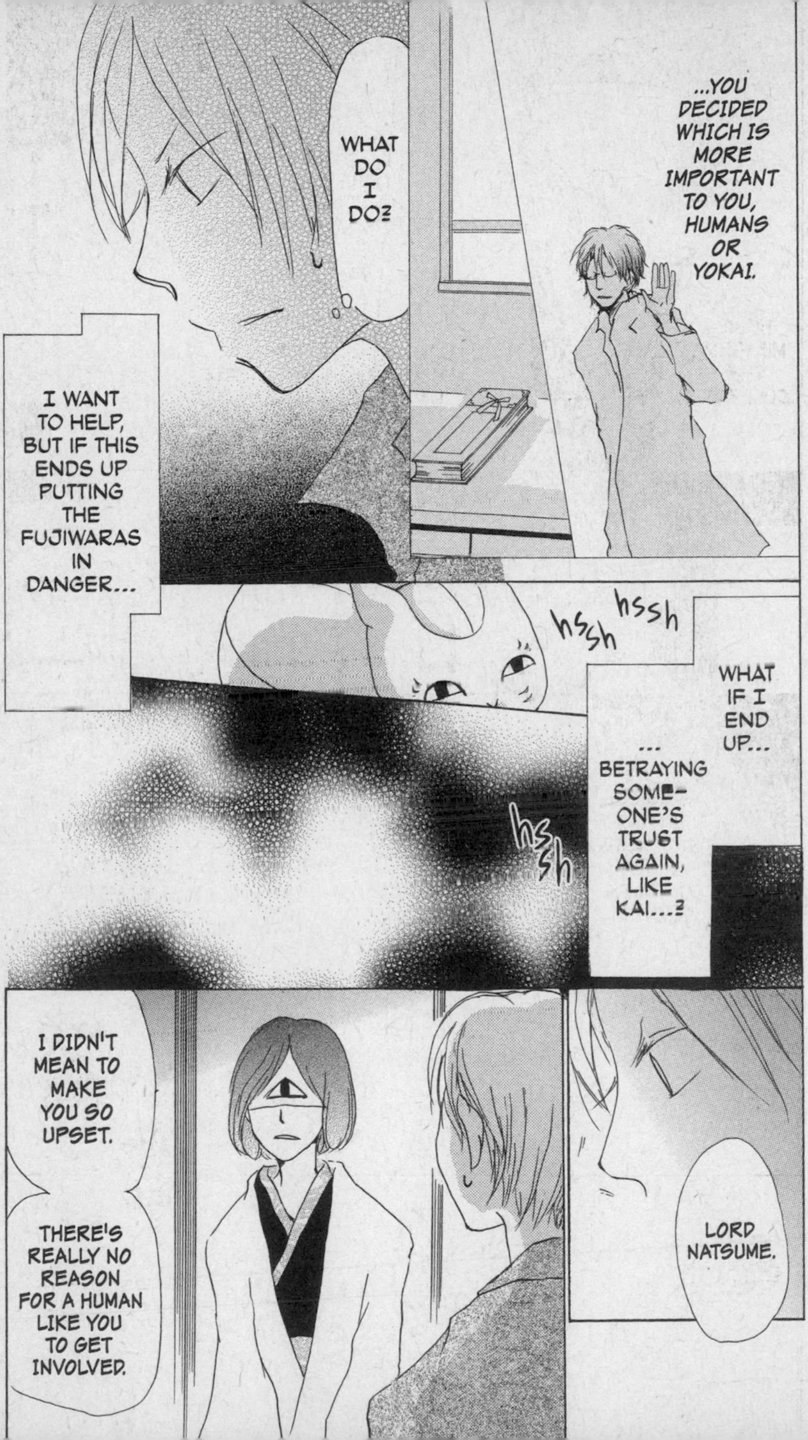

...YOU DECIDED WHICH IS MORE IMPORTANT TO YOU, HUMANS OR YOKAI.
WHAT DO I DO?
I WANT TO HELP, BUT IF THIS ENDS UP PUTTING THE FUJIWARAS IN DANGER...
hssh
hssh
WHAT IF I END UP...
...BETRAYING SOME-ONE'S TRUST AGAIN, LIKE KAI...?
hssh
LORD NATSUME.
I DIDN'T MEAN TO MAKE YOU SO UPSET.
THERE'S REALLY NO REASON FOR A HUMAN LIKE YOU TO GET INVOLVED.

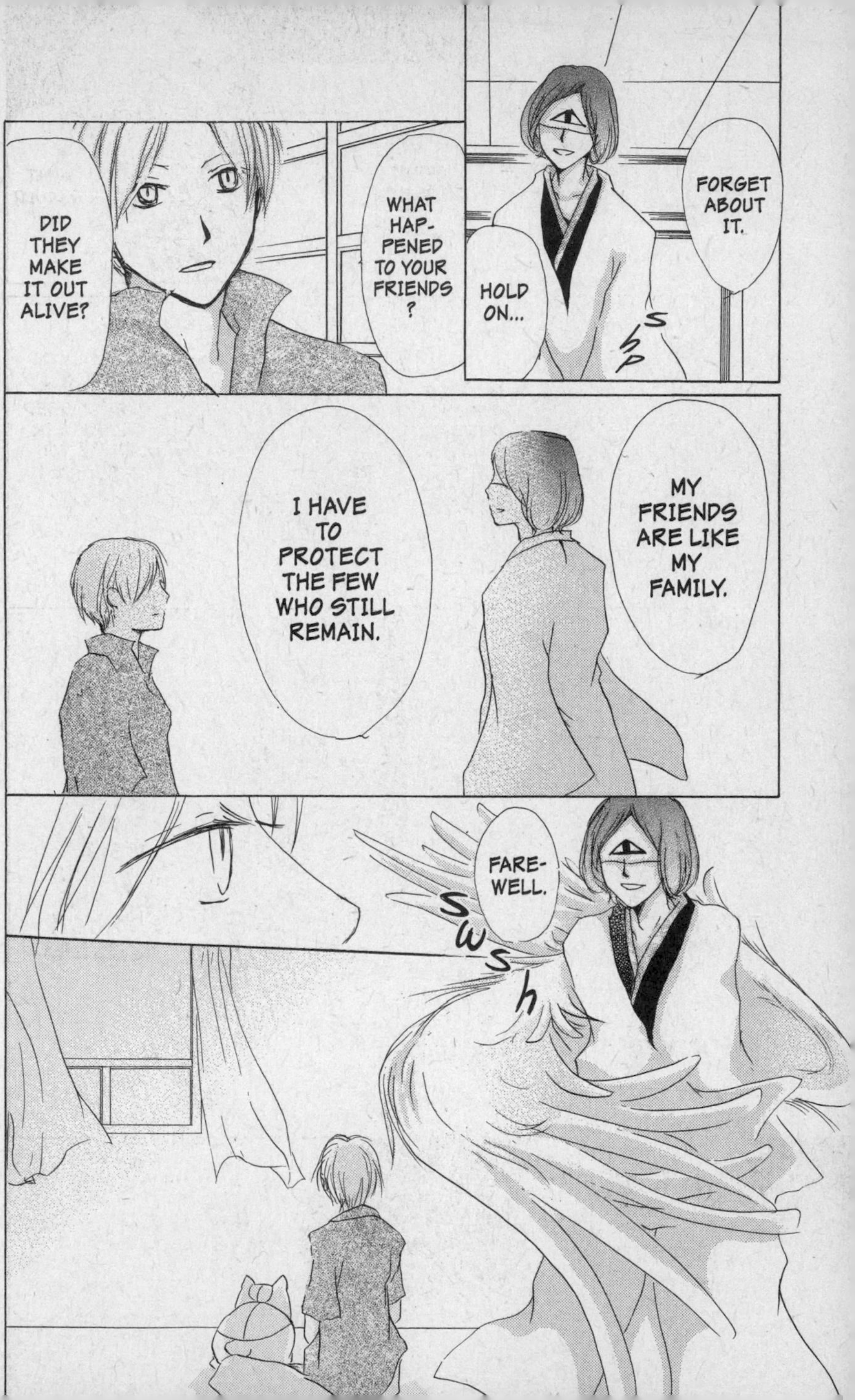
FORGET ABOUT IT.
SHP
HOLD ON...
WHAT HAP-PENED TO YOUR FRIENDS?
DID THEY MAKE IT OUT ALIVE?
MY FRIENDS ARE LIKE MY FAMILY.
I HAVE TO PROTECT THE FEW WHO STILL REMAIN.
FARE-WELL.
SWSH

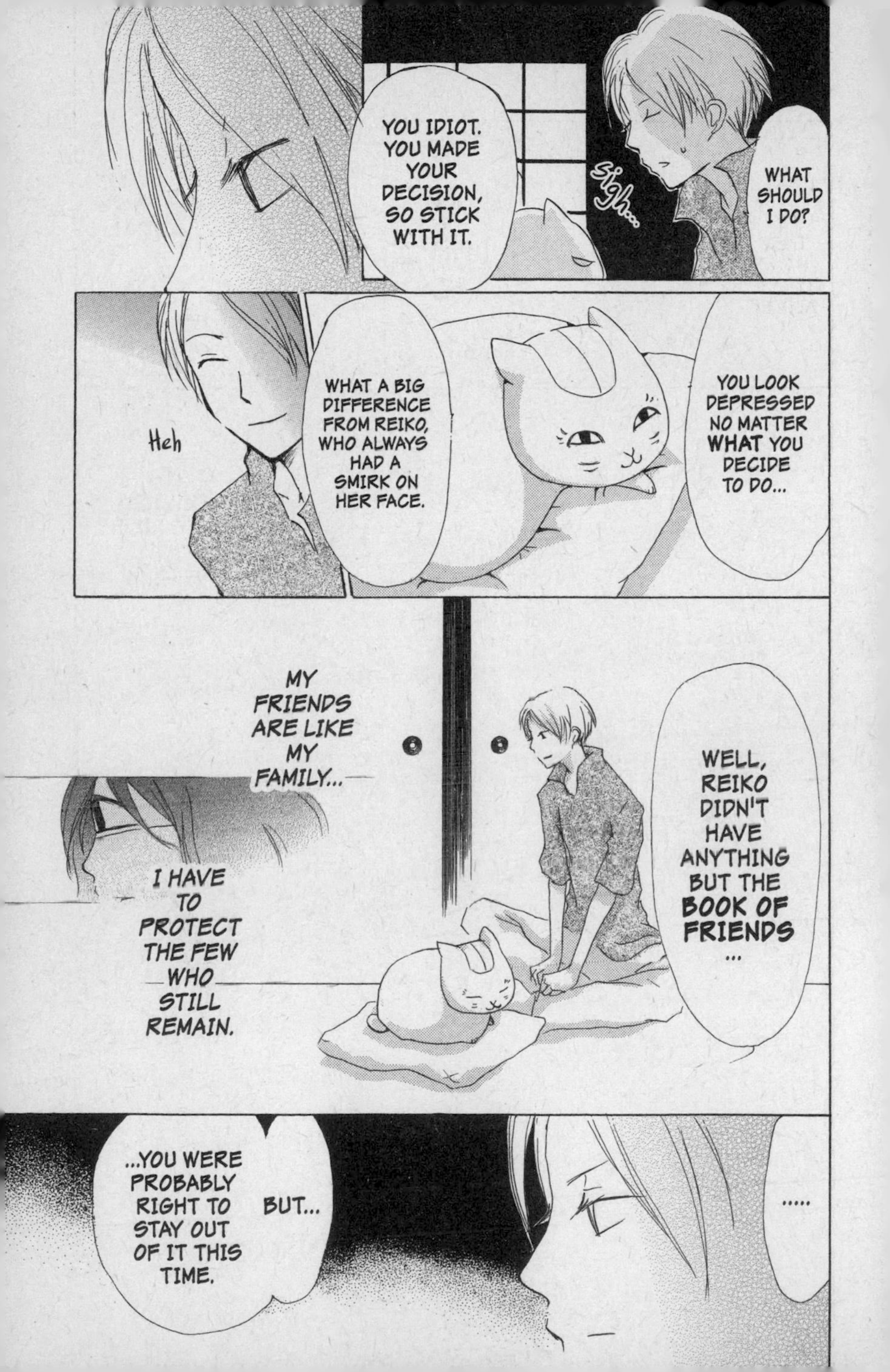

WHAT SHOULD I DO?
Sigh...
YOU IDIOT. YOU MADE YOUR DECISION, SO STICK WITH IT.
YOU LOOK DEPRESSED NO MATTER WHAT YOU DECIDE TO DO...
WHAT A BIG DIFFERENCE FROM REIKO, WHO ALWAYS HAD A SMIRK ON HER FACE.
Heh
WELL, REIKO DIDN'T HAVE ANYTHING BUT THE BOOK OF FRIENDS...
MY FRIENDS ARE LIKE MY FAMILY...
I HAVE TO PROTECT THE FEW WHO STILL REMAIN.
.....
BUT...
...YOU WERE PROBABLY RIGHT TO STAY OUT OF IT THIS TIME.

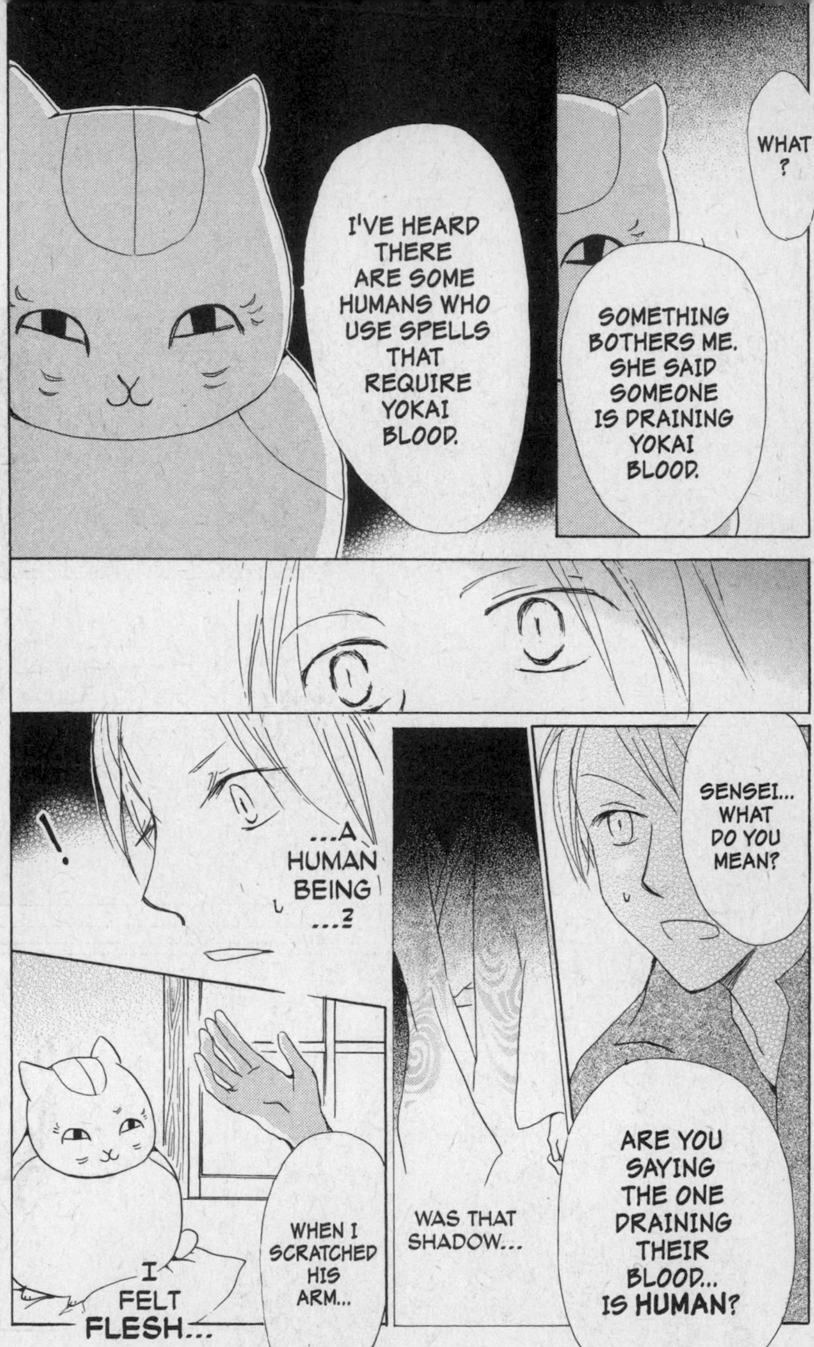
WHAT ?
SOMETHING BOTHERS ME. SHE SAID SOMEONE IS DRAINING YOKAI BLOOD.
I'VE HEARD THERE ARE SOME HUMANS WHO USE SPELLS THAT REQUIRE YOKAI BLOOD.
SENSEI... WHAT DO YOU MEAN?
ARE YOU SAYING THE ONE DRAINING THEIR BLOOD... IS HUMAN?
WAS THAT SHADOW...
!
...A HUMAN BEING ...?
WHEN I SCRATCHED HIS ARM...
I FELT FLESH...

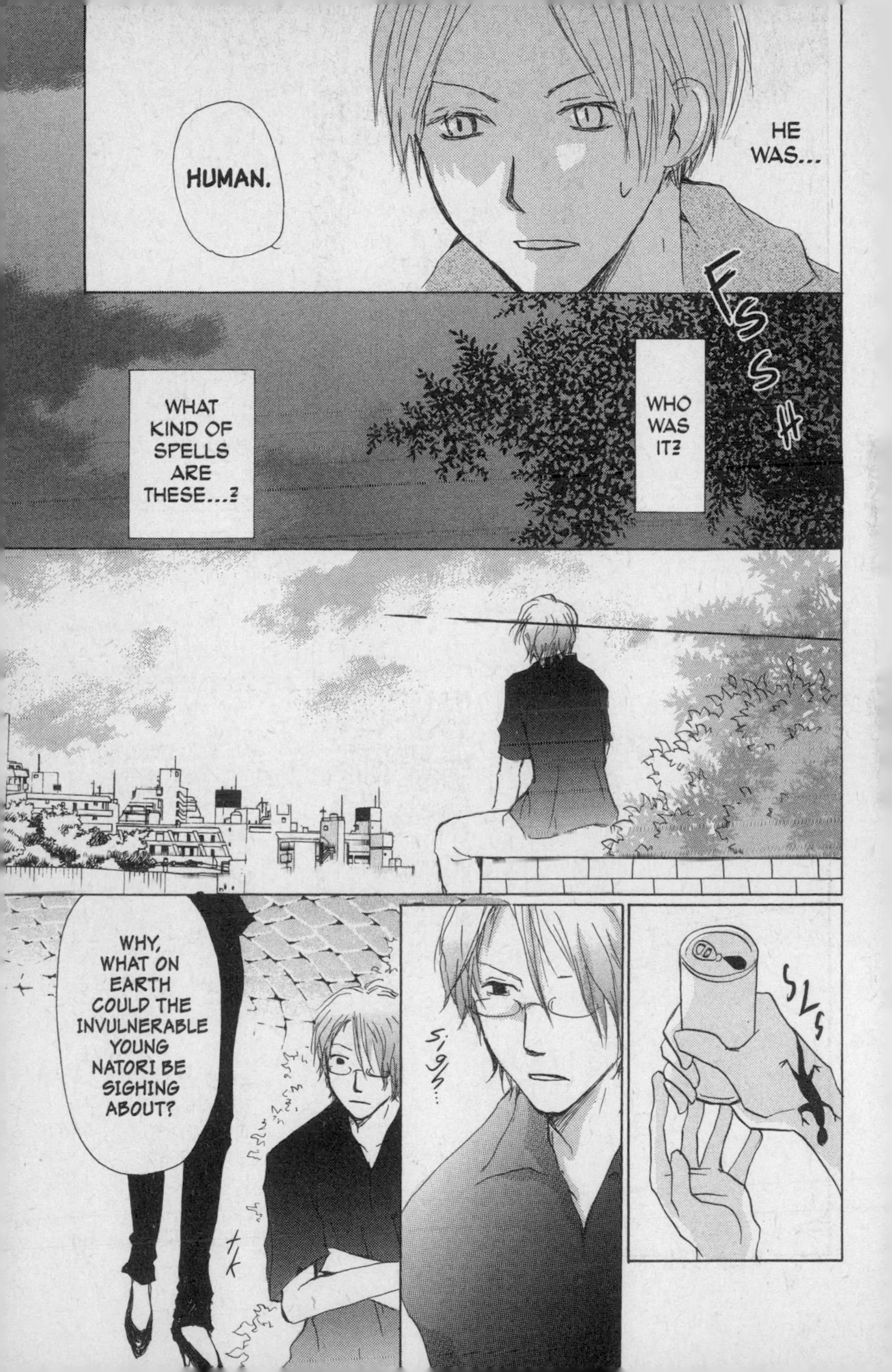

HE WAS...
HUMAN.
FSSH
WHO WAS IT?
WHAT KIND OF SPELLS ARE THESE...?
SLS
SIGH...
TK
WHY, WHAT ON EARTH COULD THE INVULNERABLE YOUNG NATORI BE SIGHING ABOUT?

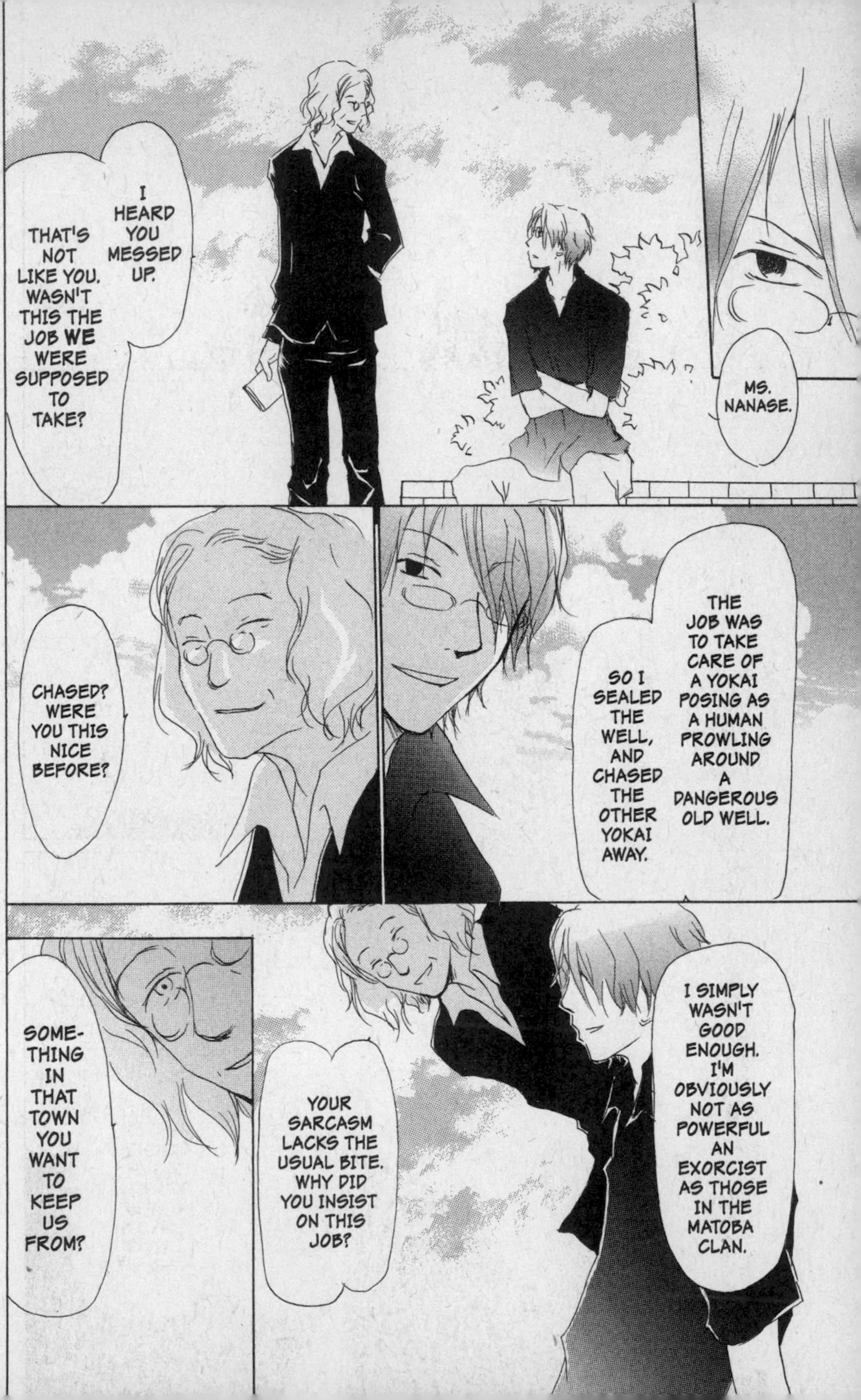
MS. NANASE.
I HEARD YOU MESSED UP.
THAT'S NOT LIKE YOU. WASN'T THIS THE JOB WE WERE SUPPOSED TO TAKE?
THE JOB WAS TO TAKE CARE OF A YOKAI POSING AS A HUMAN PROWLING AROUND A DANGEROUS OLD WELL.
SO I SEALED THE WELL, AND CHASED THE OTHER YOKAI AWAY.
CHASED? WERE YOU THIS NICE BEFORE?
I SIMPLY WASN'T GOOD ENOUGH. I'M OBVIOUSLY NOT AS POWERFUL AN EXORCIST AS THOSE IN THE MATOBA CLAN.
YOUR SARCASM LACKS THE USUAL BITE. WHY DID YOU INSIST ON THIS JOB?
SOMETHING IN THAT TOWN YOU WANT TO KEEP US FROM?

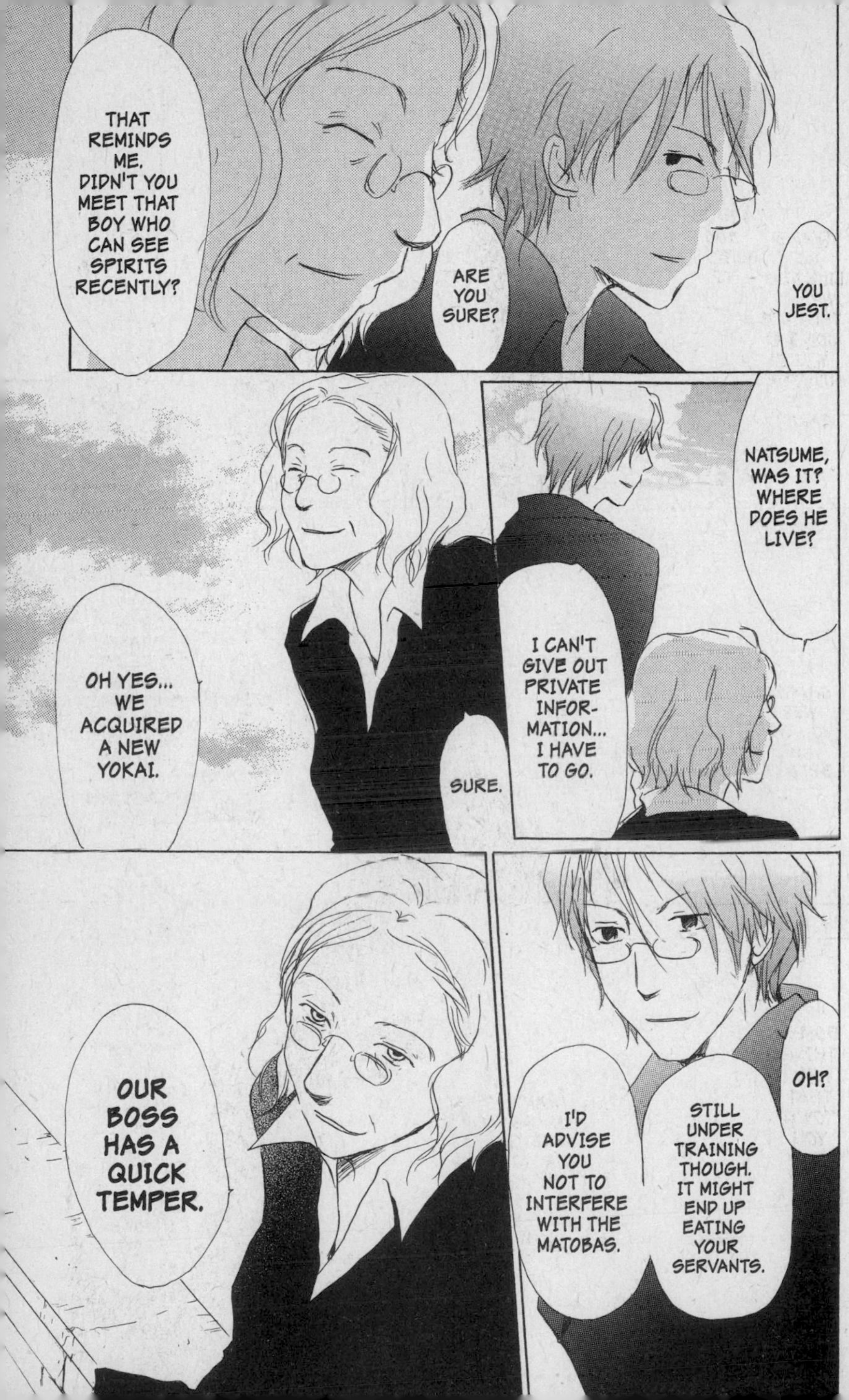
YOU JEST.
ARE YOU SURE?
THAT REMINDS ME. DIDN'T YOU MEET THAT BOY WHO CAN SEE SPIRITS RECENTLY?
NATSUME, WAS IT? WHERE DOES HE LIVE?
I CAN'T GIVE OUT PRIVATE INFOR-MATION... I HAVE TO GO.
SURE.
OH YES... WE ACQUIRED A NEW YOKAI.
OH?
STILL UNDER TRAINING THOUGH. IT MIGHT END UP EATING YOUR SERVANTS.
I'D ADVISE YOU NOT TO INTERFERE WITH THE MATOBAS.
OUR BOSS HAS A QUICK TEMPER.

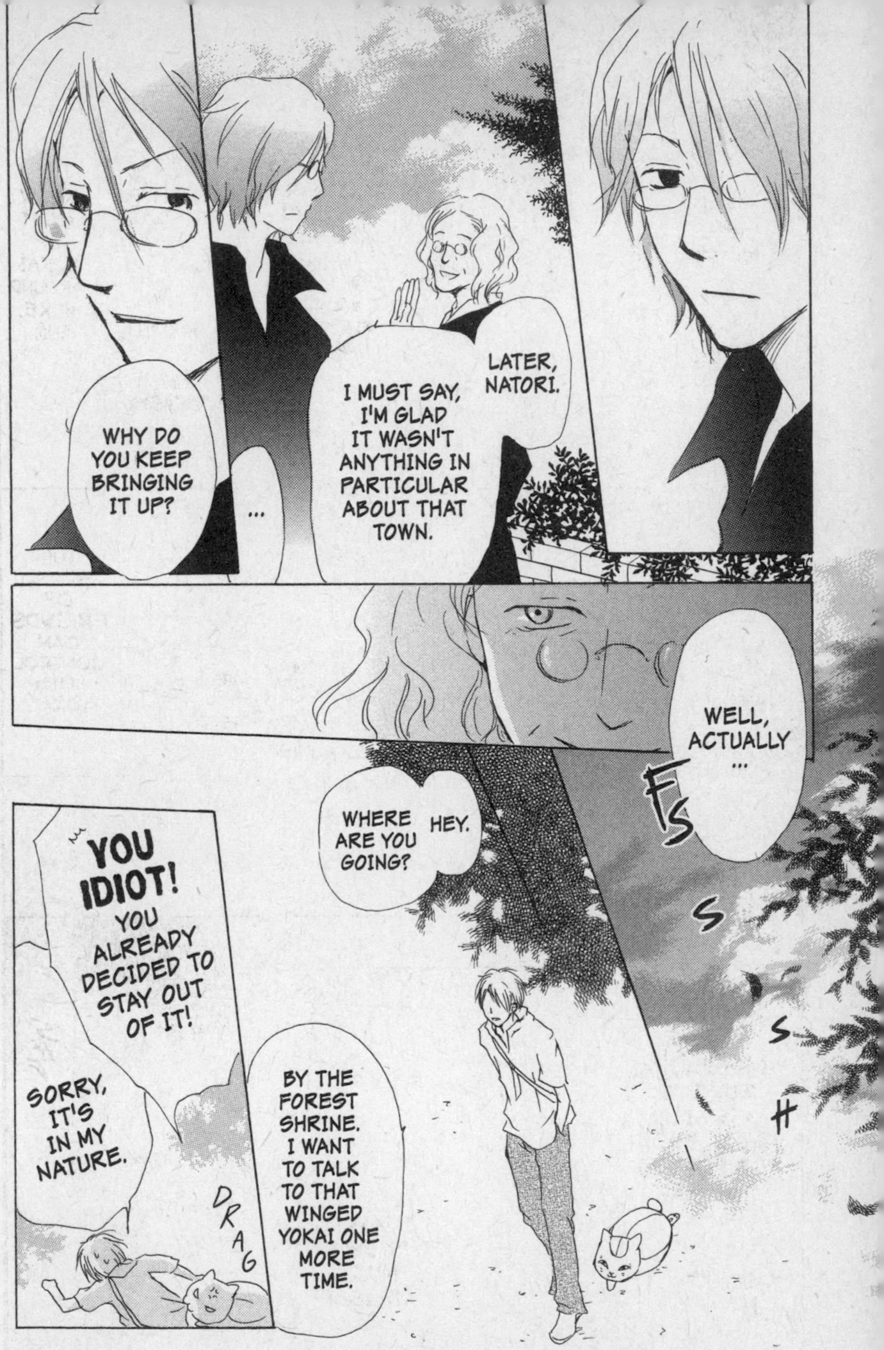
LATER, NATORI.
I MUST SAY, I'M GLAD IT WASN'T ANYTHING IN PARTICULAR ABOUT THAT TOWN.
...
WHY DO YOU KEEP BRINGING IT UP?
WELL, ACTUALLY ...
FSSSH
HEY.
WHERE ARE YOU GOING?
BY THE FOREST SHRINE. I WANT TO TALK TO THAT WINGED YOKAI ONE MORE TIME.
YOU IDIOT! YOU ALREADY DECIDED TO STAY OUT OF IT!
SORRY, IT'S IN MY NATURE.
DRAG

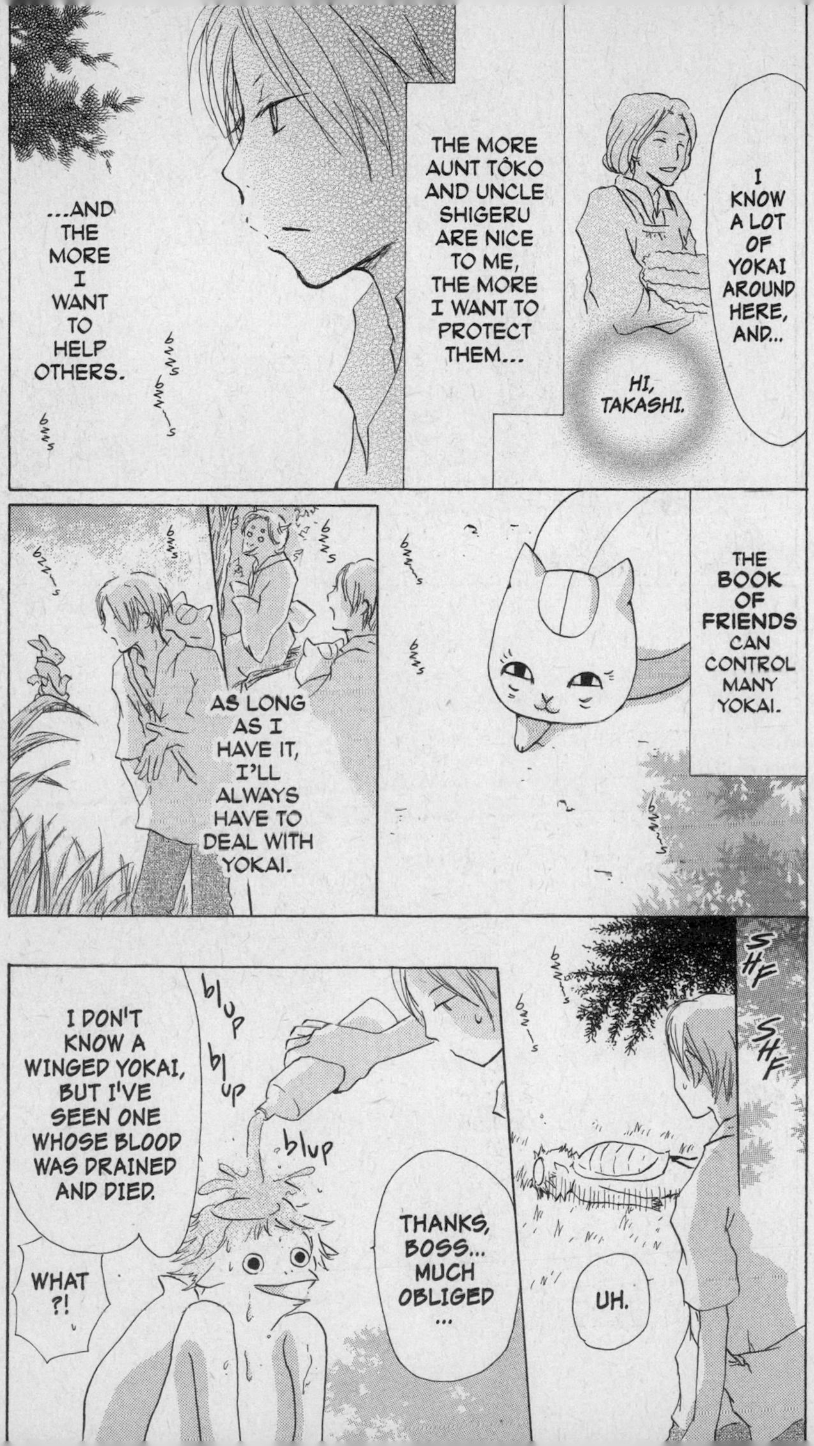
I KNOW A LOT OF YOKAI AROUND HERE, AND...
HI, TAKASHI.
THE MORE AUNT TÔKO AND UNCLE SHIGERU ARE NICE TO ME, THE MORE I WANT TO PROTECT THEM...
...AND THE MORE I WANT TO HELP OTHERS.
bzzs
THE BOOK OF FRIENDS CAN CONTROL MANY YOKAI.
AS LONG AS I HAVE IT, I'LL ALWAYS HAVE TO DEAL WITH YOKAI.
SHF
SHF
UH.
THANKS, BOSS... MUCH OBLIGED...
blup
blup
blup
I DON'T KNOW A WINGED YOKAI, BUT I'VE SEEN ONE WHOSE BLOOD WAS DRAINED AND DIED.
WHAT?!

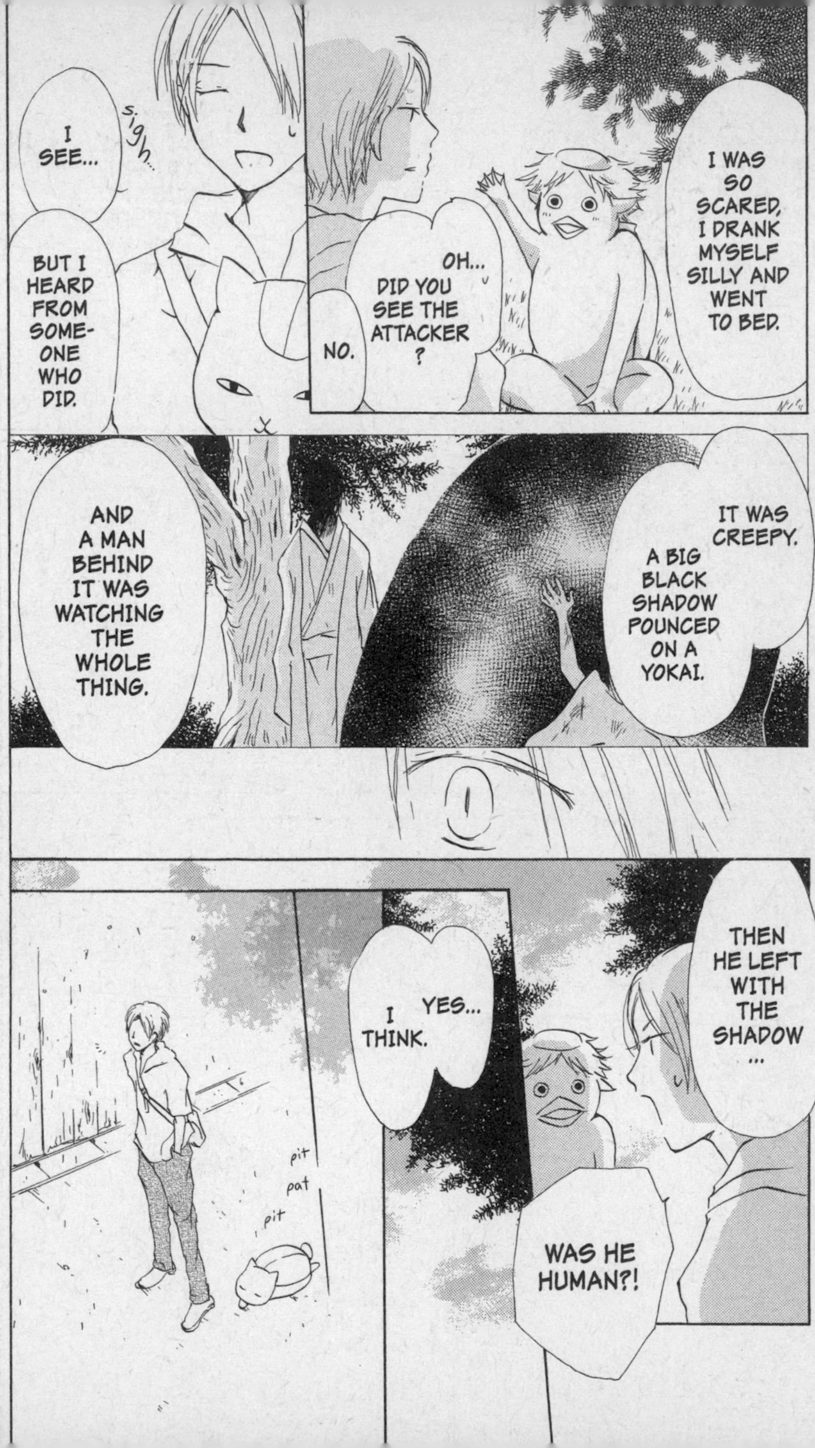
I WAS SO SCARED, I DRANK MYSELF SILLY AND WENT TO BED.
OH... DID YOU SEE THE ATTACKER?
NO.
sigh...
I SEE...
BUT I HEARD FROM SOME-ONE WHO DID.
IT WAS CREEPY.
A BIG BLACK SHADOW POUNCED ON A YOKAI.
AND A MAN BEHIND IT WAS WATCHING THE WHOLE THING.
THEN HE LEFT WITH THE SHADOW...
WAS HE HUMAN?!
YES... I THINK.
pit
pat
pit

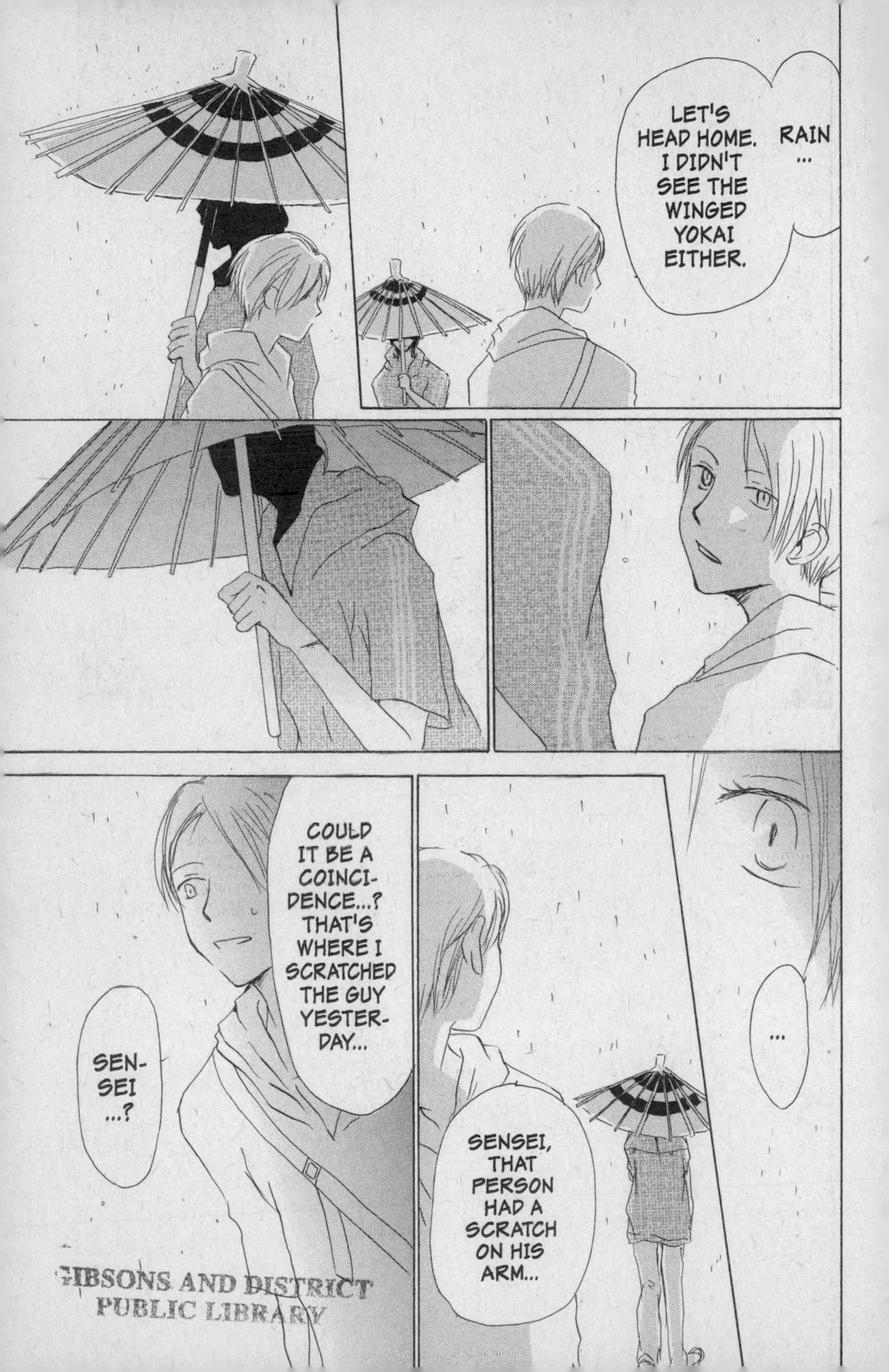
RAIN ...
LET'S HEAD HOME. I DIDN'T SEE THE WINGED YOKAI EITHER.
...
SENSEI, THAT PERSON HAD A SCRATCH ON HIS ARM...
COULD IT BE A COINCIDENCE...? THAT'S WHERE I SCRATCHED THE GUY YESTERDAY...
SENSEI ...?

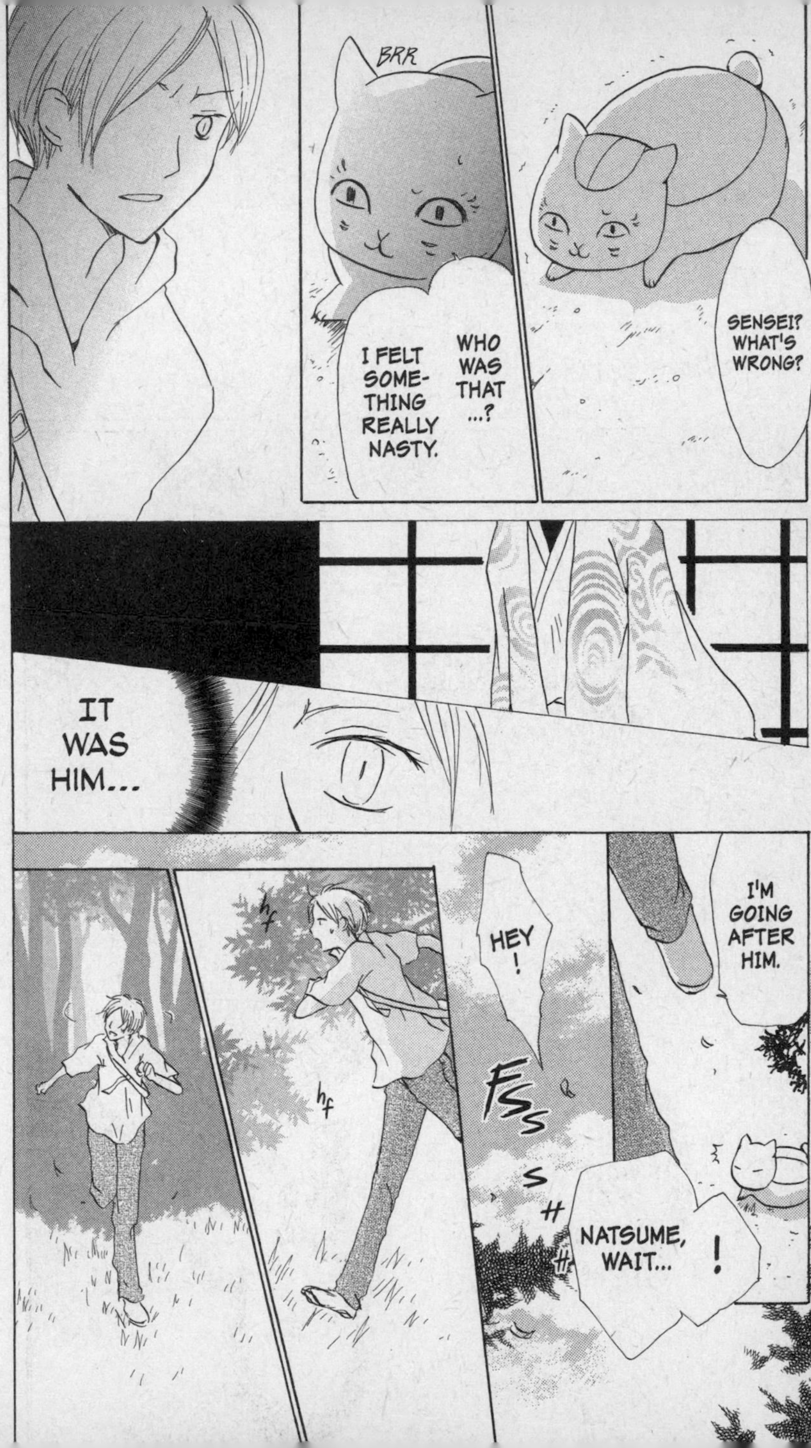
SENSEI? WHAT'S WRONG?
BRR
WHO WAS THAT ...?
I FELT SOMETHING REALLY NASTY.
IT WAS HIM...
I'M GOING AFTER HIM.
HEY!
FSSSHH
NATSUME, WAIT...!
hf
hf

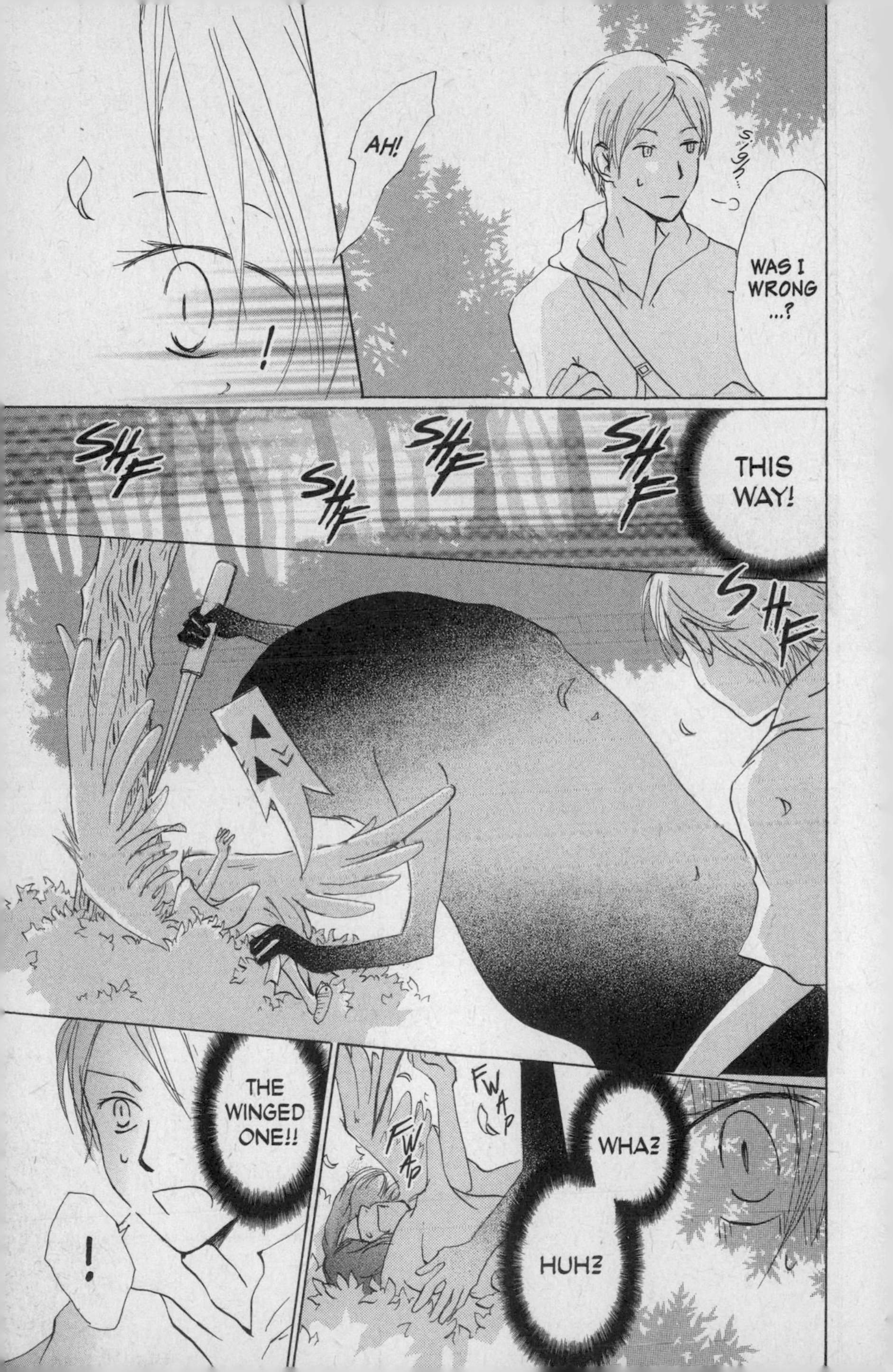
sigh...
WAS I WRONG ...?
AH!
!
THIS WAY!
SHF
SHF
SHF
SHF
SHF
WHA?
HUH?
FWAP
FWAP
THE WINGED ONE!!
!

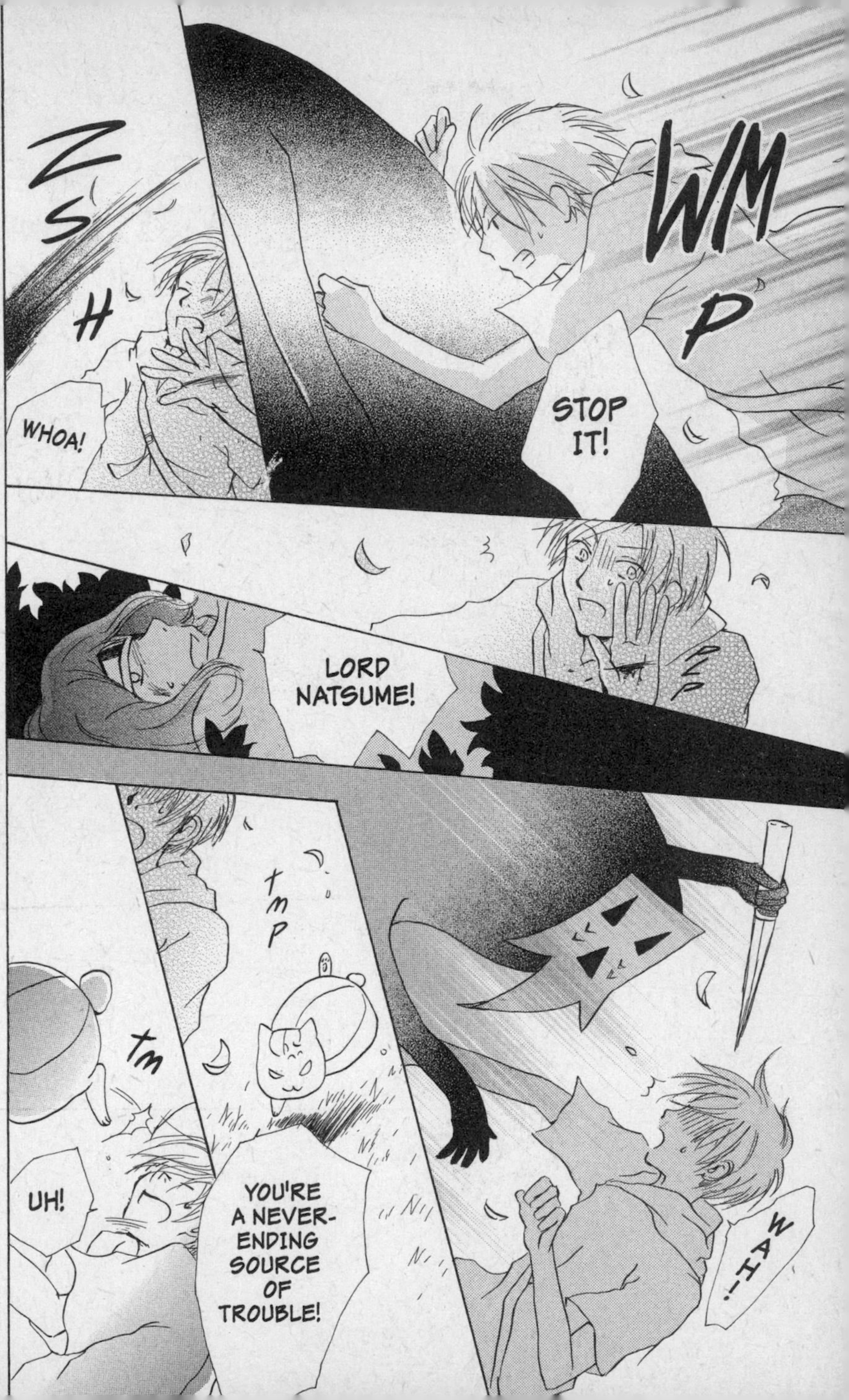
WMP
STOP IT!
ZSH
WHOA!
LORD NATSUME!
WAH!
tmp
YOU'RE A NEVER-ENDING SOURCE OF TROUBLE!
tm
UH!

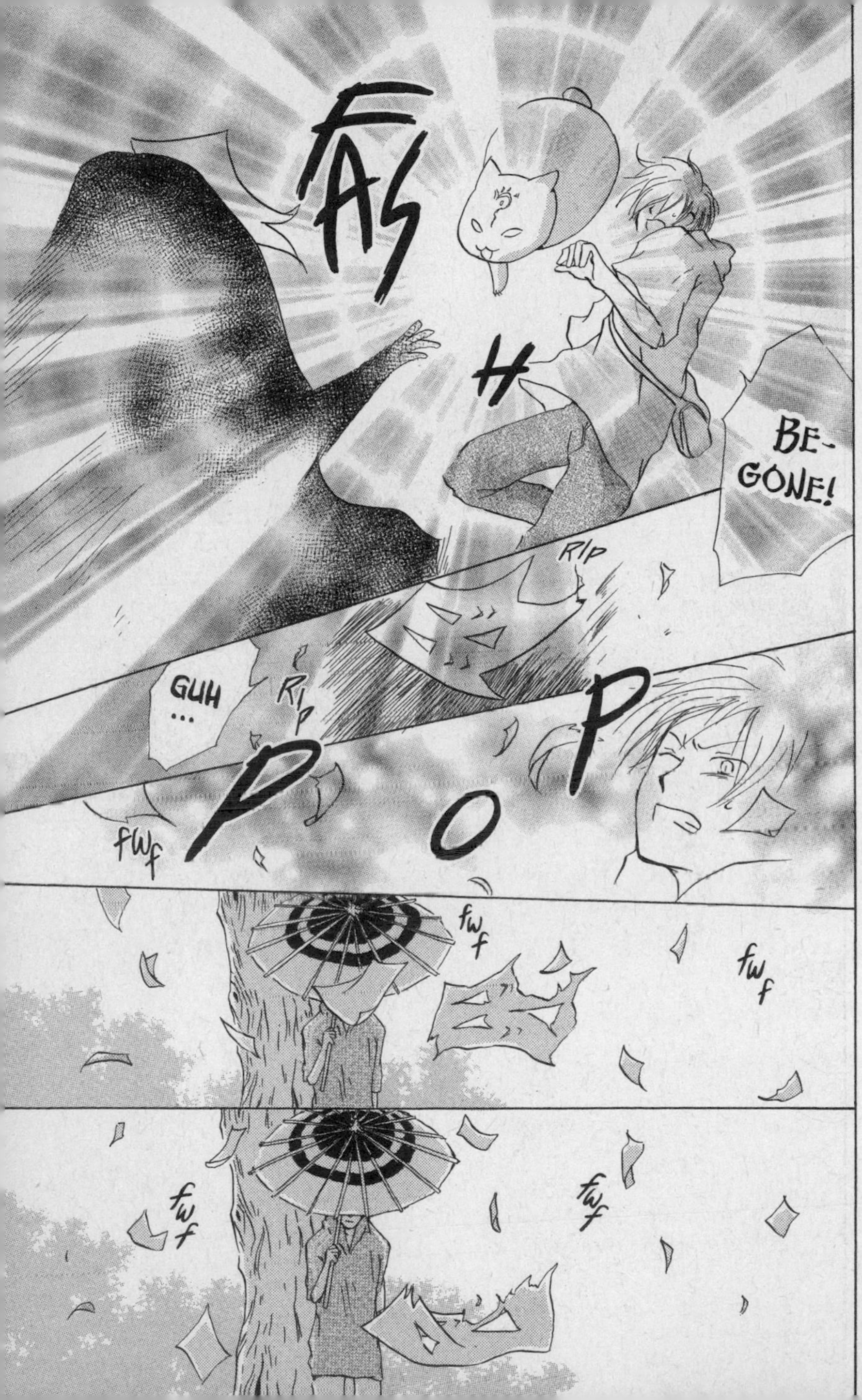
FASH
BE-GONE!
RIP
POP
RIP
GUH ...
FWF
FWF
FWF
FWF
FWF

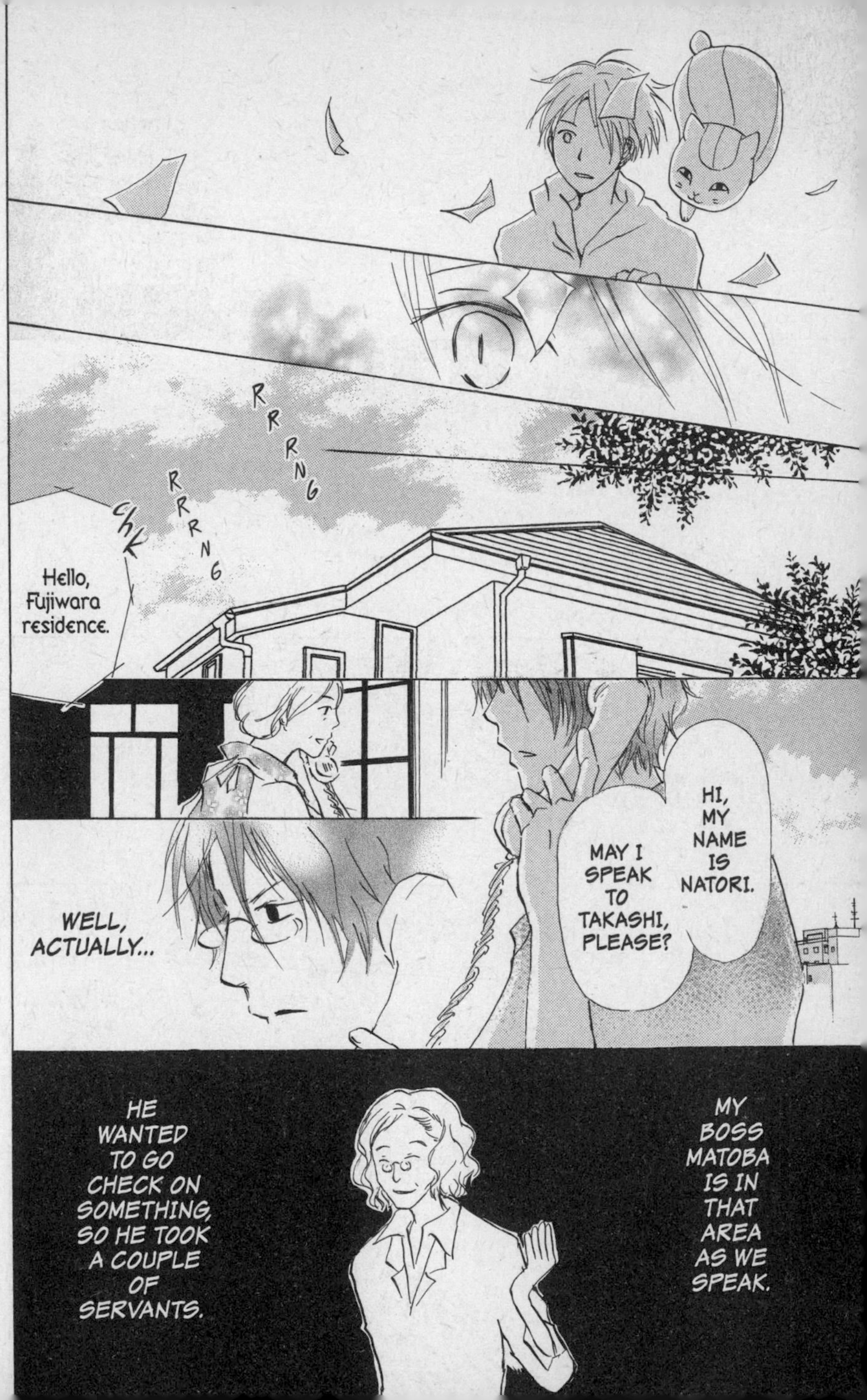

RRRNG
RRRNG
chk
Hello, Fujiwara residence.
HI, MY NAME IS NATORI.
MAY I SPEAK TO TAKASHI, PLEASE?
WELL, ACTUALLY...
MY BOSS MATOBA IS IN THAT AREA AS WE SPEAK.
HE WANTED TO GO CHECK ON SOMETHING, SO HE TOOK A COUPLE OF SERVANTS.

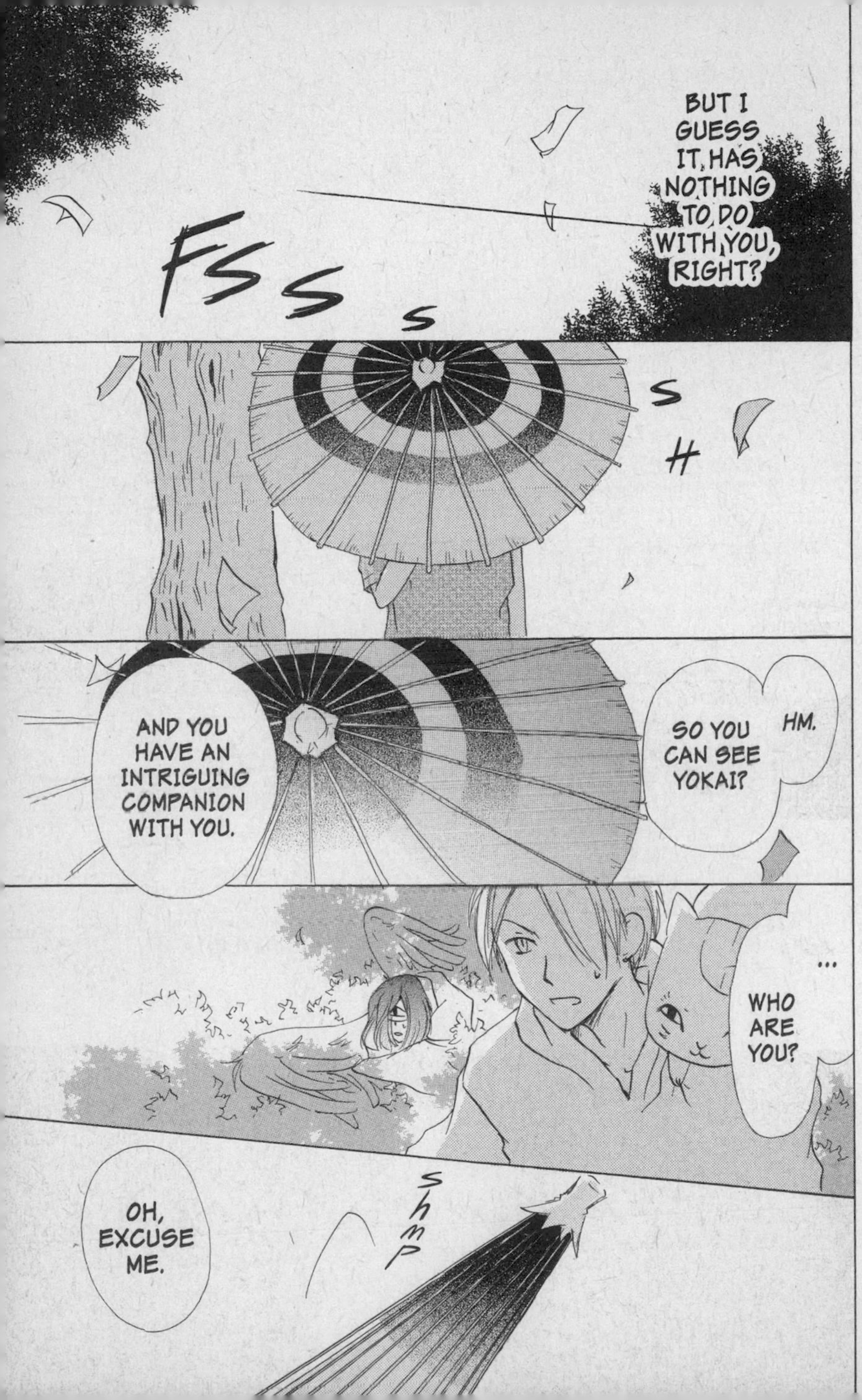
BUT I GUESS IT HAS NOTHING TO DO WITH YOU, RIGHT?
FSSSSH
HM.
SO YOU CAN SEE YOKAI?
AND YOU HAVE AN INTRIGUING COMPANION WITH YOU.
...
WHO ARE YOU?
SHMP
OH, EXCUSE ME.

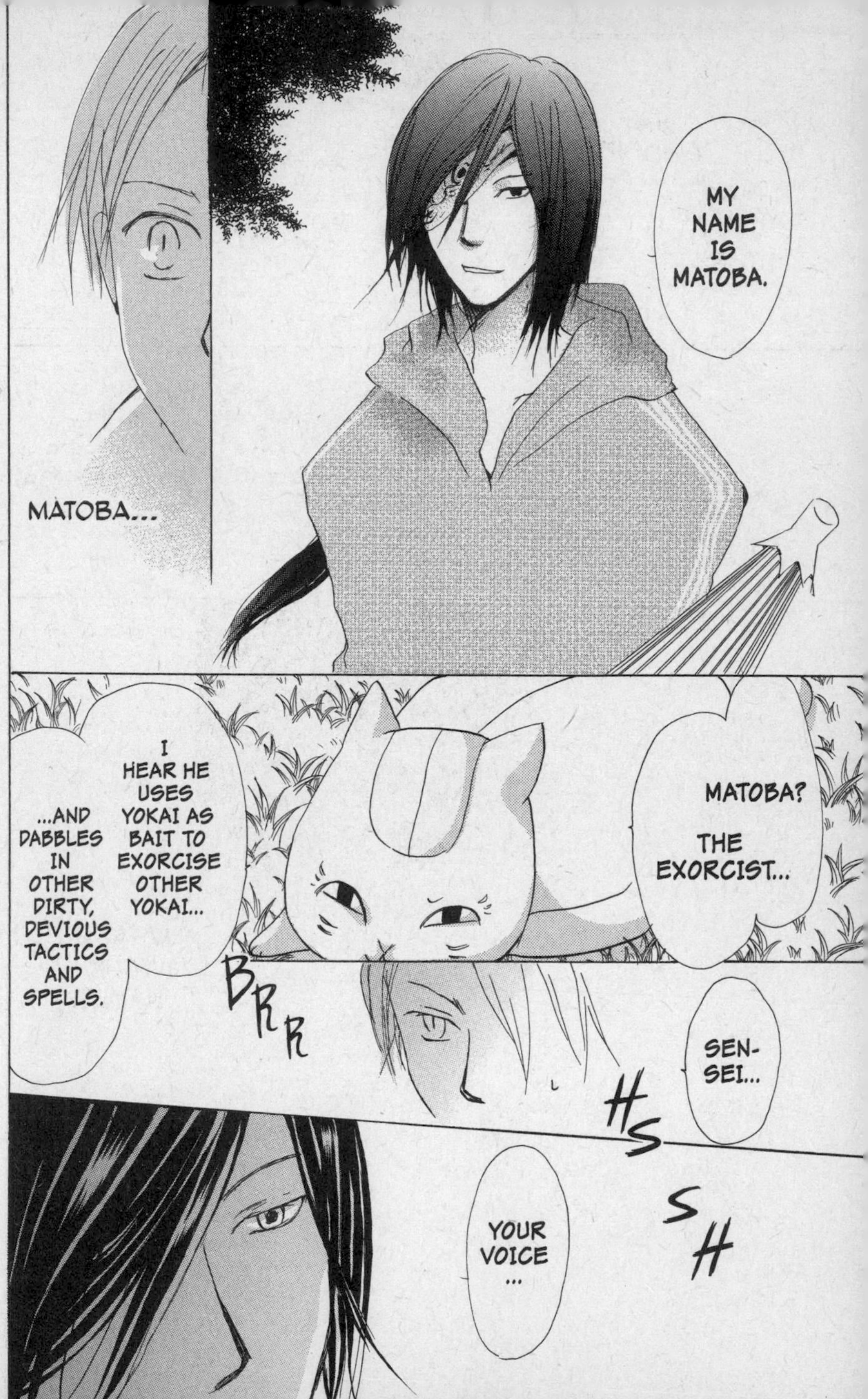
MY NAME IS MATOBA.
MATOBA...
MATOBA? THE EXORCIST...
I HEAR HE USES YOKAI AS BAIT TO EXORCISE OTHER YOKAI...
...AND DABBLES IN OTHER DIRTY, DEVIOUS TACTICS AND SPELLS.
BRR
SEN-SEI...
HSS
SH
YOUR VOICE ...

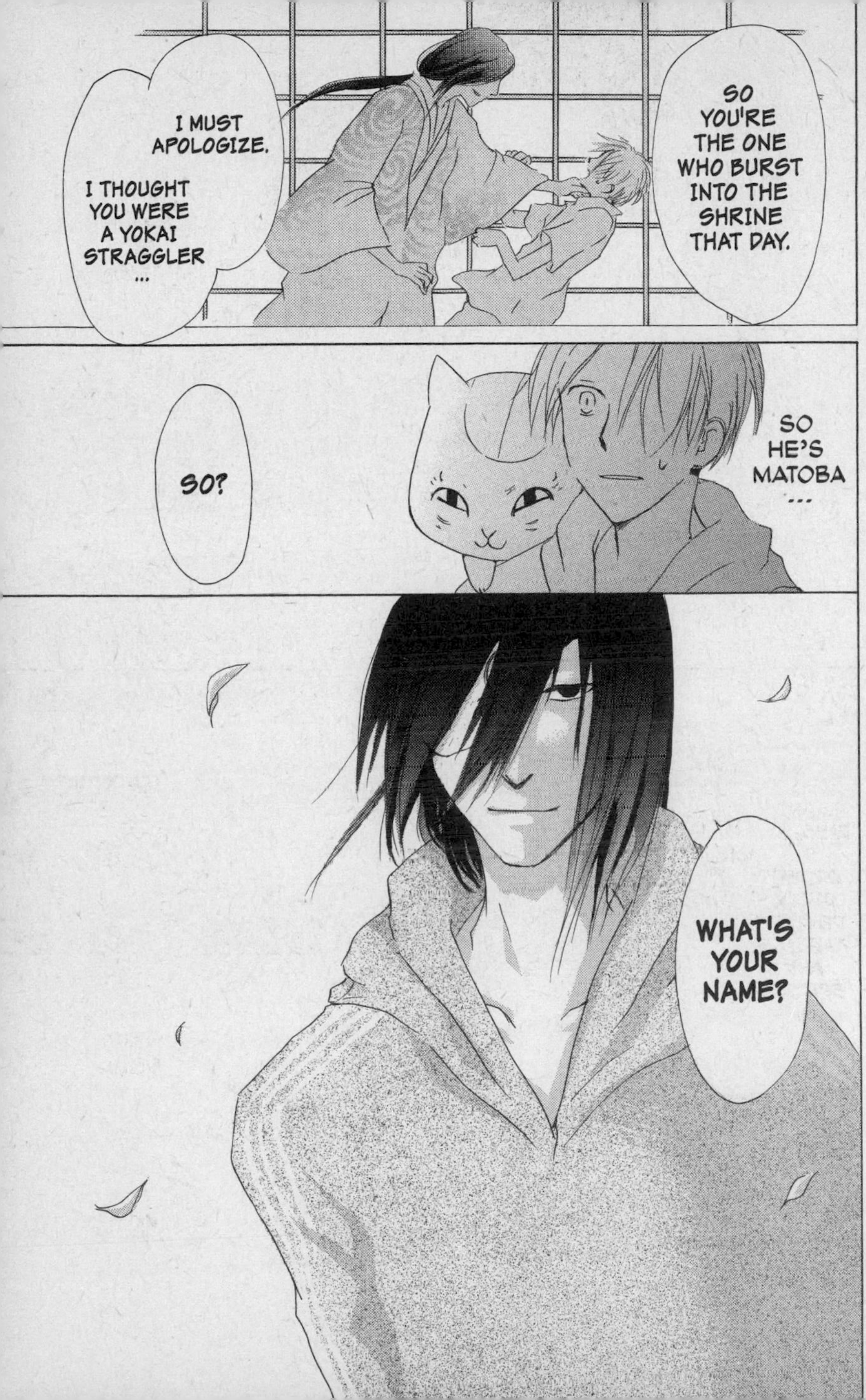
SO YOU'RE THE ONE WHO BURST INTO THE SHRINE THAT DAY.
I MUST APOLOGIZE.
I THOUGHT YOU WERE A YOKAI STRAGGLER ...
SO HE'S MATOBA ...
SO?
WHAT'S YOUR NAME?

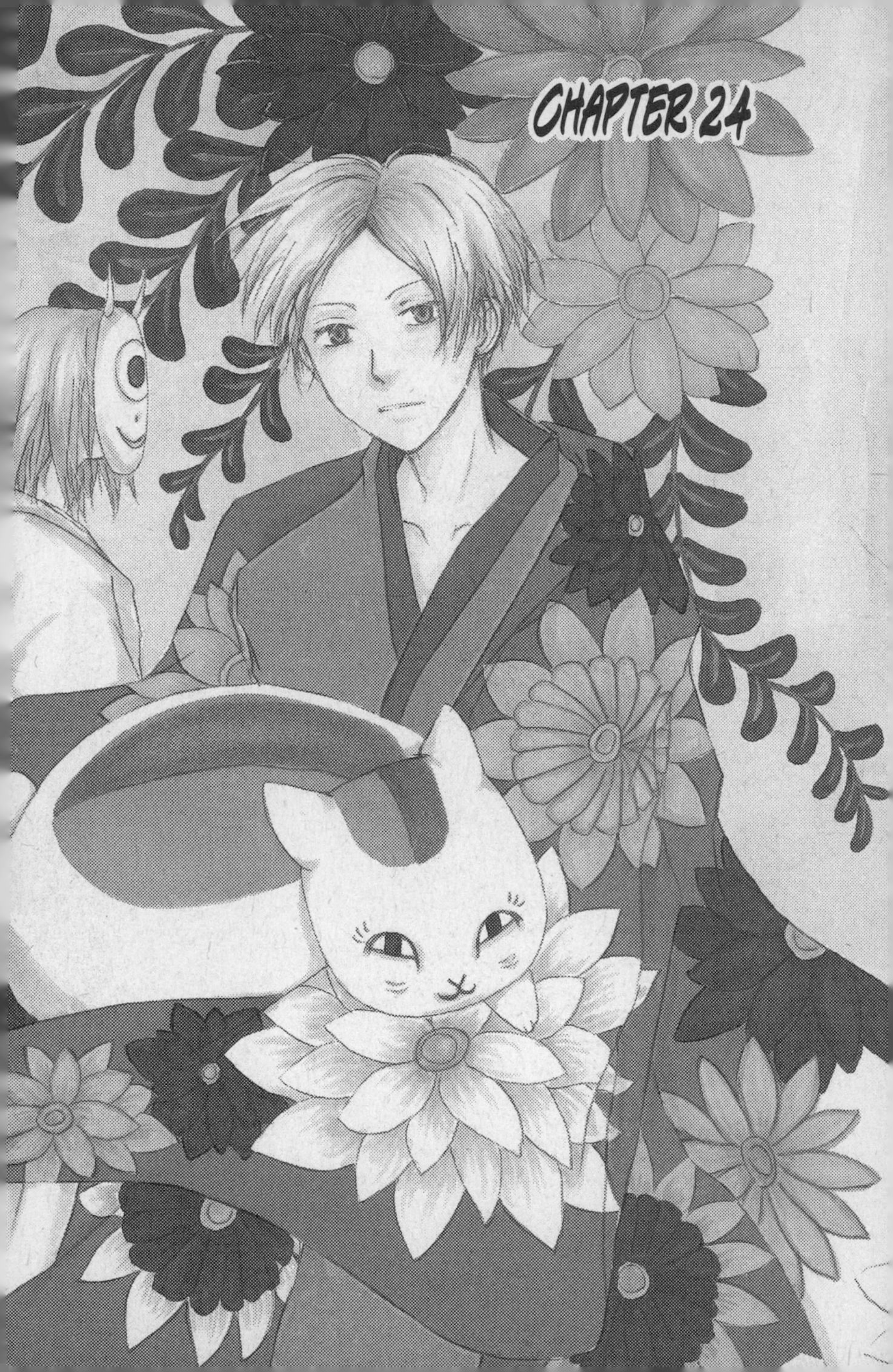
CHAPTER 24

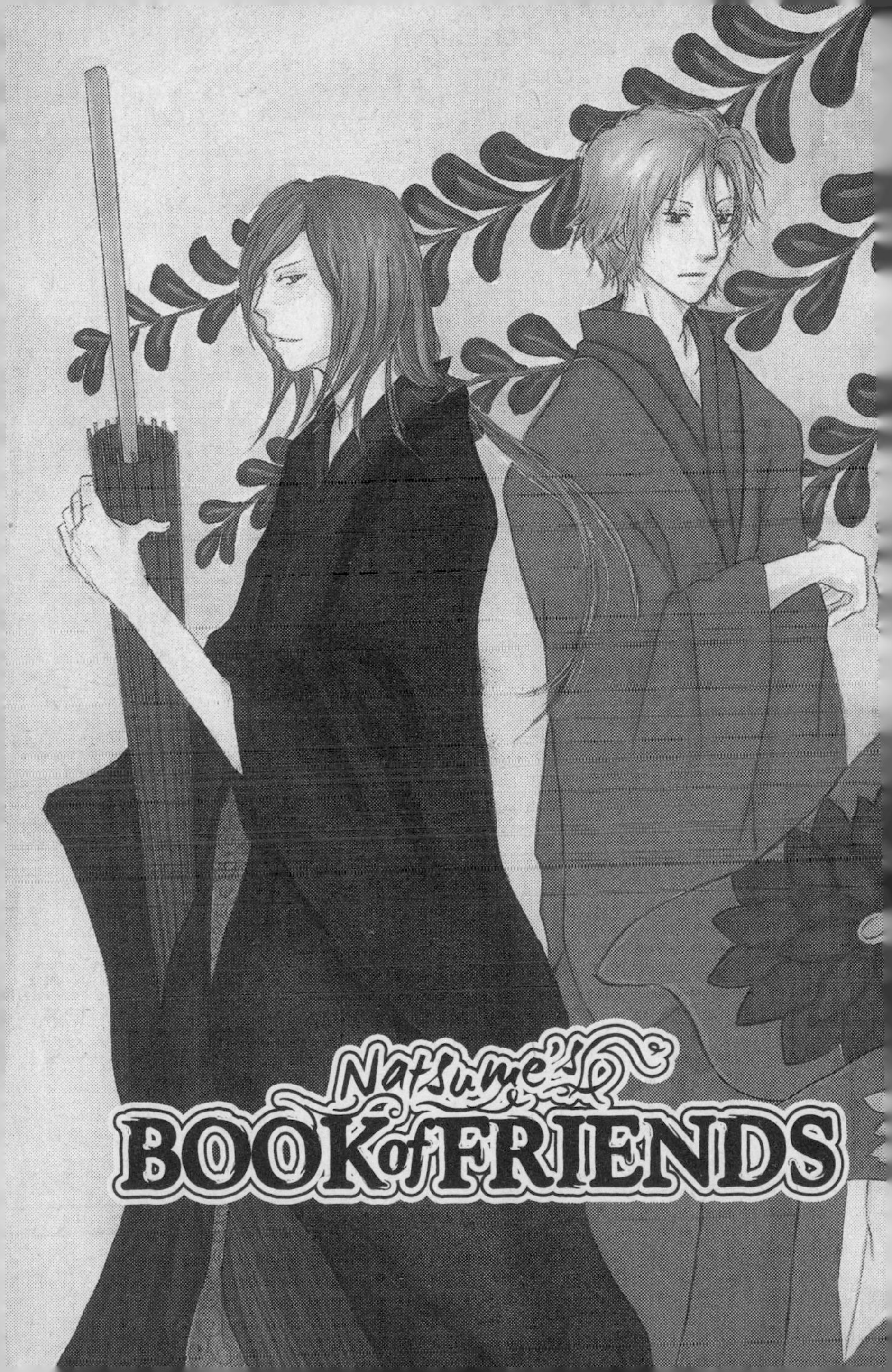
Natsume's
BOOK of FRIENDS

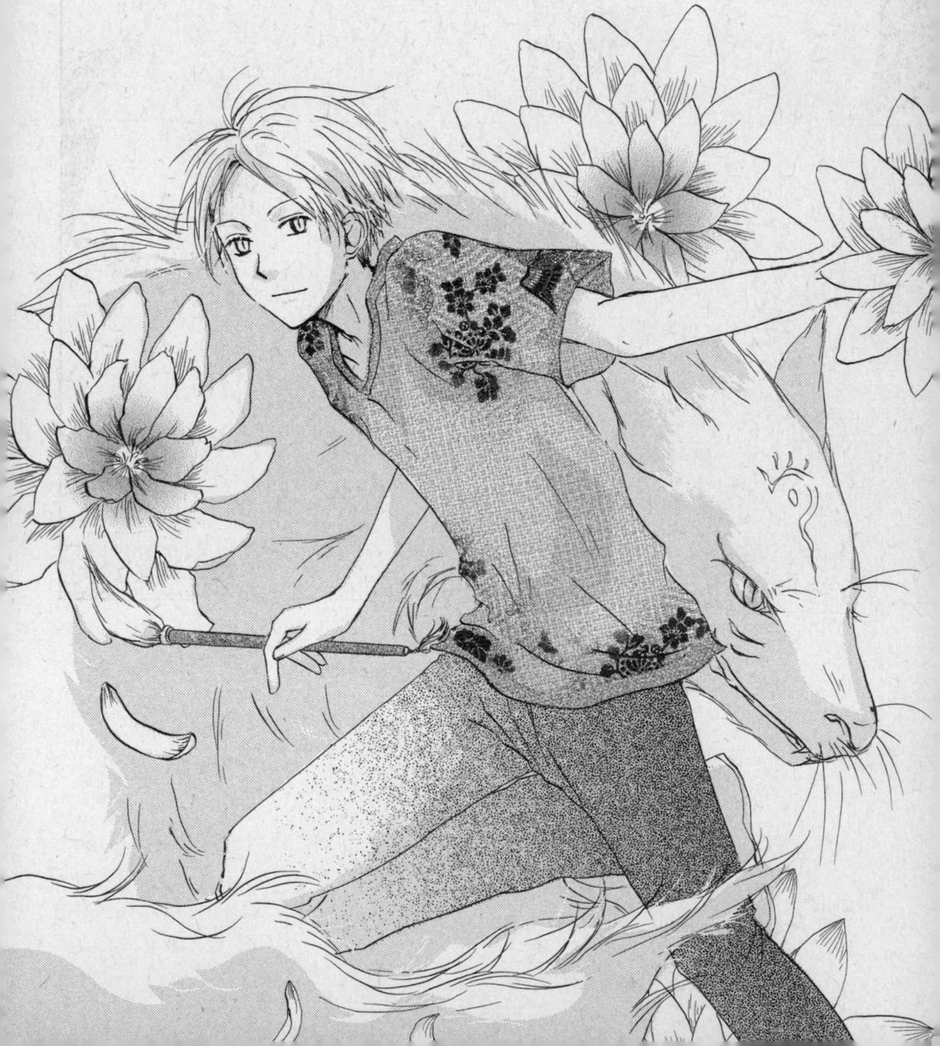

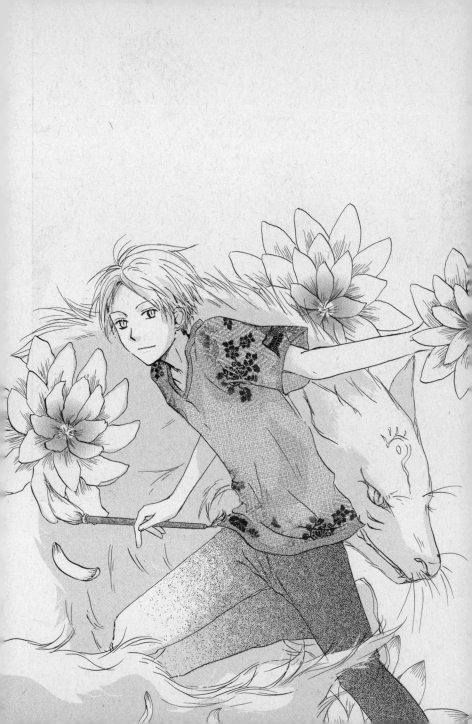

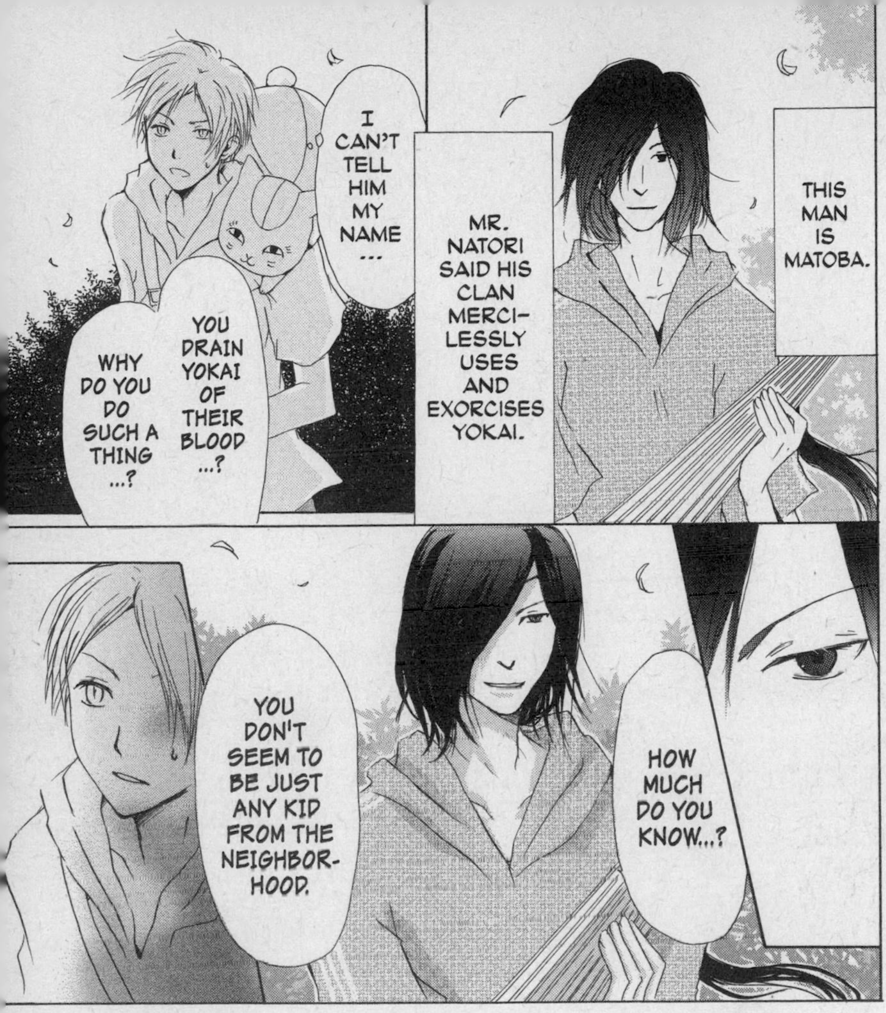
THIS MAN IS MATOBA.
MR. NATORI SAID HIS CLAN MERCILESSLY USES AND EXORCISES YOKAI.
I CAN'T TELL HIM MY NAME...
YOU DRAIN YOKAI OF THEIR BLOOD...?
WHY DO YOU DO SUCH A THING...?
HOW MUCH DO YOU KNOW...?
YOU DON'T SEEM TO BE JUST ANY KID FROM THE NEIGHBORHOOD.

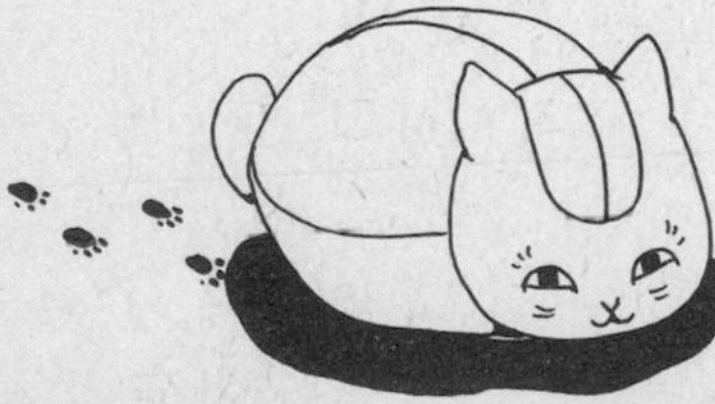

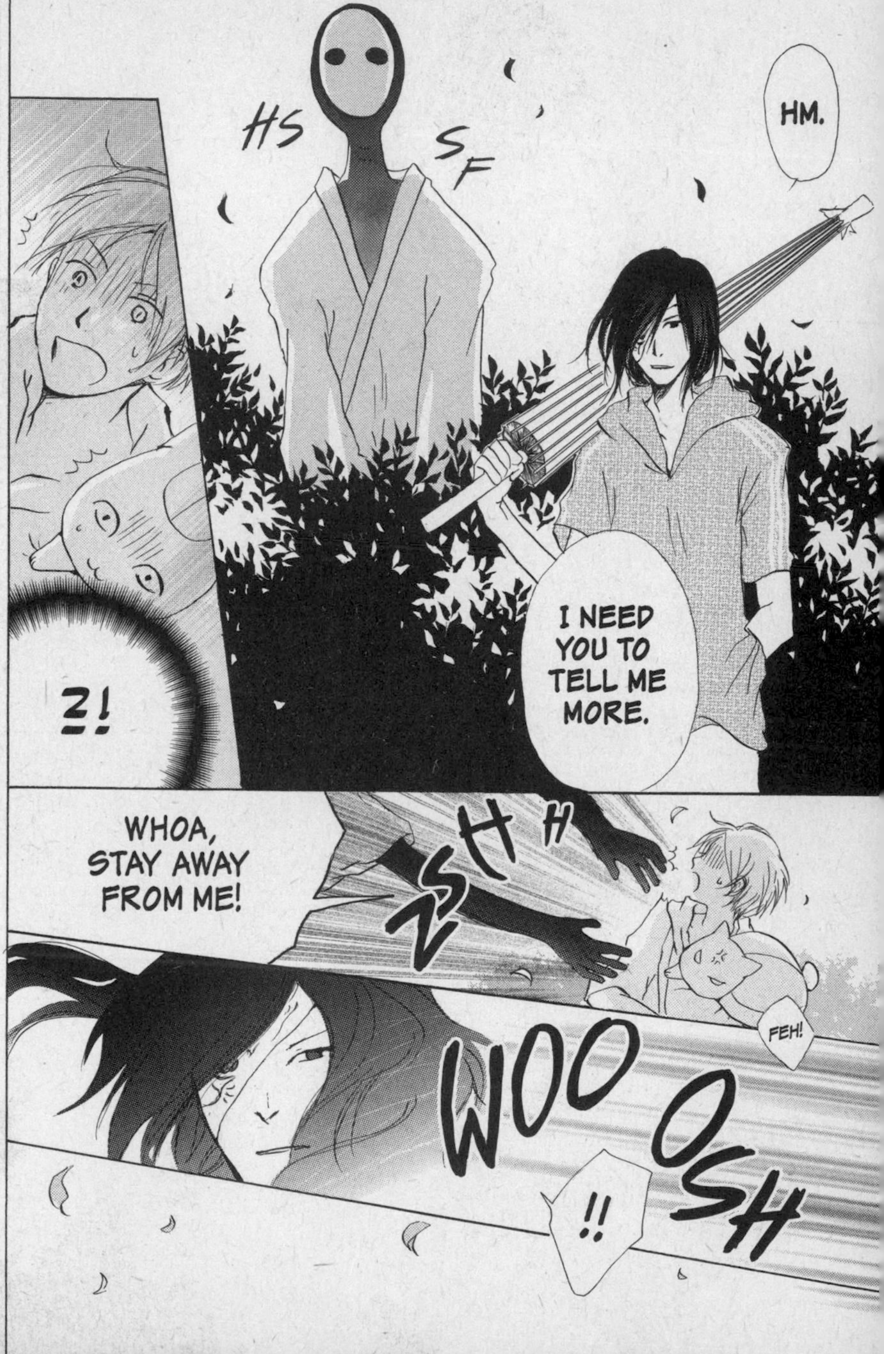
HM.
I NEED YOU TO TELL ME MORE.
HS
SF
Z!
WHOA, STAY AWAY FROM ME!
ZSHH
FEH!
WOOOSH
!!

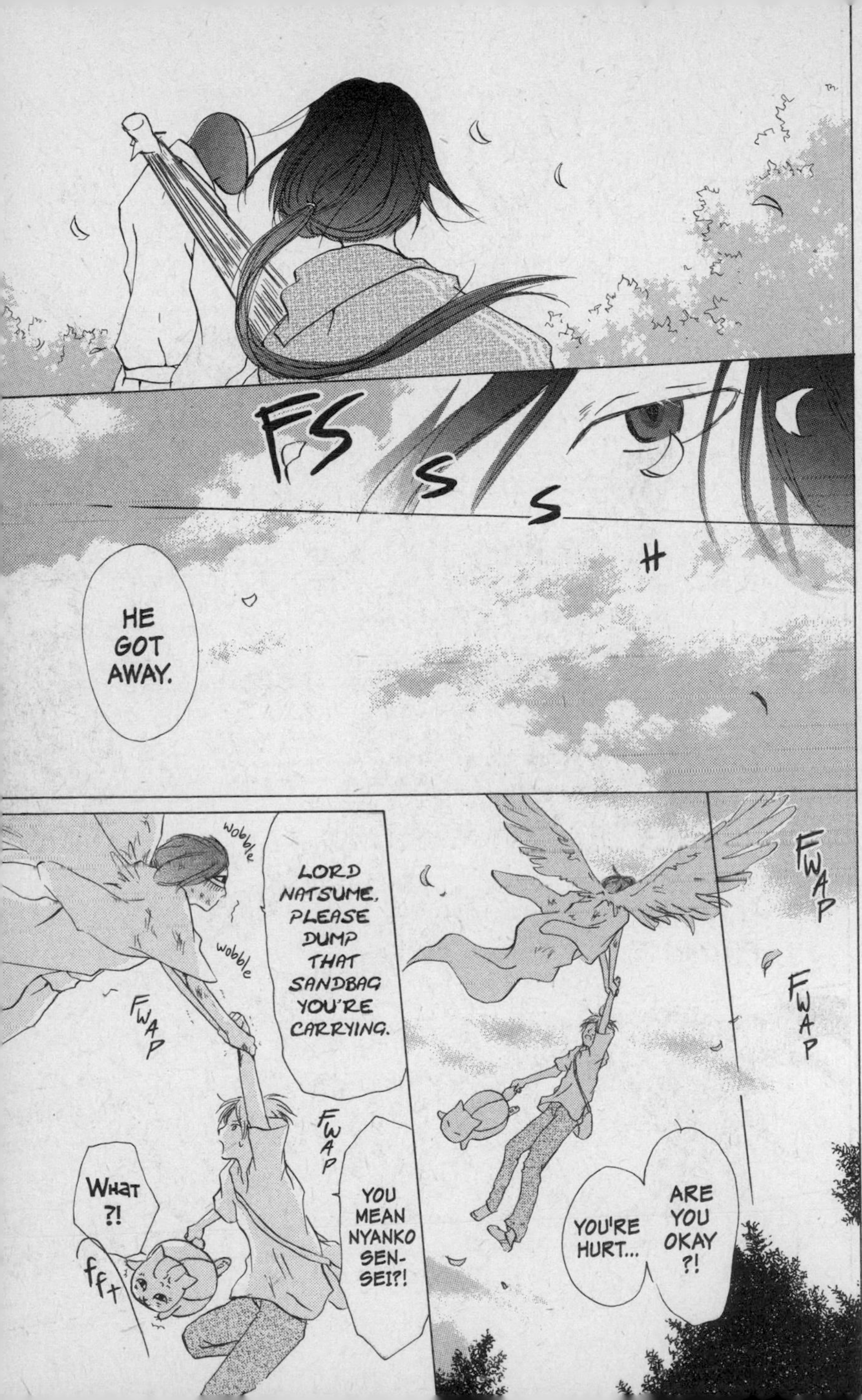
FSSH
HE GOT AWAY.
FWAP
FWAP
ARE YOU OKAY?!
YOU'RE HURT...
wobble
wobble
LORD NATSUME, PLEASE DUMP THAT SANDBAG YOU'RE CARRYING.
FWAP
FWAP
YOU MEAN NYANKO SENSEI?!
WHAT?!
fft

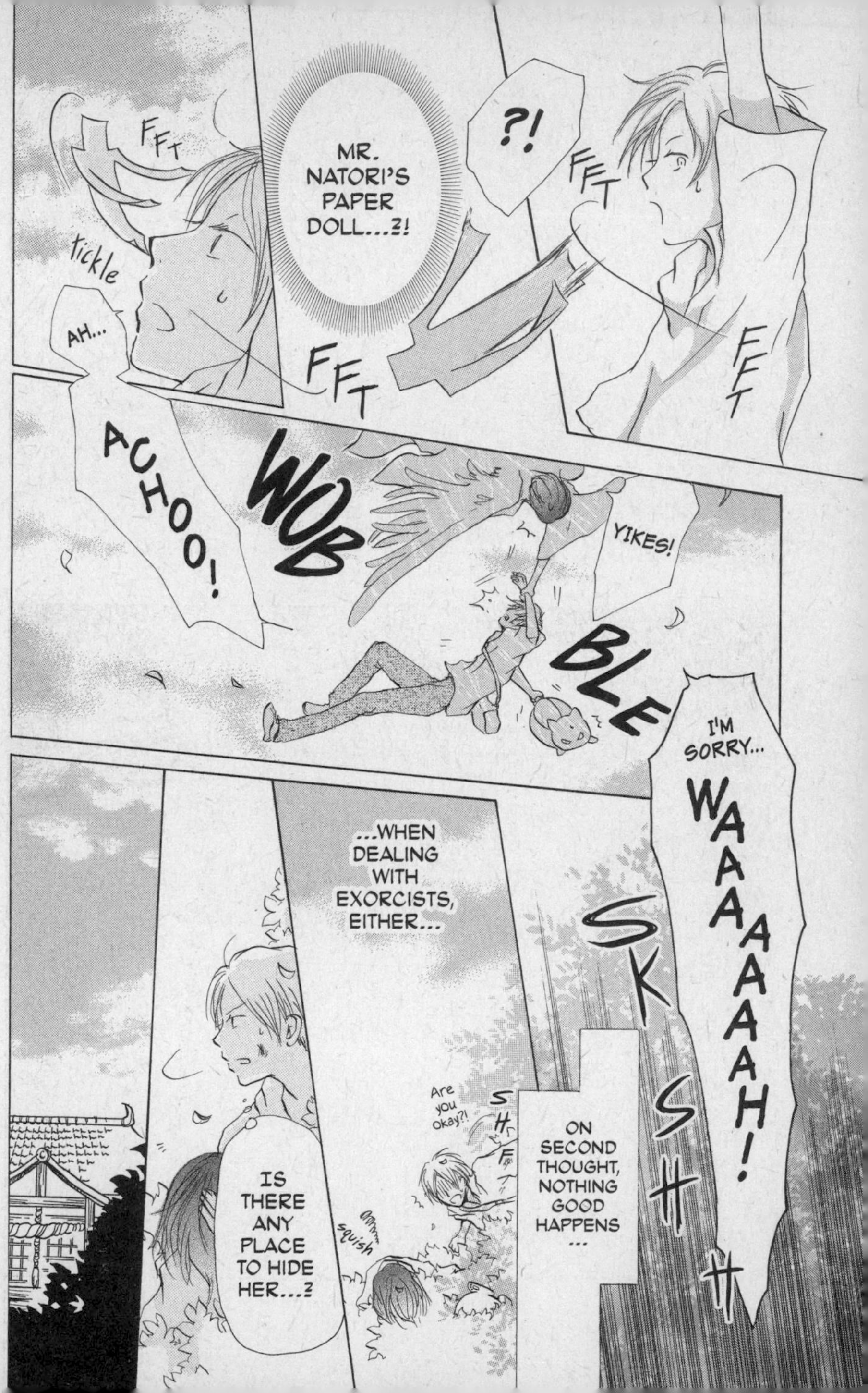
?!
FFFT
FFFT
MR. NATORI'S PAPER DOLL...?!
FFFT
FFT
tickle
AH...
YIKES!
WOB
BLE
ACHOO!
I'M SORRY...
WAAAAAAAH!
SKSH
SH
ON SECOND THOUGHT, NOTHING GOOD HAPPENS ...
Are you okay?!
SHF
squish
...WHEN DEALING WITH EXORCISTS, EITHER...
IS THERE ANY PLACE TO HIDE HER...?

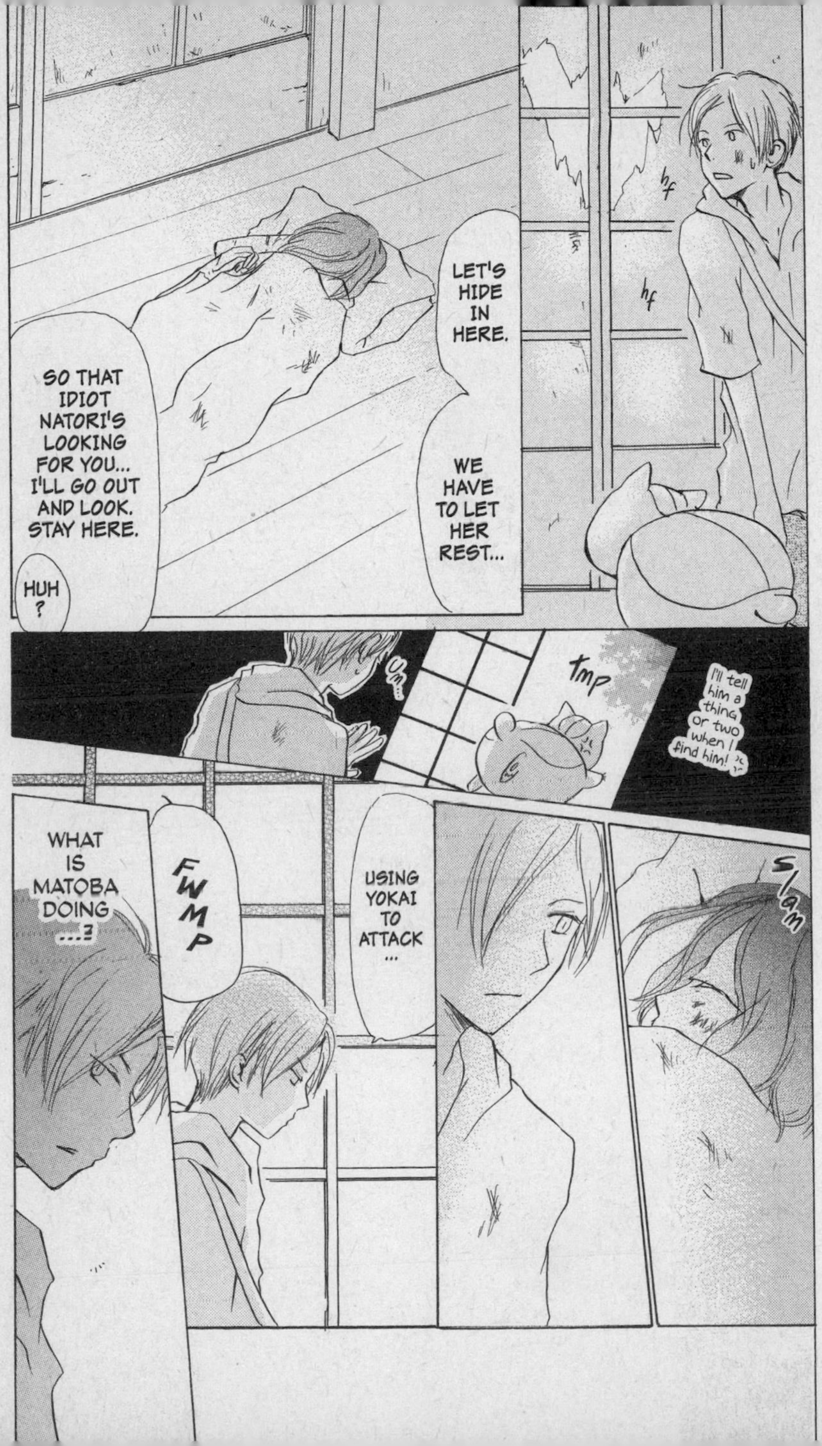
hf
hf
LET'S HIDE IN HERE.
WE HAVE TO LET HER REST...
SO THAT IDIOT NATORI'S LOOKING FOR YOU... I'LL GO OUT AND LOOK. STAY HERE.
HUH?
I'll tell him a thing or two when I find him!
tmp
Um...
Slam
USING YOKAI TO ATTACK ...
FWMP
WHAT IS MATOBA DOING ...?

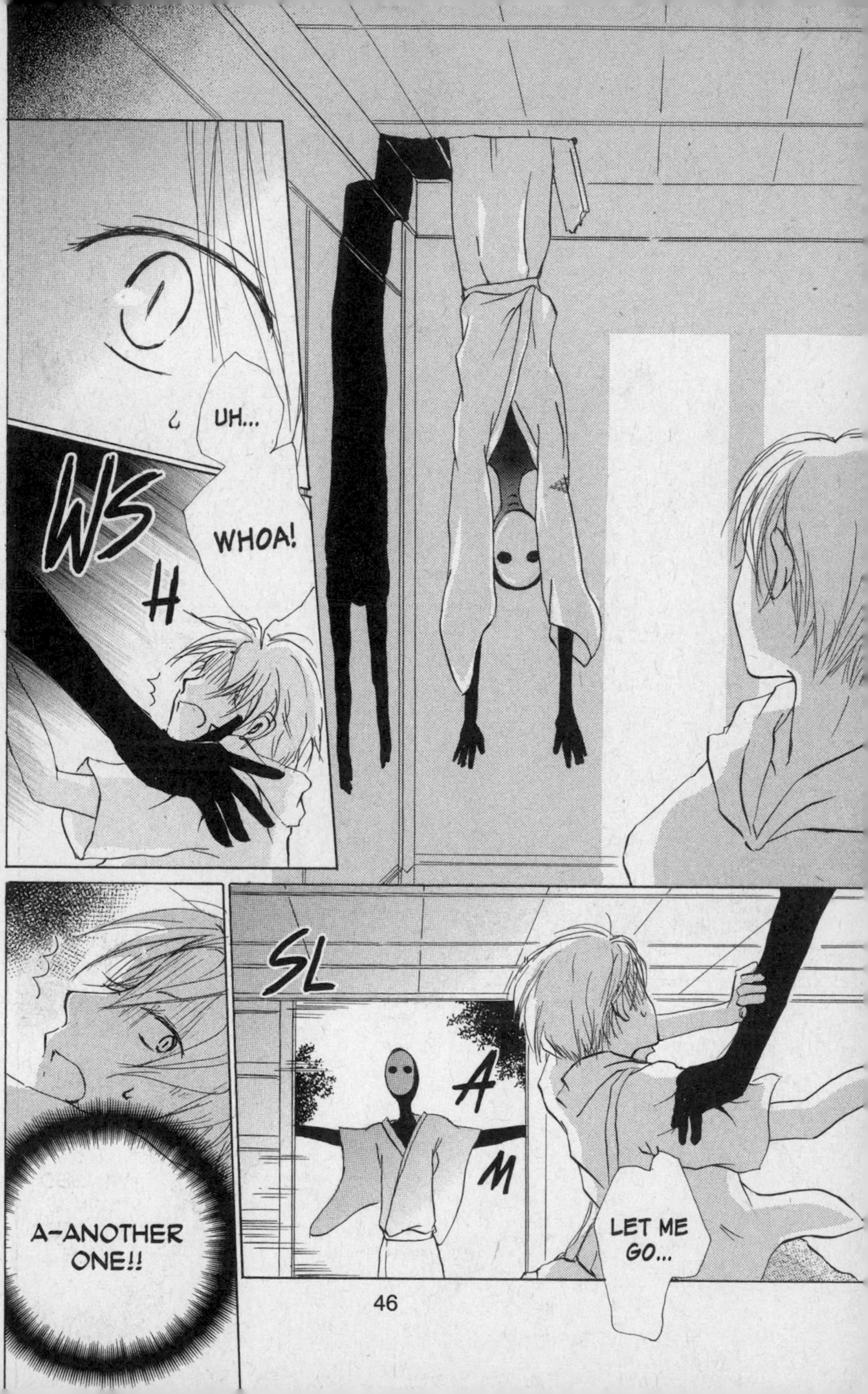
UH...
WSH
WHOA!
SLAM
LET ME GO...
A-ANOTHER ONE!!

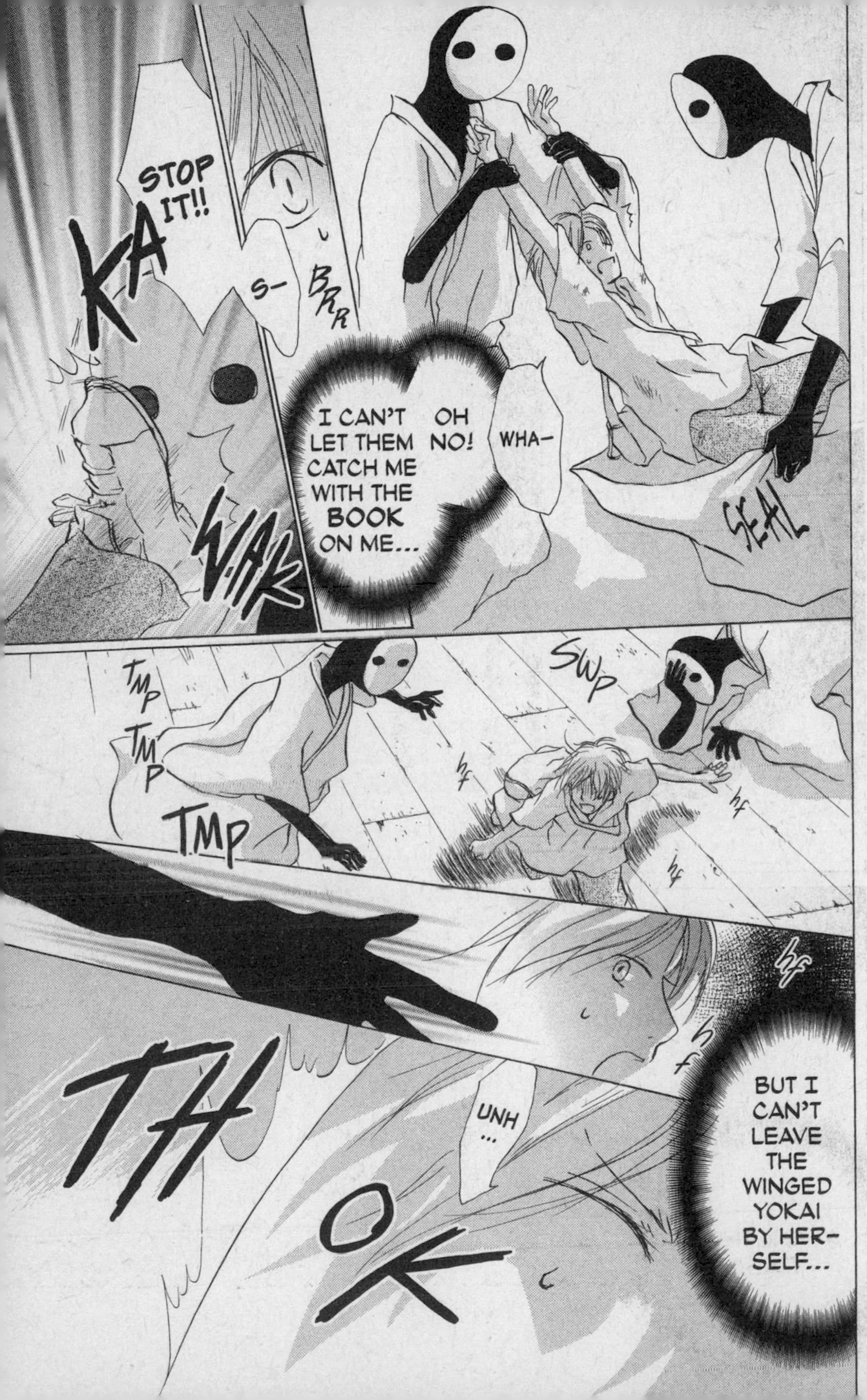
SEAL
WHA-
OH NO!
I CAN'T LET THEM CATCH ME WITH THE BOOK ON ME...
S-
BRR
STOP IT!!
KA
WAK
SWP
hf
hf
hf
TMP
TMP
TMP
TMP
hf
hf
BUT I CAN'T LEAVE THE WINGED YOKAI BY HER-SELF...
UNH...
THOK

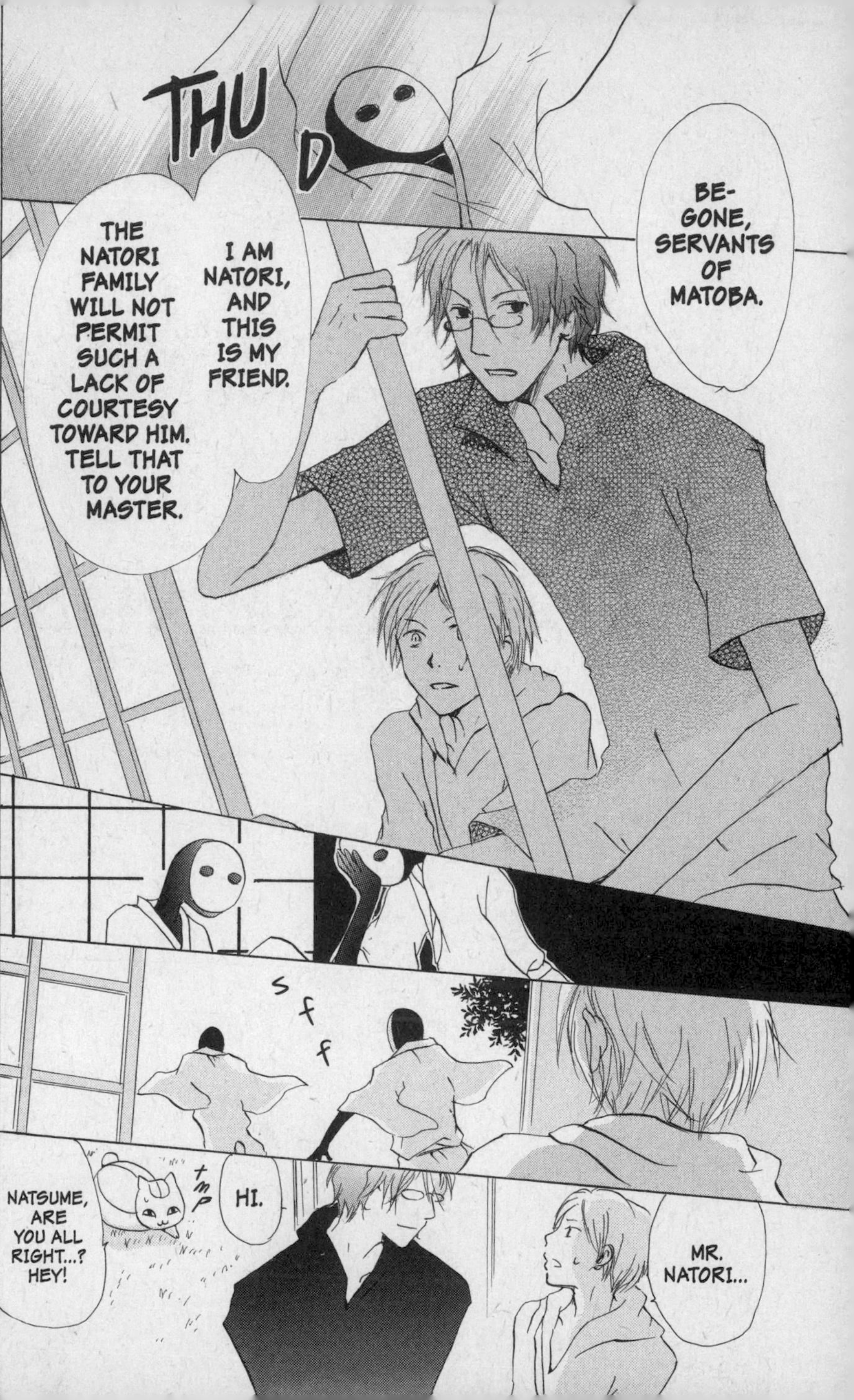
THUD
BE-GONE, SERVANTS OF MATOBA.
I AM NATORI, AND THIS IS MY FRIEND.
THE NATORI FAMILY WILL NOT PERMIT SUCH A LACK OF COURTESY TOWARD HIM. TELL THAT TO YOUR MASTER.
sff
MR. NATORI...
HI.
tmp
NATSUME, ARE YOU ALL RIGHT...? HEY!

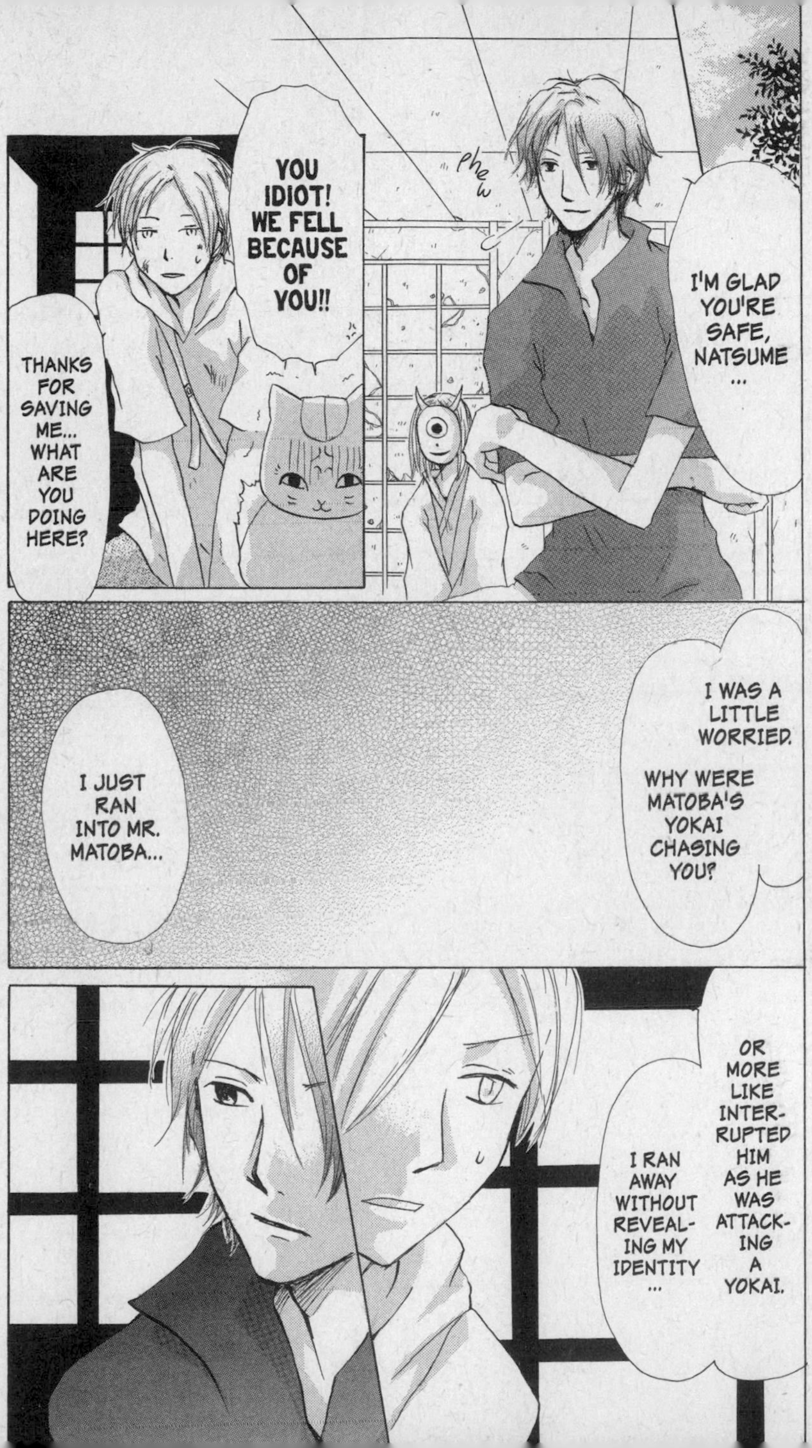
I'M GLAD YOU'RE SAFE, NATSUME ...
phew
YOU IDIOT! WE FELL BECAUSE OF YOU!!
THANKS FOR SAVING ME... WHAT ARE YOU DOING HERE?
I WAS A LITTLE WORRIED.
WHY WERE MATOBA'S YOKAI CHASING YOU?
I JUST RAN INTO MR. MATOBA...
OR MORE LIKE INTER-RUPTED HIM AS HE WAS ATTACK-ING A YOKAI.
I RAN AWAY WITHOUT REVEAL-ING MY IDENTITY ...

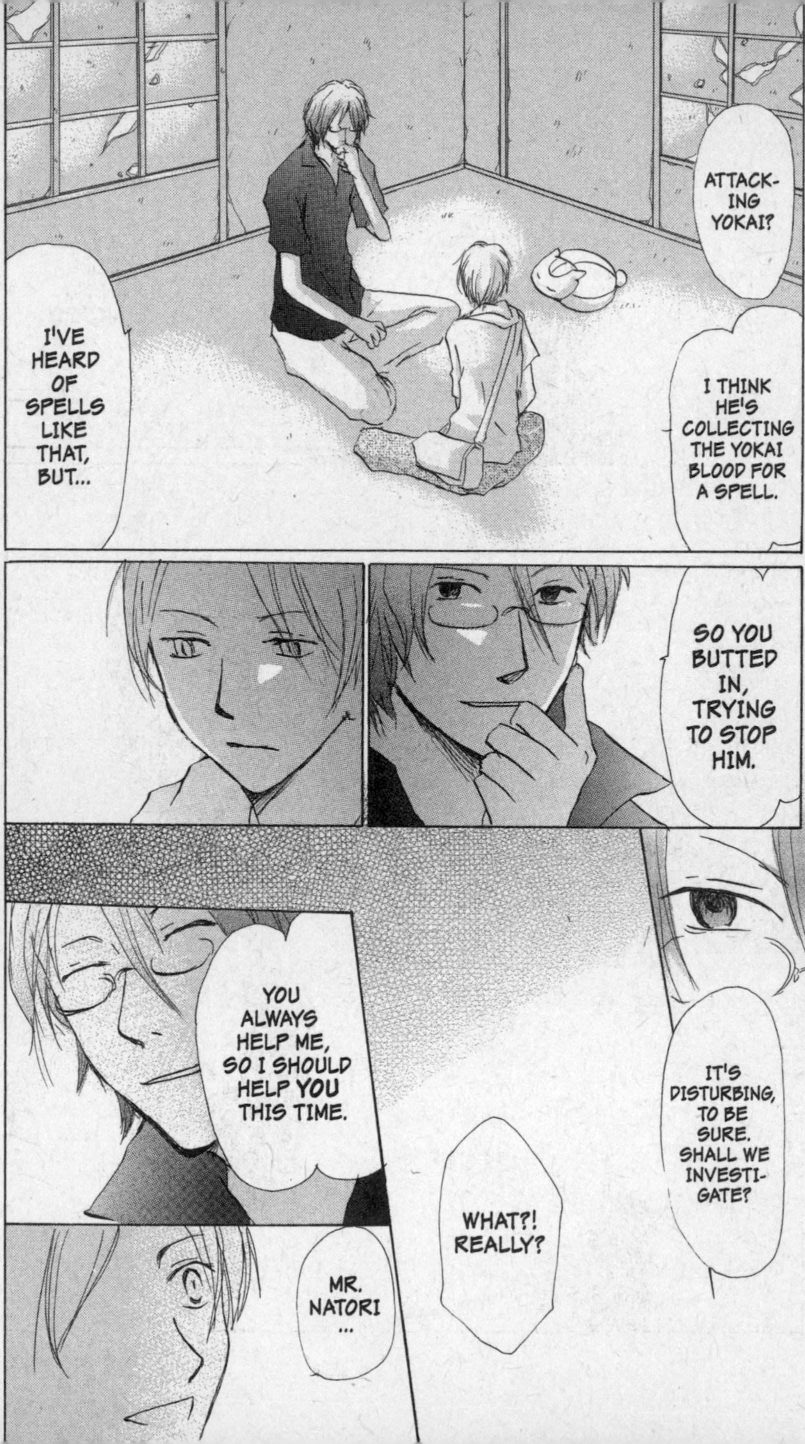
ATTACK-ING YOKAI?
I THINK HE'S COLLECTING THE YOKAI BLOOD FOR A SPELL.
I'VE HEARD OF SPELLS LIKE THAT, BUT...
SO YOU BUTTED IN, TRYING TO STOP HIM.
IT'S DISTURBING, TO BE SURE. SHALL WE INVESTI-GATE?
WHAT?! REALLY?
YOU ALWAYS HELP ME, SO I SHOULD HELP YOU THIS TIME.
MR. NATORI...

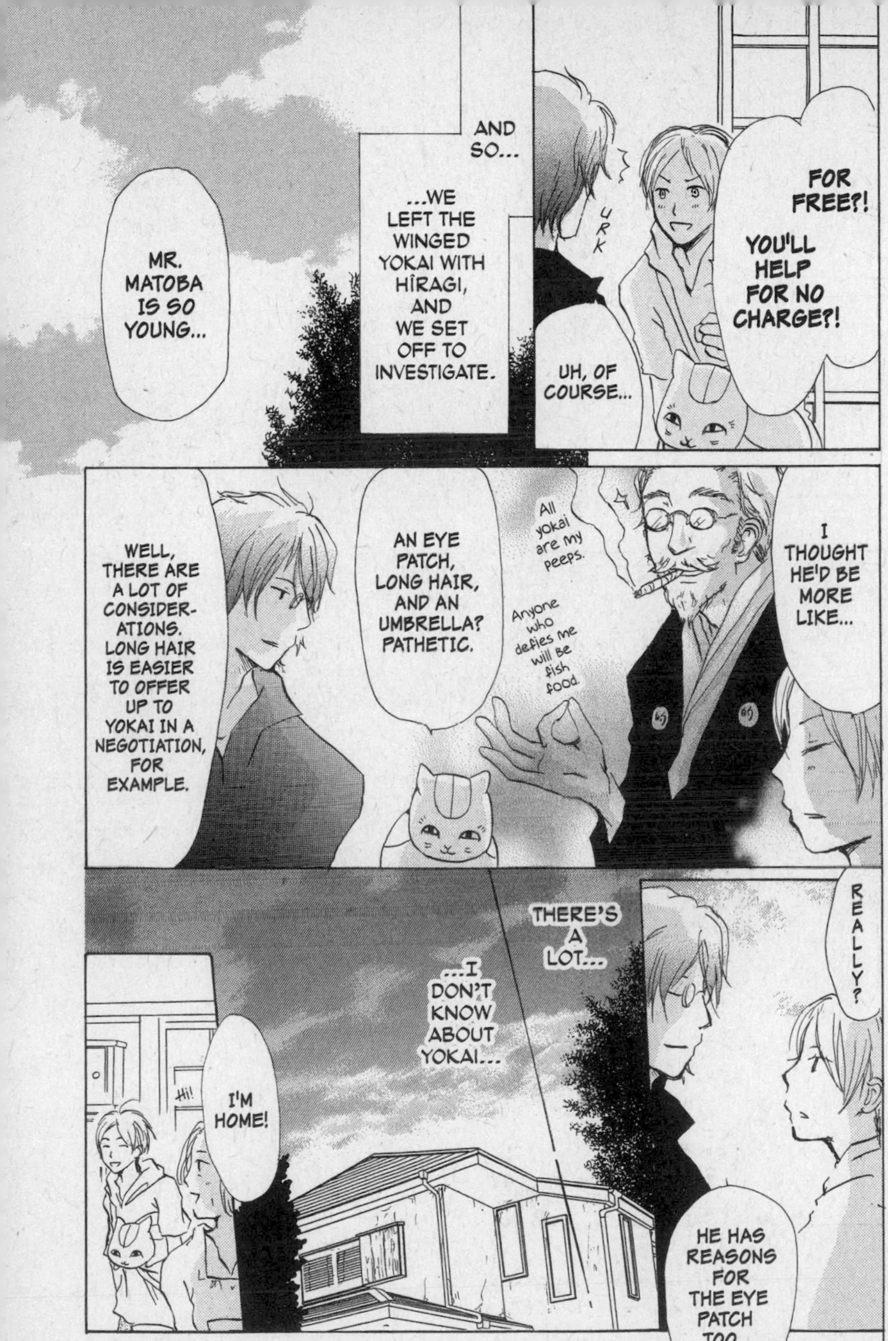
FOR FREE?!
YOU'LL HELP FOR NO CHARGE?!
URK
UH, OF COURSE...
AND SO...
...WE LEFT THE WINGED YOKAI WITH HÎRAGI, AND WE SET OFF TO INVESTIGATE.
MR. MATOBA IS SO YOUNG...
I THOUGHT HE'D BE MORE LIKE...
All yokai are my peeps.
Anyone who defies me will be fish food.
AN EYE PATCH, LONG HAIR, AND AN UMBRELLA? PATHETIC.
WELL, THERE ARE A LOT OF CONSIDER-ATIONS. LONG HAIR IS EASIER TO OFFER UP TO YOKAI IN A NEGOTIATION, FOR EXAMPLE.
REALLY?
HE HAS REASONS FOR THE EYE PATCH TOO...
THERE'S A LOT...
...I DON'T KNOW ABOUT YOKAI...
I'M HOME!
Hi!

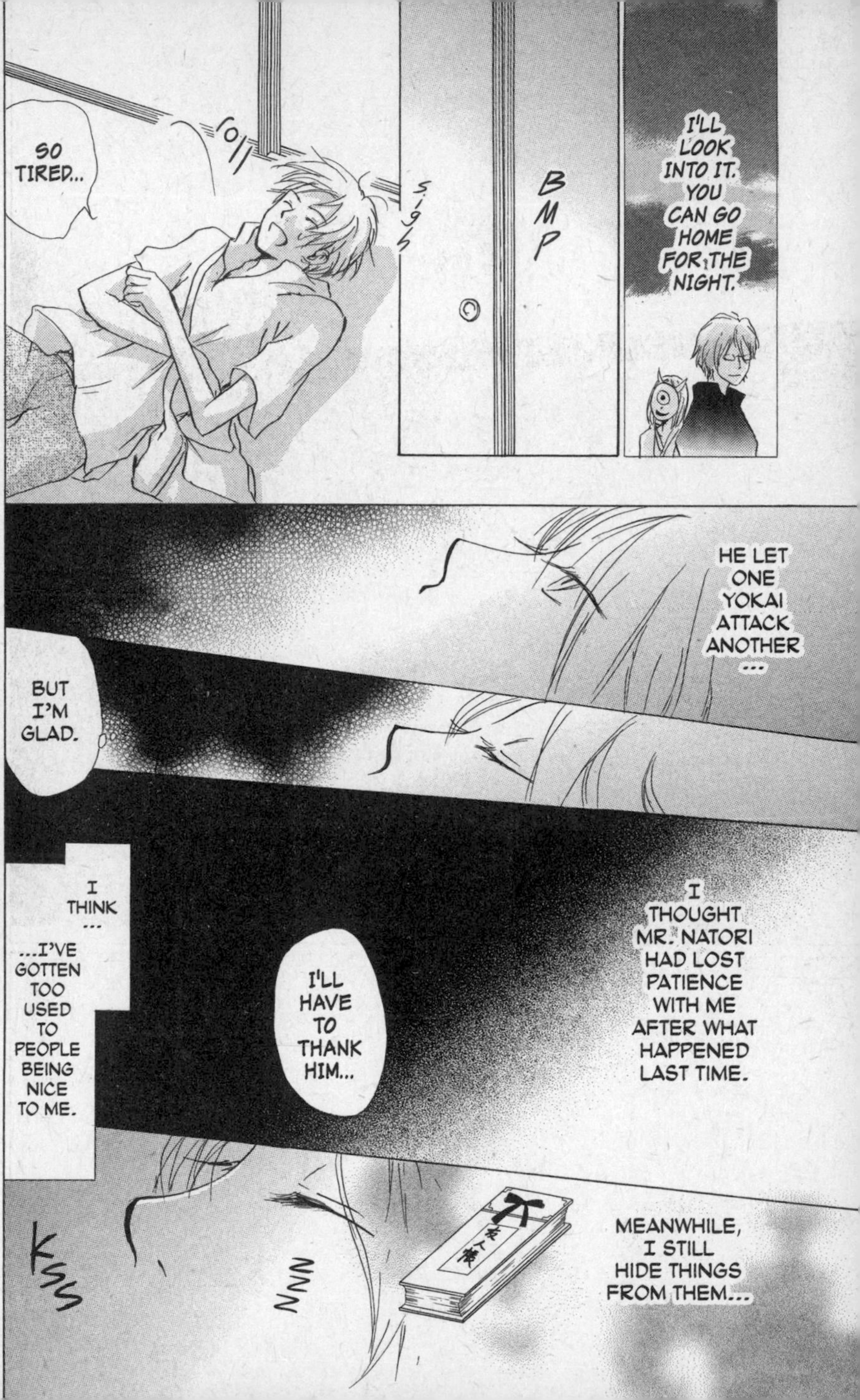
I'LL LOOK INTO IT. YOU CAN GO HOME FOR THE NIGHT.
BMP
SO TIRED...
CLOP
SIGH
HE LET ONE YOKAI ATTACK ANOTHER...
BUT I'M GLAD.
I THOUGHT MR. NATORI HAD LOST PATIENCE WITH ME AFTER WHAT HAPPENED LAST TIME.
I'LL HAVE TO THANK HIM...
I THINK...
...I'VE GOTTEN TOO USED TO PEOPLE BEING NICE TO ME.
MEANWHILE, I STILL HIDE THINGS FROM THEM...
ZZZ
KSS

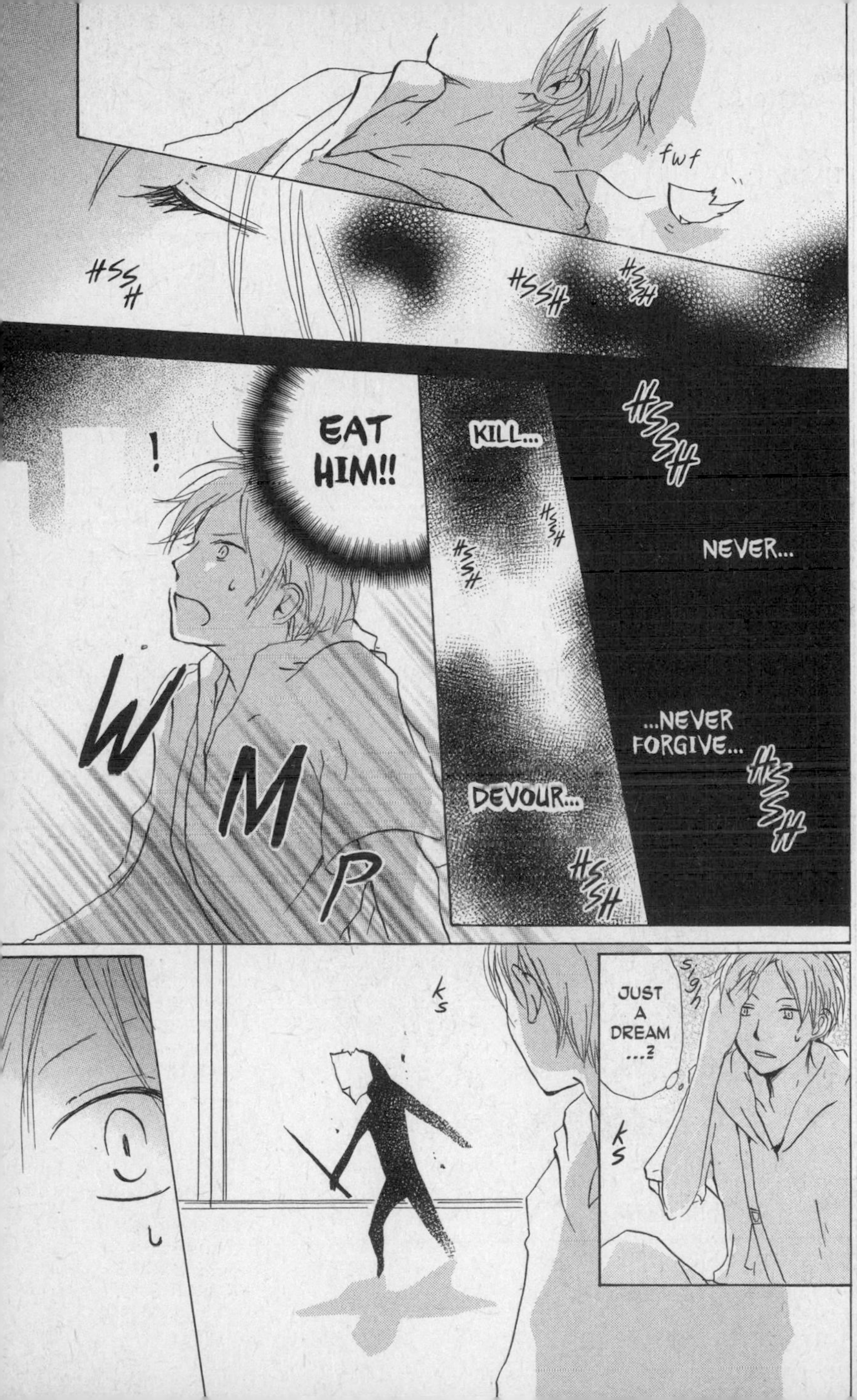
fwf
HSSH
HSSH
HSSH
HSSH
NEVER...
...NEVER FORGIVE...
HSSH
KILL...
HSSH
HSSH
DEVOUR...
HSSH
EAT HIM!!
!
WMP
sigh
JUST A DREAM ...?
ks
ks

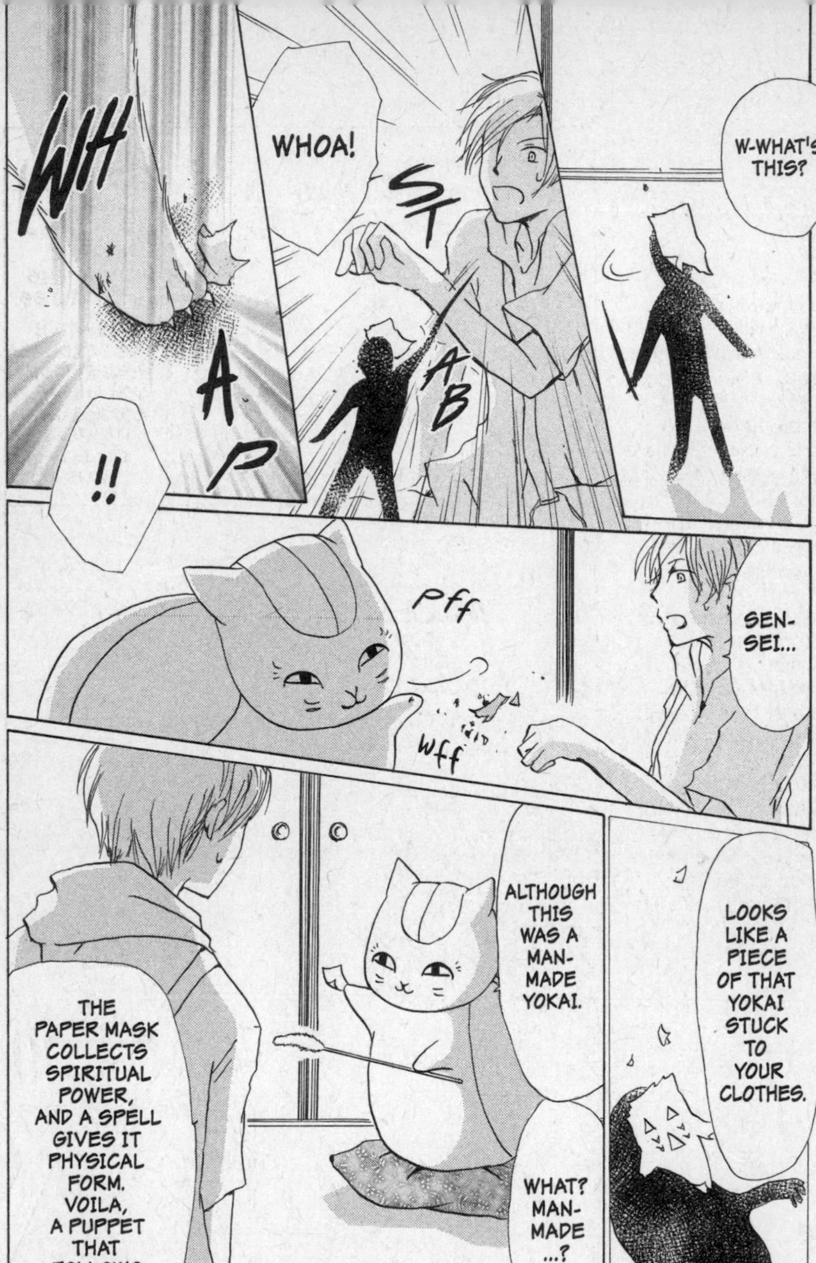
W-WHAT'S THIS?
WHOA!
STAB
WHAP
!!
SEN-SEI...
pff
wff
LOOKS LIKE A PIECE OF THAT YOKAI STUCK TO YOUR CLOTHES.
ALTHOUGH THIS WAS A MAN-MADE YOKAI.
WHAT? MAN-MADE ...?
THE PAPER MASK COLLECTS SPIRITUAL POWER, AND A SPELL GIVES IT PHYSICAL FORM. VOILA, A PUPPET THAT FOLLOWS COMMANDS.

## 02

❀Fan Book: part 1

Having a Natsume anime gave us the opportunity to make an official fan book. I feel so much indescribable joy from having some-one pick up my work and make something like this for it. It's very fun, cute, and humorous, so please check it out.

It was a good oppor-tunity for me to write up simple profiles for the characters. They're only rough guides, so if they sound different from what you imagined the characters to be like, please feel free to imagine them as you see fit.

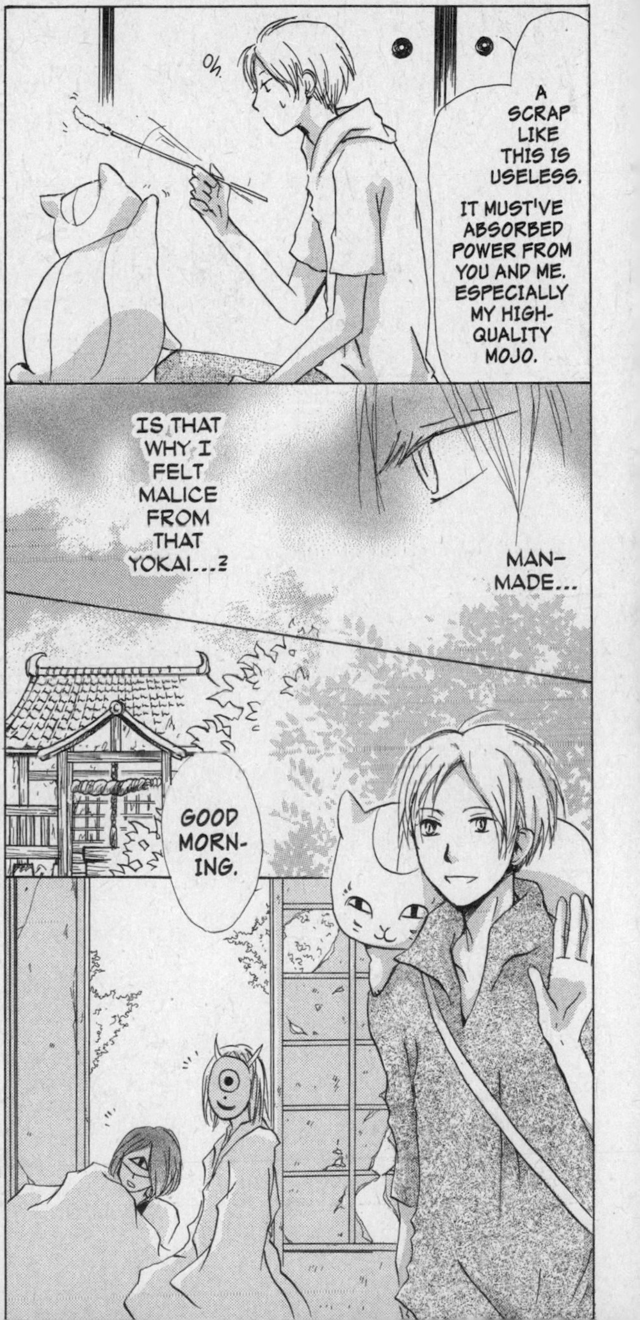
A SCRAP LIKE THIS IS USELESS.
IT MUST'VE ABSORBED POWER FROM YOU AND ME. ESPECIALLY MY HIGH-QUALITY MOJO.
Oh.
MAN-MADE...
IS THAT WHY I FELT MALICE FROM THAT YOKAI...?
GOOD MORNING.

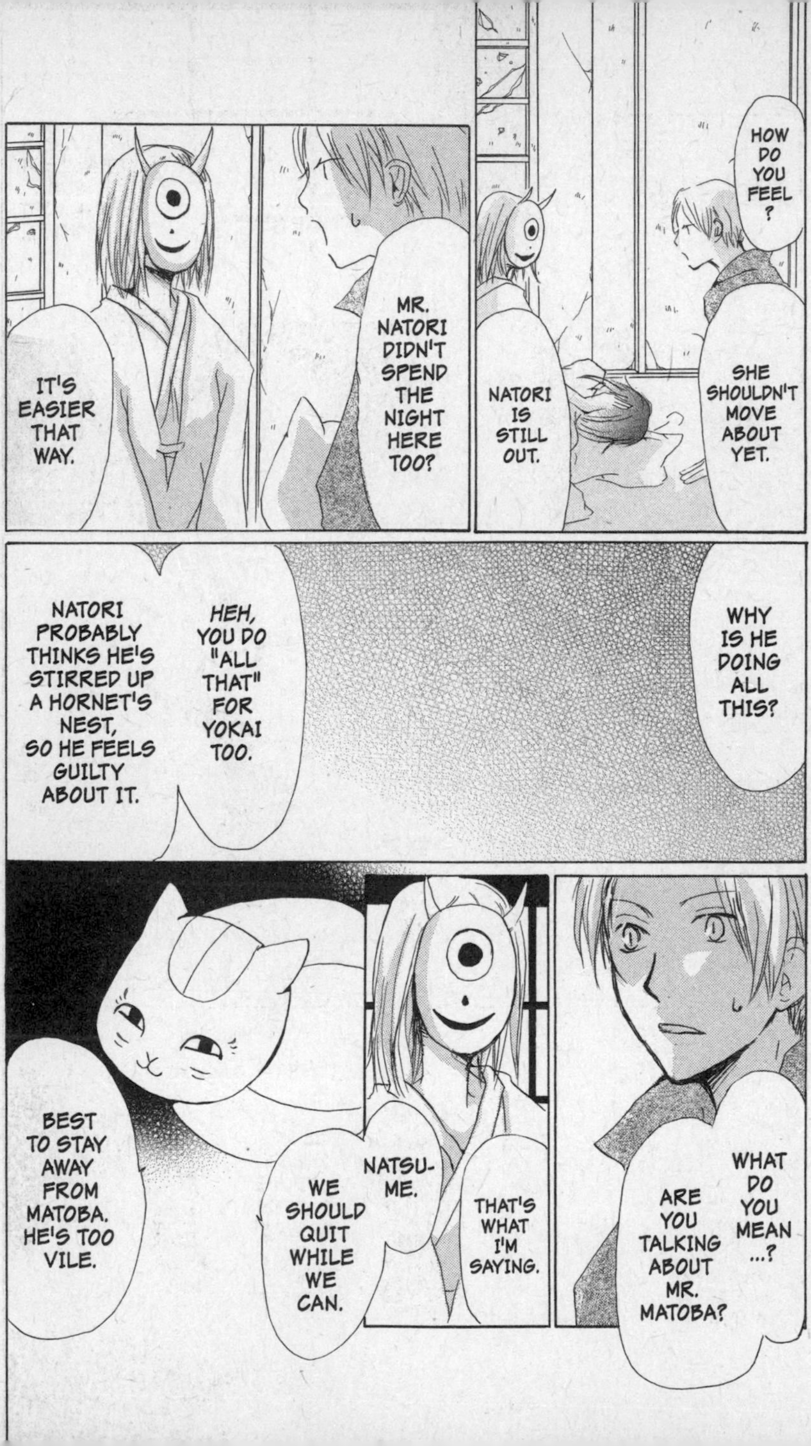
HOW DO YOU FEEL?
SHE SHOULDN'T MOVE ABOUT YET.
NATORI IS STILL OUT.
MR. NATORI DIDN'T SPEND THE NIGHT HERE TOO?
IT'S EASIER THAT WAY.
WHY IS HE DOING ALL THIS?
HEH, YOU DO "ALL THAT" FOR YOKAI TOO.
NATORI PROBABLY THINKS HE'S STIRRED UP A HORNET'S NEST, SO HE FEELS GUILTY ABOUT IT.
WHAT DO YOU MEAN ...?
ARE YOU TALKING ABOUT MR. MATOBA?
NATSUME.
THAT'S WHAT I'M SAYING.
WE SHOULD QUIT WHILE WE CAN.
BEST TO STAY AWAY FROM MATOBA. HE'S TOO VILE.

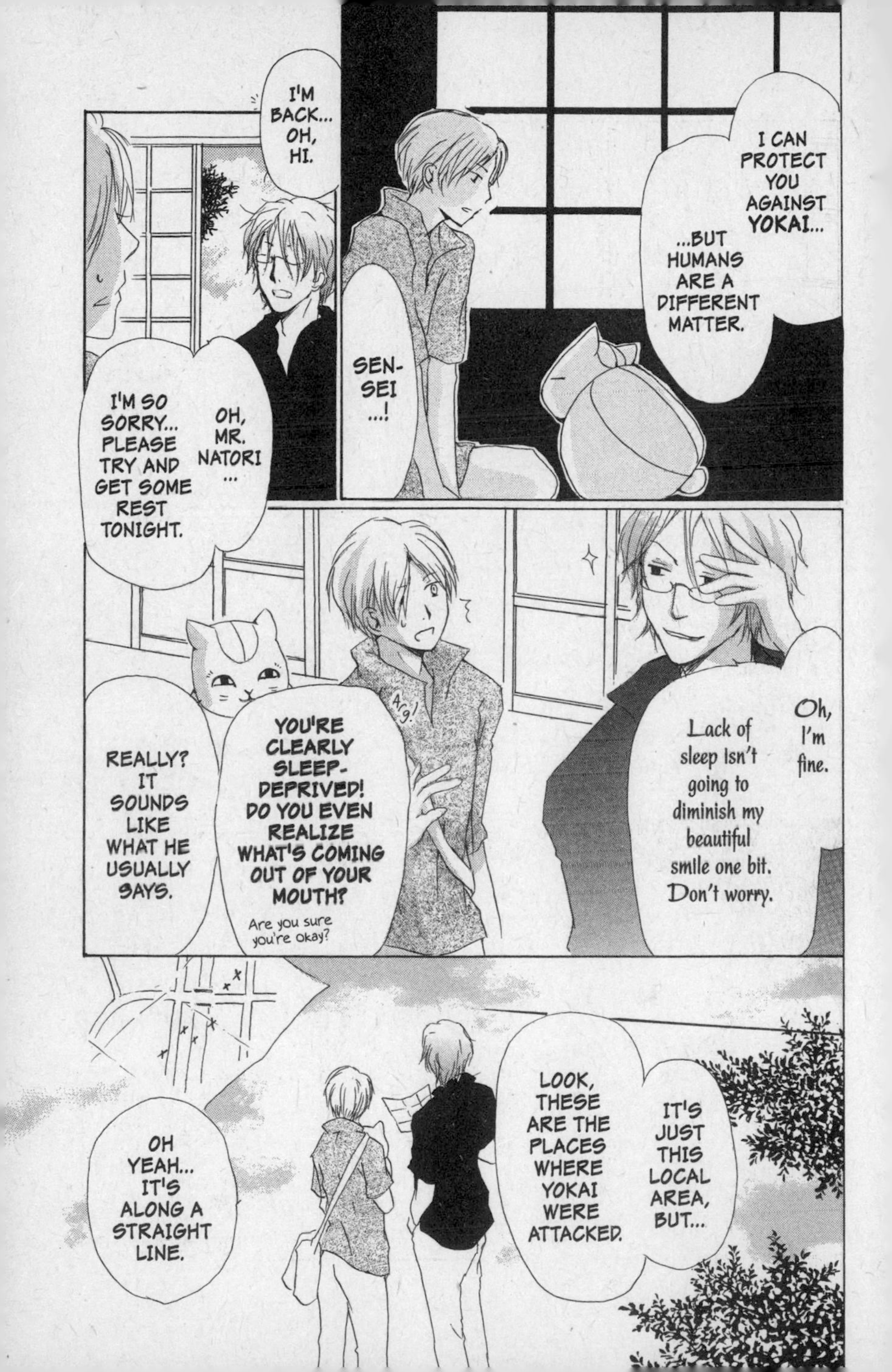
I CAN PROTECT YOU AGAINST YOKAI...
...BUT HUMANS ARE A DIFFERENT MATTER.
SEN-SEI ...!
I'M BACK... OH, HI.
OH, MR. NATORI ...
I'M SO SORRY... PLEASE TRY AND GET SOME REST TONIGHT.
Oh, I'm fine.
Lack of sleep isn't going to diminish my beautiful smile one bit. Don't worry.
Arg!
YOU'RE CLEARLY SLEEP-DEPRIVED! DO YOU EVEN REALIZE WHAT'S COMING OUT OF YOUR MOUTH?
Are you sure you're okay?
REALLY? IT SOUNDS LIKE WHAT HE USUALLY SAYS.
IT'S JUST THIS LOCAL AREA, BUT...
LOOK, THESE ARE THE PLACES WHERE YOKAI WERE ATTACKED.
OH YEAH... IT'S ALONG A STRAIGHT LINE.

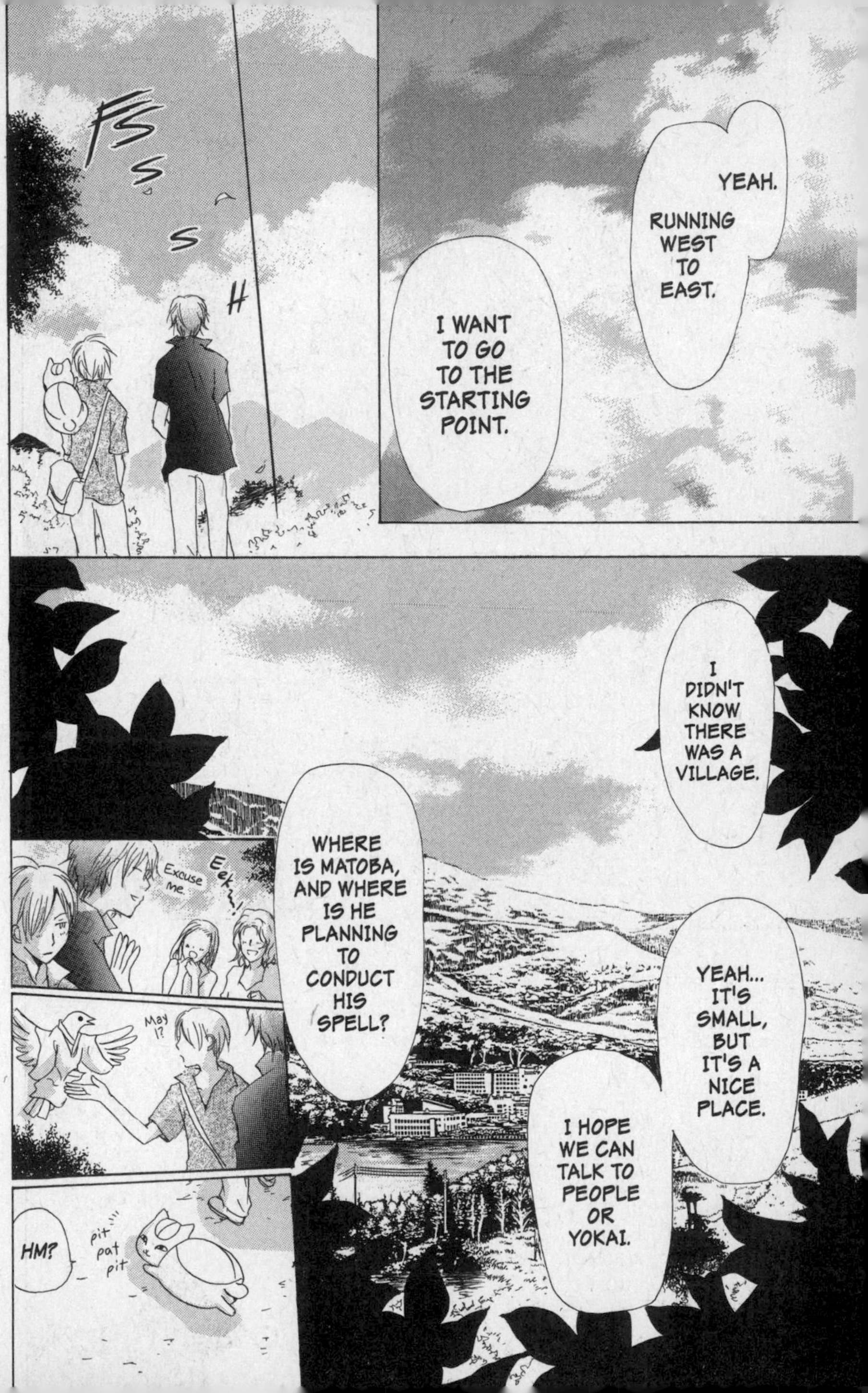
YEAH.
RUNNING WEST TO EAST.
I WANT TO GO TO THE STARTING POINT.
FSSSH
I DIDN'T KNOW THERE WAS A VILLAGE.
YEAH... IT'S SMALL, BUT IT'S A NICE PLACE.
I HOPE WE CAN TALK TO PEOPLE OR YOKAI.
WHERE IS MATOBA, AND WHERE IS HE PLANNING TO CONDUCT HIS SPELL?
Excuse me.
Eek!
May I?
HM?
pit pat pit

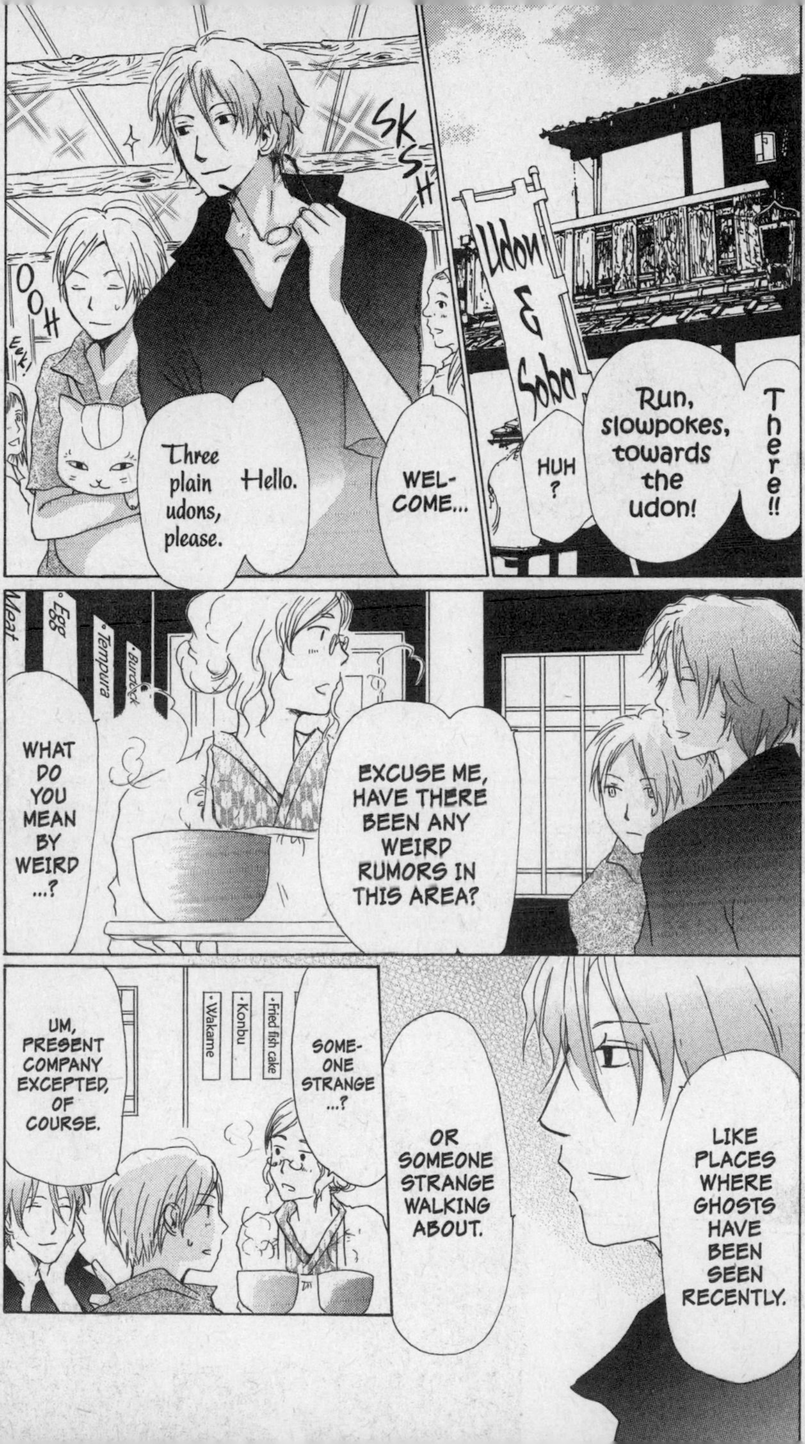

There!!
Run, slowpokes, towards the udon!
HUH?
Udon & Soba
WEL-COME...
Hello.
Three plain udons, please.
SKSH
OOH
Eek!
EXCUSE ME, HAVE THERE BEEN ANY WEIRD RUMORS IN THIS AREA?
WHAT DO YOU MEAN BY WEIRD...?
•Burdock
•Tempura
•Egg
•Meat
LIKE PLACES WHERE GHOSTS HAVE BEEN SEEN RECENTLY.
OR SOMEONE STRANGE WALKING ABOUT.
SOME-ONE STRANGE...?
•Fried fish cake
•Konbu
•Wakame
UM, PRESENT COMPANY EXCEPTED, OF COURSE.

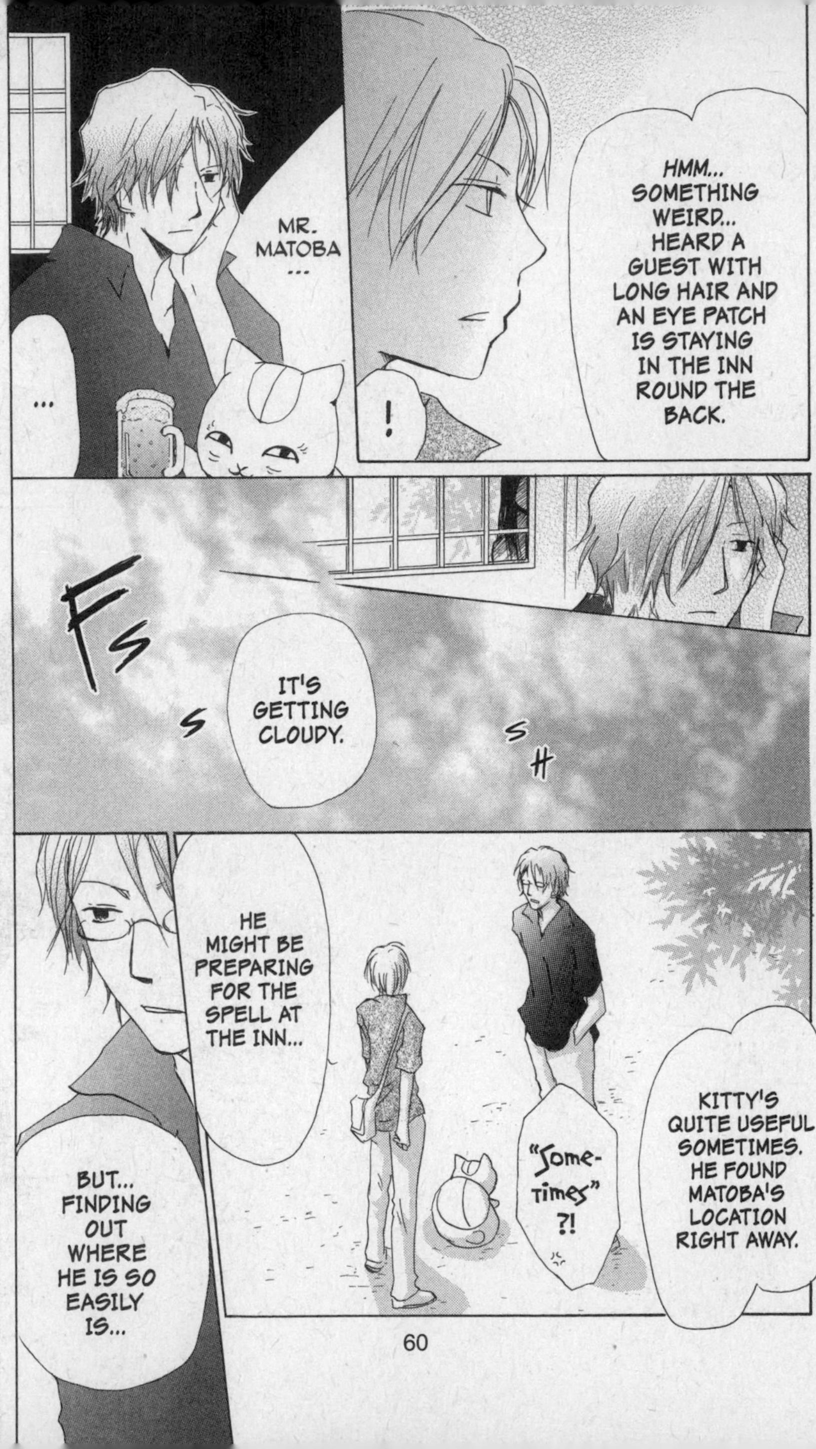
HMM... SOMETHING WEIRD... HEARD A GUEST WITH LONG HAIR AND AN EYE PATCH IS STAYING IN THE INN ROUND THE BACK.
!
MR. MATOBA ...
...
FSS
SH
IT'S GETTING CLOUDY.
KITTY'S QUITE USEFUL SOMETIMES. HE FOUND MATOBA'S LOCATION RIGHT AWAY.
"Some-times" ?!
HE MIGHT BE PREPARING FOR THE SPELL AT THE INN...
BUT... FINDING OUT WHERE HE IS SO EASILY IS...

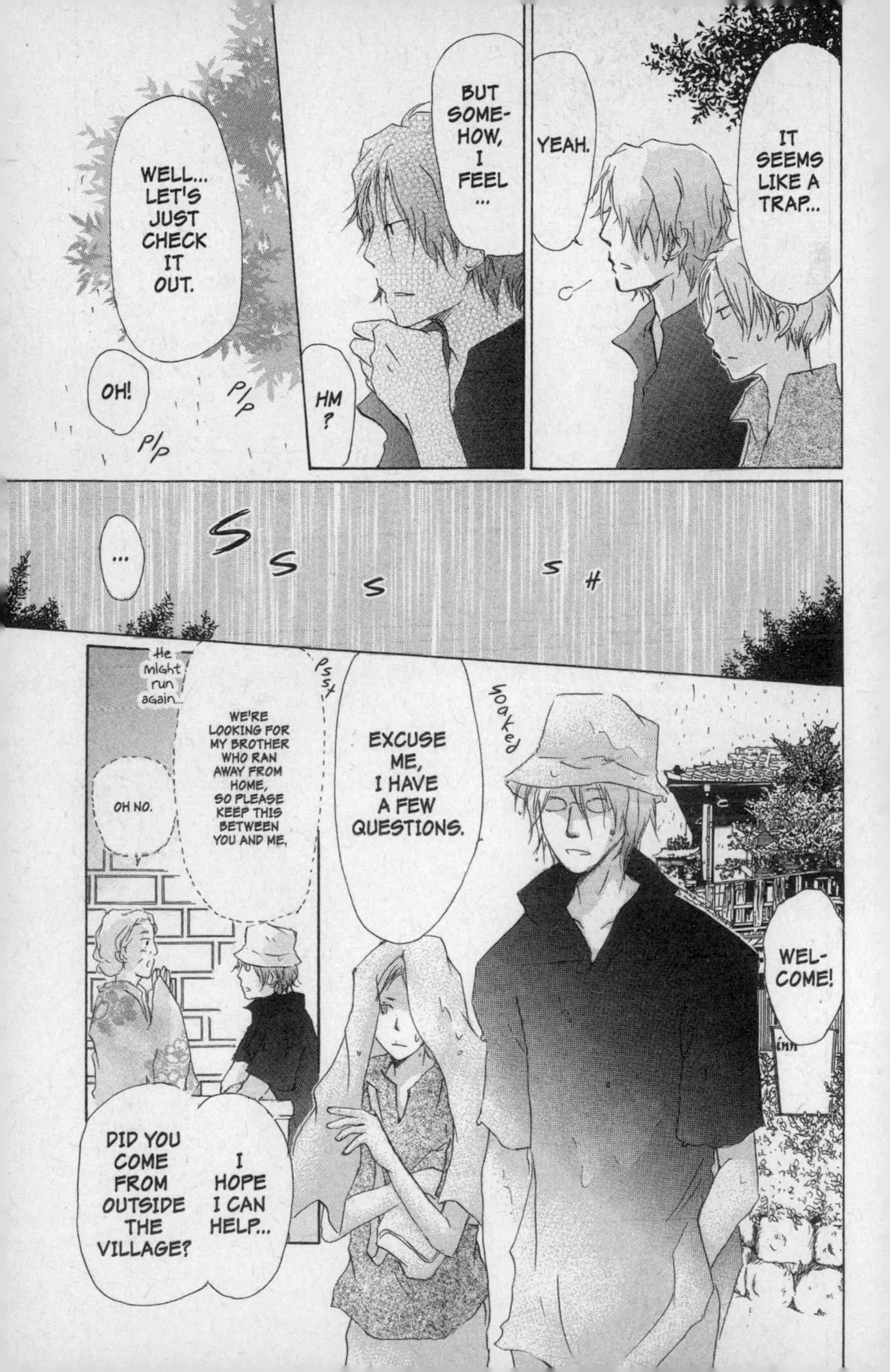
IT SEEMS LIKE A TRAP...
YEAH.
BUT SOMEHOW, I FEEL ...
HM?
WELL... LET'S JUST CHECK IT OUT.
P/P
OH!
P/P
SSSSH
...
soaked
WELCOME!
inn
EXCUSE ME, I HAVE A FEW QUESTIONS.
Psst
WE'RE LOOKING FOR MY BROTHER WHO RAN AWAY FROM HOME, SO PLEASE KEEP THIS BETWEEN YOU AND ME.
He might run again...
OH NO.
I HOPE I CAN HELP...
DID YOU COME FROM OUTSIDE THE VILLAGE?

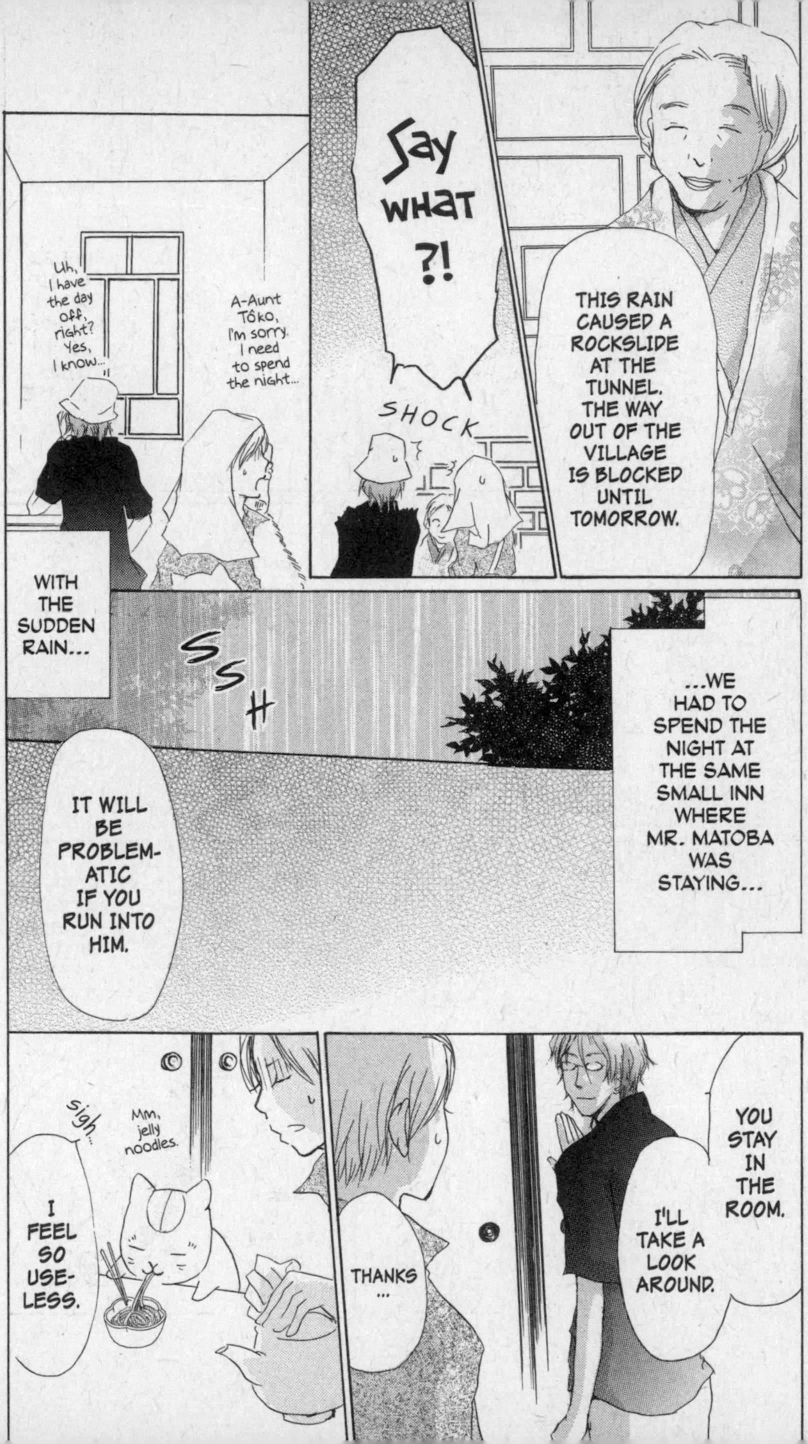
THIS RAIN CAUSED A ROCKSLIDE AT THE TUNNEL. THE WAY OUT OF THE VILLAGE IS BLOCKED UNTIL TOMORROW.
SAY WHAT ?!
SHOCK
A-Aunt Tôko, I'm sorry. I need to spend the night...
Uh, I have the day off, right? Yes, I know...
WITH THE SUDDEN RAIN...
SSH
...WE HAD TO SPEND THE NIGHT AT THE SAME SMALL INN WHERE MR. MATOBA WAS STAYING...
IT WILL BE PROBLEMATIC IF YOU RUN INTO HIM.
YOU STAY IN THE ROOM.
I'LL TAKE A LOOK AROUND.
THANKS...
Mm, jelly noodles.
sigh...
I FEEL SO USELESS.

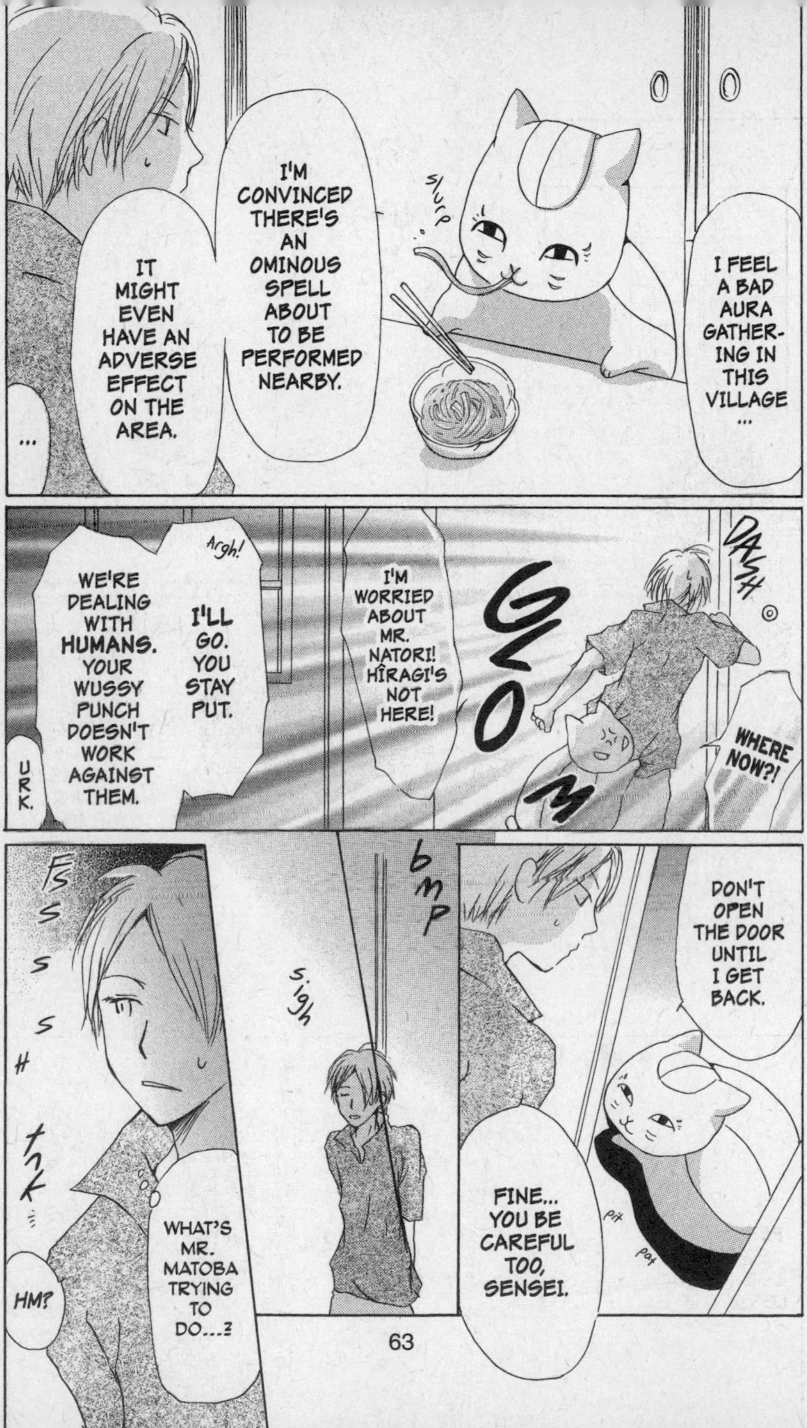
I FEEL A BAD AURA GATHERING IN THIS VILLAGE ...
slurp
I'M CONVINCED THERE'S AN OMINOUS SPELL ABOUT TO BE PERFORMED NEARBY.
IT MIGHT EVEN HAVE AN ADVERSE EFFECT ON THE AREA.
...
DASH
WHERE NOW?!
GZOM
I'M WORRIED ABOUT MR. NATORI! HÎRAGI'S NOT HERE!
Argh!
I'LL GO. YOU STAY PUT.
WE'RE DEALING WITH HUMANS. YOUR WUSSY PUNCH DOESN'T WORK AGAINST THEM.
URK.
DON'T OPEN THE DOOR UNTIL I GET BACK.
pit
pat
FINE... YOU BE CAREFUL TOO, SENSEI.
bmp
sigh
FSSSH
tnk
WHAT'S MR. MATOBA TRYING TO DO...?
HM?

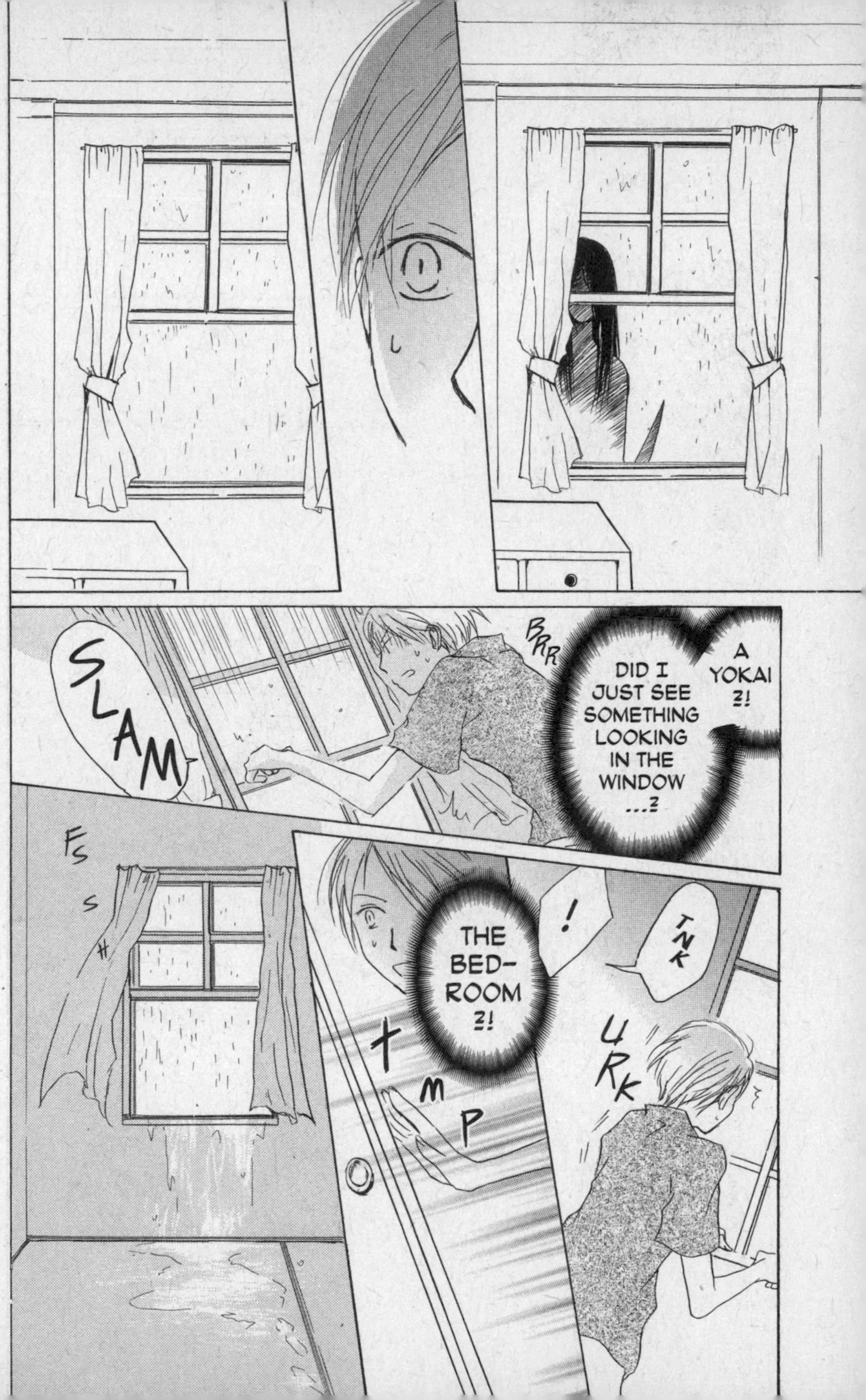
A YOKAI ?!
DID I JUST SEE SOMETHING LOOKING IN THE WINDOW ...?
BRRR
SLAM
TNK
!
THE BED-ROOM ?!
URK
THMP
FSSH

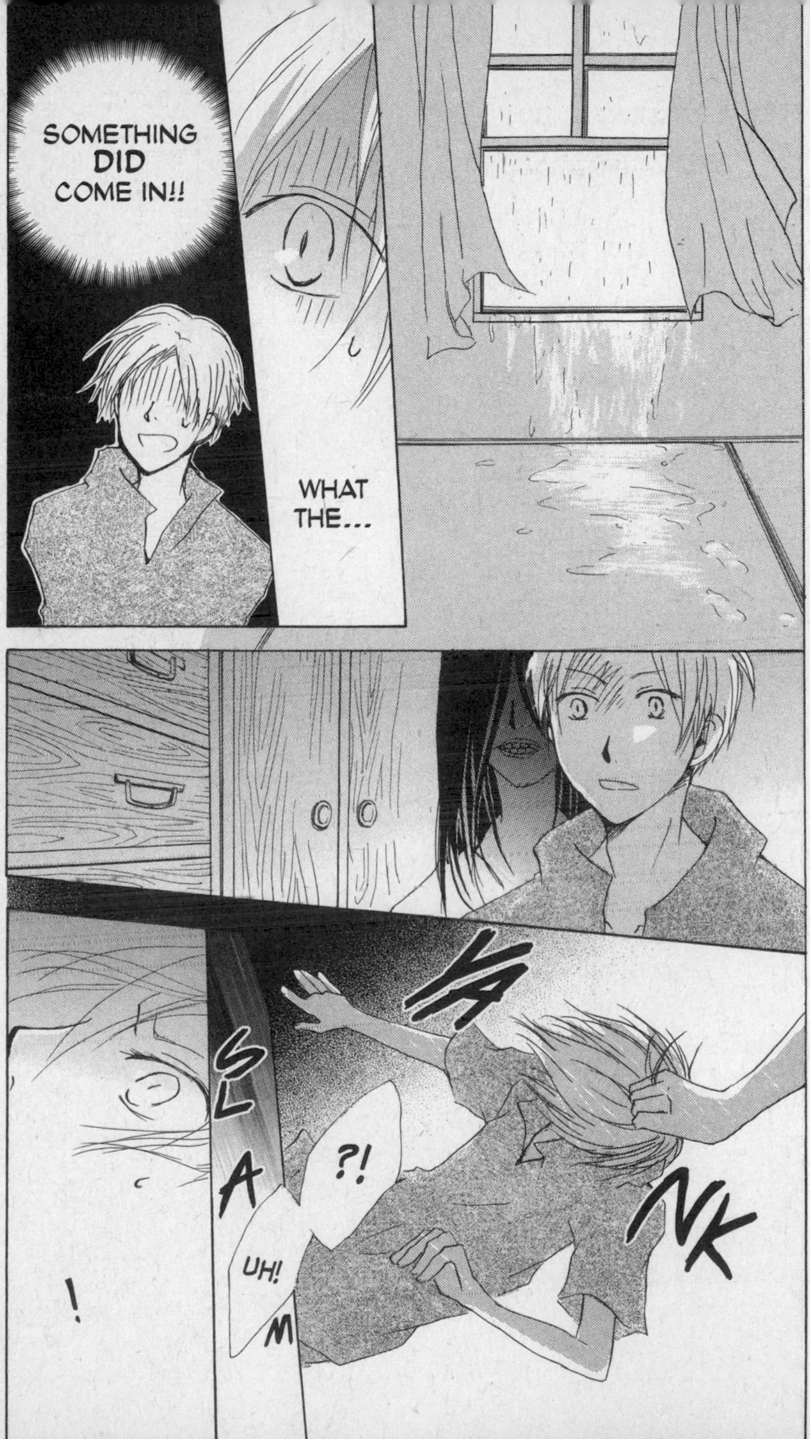
WHAT THE...
SOMETHING DID COME IN!!
YANK
?!
UH!
SLAM
!

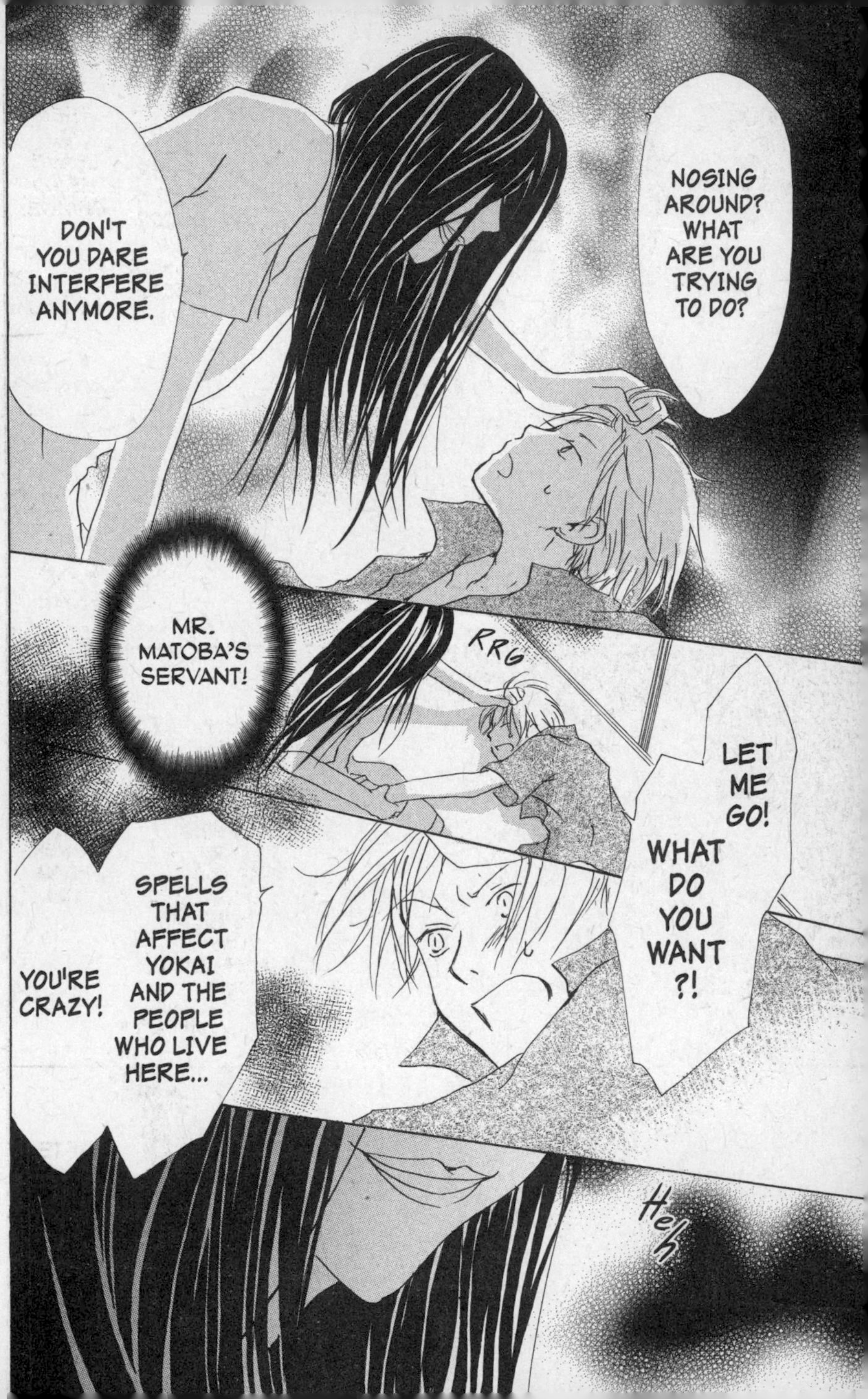
NOSING AROUND? WHAT ARE YOU TRYING TO DO?
DON'T YOU DARE INTERFERE ANYMORE.
RRG
MR. MATOBA'S SERVANT!
LET ME GO!
WHAT DO YOU WANT?!
SPELLS THAT AFFECT YOKAI AND THE PEOPLE WHO LIVE HERE...
YOU'RE CRAZY!
Heh

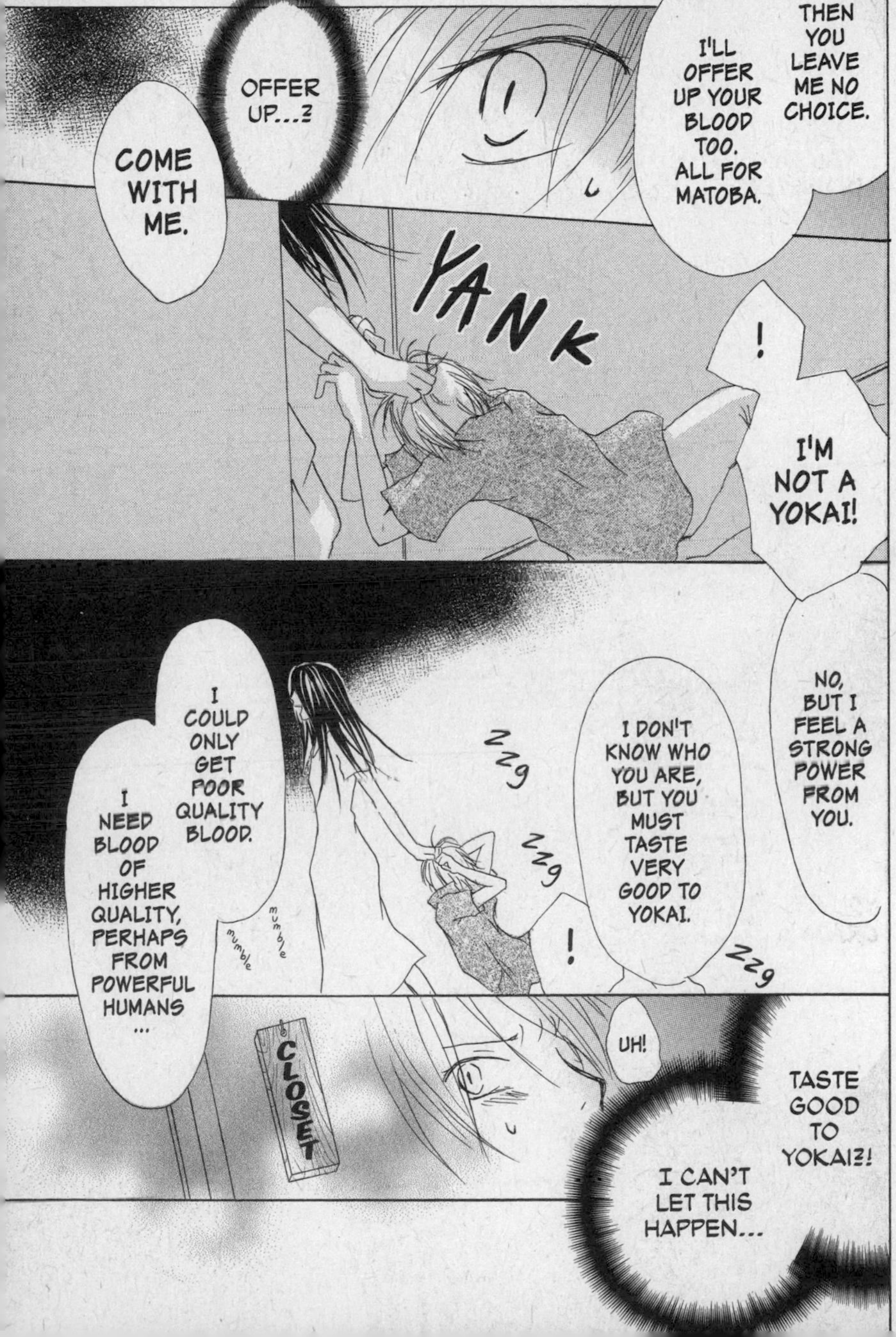
THEN YOU LEAVE ME NO CHOICE.
I'LL OFFER UP YOUR BLOOD TOO. ALL FOR MATOBA.
OFFER UP...?
COME WITH ME.
!
I'M NOT A YOKAI!
YANK
NO, BUT I FEEL A STRONG POWER FROM YOU.
I DON'T KNOW WHO YOU ARE, BUT YOU MUST TASTE VERY GOOD TO YOKAI.
ZZG
ZZG
ZZG
!
I COULD ONLY GET POOR QUALITY BLOOD.
I NEED BLOOD OF HIGHER QUALITY, PERHAPS FROM POWERFUL HUMANS ...
mumble mumble
TASTE GOOD TO YOKAI?!
UH!
I CAN'T LET THIS HAPPEN...
CLOSET

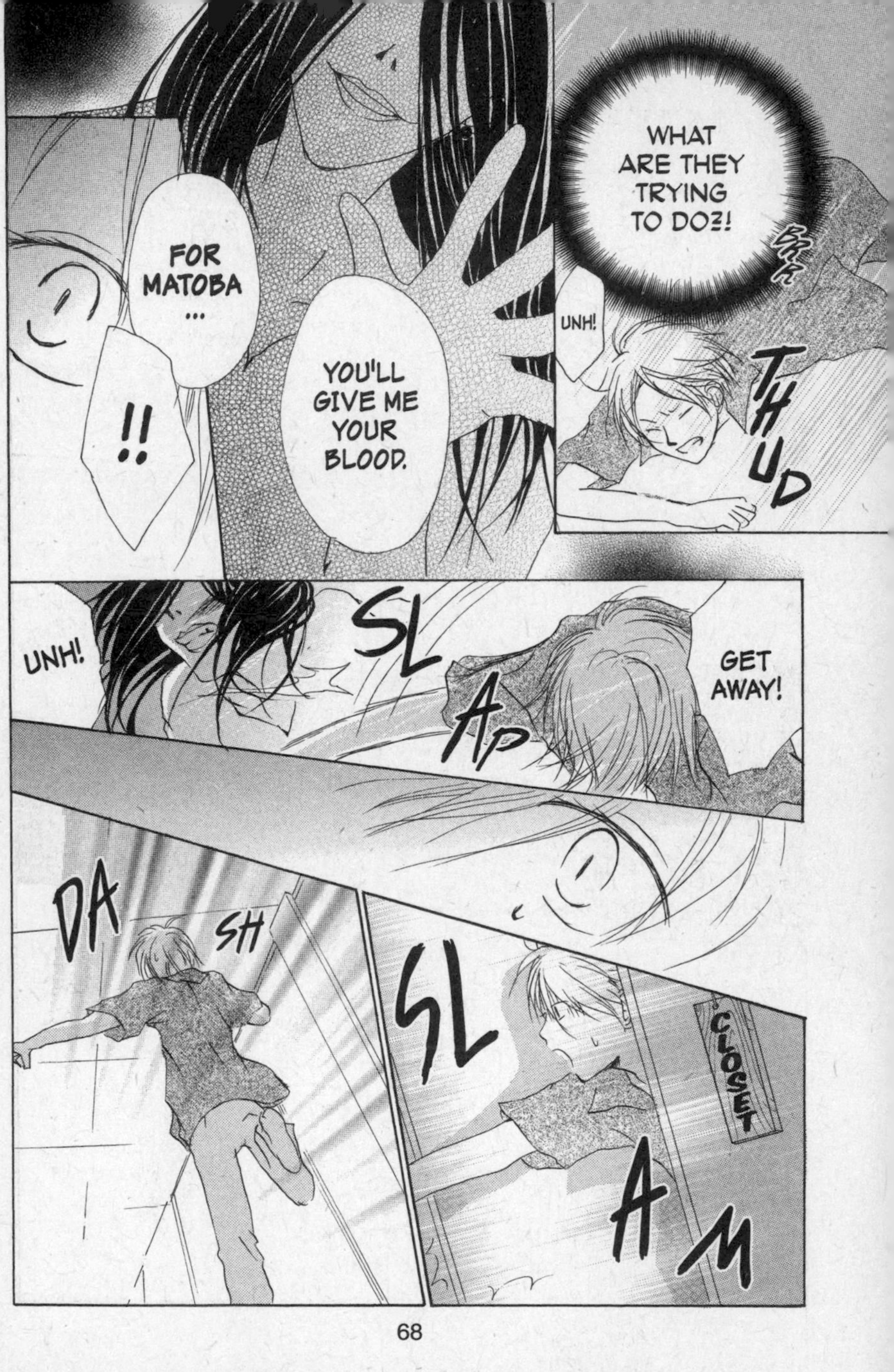

WHAT ARE THEY TRYING TO DO?!
BRR
UNH!
THUD
FOR MATOBA...
YOU'LL GIVE ME YOUR BLOOD.
!!
GET AWAY!
SLAP
UNH!
SLAM
CLOSET
DASH

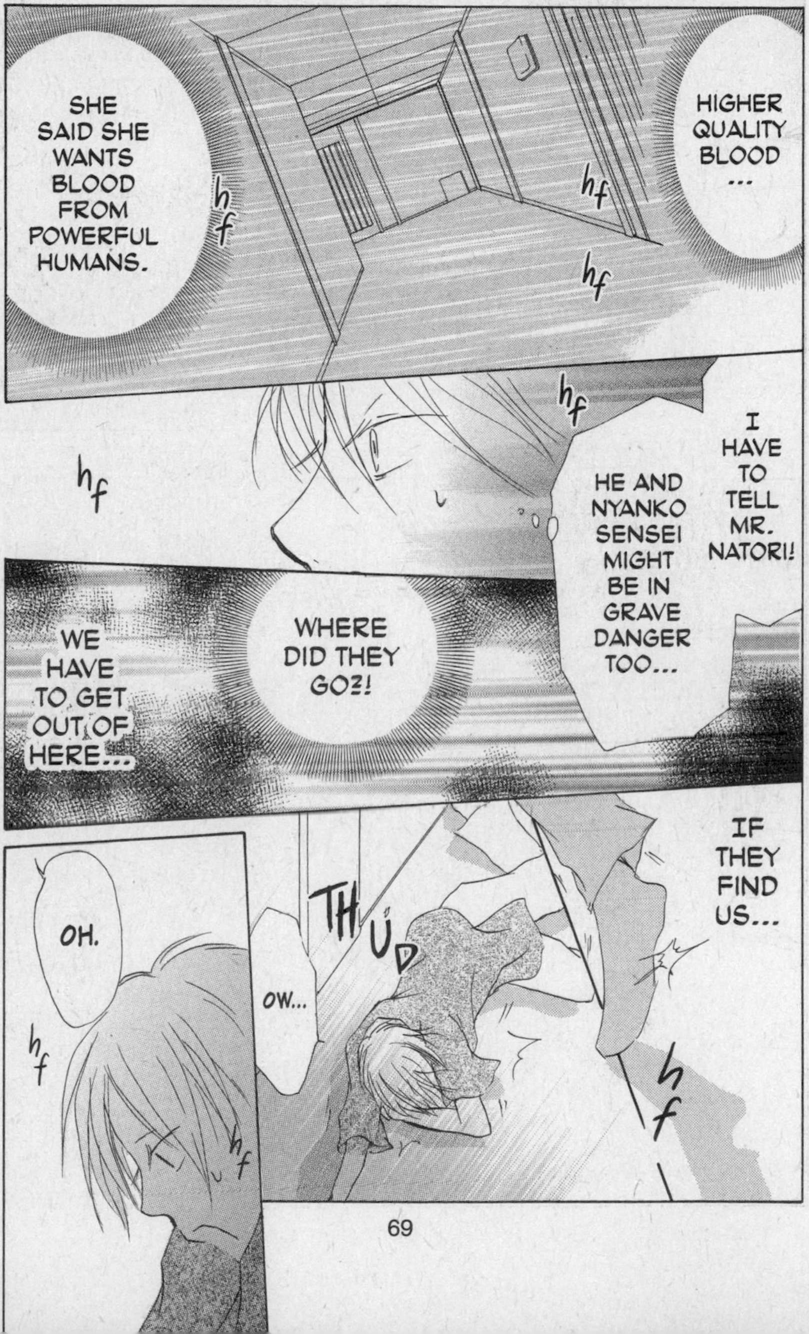
HIGHER QUALITY BLOOD ...
hf
hf
SHE SAID SHE WANTS BLOOD FROM POWERFUL HUMANS.
hf
hf
I HAVE TO TELL MR. NATORI!
HE AND NYANKO SENSEI MIGHT BE IN GRAVE DANGER TOO...
hf
WHERE DID THEY GO?!
WE HAVE TO GET OUT OF HERE...
IF THEY FIND US...
hf
THUD
OW...
OH.
hf
hf

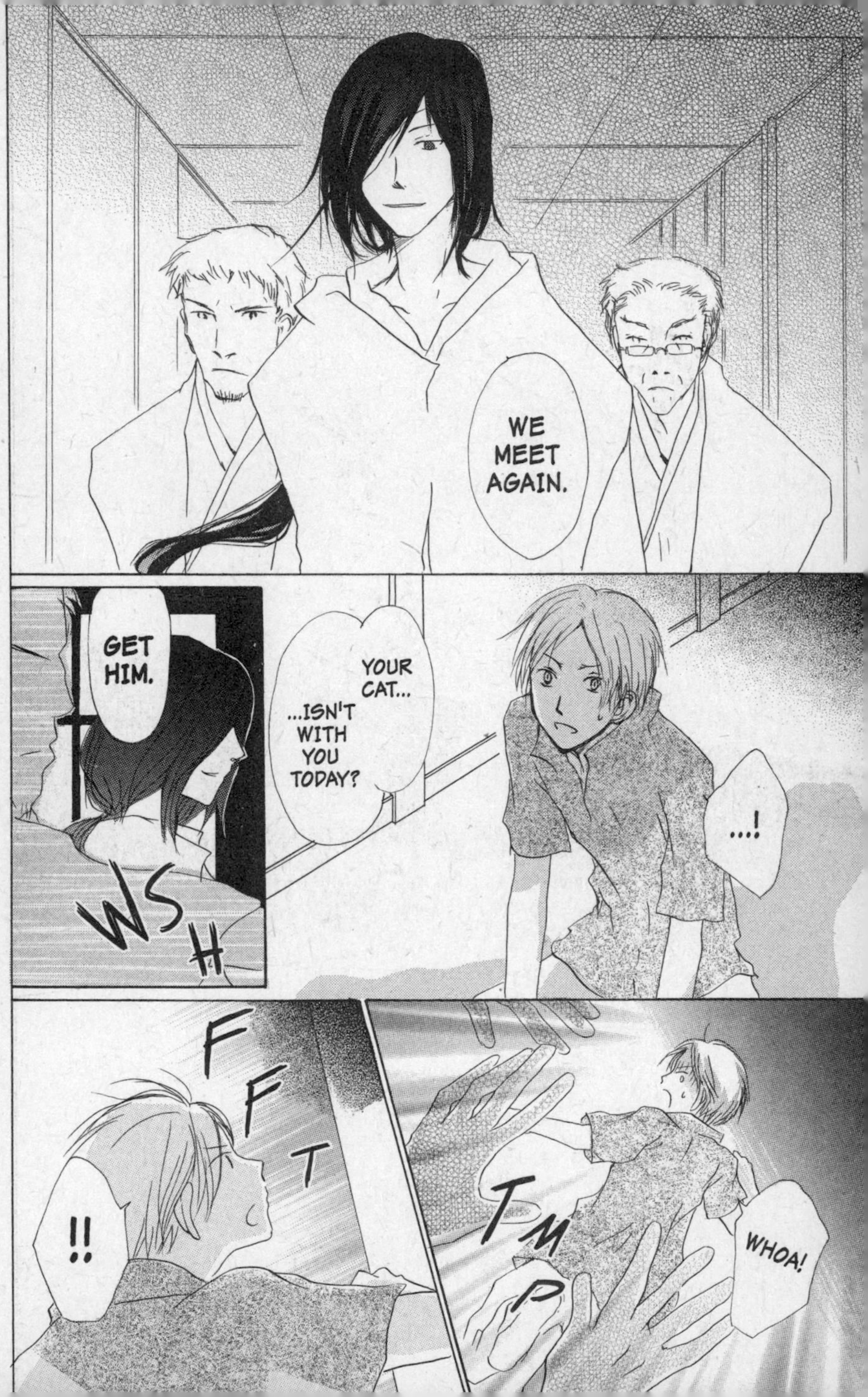
WE MEET AGAIN.
...!
YOUR CAT...
...ISN'T WITH YOU TODAY?
GET HIM.
WSH
WHOA!
TMP
FFFT
!!

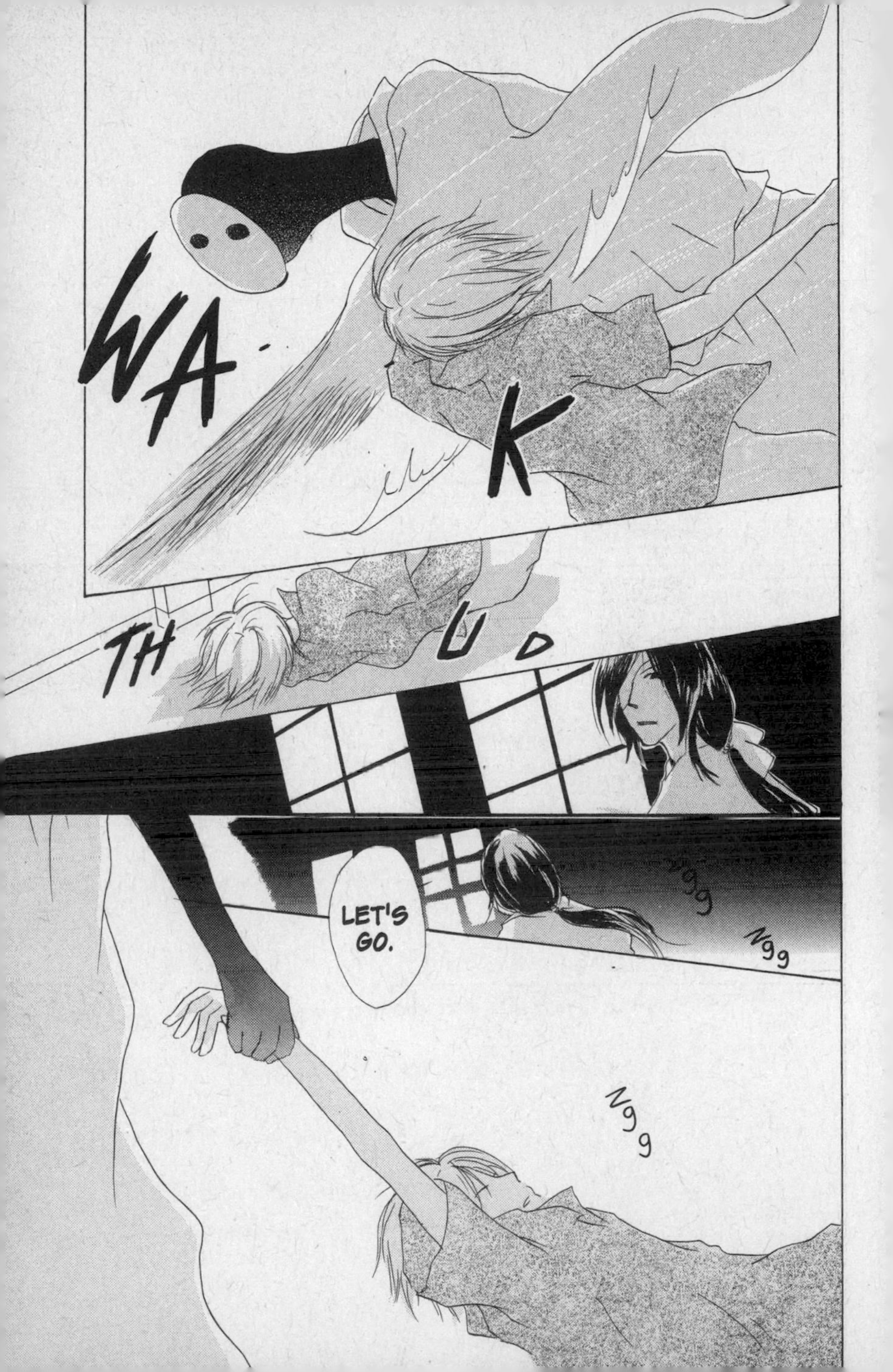
WAK
THUD
Zgg
Zgg
LET'S GO.
Zgg

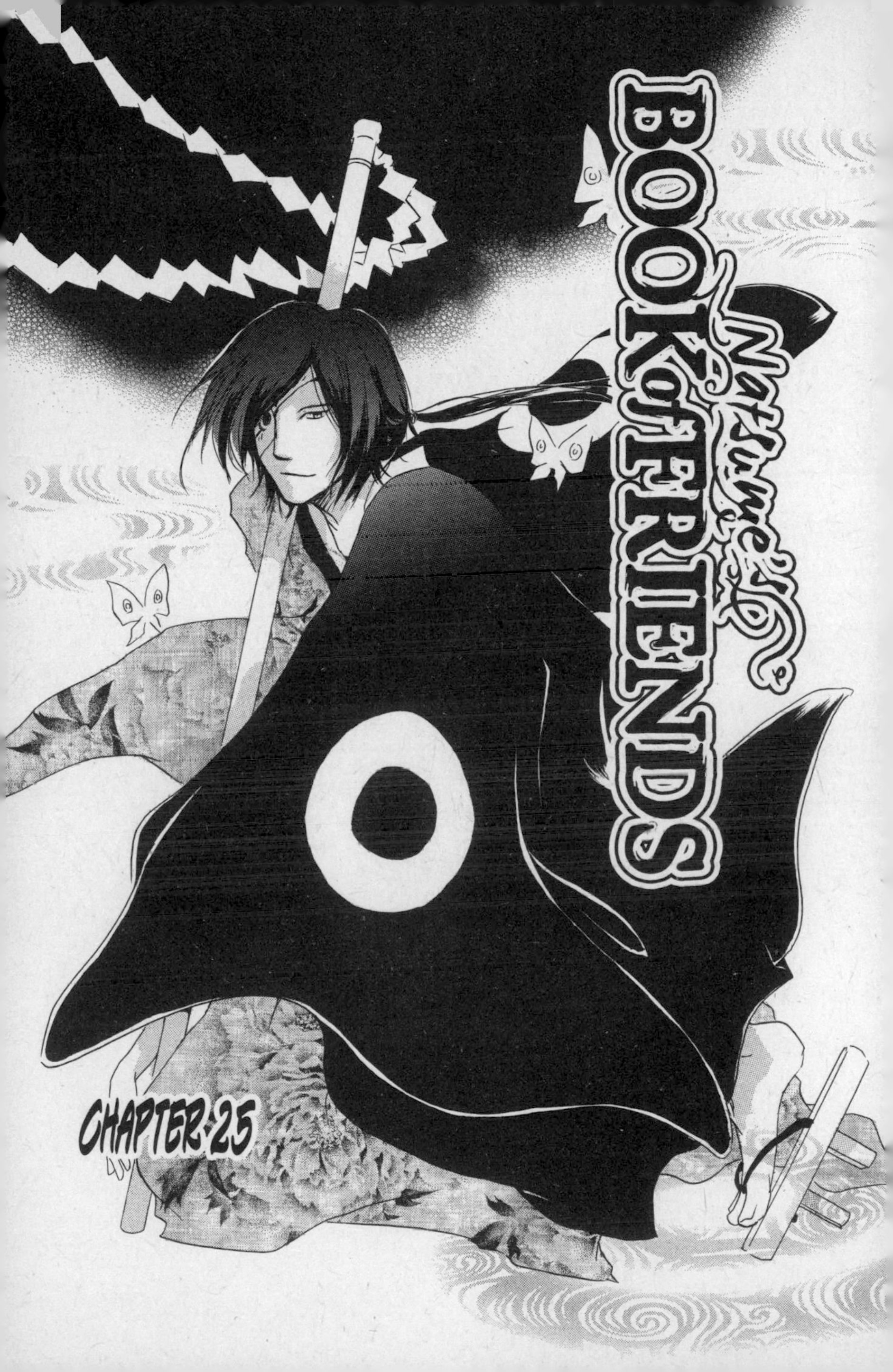
Natsume's
BOOK of FRIENDS
CHAPTER 25

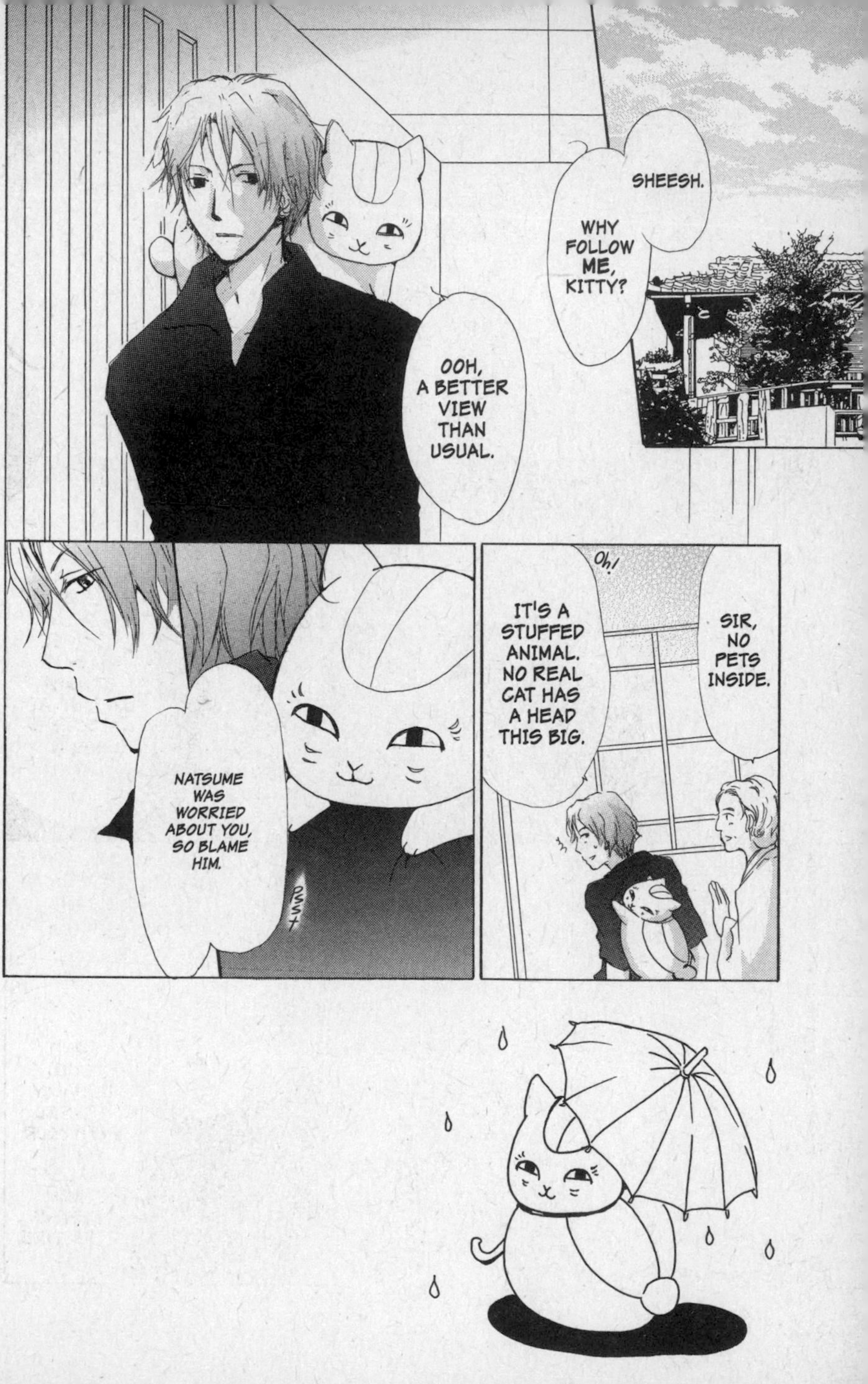
SHEESH.
WHY FOLLOW ME, KITTY?
OOH, A BETTER VIEW THAN USUAL.
SIR, NO PETS INSIDE.
Oh!
IT'S A STUFFED ANIMAL. NO REAL CAT HAS A HEAD THIS BIG.
NATSUME WAS WORRIED ABOUT YOU, SO BLAME HIM.
PSST

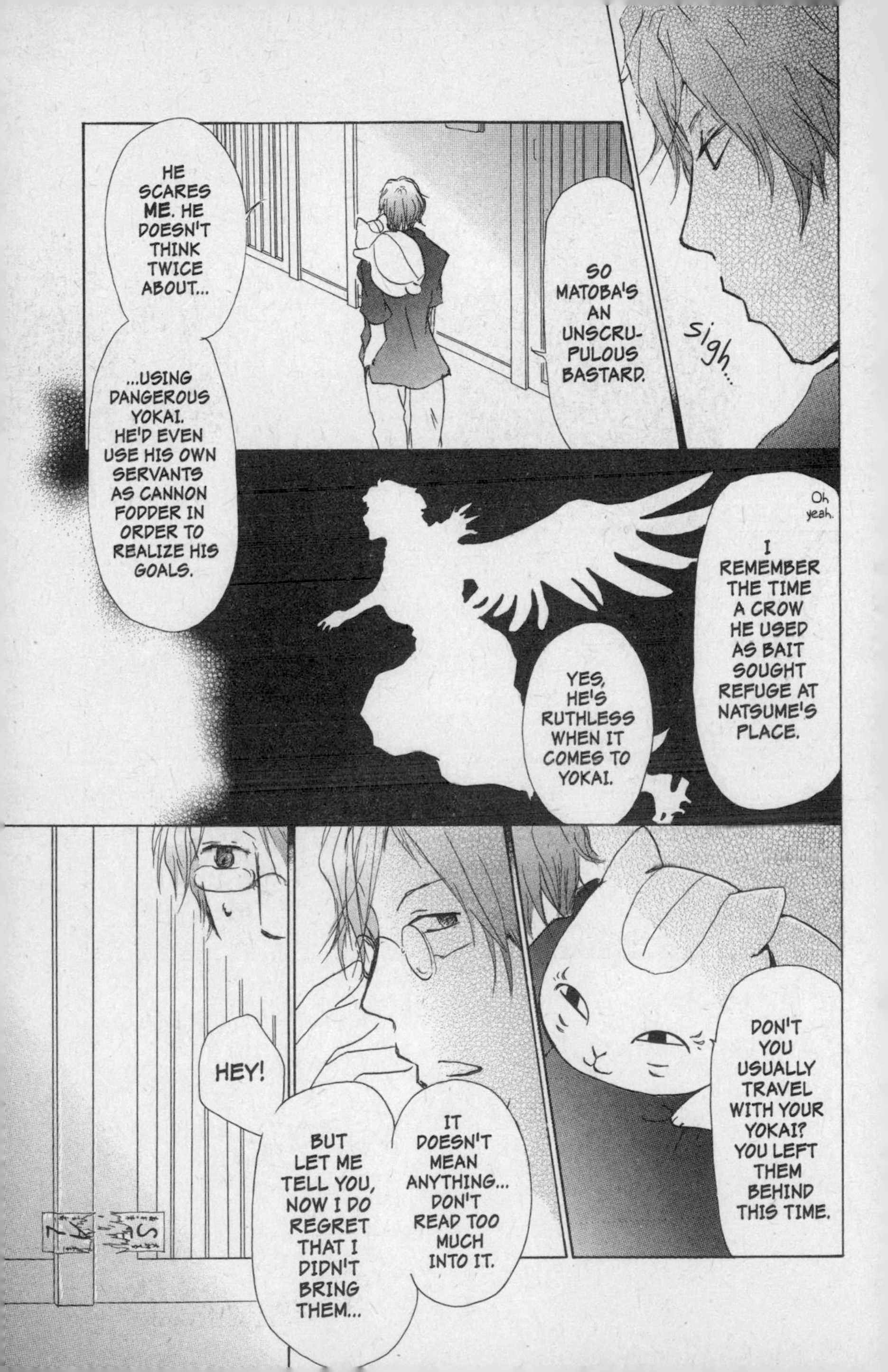
SO MATOBA'S AN UNSCRU-PULOUS BASTARD.
sigh...
HE SCARES ME. HE DOESN'T THINK TWICE ABOUT...
...USING DANGEROUS YOKAI. HE'D EVEN USE HIS OWN SERVANTS AS CANNON FODDER IN ORDER TO REALIZE HIS GOALS.
Oh yeah.
I REMEMBER THE TIME A CROW HE USED AS BAIT SOUGHT REFUGE AT NATSUME'S PLACE.
YES, HE'S RUTHLESS WHEN IT COMES TO YOKAI.
DON'T YOU USUALLY TRAVEL WITH YOUR YOKAI? YOU LEFT THEM BEHIND THIS TIME.
IT DOESN'T MEAN ANYTHING... DON'T READ TOO MUCH INTO IT.
BUT LET ME TELL YOU, NOW I DO REGRET THAT I DIDN'T BRING THEM...
HEY!

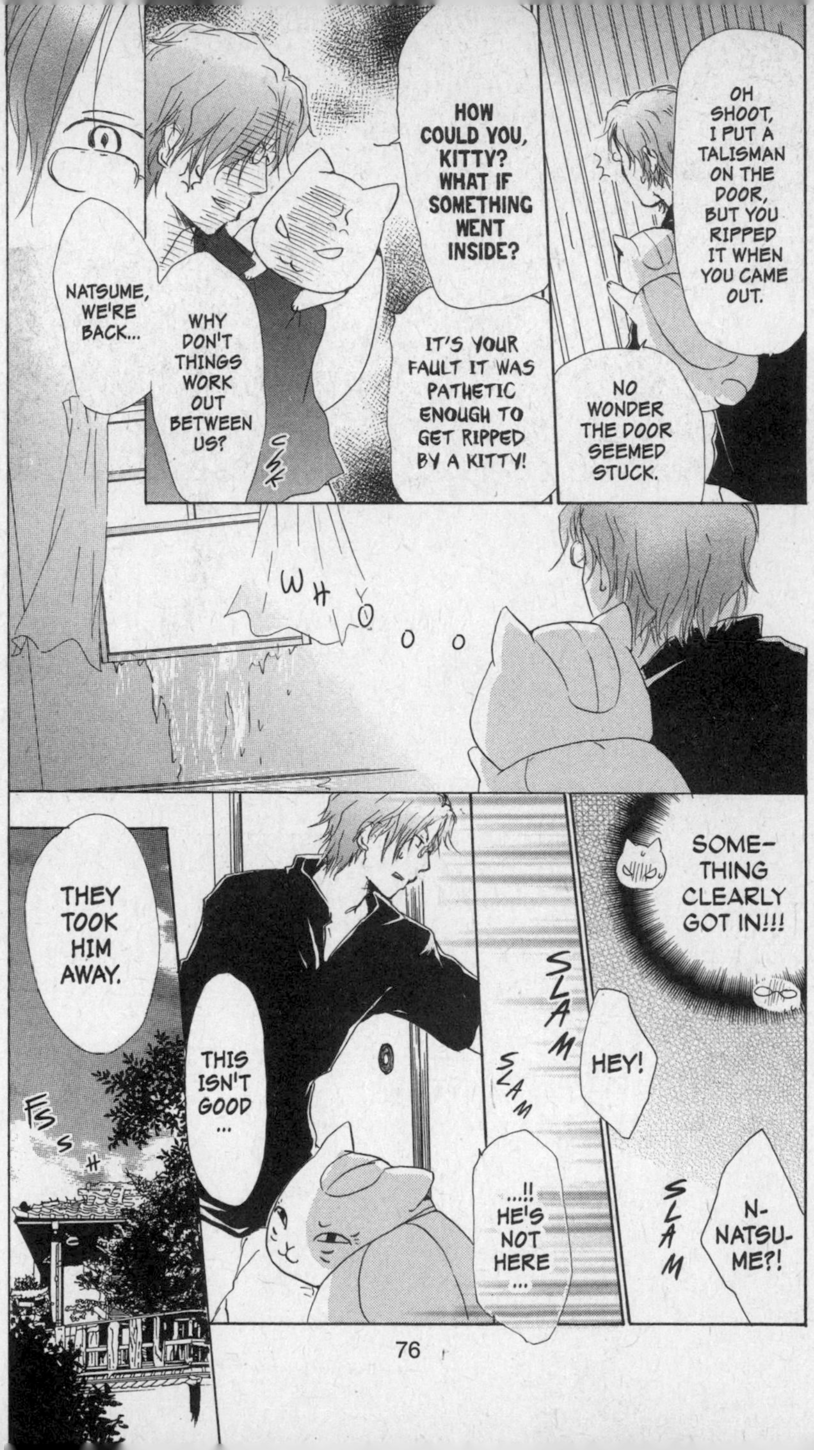
OH SHOOT, I PUT A TALISMAN ON THE DOOR, BUT YOU RIPPED IT WHEN YOU CAME OUT.
NO WONDER THE DOOR SEEMED STUCK.
HOW COULD YOU, KITTY? WHAT IF SOMETHING WENT INSIDE?
IT'S YOUR FAULT IT WAS PATHETIC ENOUGH TO GET RIPPED BY A KITTY!
WHY DON'T THINGS WORK OUT BETWEEN US?
CLNK
NATSUME, WE'RE BACK...
WHOOOO
SOME-THING CLEARLY GOT IN!!!
SLAM
HEY!
SLAM
N-NATSU-ME?!
SLAM
...!! HE'S NOT HERE ...
THIS ISN'T GOOD ...
THEY TOOK HIM AWAY.
FSSH

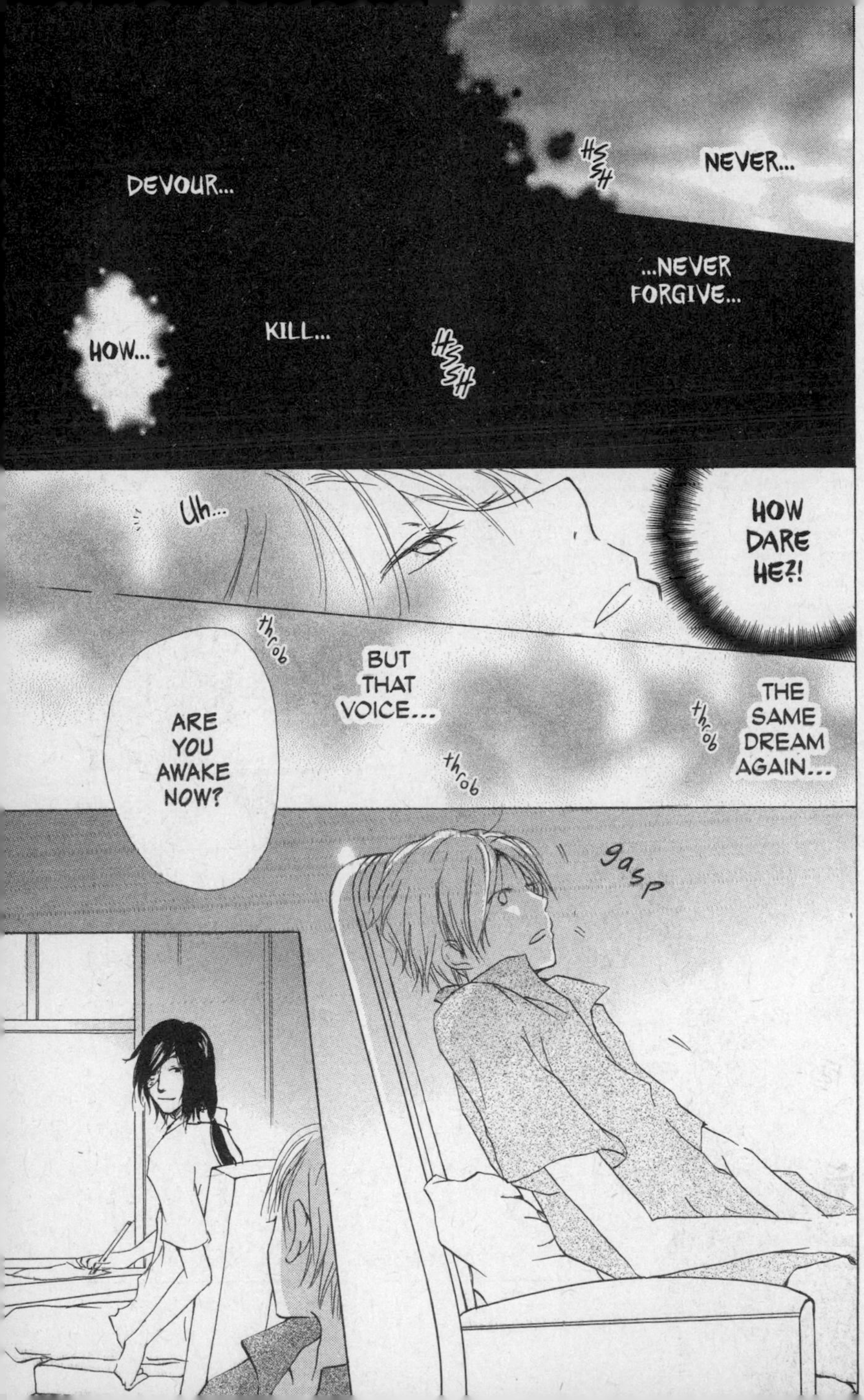
NEVER...
HSSH
...NEVER FORGIVE...
DEVOUR...
HSSH
KILL...
HOW...
HOW DARE HE?!
Uh...
THE SAME DREAM AGAIN...
throb
throb
BUT THAT VOICE...
throb
ARE YOU AWAKE NOW?
gasp

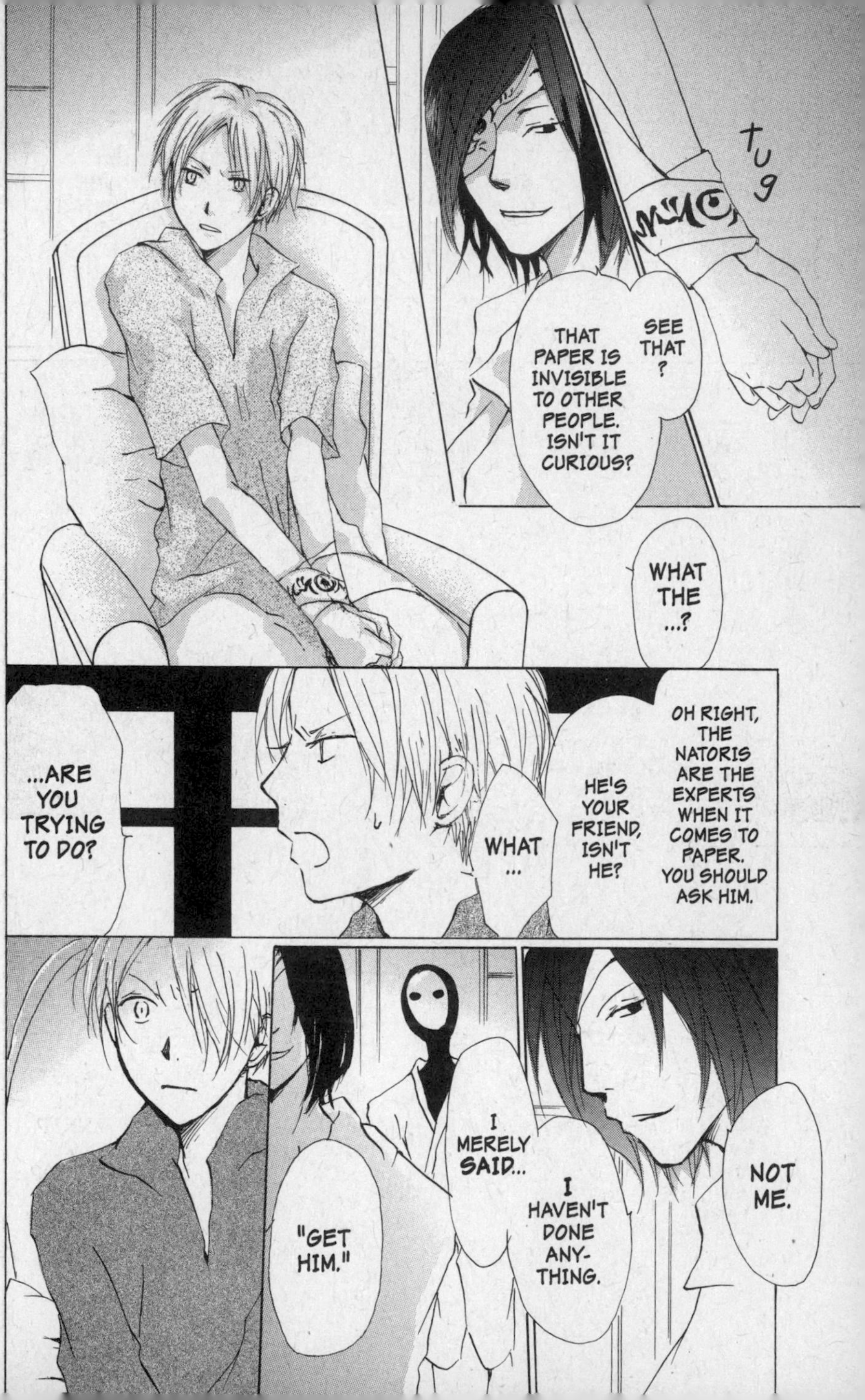
TUG
SEE THAT?
THAT PAPER IS INVISIBLE TO OTHER PEOPLE. ISN'T IT CURIOUS?
WHAT THE ...?
OH RIGHT, THE NATORIS ARE THE EXPERTS WHEN IT COMES TO PAPER. YOU SHOULD ASK HIM.
HE'S YOUR FRIEND, ISN'T HE?
WHAT ...
...ARE YOU TRYING TO DO?
NOT ME.
I HAVEN'T DONE ANY-THING.
I MERELY SAID...
"GET HIM."

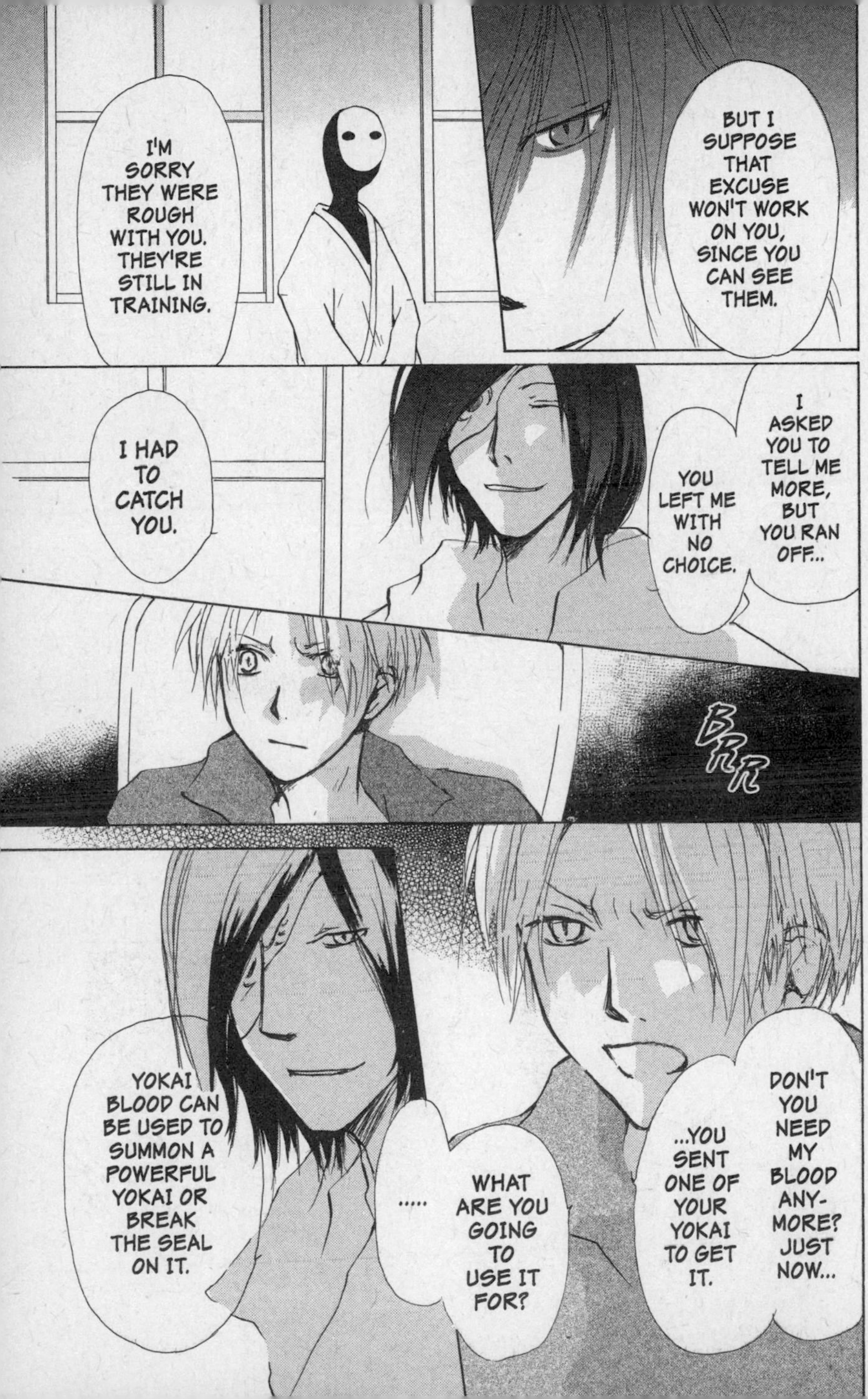
BUT I SUPPOSE THAT EXCUSE WON'T WORK ON YOU, SINCE YOU CAN SEE THEM.
I'M SORRY THEY WERE ROUGH WITH YOU. THEY'RE STILL IN TRAINING.
I ASKED YOU TO TELL ME MORE, BUT YOU RAN OFF...
YOU LEFT ME WITH NO CHOICE.
I HAD TO CATCH YOU.
BRR
DON'T YOU NEED MY BLOOD ANY-MORE? JUST NOW...
...YOU SENT ONE OF YOUR YOKAI TO GET IT.
WHAT ARE YOU GOING TO USE IT FOR?
.....
YOKAI BLOOD CAN BE USED TO SUMMON A POWERFUL YOKAI OR BREAK THE SEAL ON IT.

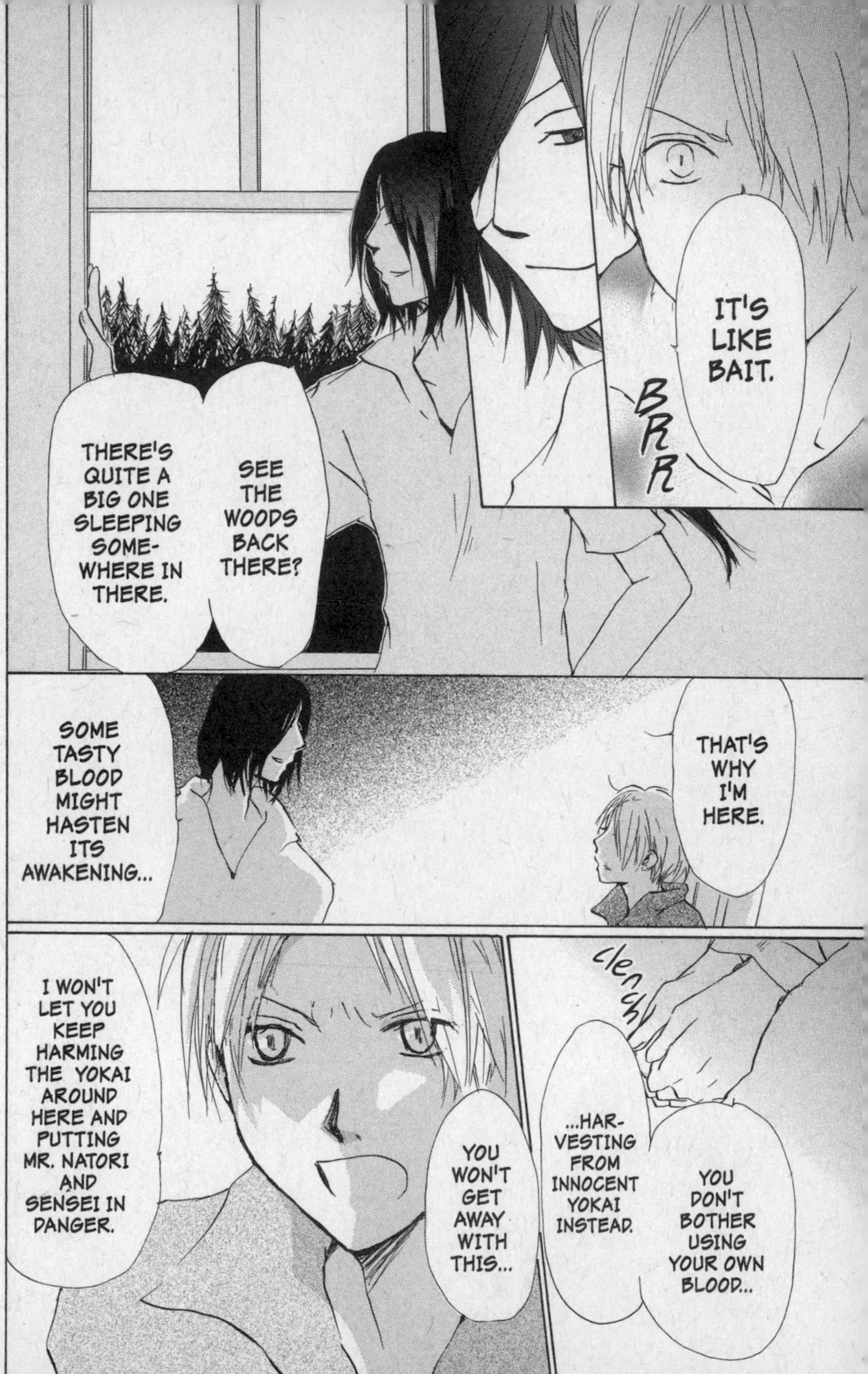
IT'S LIKE BAIT.
BRR
SEE THE WOODS BACK THERE?
THERE'S QUITE A BIG ONE SLEEPING SOME-WHERE IN THERE.
THAT'S WHY I'M HERE.
SOME TASTY BLOOD MIGHT HASTEN ITS AWAKENING...
clench
YOU DON'T BOTHER USING YOUR OWN BLOOD...
...HAR-VESTING FROM INNOCENT YOKAI INSTEAD.
YOU WON'T GET AWAY WITH THIS...
I WON'T LET YOU KEEP HARMING THE YOKAI AROUND HERE AND PUTTING MR. NATORI AND SENSEI IN DANGER.

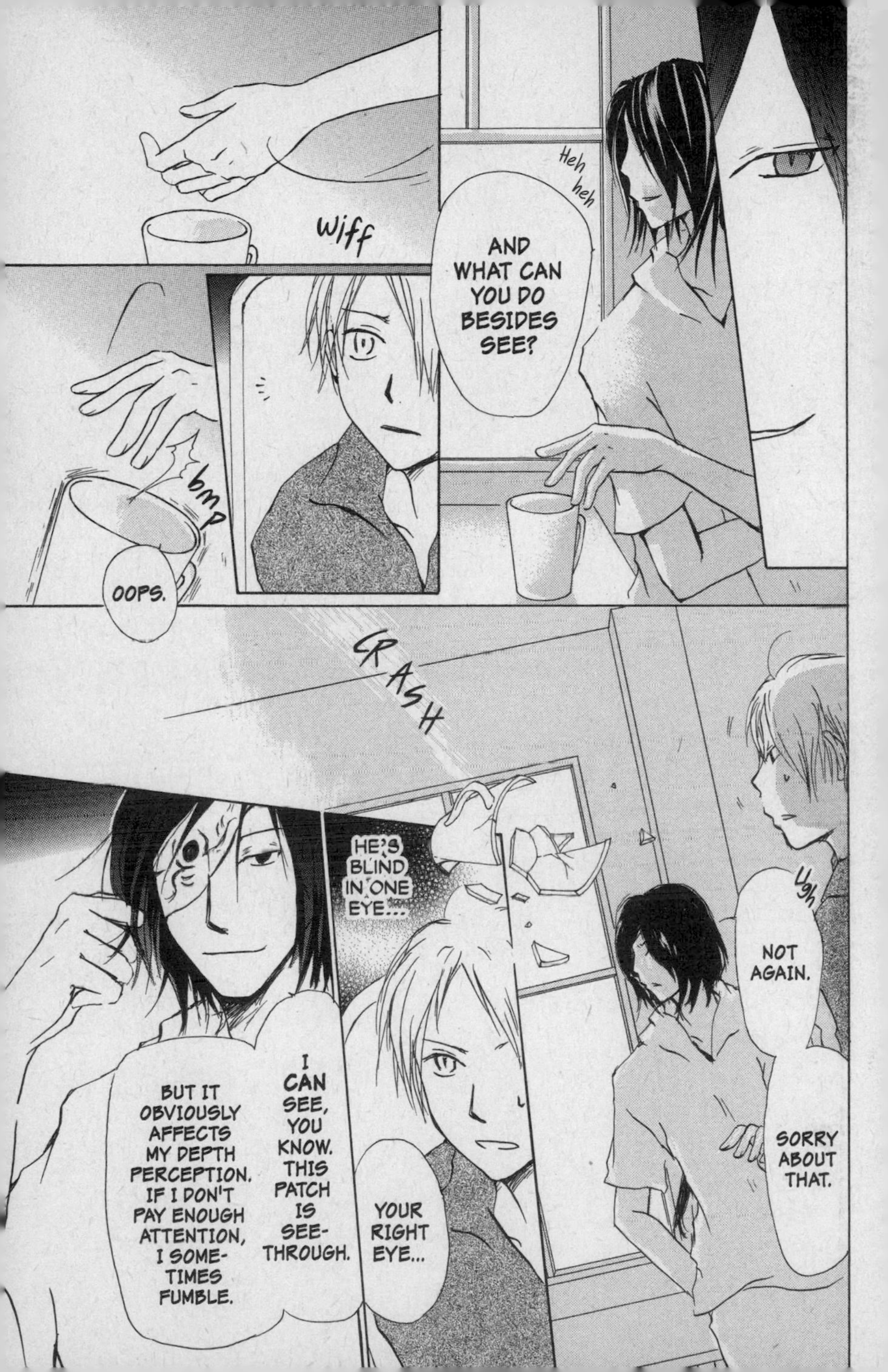
Heh heh
AND WHAT CAN YOU DO BESIDES SEE?
wiff
bmp
OOPS.
CRASH
Ugh
NOT AGAIN.
SORRY ABOUT THAT.
HE'S BLIND IN ONE EYE...
YOUR RIGHT EYE...
I CAN SEE, YOU KNOW. THIS PATCH IS SEE-THROUGH.
BUT IT OBVIOUSLY AFFECTS MY DEPTH PERCEPTION. IF I DON'T PAY ENOUGH ATTENTION, I SOMETIMES FUMBLE.

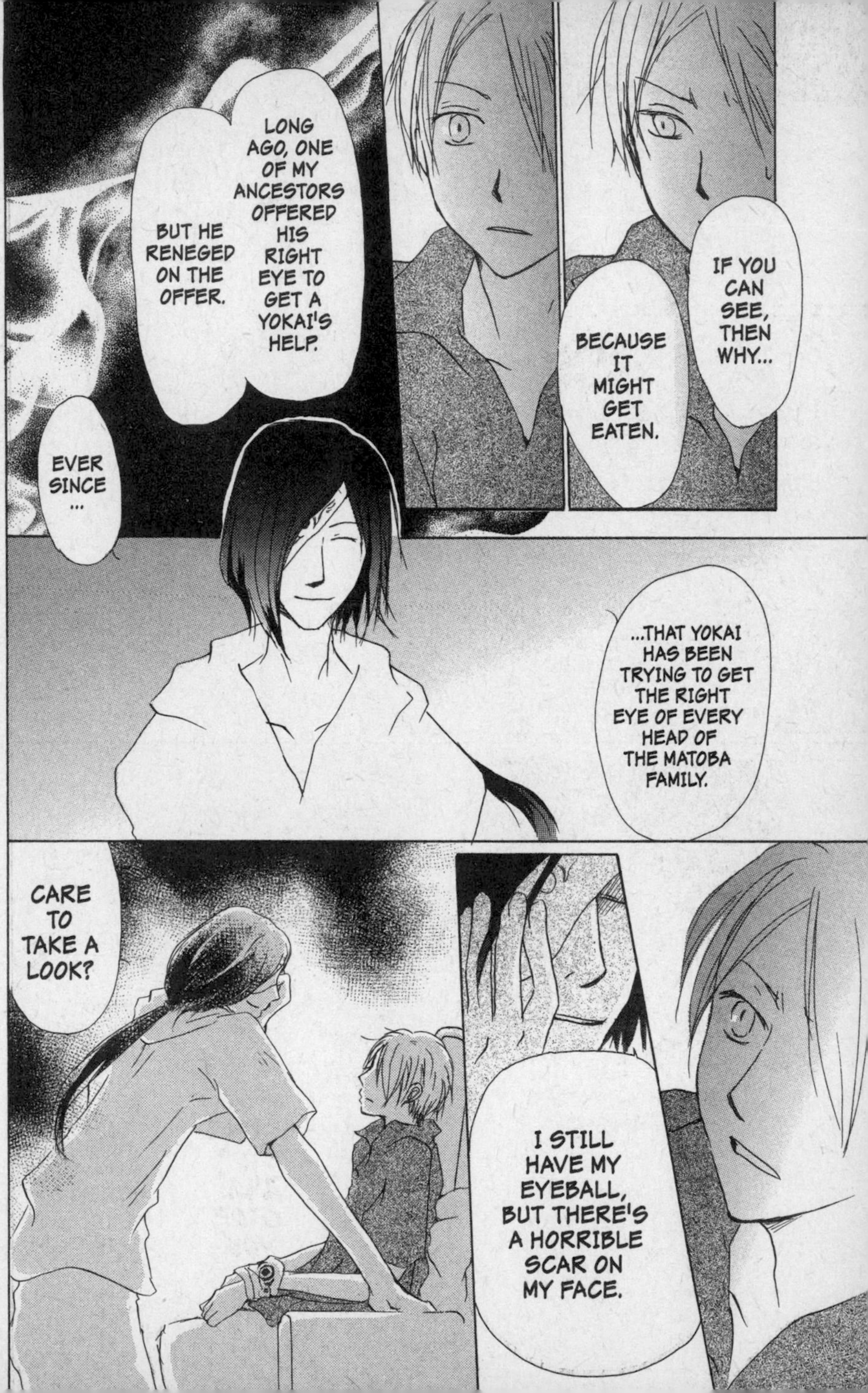
IF YOU CAN SEE, THEN WHY...
BECAUSE IT MIGHT GET EATEN.
LONG AGO, ONE OF MY ANCESTORS OFFERED HIS RIGHT EYE TO GET A YOKAI'S HELP.
BUT HE RENEGED ON THE OFFER.
EVER SINCE ...
...THAT YOKAI HAS BEEN TRYING TO GET THE RIGHT EYE OF EVERY HEAD OF THE MATOBA FAMILY.
I STILL HAVE MY EYEBALL, BUT THERE'S A HORRIBLE SCAR ON MY FACE.
CARE TO TAKE A LOOK?

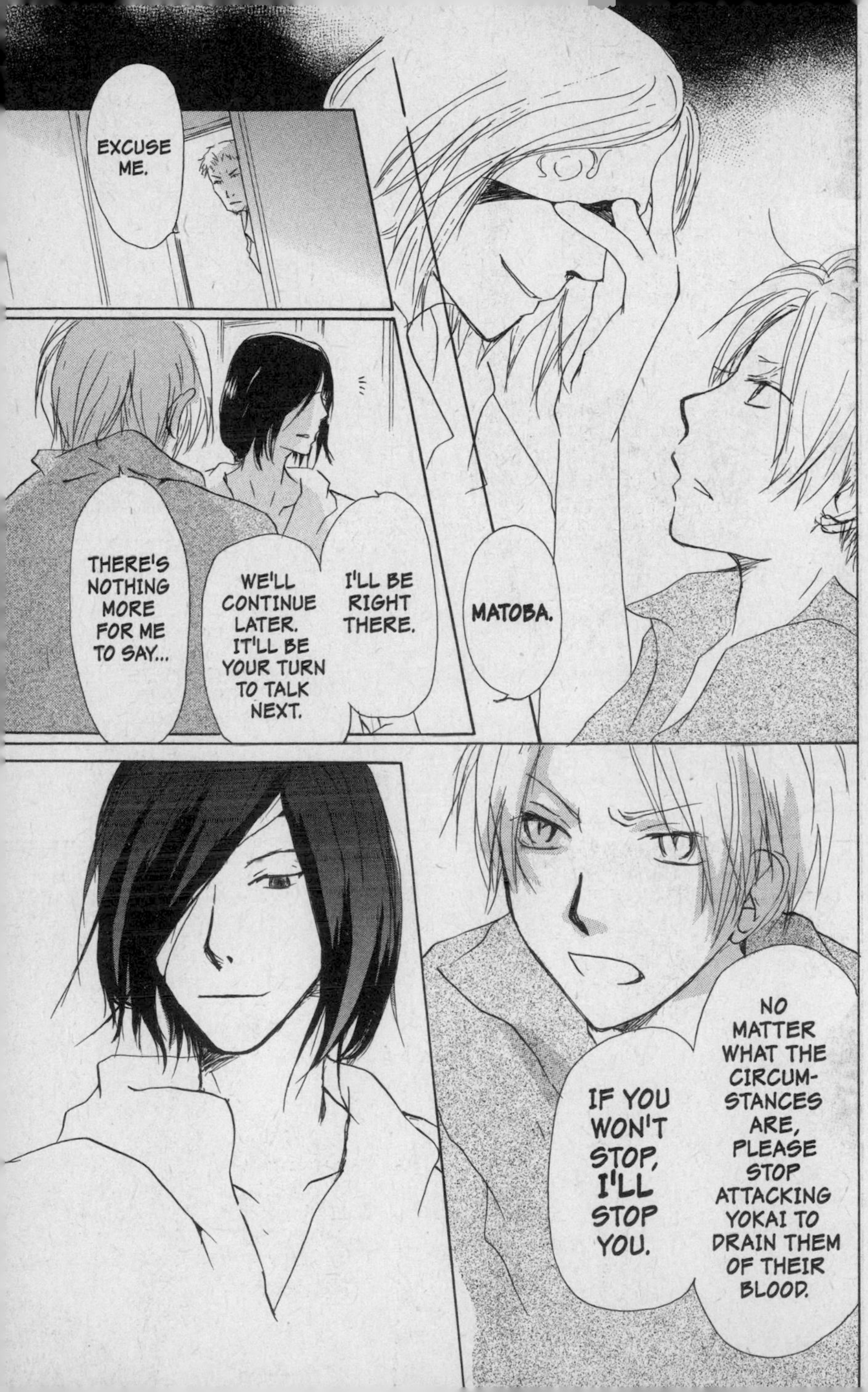
MATOBA.
EXCUSE ME.
I'LL BE RIGHT THERE.
WE'LL CONTINUE LATER. IT'LL BE YOUR TURN TO TALK NEXT.
THERE'S NOTHING MORE FOR ME TO SAY...
NO MATTER WHAT THE CIRCUM-STANCES ARE, PLEASE STOP ATTACKING YOKAI TO DRAIN THEM OF THEIR BLOOD.
IF YOU WON'T STOP, I'LL STOP YOU.

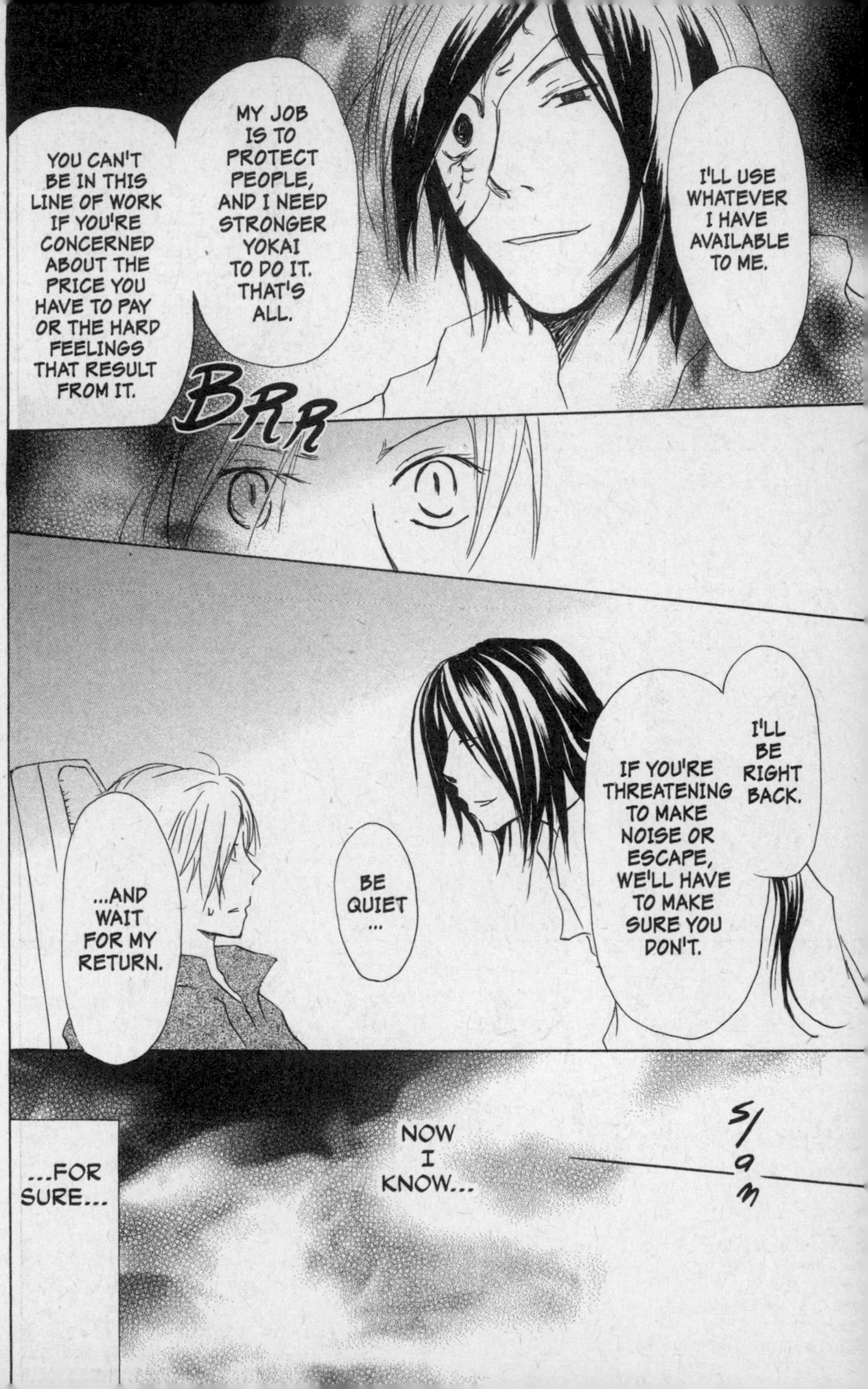
I'LL USE WHATEVER I HAVE AVAILABLE TO ME.
MY JOB IS TO PROTECT PEOPLE, AND I NEED STRONGER YOKAI TO DO IT. THAT'S ALL.
YOU CAN'T BE IN THIS LINE OF WORK IF YOU'RE CONCERNED ABOUT THE PRICE YOU HAVE TO PAY OR THE HARD FEELINGS THAT RESULT FROM IT.
BRR
I'LL BE RIGHT BACK.
IF YOU'RE THREATENING TO MAKE NOISE OR ESCAPE, WE'LL HAVE TO MAKE SURE YOU DON'T.
BE QUIET...
...AND WAIT FOR MY RETURN.
Slam
NOW I KNOW...
...FOR SURE...

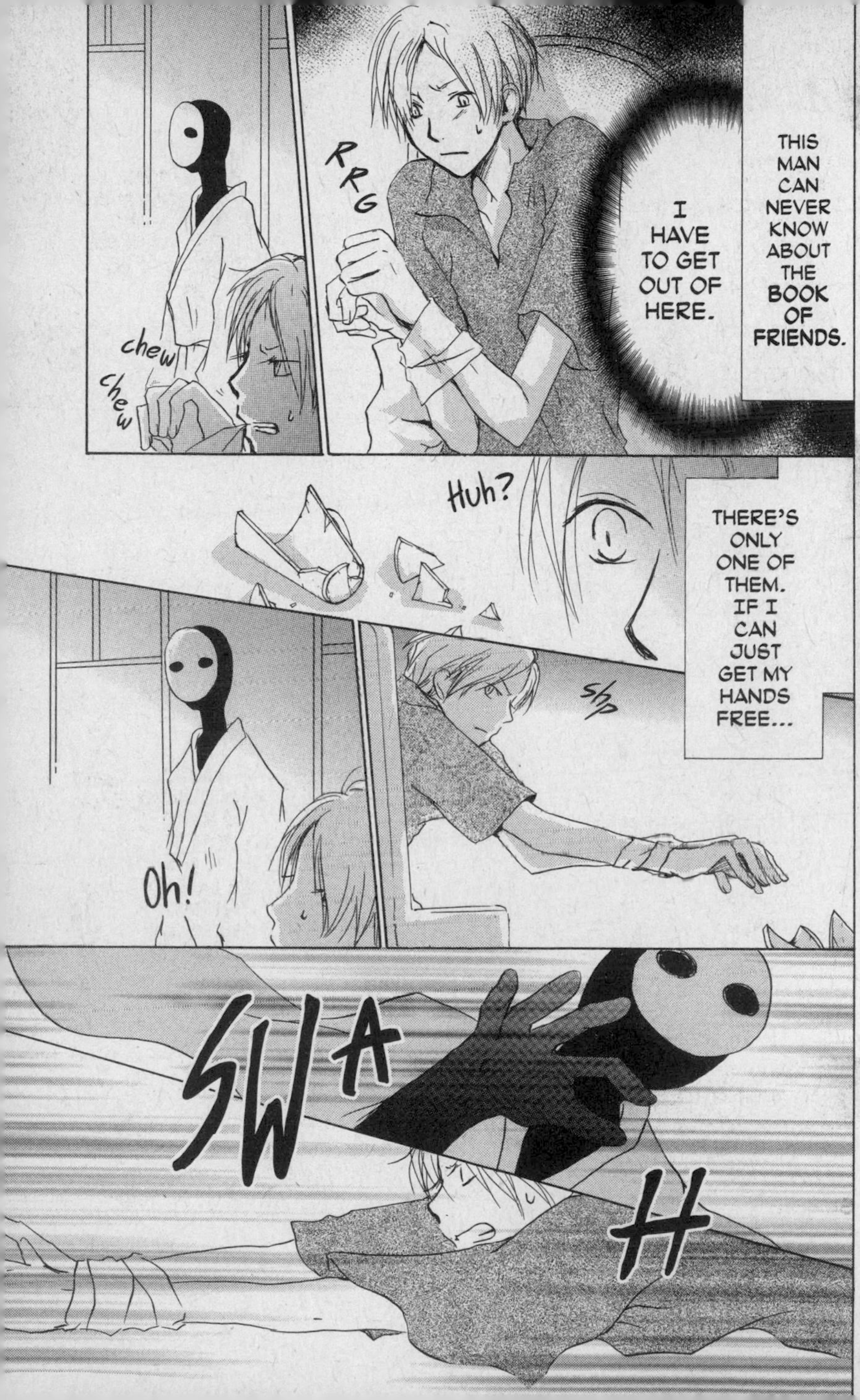
THIS MAN CAN NEVER KNOW ABOUT THE BOOK OF FRIENDS.
I HAVE TO GET OUT OF HERE.
RRG
chew chew
THERE'S ONLY ONE OF THEM. IF I CAN JUST GET MY HANDS FREE...
Huh?
shp
Oh!
SWAH

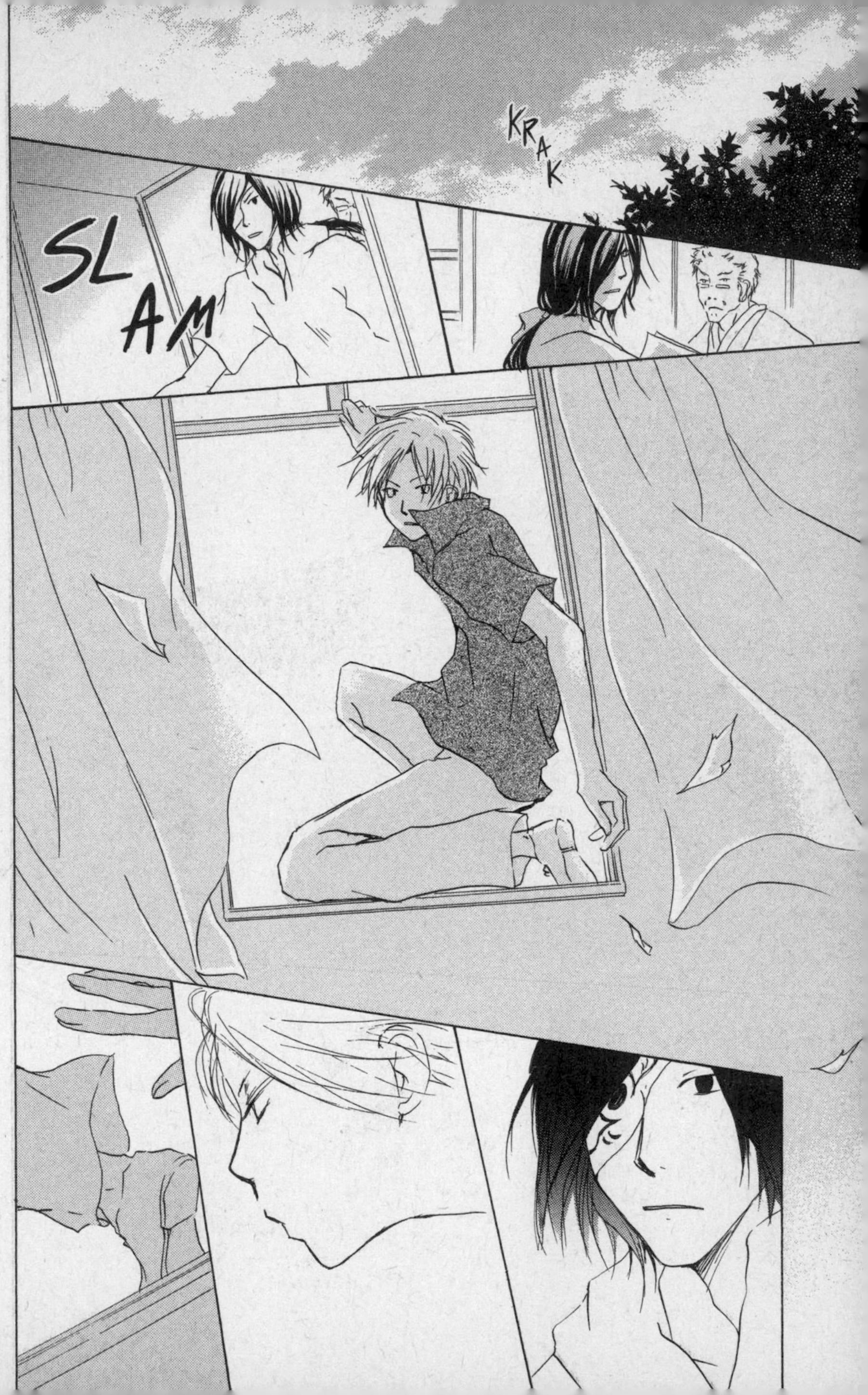
KRAK
SLAM

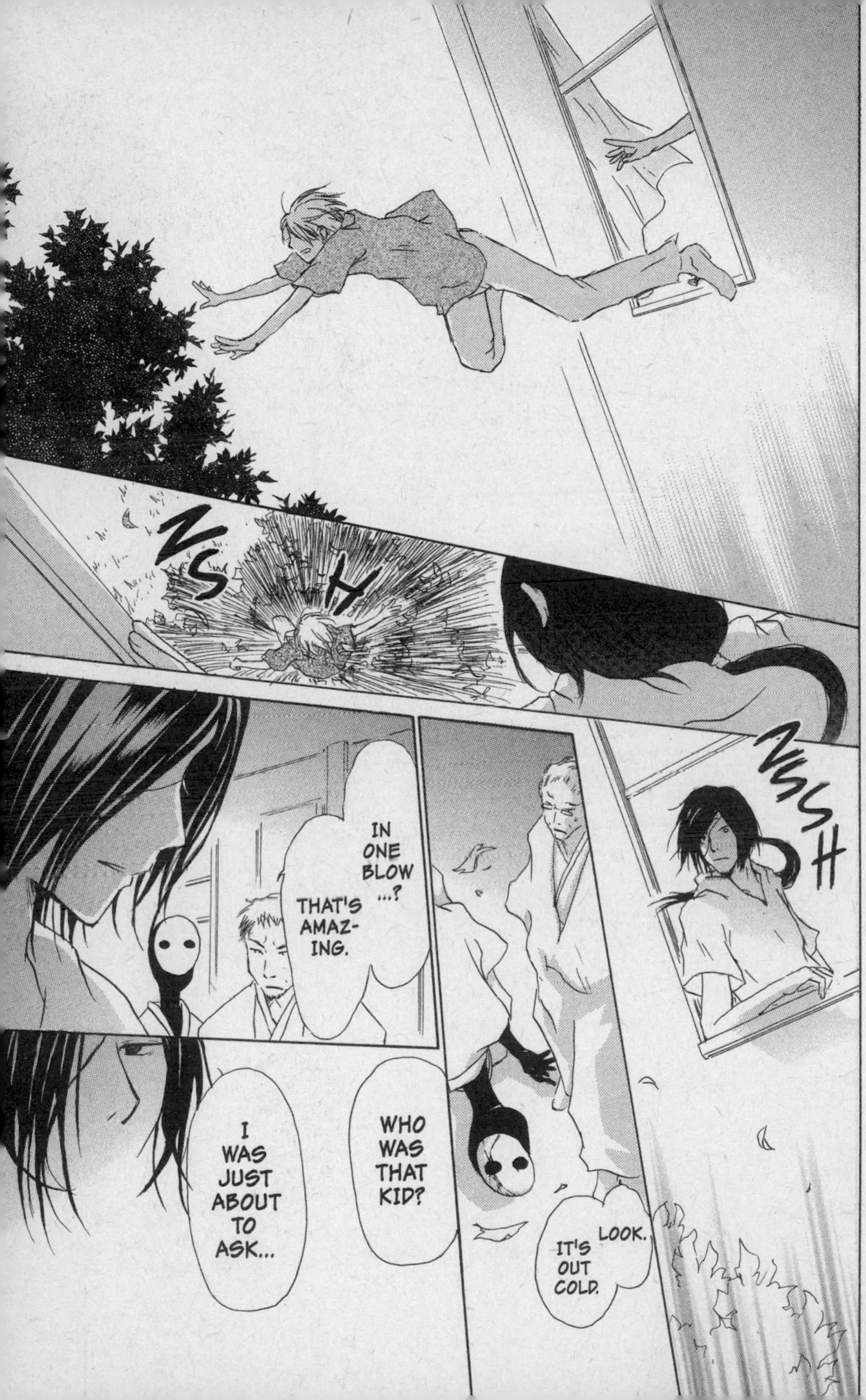
NSH
NSSH
LOOK.
IT'S OUT COLD.
IN ONE BLOW ...?
THAT'S AMAZ-ING.
WHO WAS THAT KID?
I WAS JUST ABOUT TO ASK...

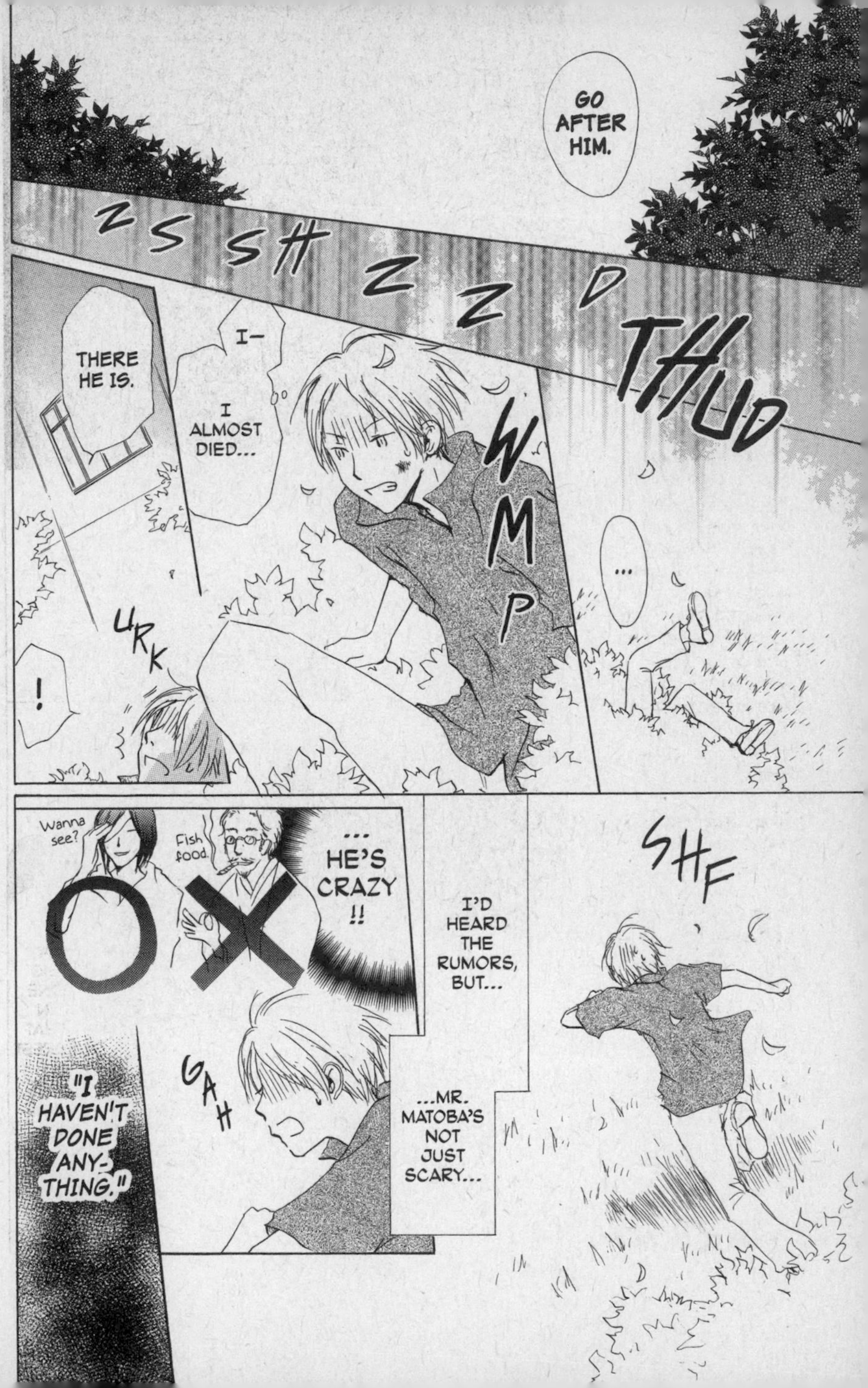
GO AFTER HIM.
ZSSHZZZD
THUD
WMP
...
I— I ALMOST DIED...
THERE HE IS.
URK
!
SHF
I'D HEARD THE RUMORS, BUT...
...MR. MATOBA'S NOT JUST SCARY...
...HE'S CRAZY!!
Wanna see?
Fish food.
GAH
"I HAVEN'T DONE ANYTHING."

## 03

❋Fan Book: part 2

Personally, I worked on the first episode imagining Natsume to be around 10th grade. I was debating whether to put him in 9th grade and show him advancing a year, but since the magazine is bimonthly, the seasons passed by until it became a moot point and it didn't match graduation season anymore. When the anime was in development, I had a conversation with the director and other staff, and we decided that 10th grade seemed right for him. So that's what he is in the manga too.

The other stats came to light in a similar fashion. Natsume and his friend Nishimura are supposed to be within half an inch of each other, so if he looks too tall or too short in some scenes, please just poke me in a letter.

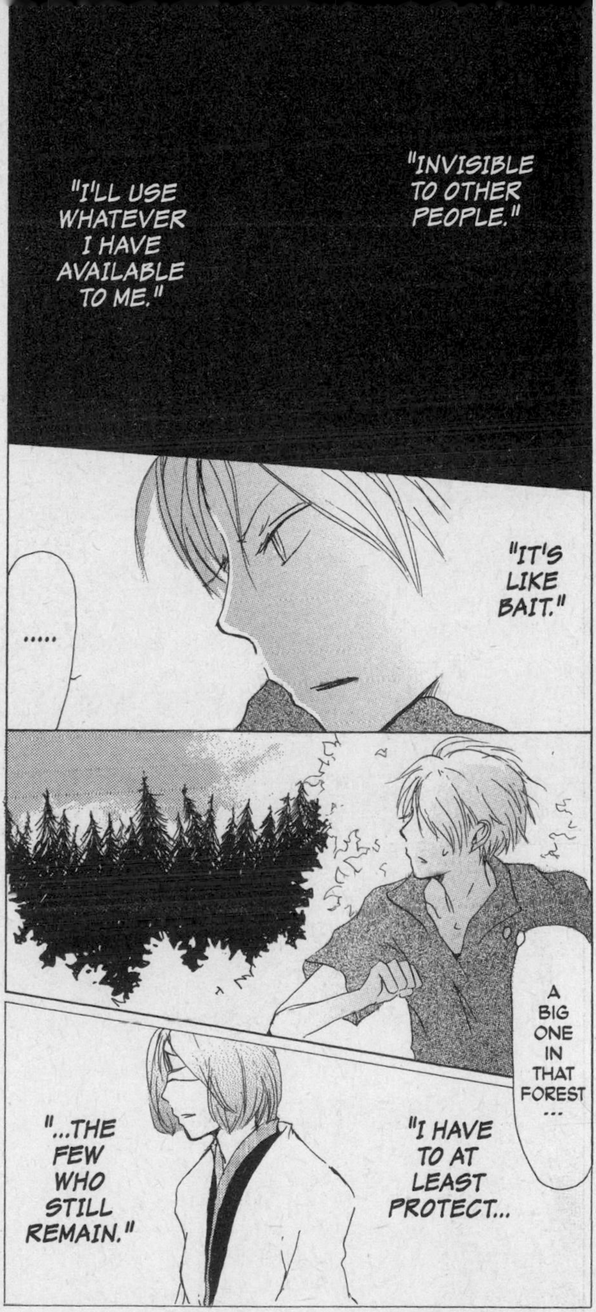
"INVISIBLE TO OTHER PEOPLE."
"I'LL USE WHATEVER I HAVE AVAILABLE TO ME."
"IT'S LIKE BAIT."
.....
A BIG ONE IN THAT FOREST...
"I HAVE TO AT LEAST PROTECT...
"...THE FEW WHO STILL REMAIN."

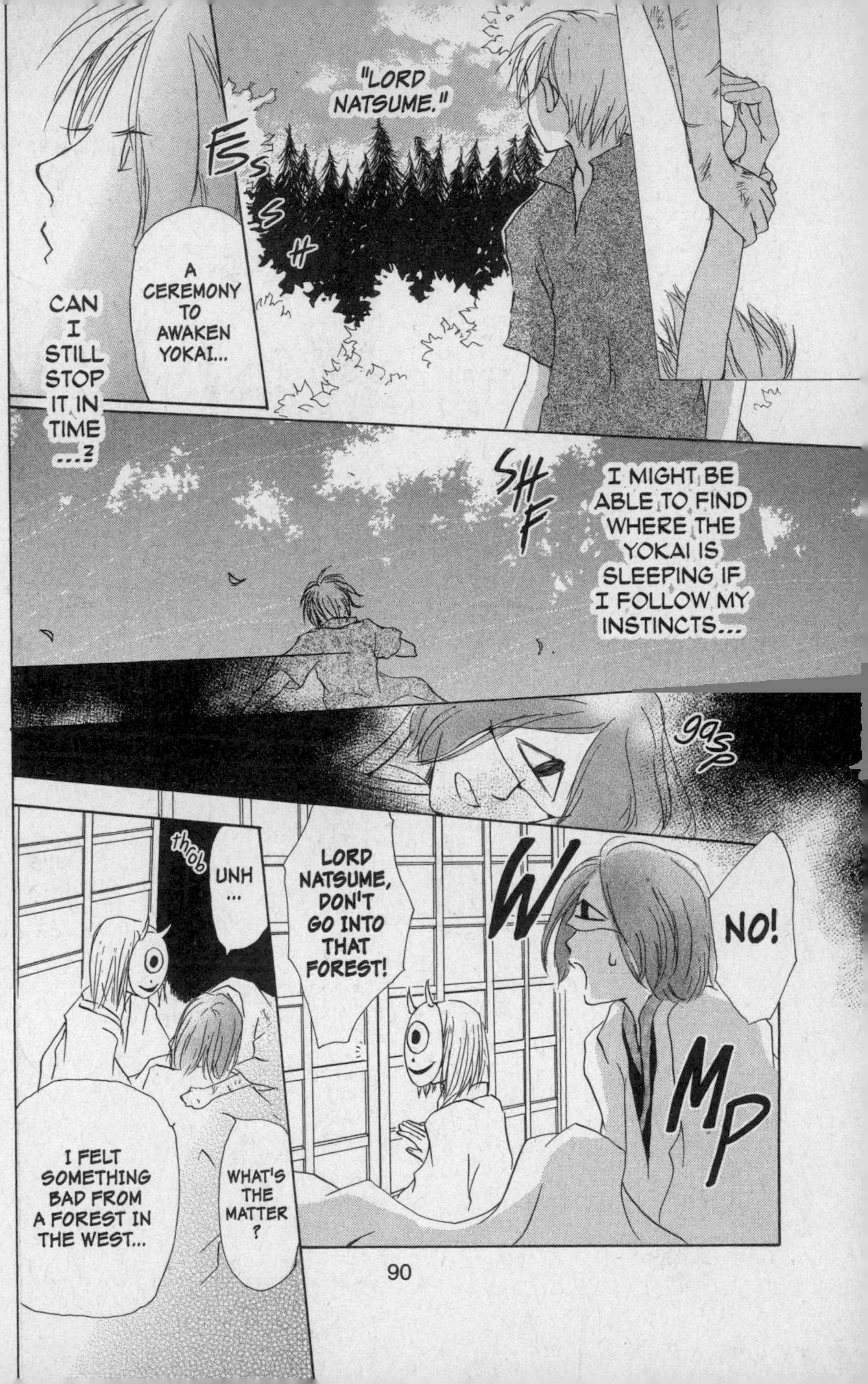
"LORD NATSUME."
FSSSH
A CEREMONY TO AWAKEN YOKAI...
CAN I STILL STOP IT IN TIME...?
SHF
I MIGHT BE ABLE TO FIND WHERE THE YOKAI IS SLEEPING IF I FOLLOW MY INSTINCTS...
gasp
NO!
WMP
LORD NATSUME, DON'T GO INTO THAT FOREST!
throb
UNH...
WHAT'S THE MATTER?
I FELT SOMETHING BAD FROM A FOREST IN THE WEST...

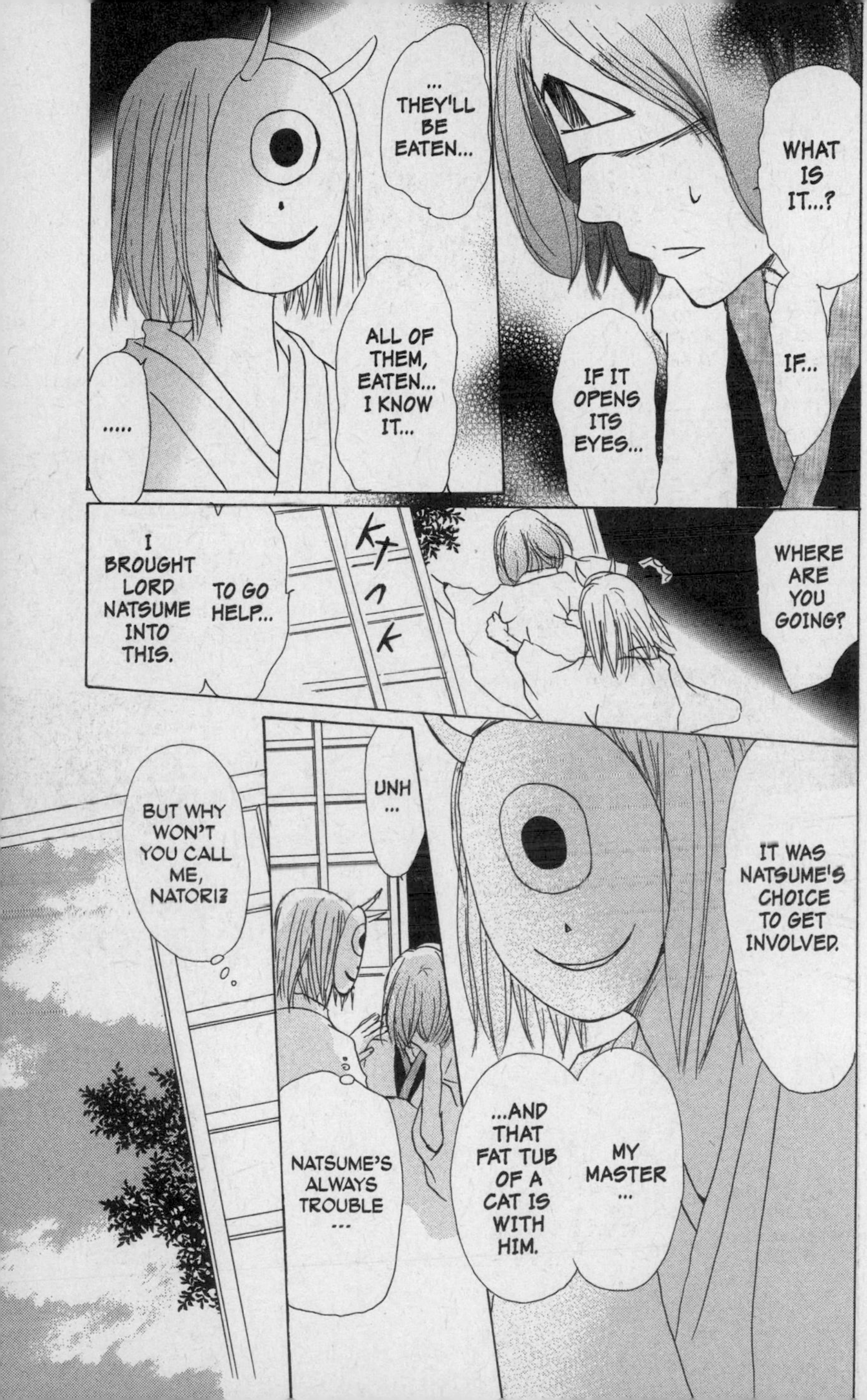
WHAT IS IT...?
IF...
IF IT OPENS ITS EYES...
... THEY'LL BE EATEN...
ALL OF THEM, EATEN... I KNOW IT...
.....
WHERE ARE YOU GOING?
TO GO HELP...
I BROUGHT LORD NATSUME INTO THIS.
IT WAS NATSUME'S CHOICE TO GET INVOLVED.
MY MASTER ...
...AND THAT FAT TUB OF A CAT IS WITH HIM.
UNH ...
BUT WHY WON'T YOU CALL ME, NATORI?
NATSUME'S ALWAYS TROUBLE ...

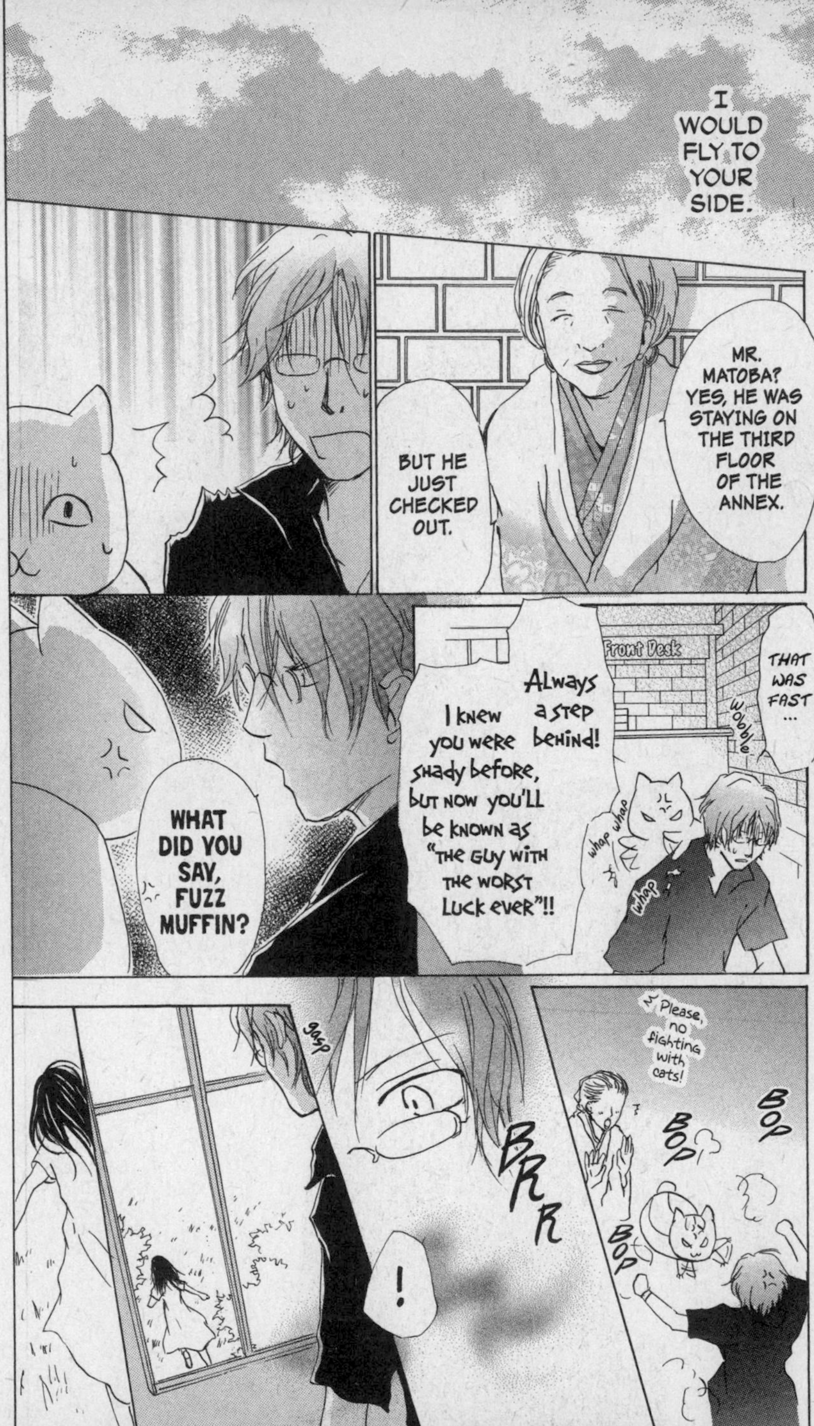
I WOULD FLY TO YOUR SIDE.
MR. MATOBA? YES, HE WAS STAYING ON THE THIRD FLOOR OF THE ANNEX.
BUT HE JUST CHECKED OUT.
Front Desk
THAT WAS FAST ...
wobble
Always a step behind!
I knew you were shady before, but now you'll be known as "the guy with the worst luck ever"!!
whap whap
whap
WHAT DID YOU SAY, FUZZ MUFFIN?
Please, no fighting with cats!
BOP
BOP
BOP
gasp
BRR
!

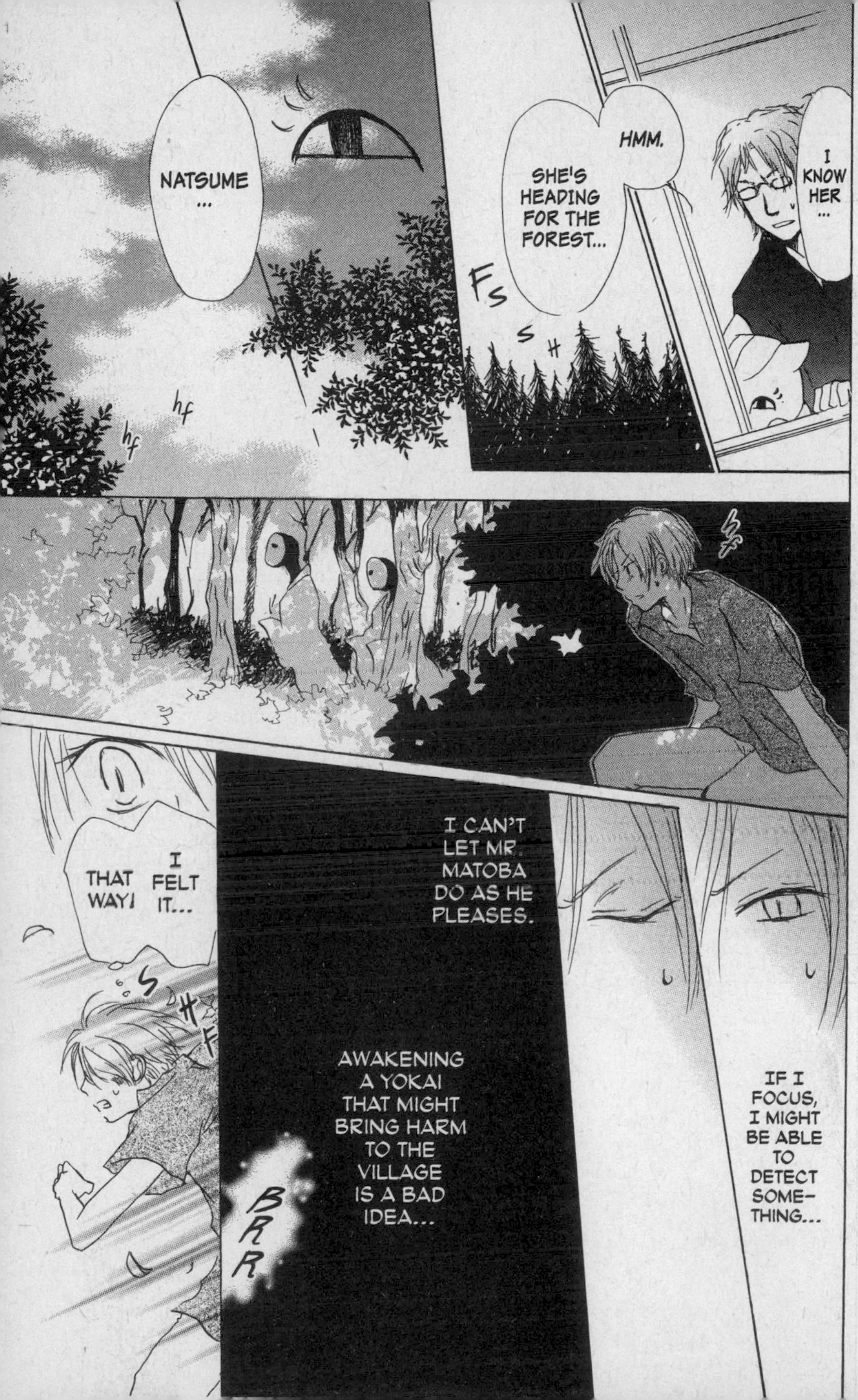
I KNOW HER...
HMM.
SHE'S HEADING FOR THE FOREST...
FSSH
NATSUME...
hf
hf
hf
IF I FOCUS, I MIGHT BE ABLE TO DETECT SOME-THING...
I CAN'T LET MR. MATOBA DO AS HE PLEASES.
AWAKENING A YOKAI THAT MIGHT BRING HARM TO THE VILLAGE IS A BAD IDEA...
BRR
I FELT IT...
THAT WAY!
SHF

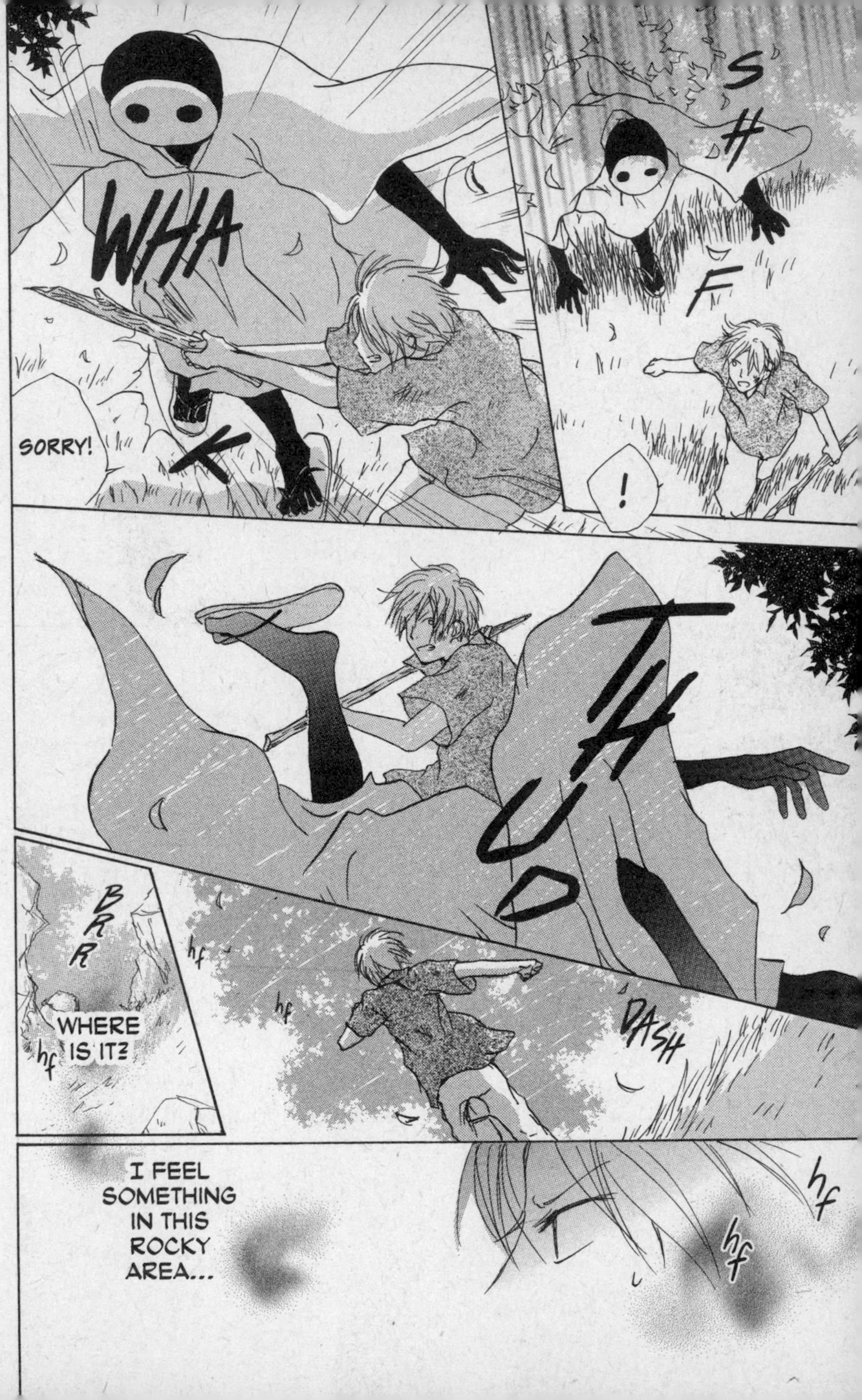
SHFF
!
WHAK
SORRY!
THUD
DASH
hf
hf
BRR
WHERE IS IT?
hf
hf
hf
I FEEL SOMETHING IN THIS ROCKY AREA...

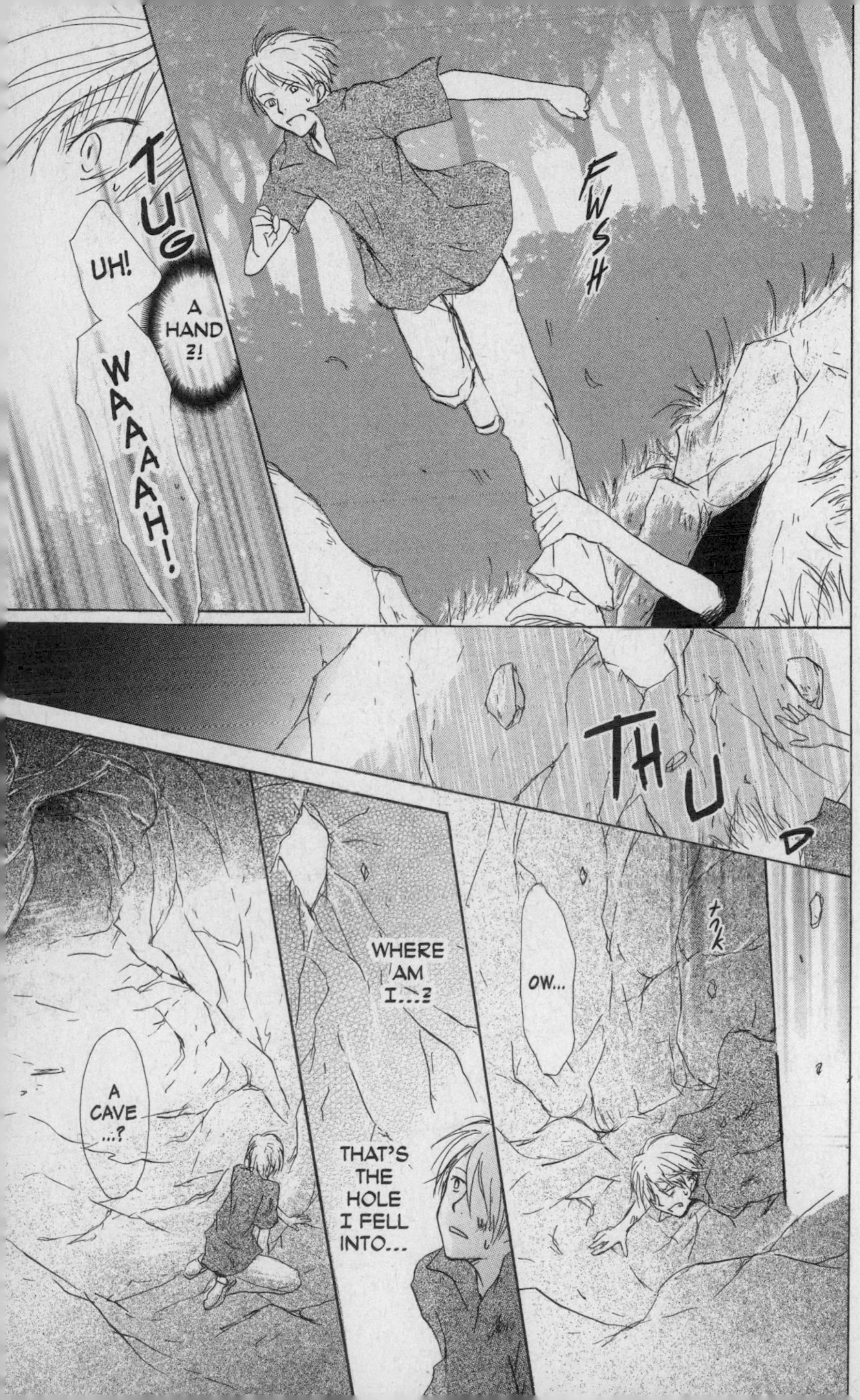
FWSH
TUG
UH!
A HAND?!
WAAAAAH!
THUD
OW...
WHERE AM I...?
THAT'S THE HOLE I FELL INTO...
A CAVE...?

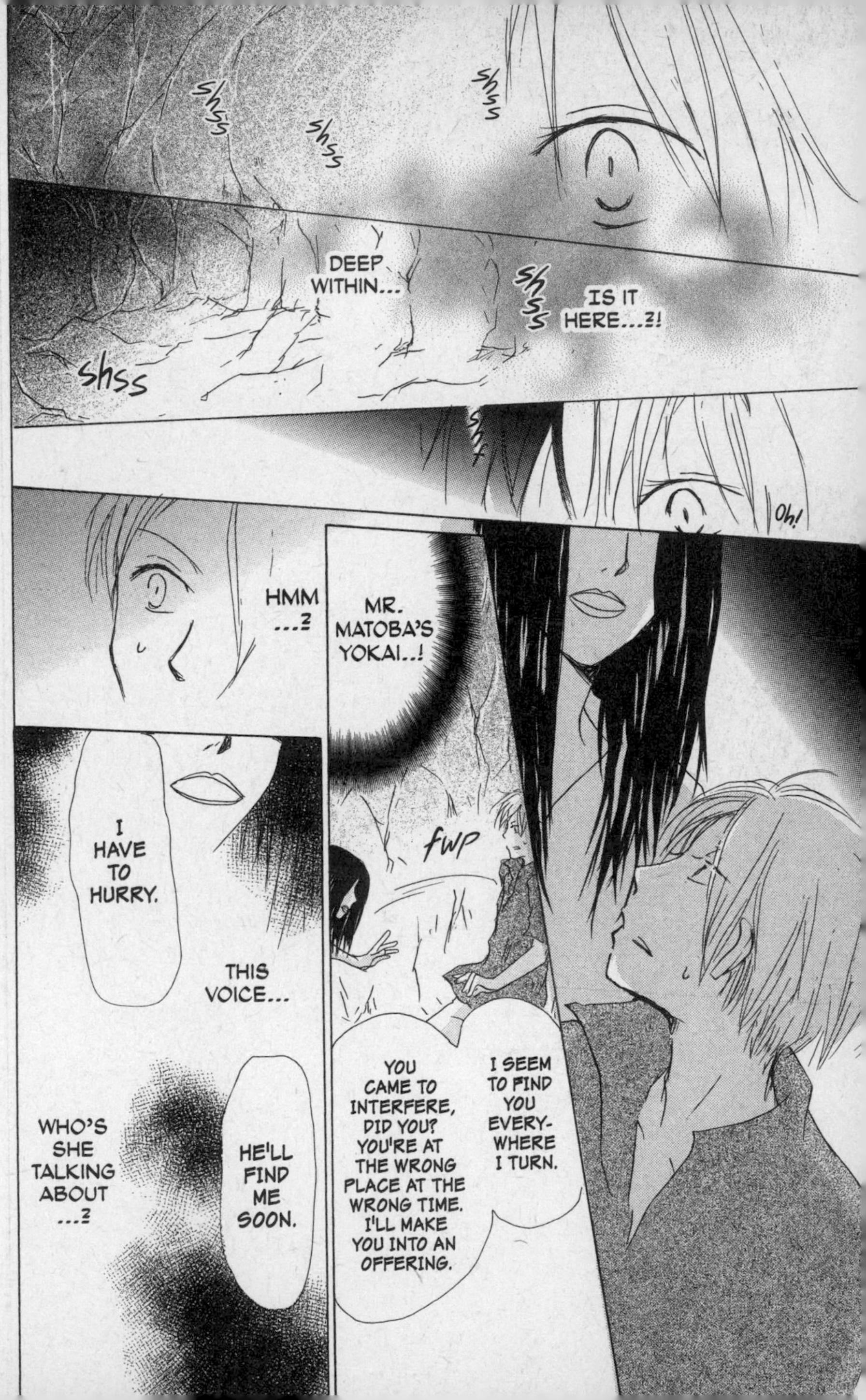
shss
shss
shss
IS IT HERE...?!
shss
DEEP WITHIN...
shss
Oh!
MR. MATOBA'S YOKAI..!
fwp
I SEEM TO FIND YOU EVERY-WHERE I TURN.
YOU CAME TO INTERFERE, DID YOU? YOU'RE AT THE WRONG PLACE AT THE WRONG TIME. I'LL MAKE YOU INTO AN OFFERING.
HMM ...?
I HAVE TO HURRY.
THIS VOICE...
HE'LL FIND ME SOON.
WHO'S SHE TALKING ABOUT ...?

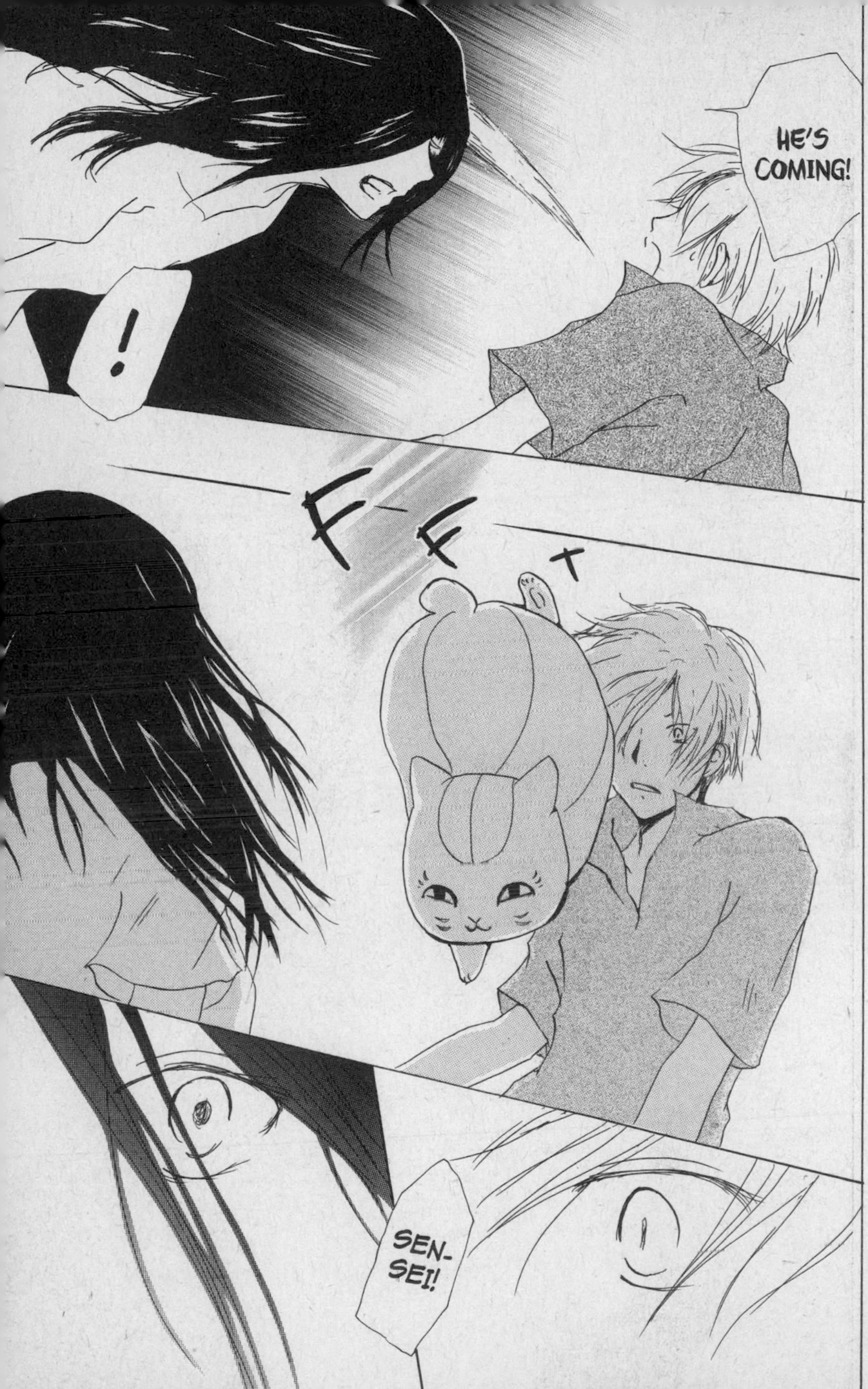
HE'S COMING!
!
FFT
SEN-SEI!

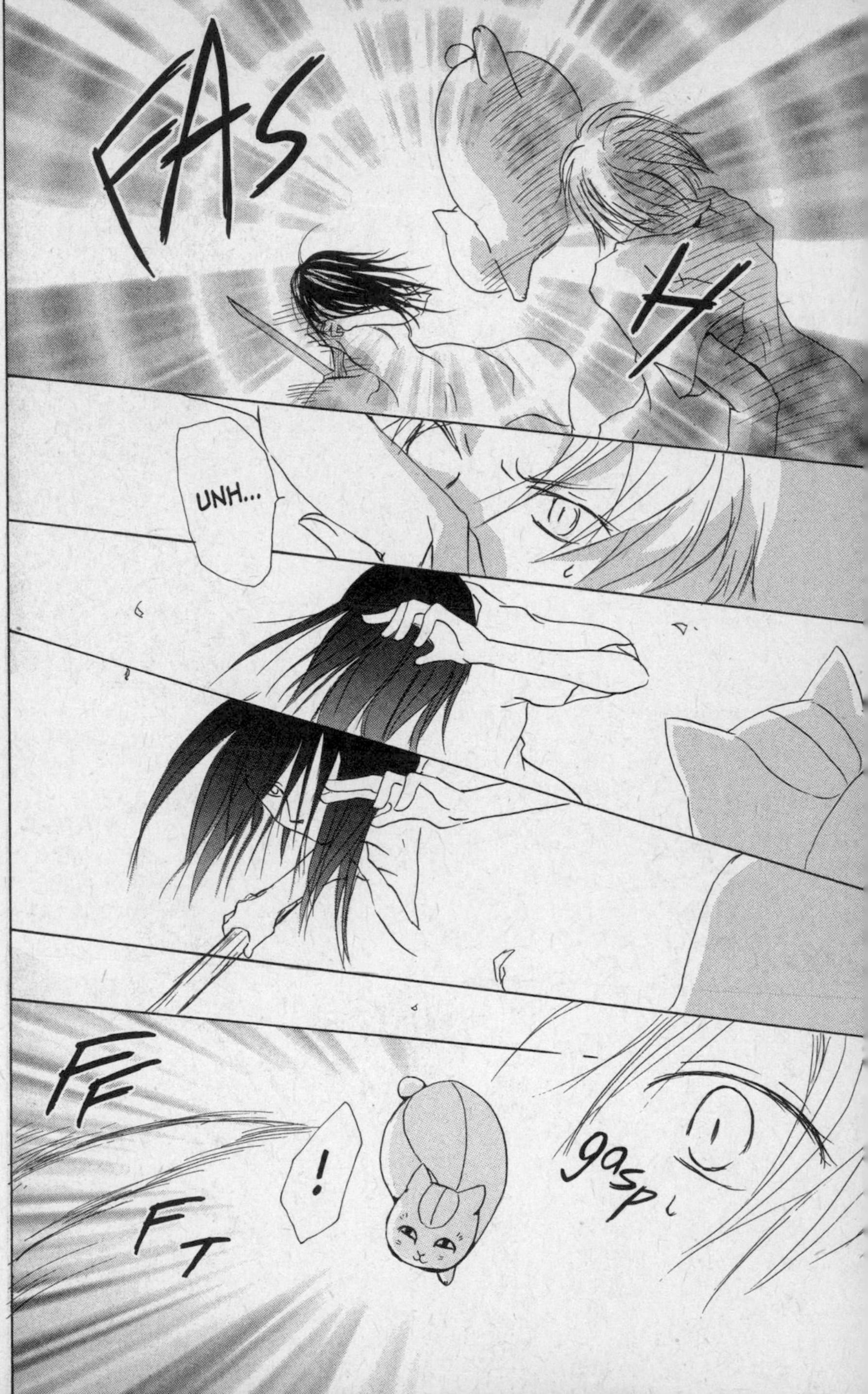

FAS
H
UNH...
gasp!
!
FF
FFT

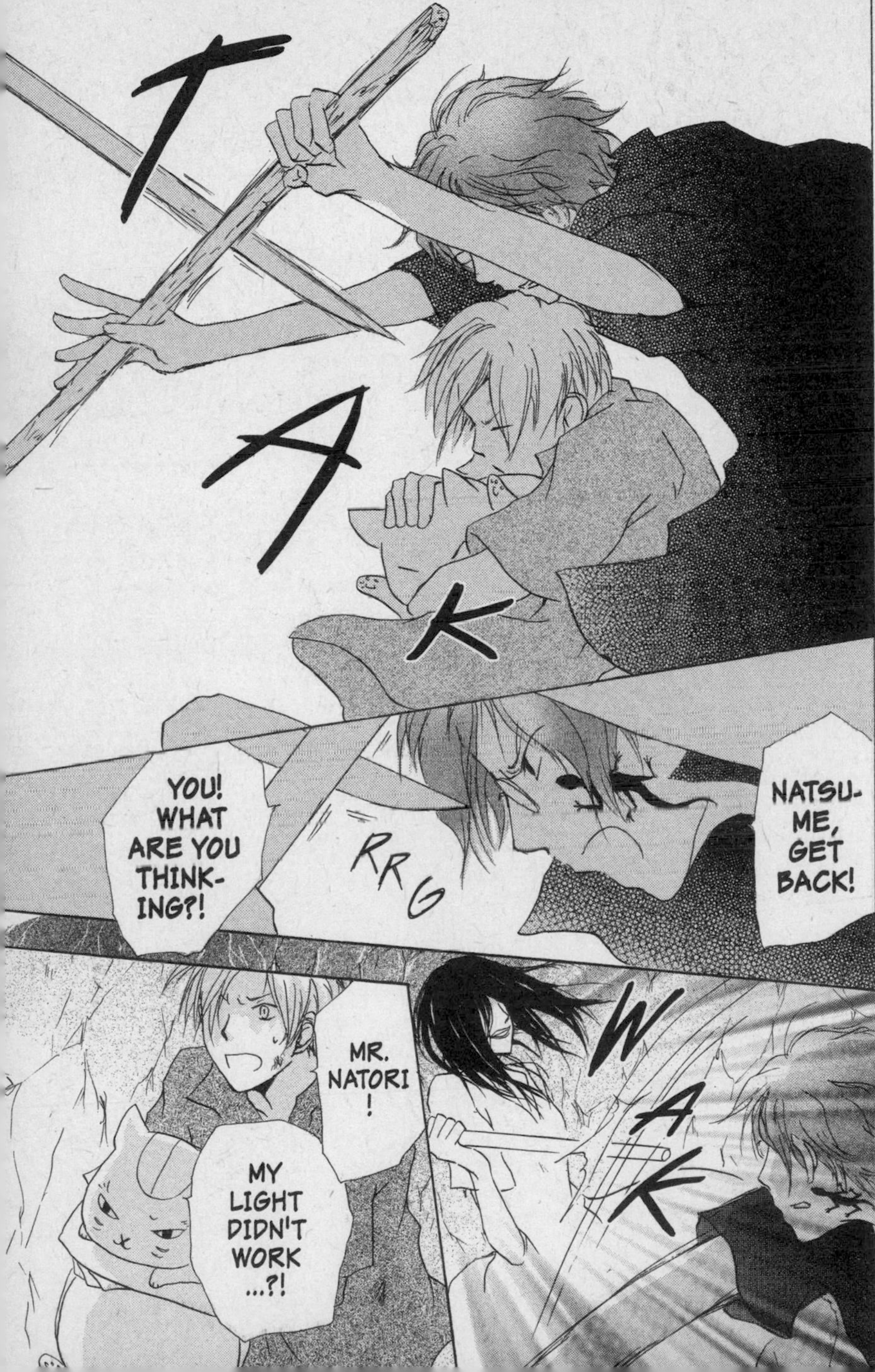
TAK
NATSUME, GET BACK!
RRG
YOU! WHAT ARE YOU THINKING?!
WAK
MR. NATORI!
MY LIGHT DIDN'T WORK...?!

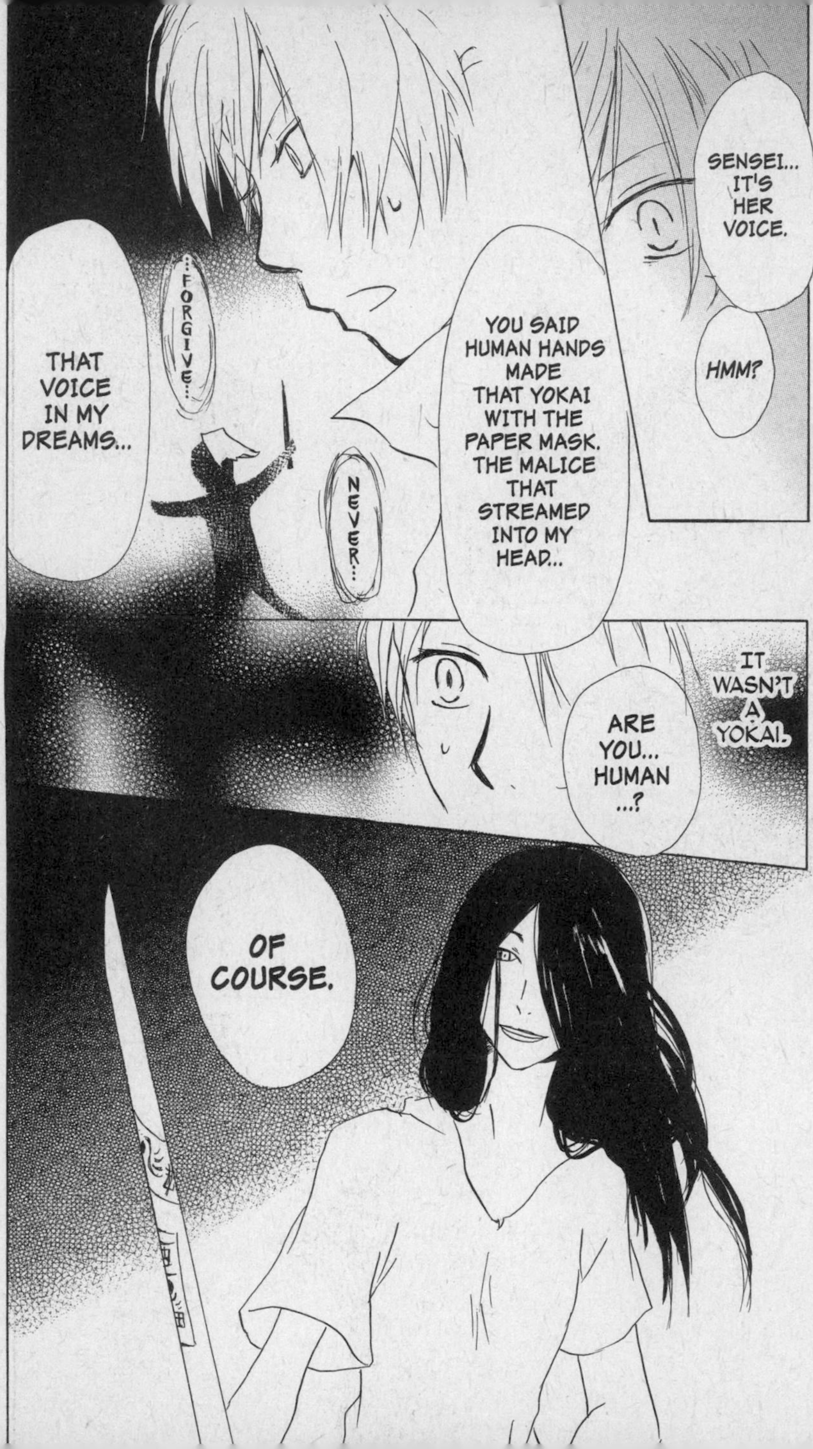
SENSEI... IT'S HER VOICE.
HMM?
YOU SAID HUMAN HANDS MADE THAT YOKAI WITH THE PAPER MASK. THE MALICE THAT STREAMED INTO MY HEAD...
NEVER...
...FORGIVE...
THAT VOICE IN MY DREAMS...
IT WASN'T A YOKAI.
ARE YOU... HUMAN ...?
OF COURSE.

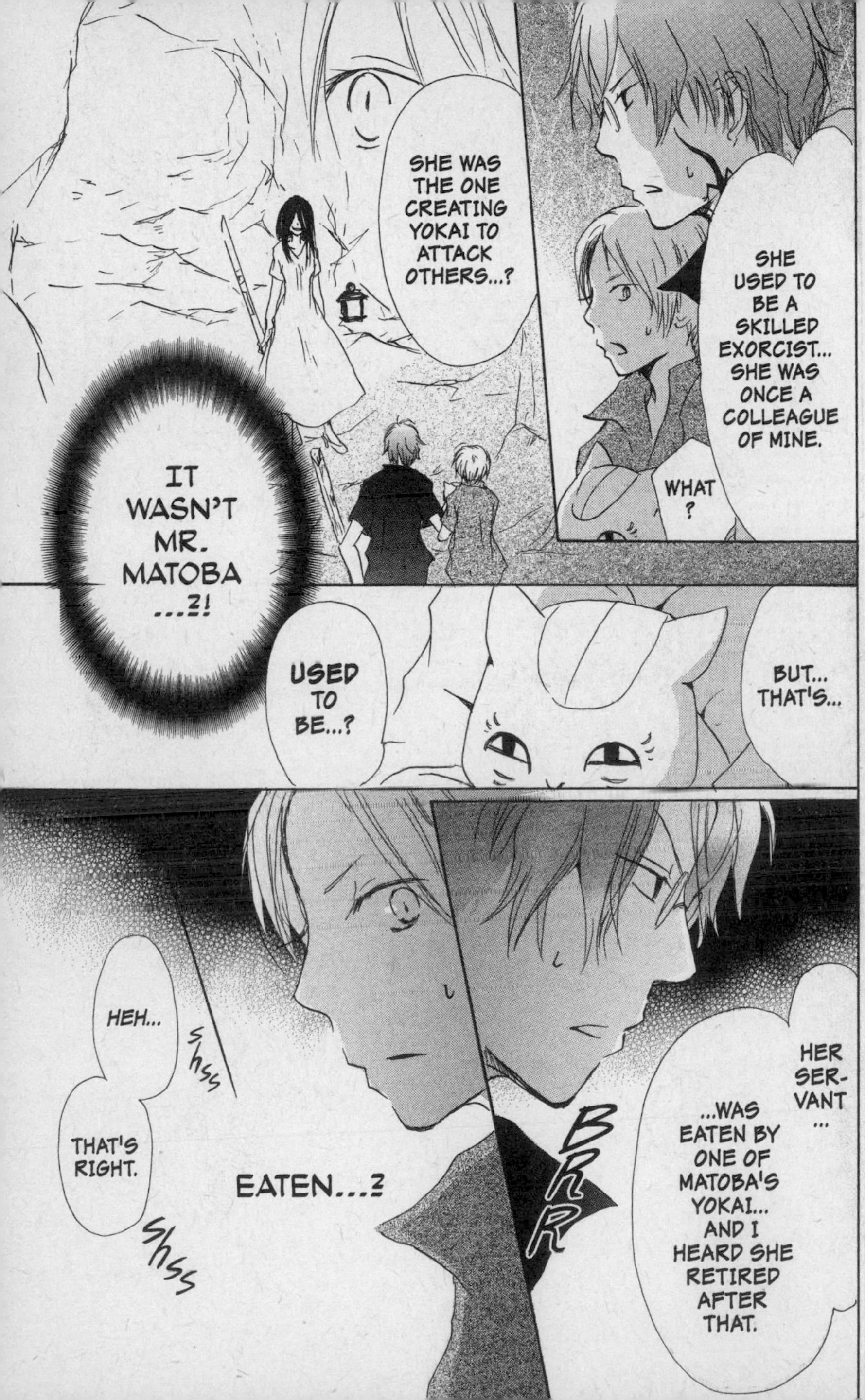
SHE USED TO BE A SKILLED EXORCIST... SHE WAS ONCE A COLLEAGUE OF MINE.
WHAT?
SHE WAS THE ONE CREATING YOKAI TO ATTACK OTHERS...?
IT WASN'T MR. MATOBA...?!
BUT... THAT'S...
USED TO BE...?
HER SERVANT...
...WAS EATEN BY ONE OF MATOBA'S YOKAI... AND I HEARD SHE RETIRED AFTER THAT.
BRR
EATEN...?
HEH...
SHSS
THAT'S RIGHT.
SHSS

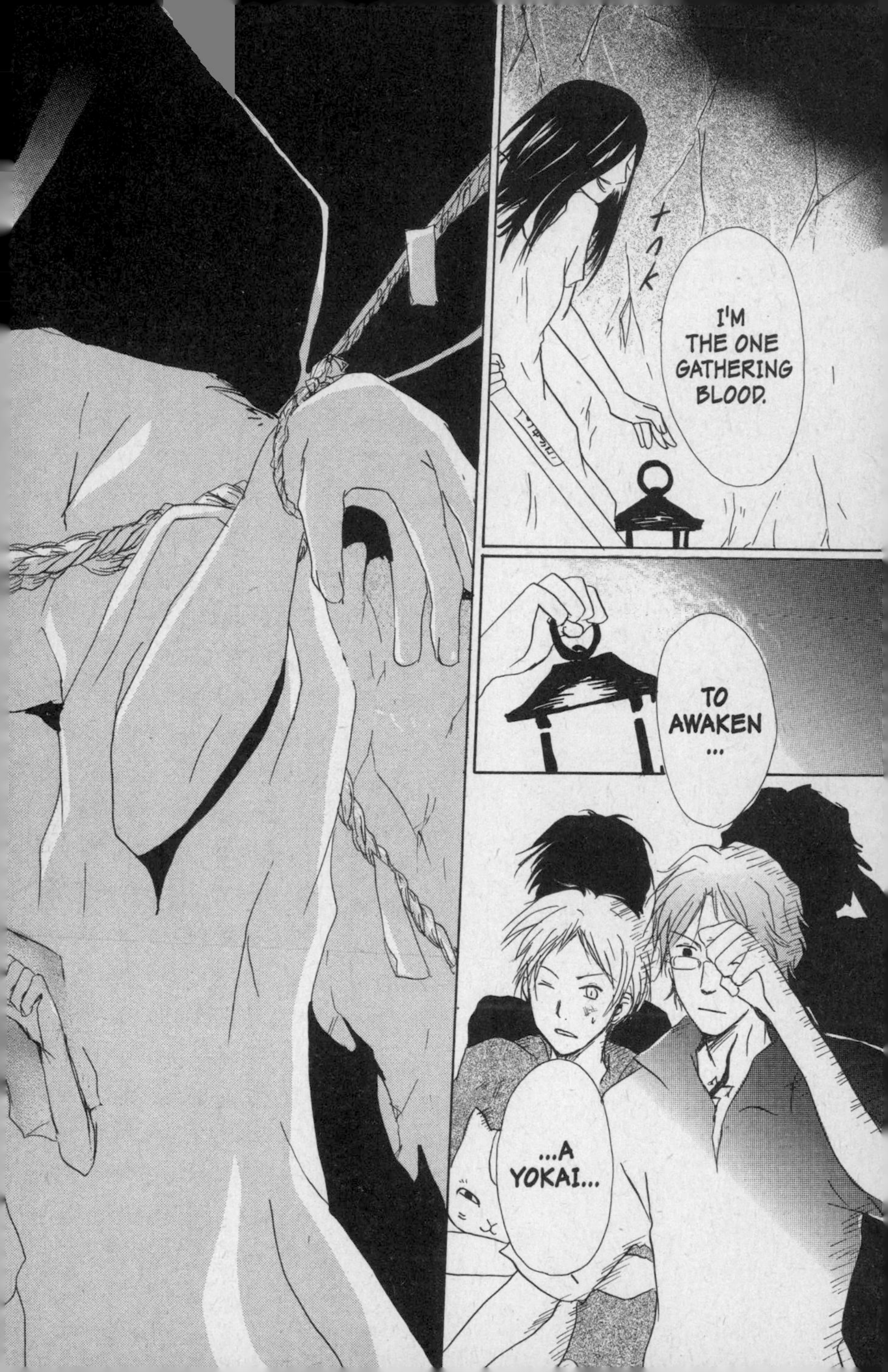
I'M THE ONE GATHERING BLOOD.
TO AWAKEN ...
...A YOKAI...

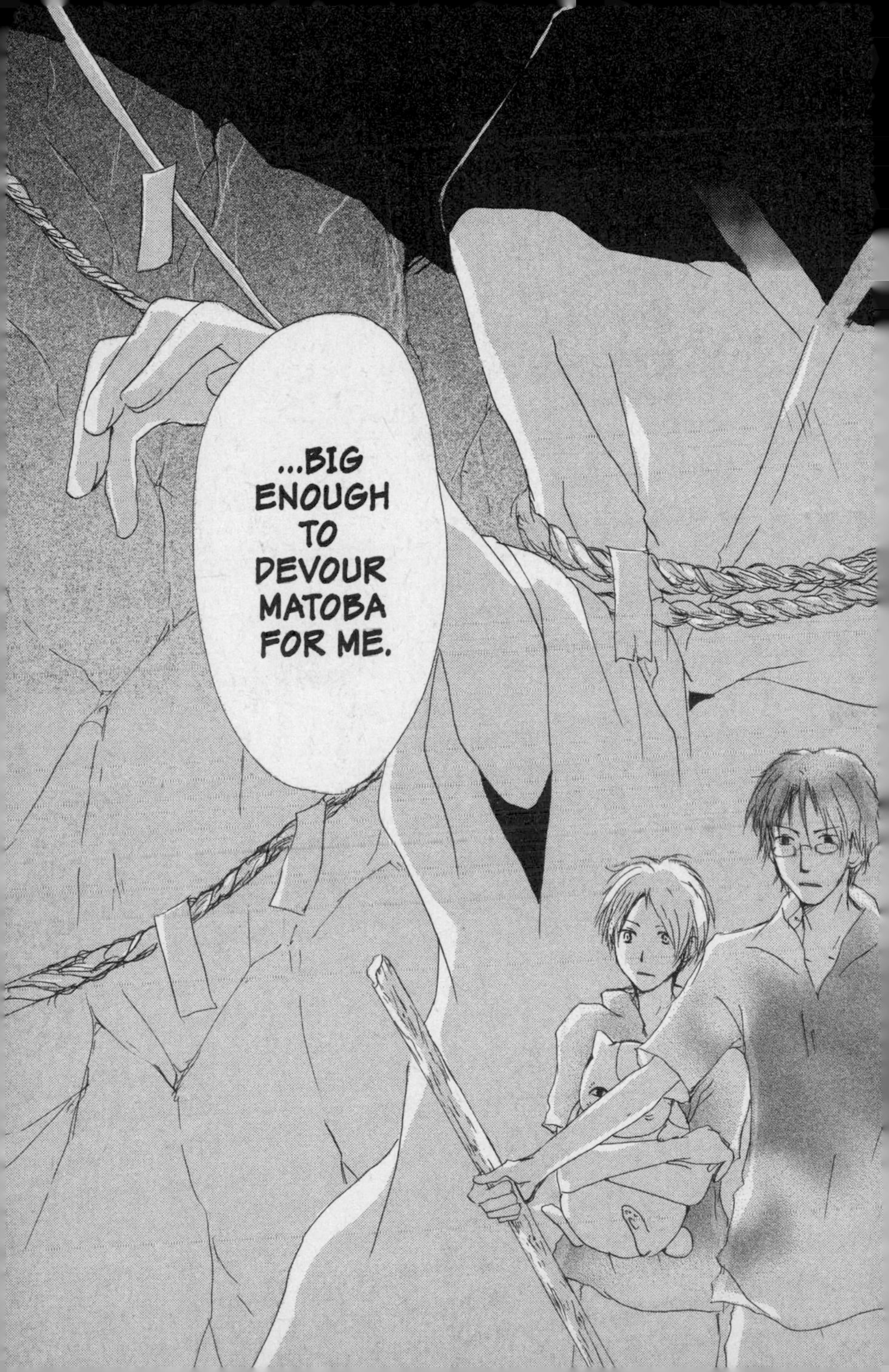
...BIG ENOUGH TO DEVOUR MATOBA FOR ME.

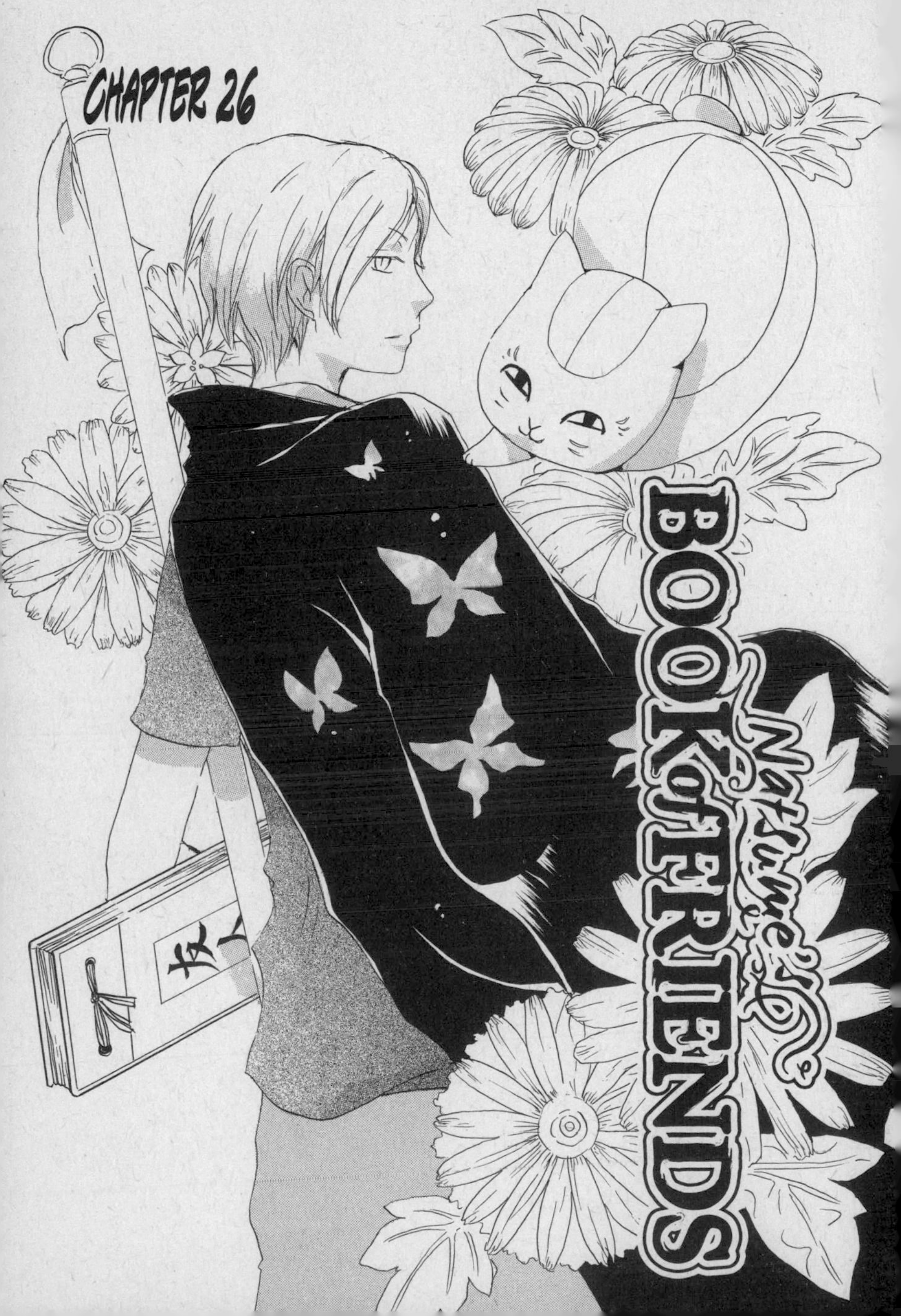
CHAPTER 26
Natsume's BOOK of FRIENDS
友人

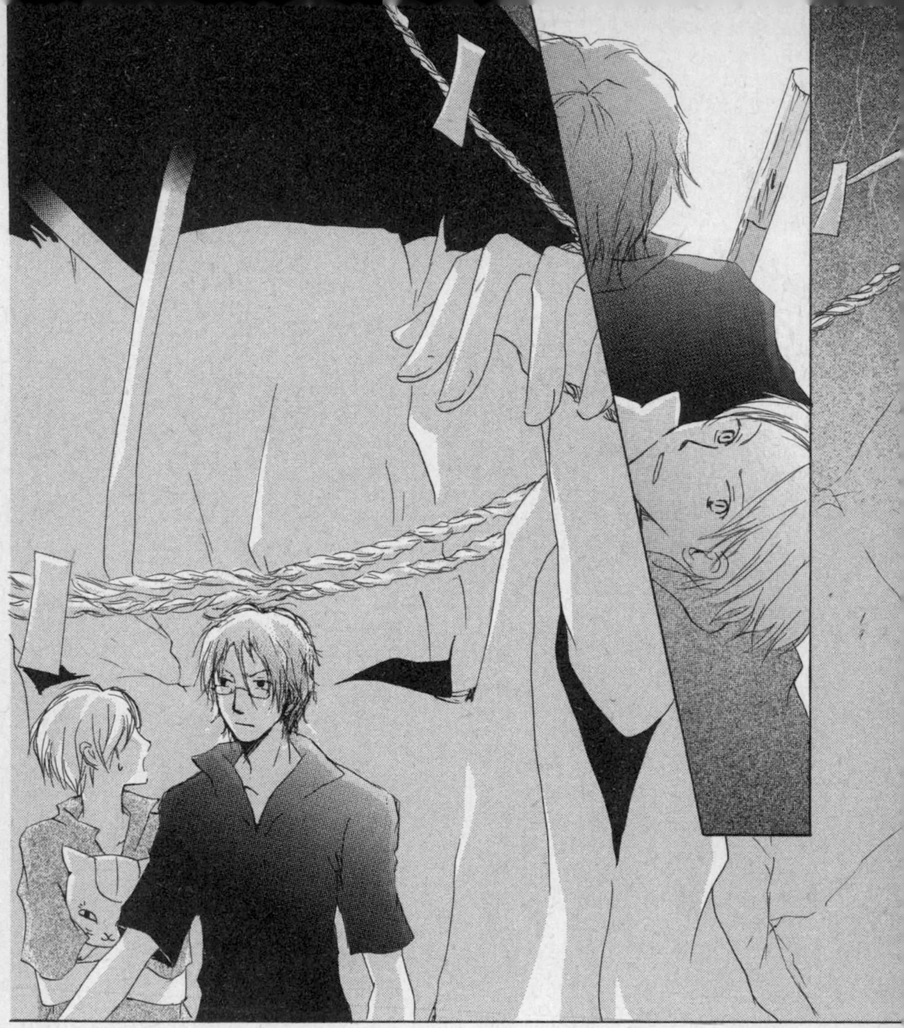

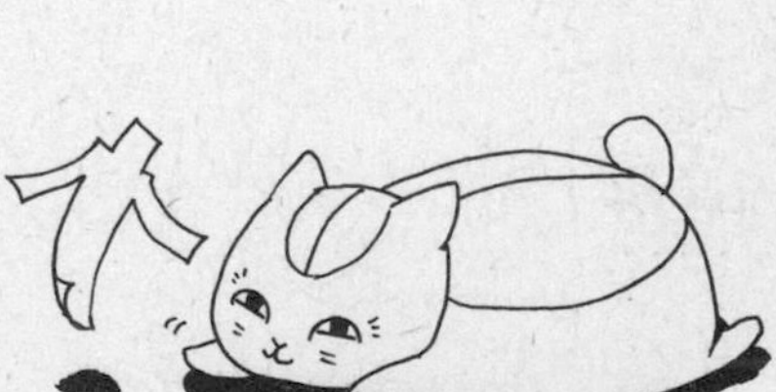

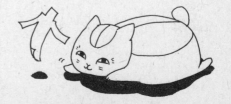

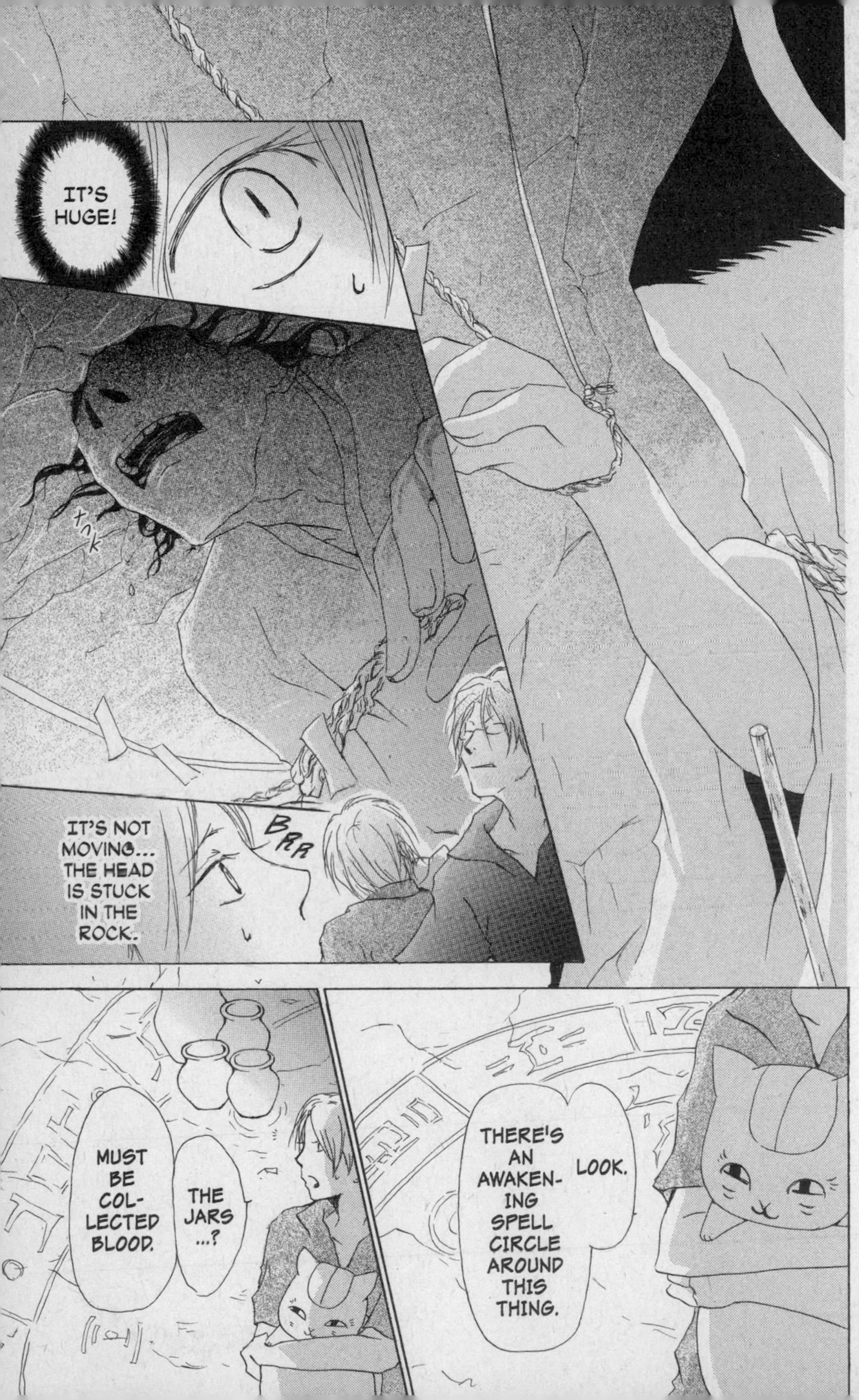
IT'S HUGE!
IT'S NOT MOVING... THE HEAD IS STUCK IN THE ROCK.
BRRR
LOOK.
THERE'S AN AWAKEN-ING SPELL CIRCLE AROUND THIS THING.
THE JARS ...?
MUST BE COL-LECTED BLOOD.

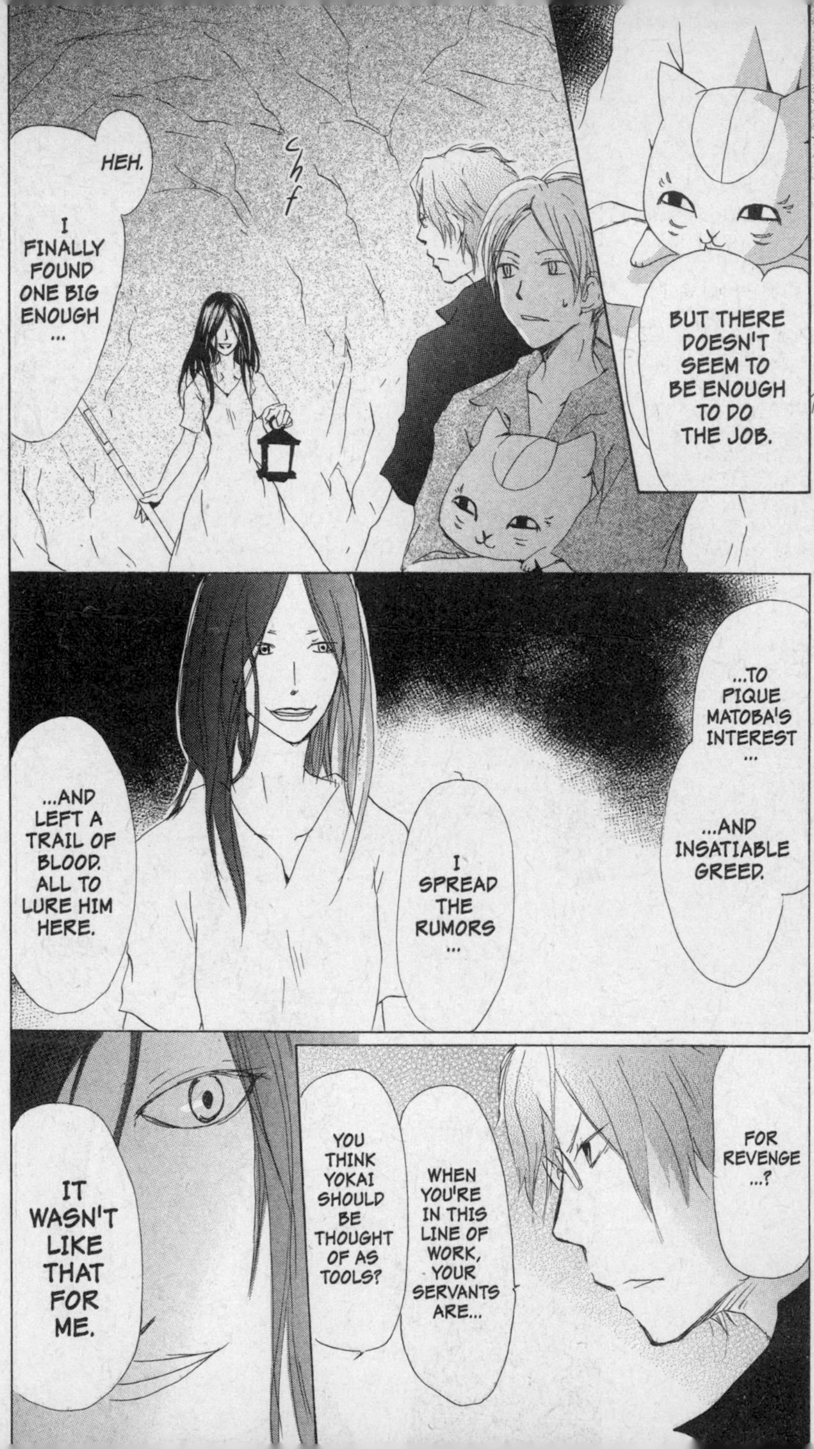
BUT THERE DOESN'T SEEM TO BE ENOUGH TO DO THE JOB.
chf
HEH.
I FINALLY FOUND ONE BIG ENOUGH ...
...TO PIQUE MATOBA'S INTEREST ...
...AND INSATIABLE GREED.
I SPREAD THE RUMORS ...
...AND LEFT A TRAIL OF BLOOD. ALL TO LURE HIM HERE.
FOR REVENGE ...?
WHEN YOU'RE IN THIS LINE OF WORK, YOUR SERVANTS ARE...
YOU THINK YOKAI SHOULD BE THOUGHT OF AS TOOLS?
IT WASN'T LIKE THAT FOR ME.

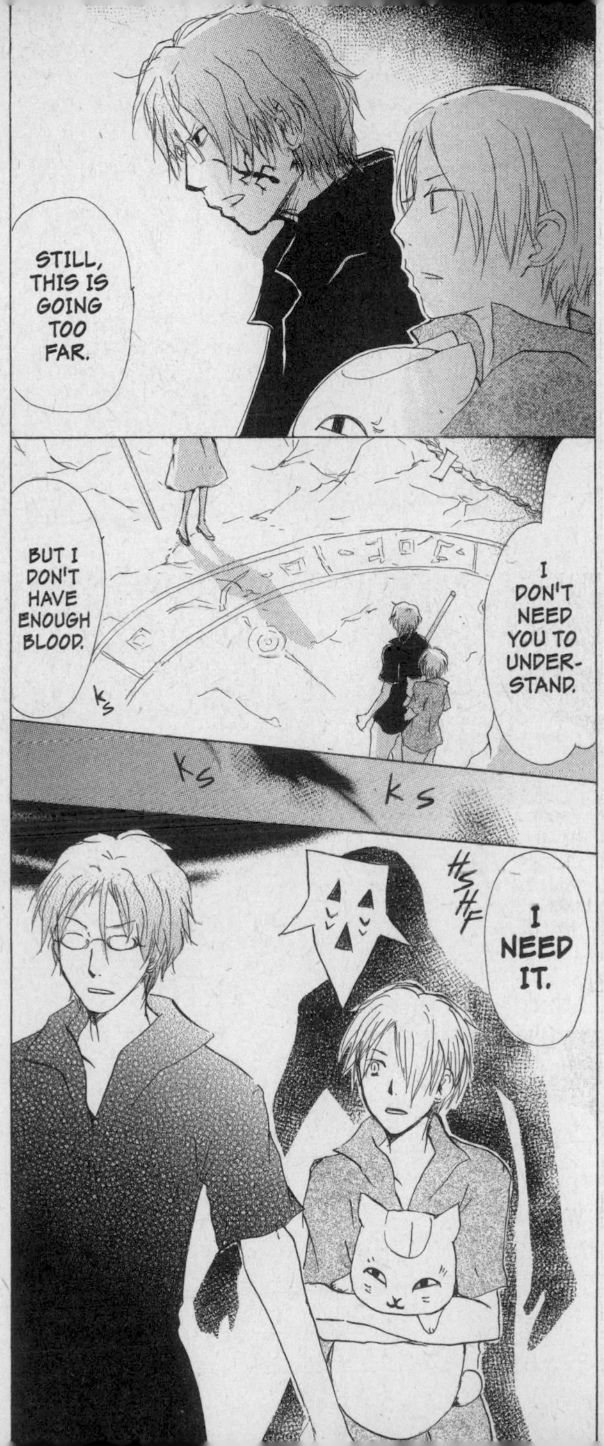
STILL, THIS IS GOING TOO FAR.
I DON'T NEED YOU TO UNDERSTAND.
BUT I DON'T HAVE ENOUGH BLOOD.
KS
KS
KS
HSHF
I NEED IT.

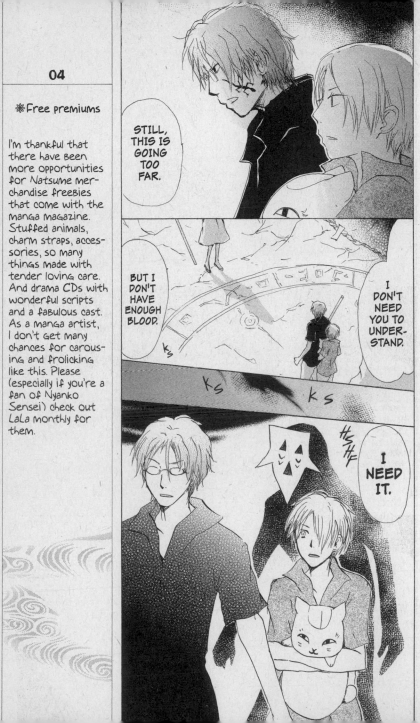

04

❋Free premiums

I'm thankful that there have been more opportunities for Natsume merchandise freebies that come with the manga magazine. Stuffed animals, charm straps, accessories, so many things made with tender loving care. And drama CDs with wonderful scripts and a fabulous cast. As a manga artist, I don't get many chances for carousing and frolicking like this. Please (especially if you're a fan of Nyanko Sensei) check out LaLa monthly for them.

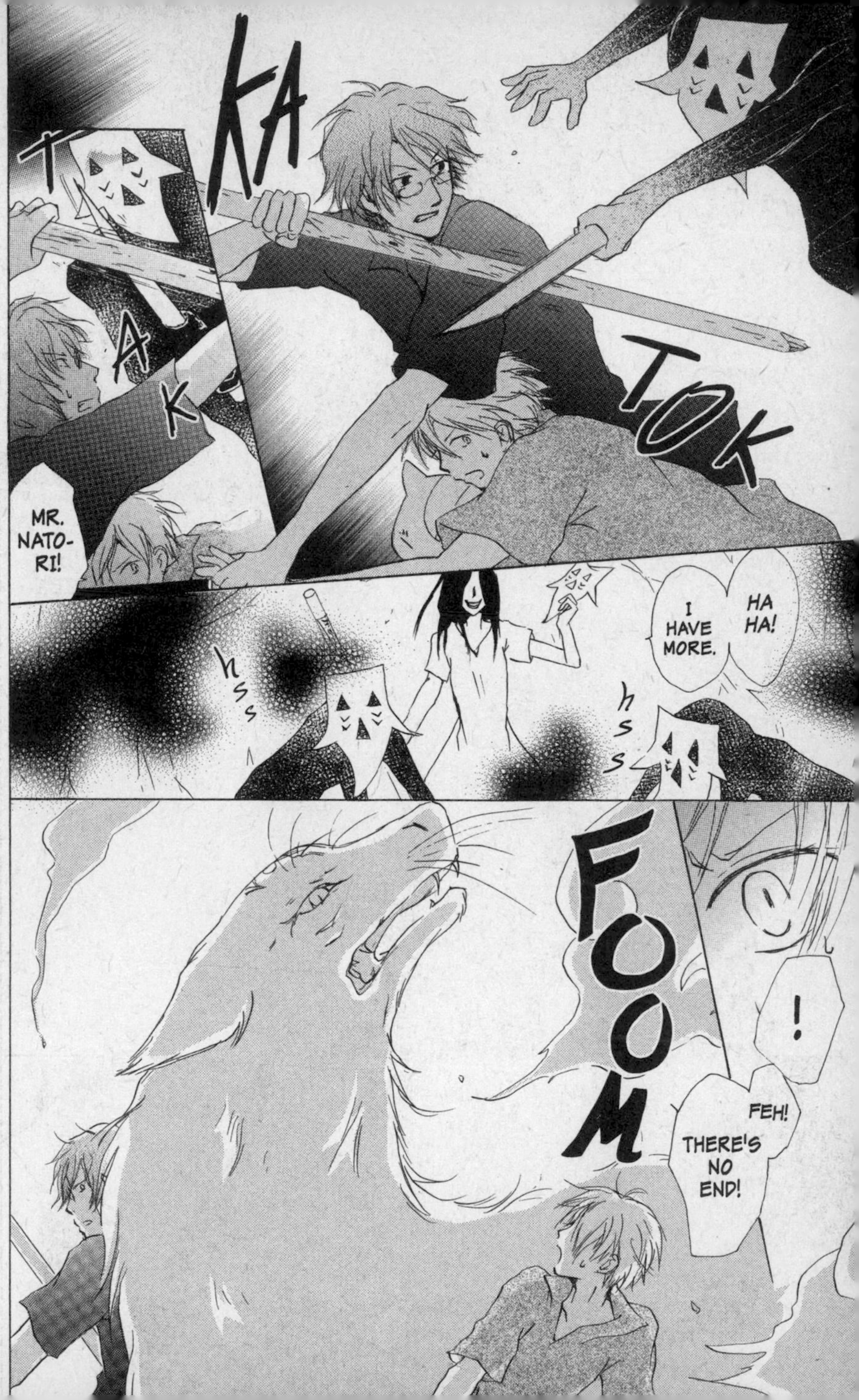
KA
TOK
TAK
MR. NATORI!
HA HA!
I HAVE MORE.
hss
hss
FOOM
!
FEH! THERE'S NO END!

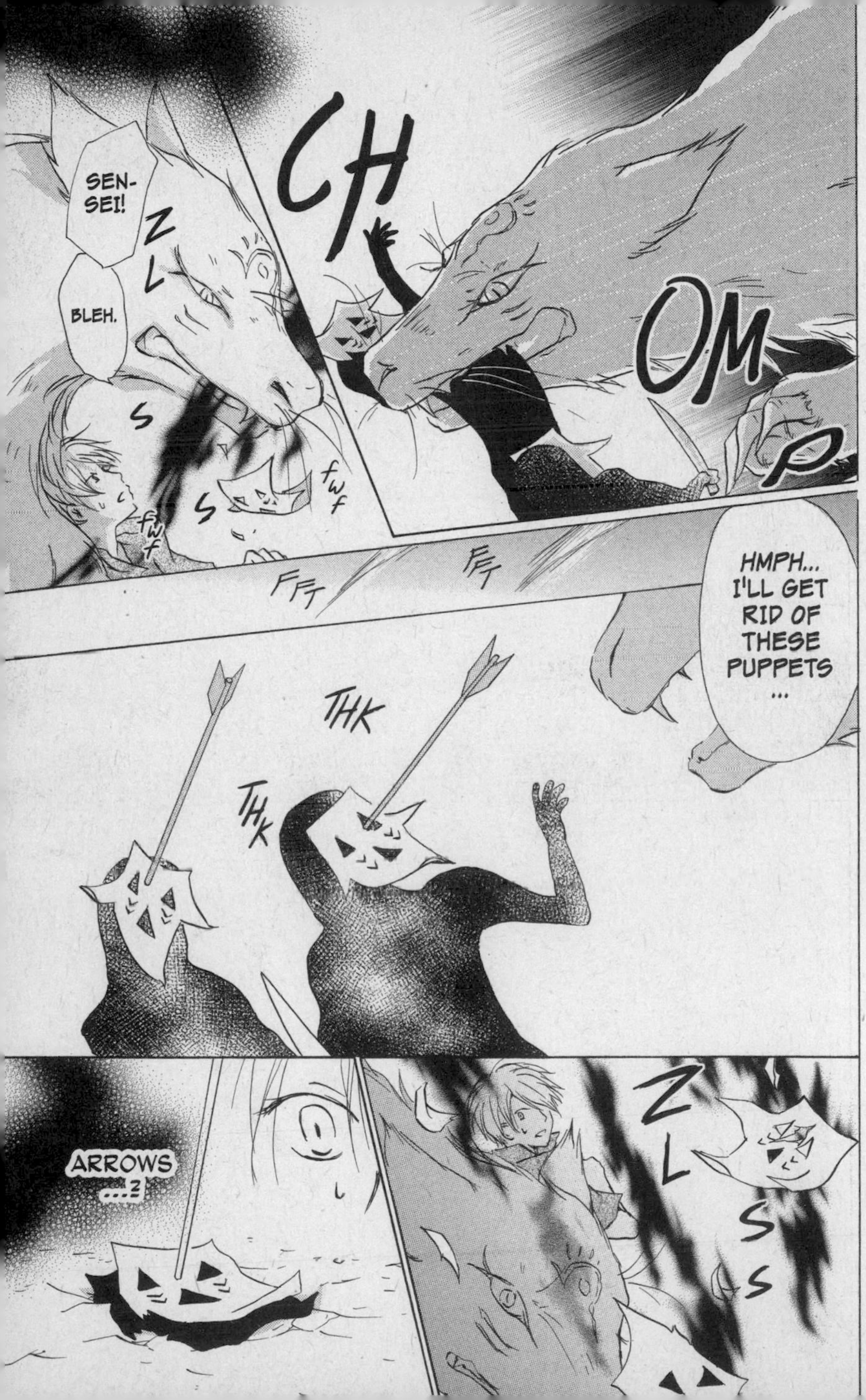
CHOMP
SEN-SEI!
ZLSS
BLEH.
fwf
fwf
FFT
FFT
HMPH... I'LL GET RID OF THESE PUPPETS...
THK
THK
ZLSS
ARROWS...?

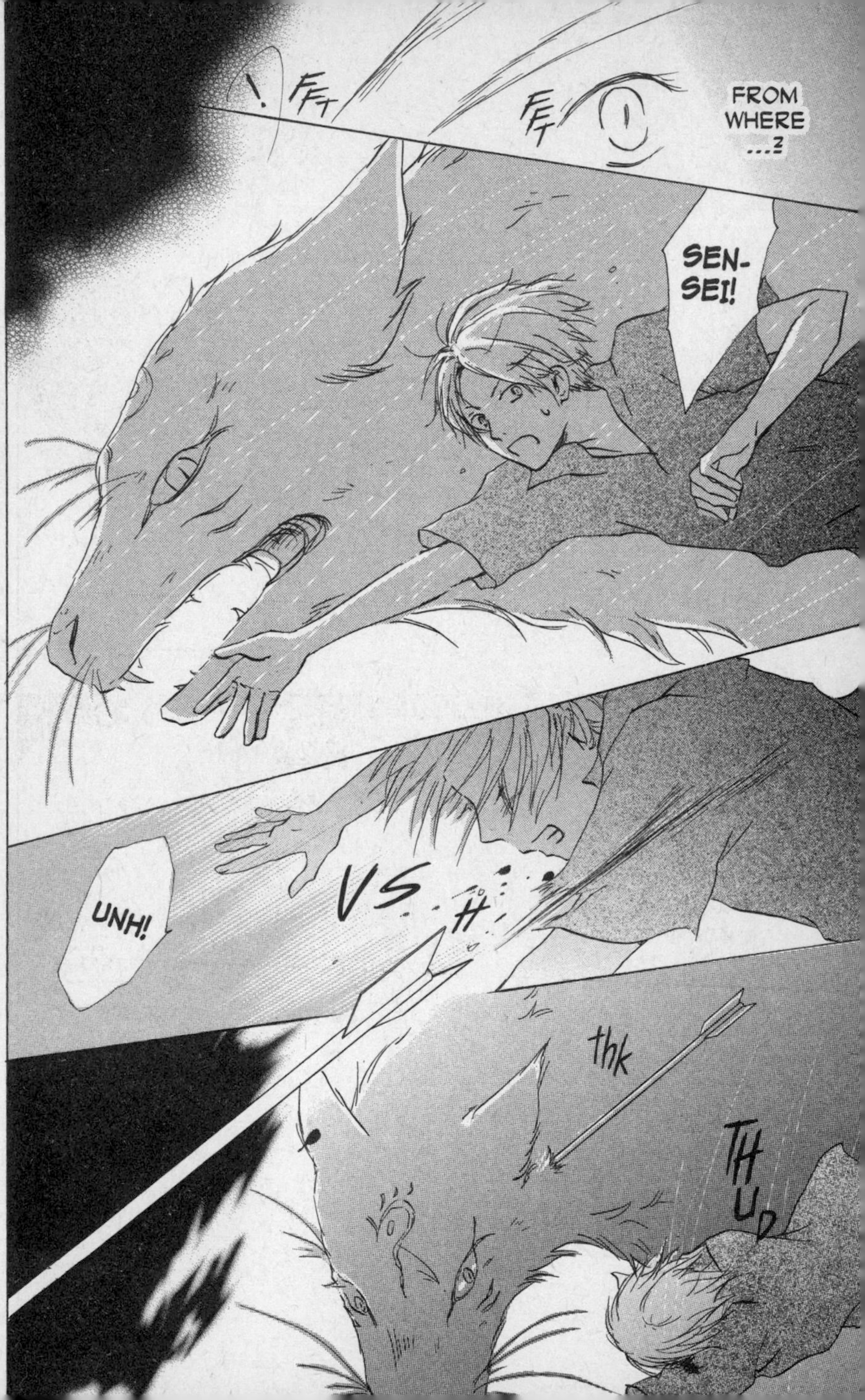
FROM WHERE ...?
FFT
FFT
SEN-SEI!
VS H
UNH!
thk
THUD

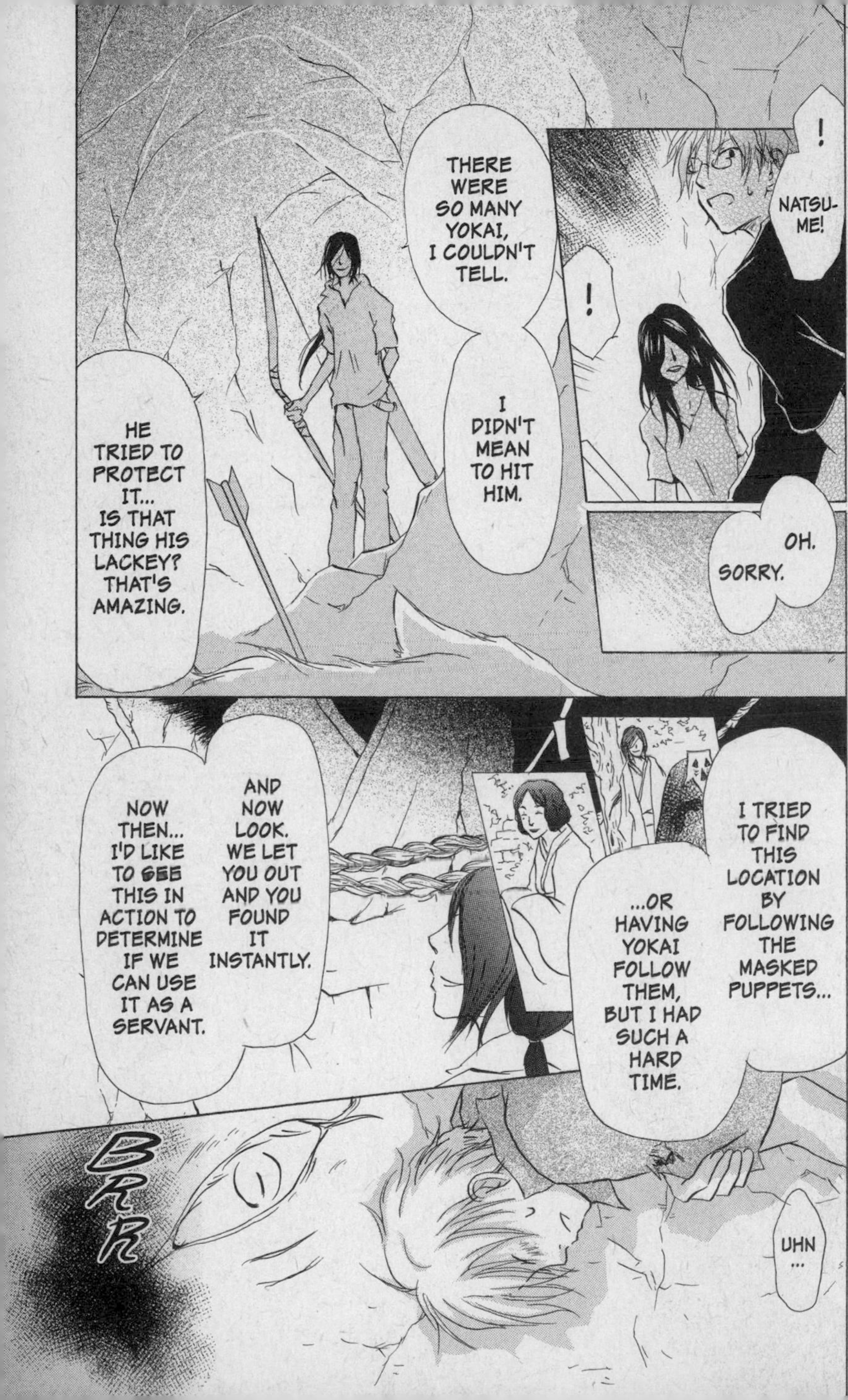
!
NATSUME!
!
OH. SORRY.
THERE WERE SO MANY YOKAI, I COULDN'T TELL.
I DIDN'T MEAN TO HIT HIM.
HE TRIED TO PROTECT IT... IS THAT THING HIS LACKEY? THAT'S AMAZING.
I TRIED TO FIND THIS LOCATION BY FOLLOWING THE MASKED PUPPETS...
...OR HAVING YOKAI FOLLOW THEM, BUT I HAD SUCH A HARD TIME.
AND NOW LOOK. WE LET YOU OUT AND YOU FOUND IT INSTANTLY.
NOW THEN... I'D LIKE TO SEE THIS IN ACTION TO DETERMINE IF WE CAN USE IT AS A SERVANT.
UHN ...
BRR

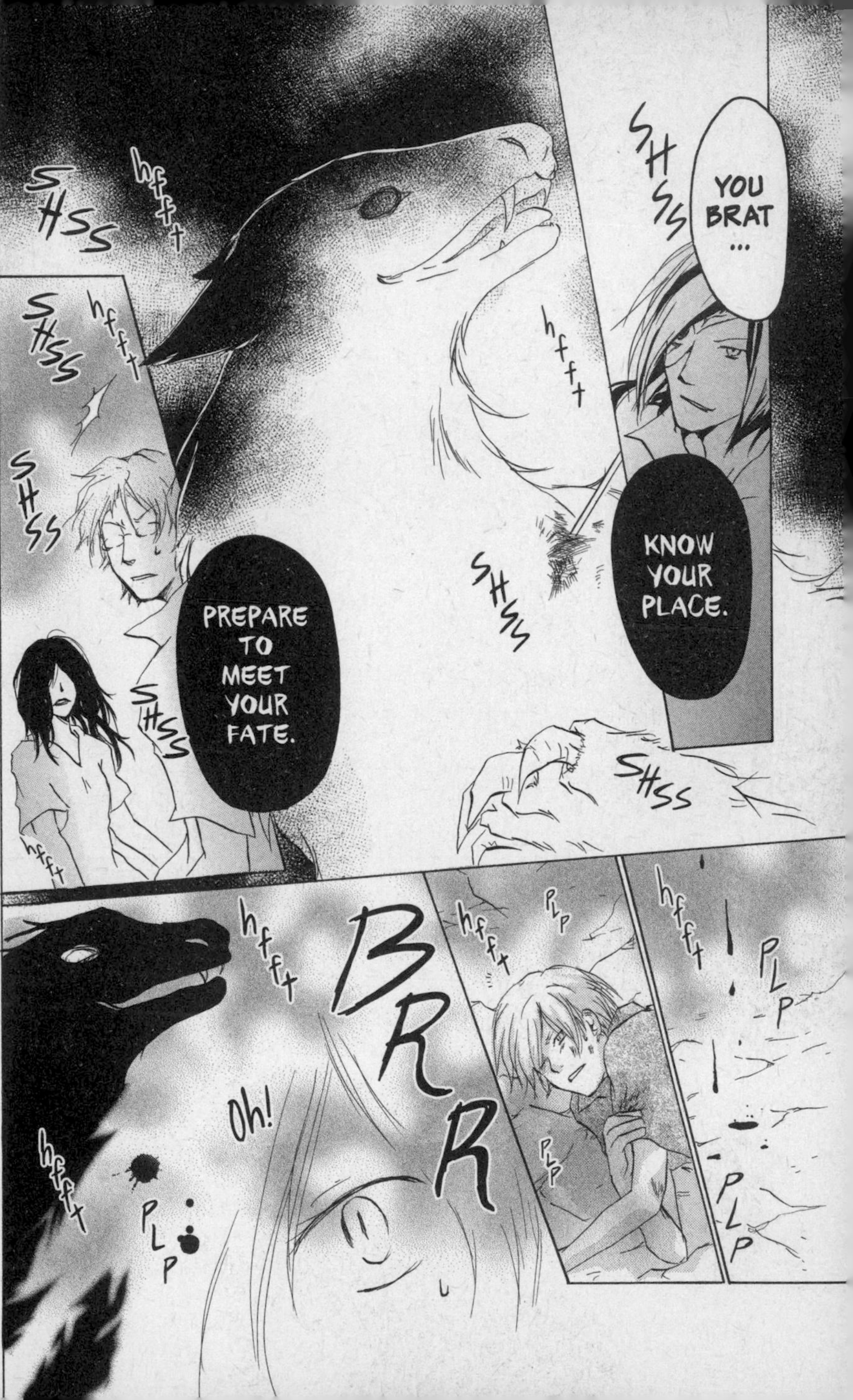
SHSS
YOU BRAT...
hffft
KNOW YOUR PLACE.
SHSS
SHSS
hffft
SHSS
SHSS
hffft
SHSS
PREPARE TO MEET YOUR FATE.
SHSS
hffft
hffft
PLP
PLP
PLP
hffft
PLP
PLP
hffft
BRR
Oh!
hffft
PLP

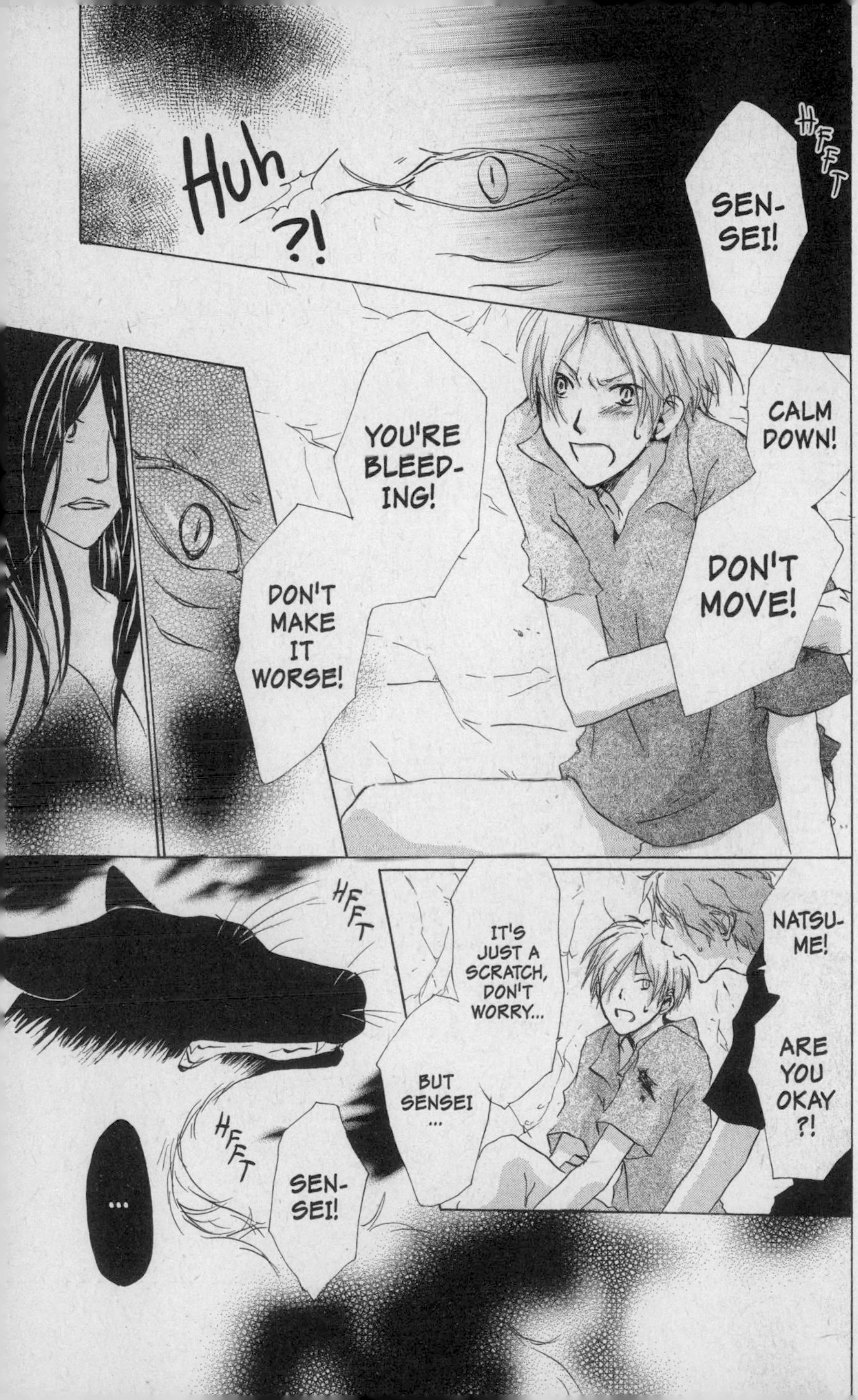
HFFT
SEN-SEI!
Huh ?!
CALM DOWN!
DON'T MOVE!
YOU'RE BLEED-ING!
DON'T MAKE IT WORSE!
NATSU-ME!
ARE YOU OKAY ?!
IT'S JUST A SCRATCH, DON'T WORRY...
BUT SENSEI ...
HFFT
HFFT
SEN-SEI!
...

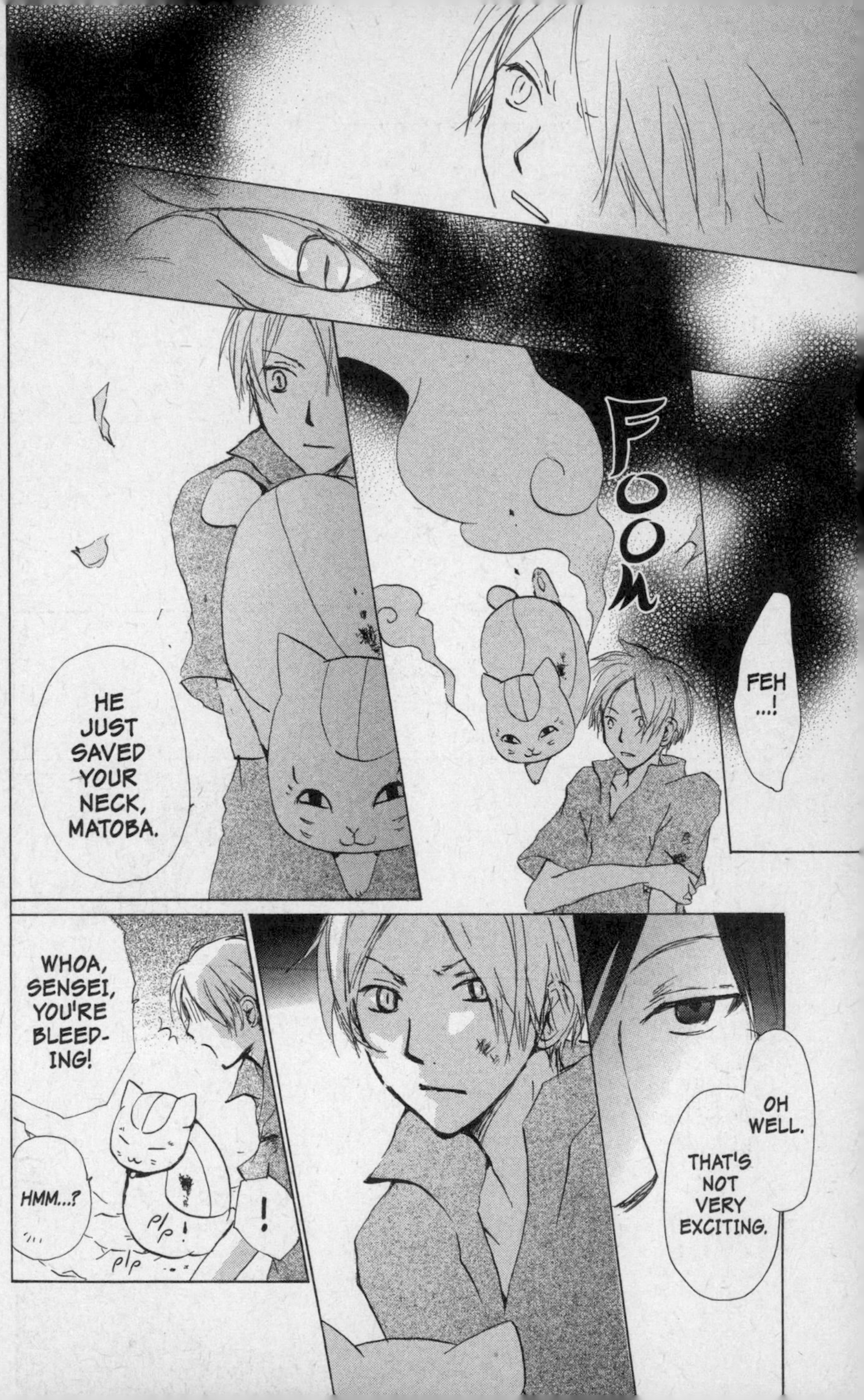
FOOM
FEH ...!
HE JUST SAVED YOUR NECK, MATOBA.
OH WELL.
THAT'S NOT VERY EXCITING.
WHOA, SENSEI, YOU'RE BLEEDING!
!
HMM...?

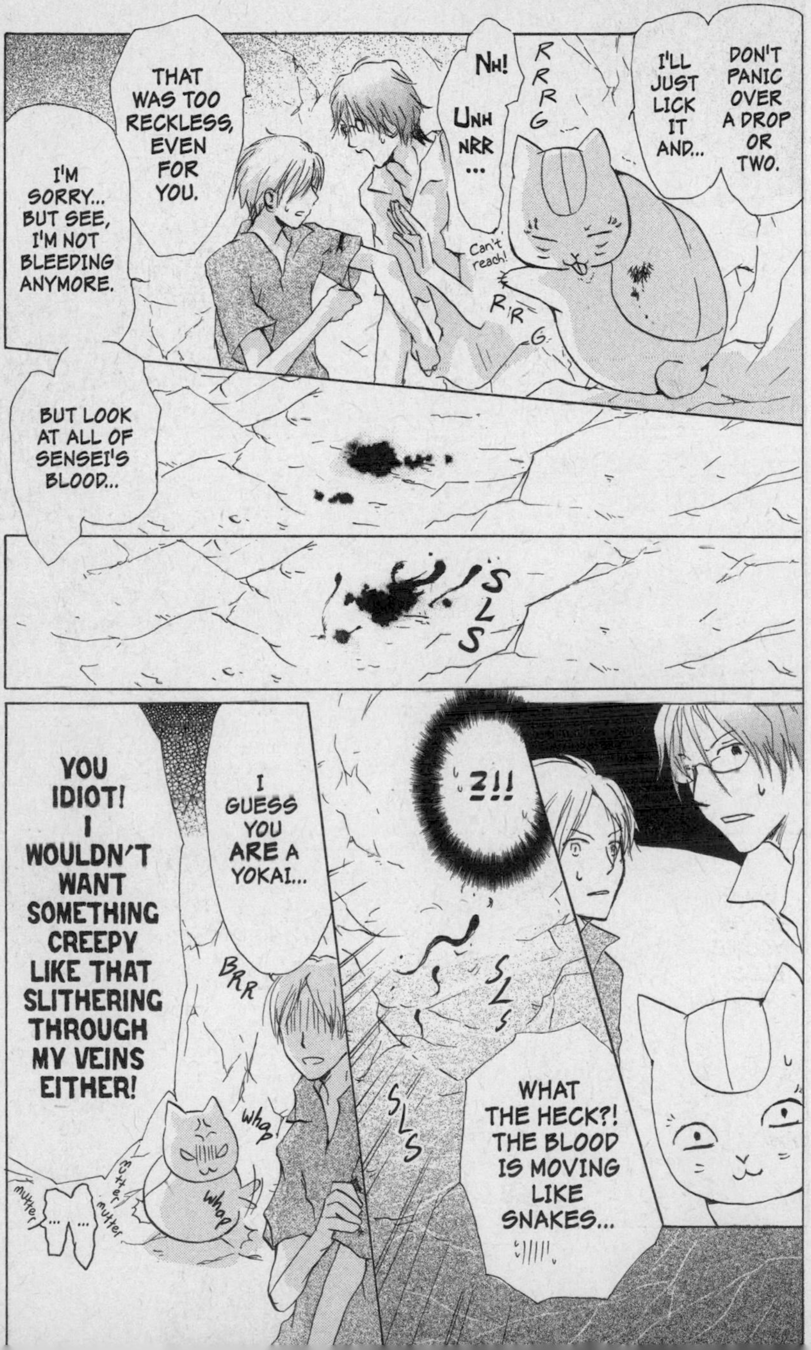
DON'T PANIC OVER A DROP OR TWO.
I'LL JUST LICK IT AND...
RRRG
NH!
UNH NRR...
Can't reach!
RRG
THAT WAS TOO RECKLESS, EVEN FOR YOU.
I'M SORRY... BUT SEE, I'M NOT BLEEDING ANYMORE.
BUT LOOK AT ALL OF SENSEI'S BLOOD...
SLS
Z!!
SLS
WHAT THE HECK?! THE BLOOD IS MOVING LIKE SNAKES...
I GUESS YOU ARE A YOKAI...
BRR
YOU IDIOT! I WOULDN'T WANT SOMETHING CREEPY LIKE THAT SLITHERING THROUGH MY VEINS EITHER!
SLS
whap
whap
mutter mutter
mutter
... ...

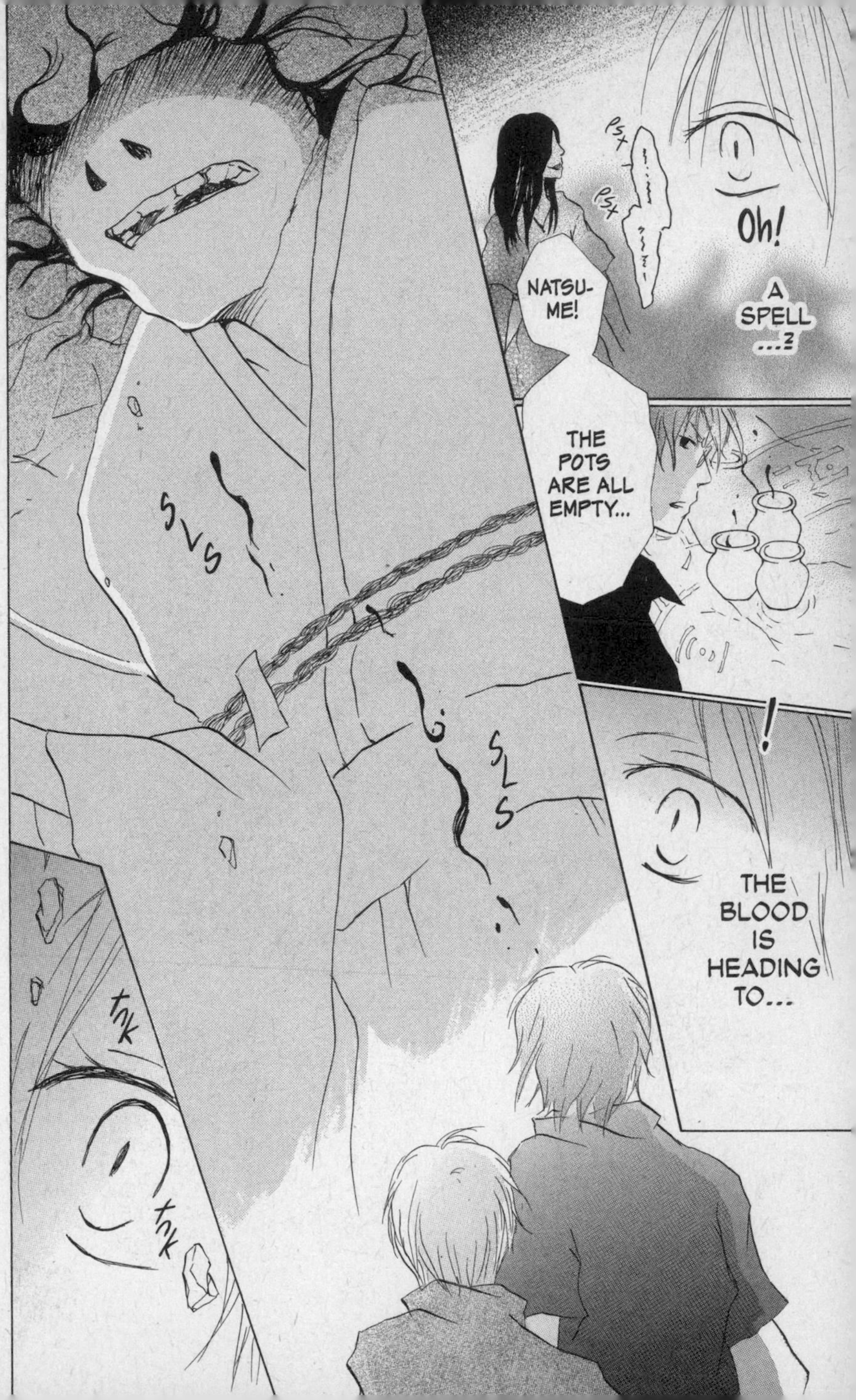
Oh!
A SPELL ...?
psx
psx
NATSU-ME!
THE POTS ARE ALL EMPTY...
!
THE BLOOD IS HEADING TO...
SLS
SLS
tnk
tnk

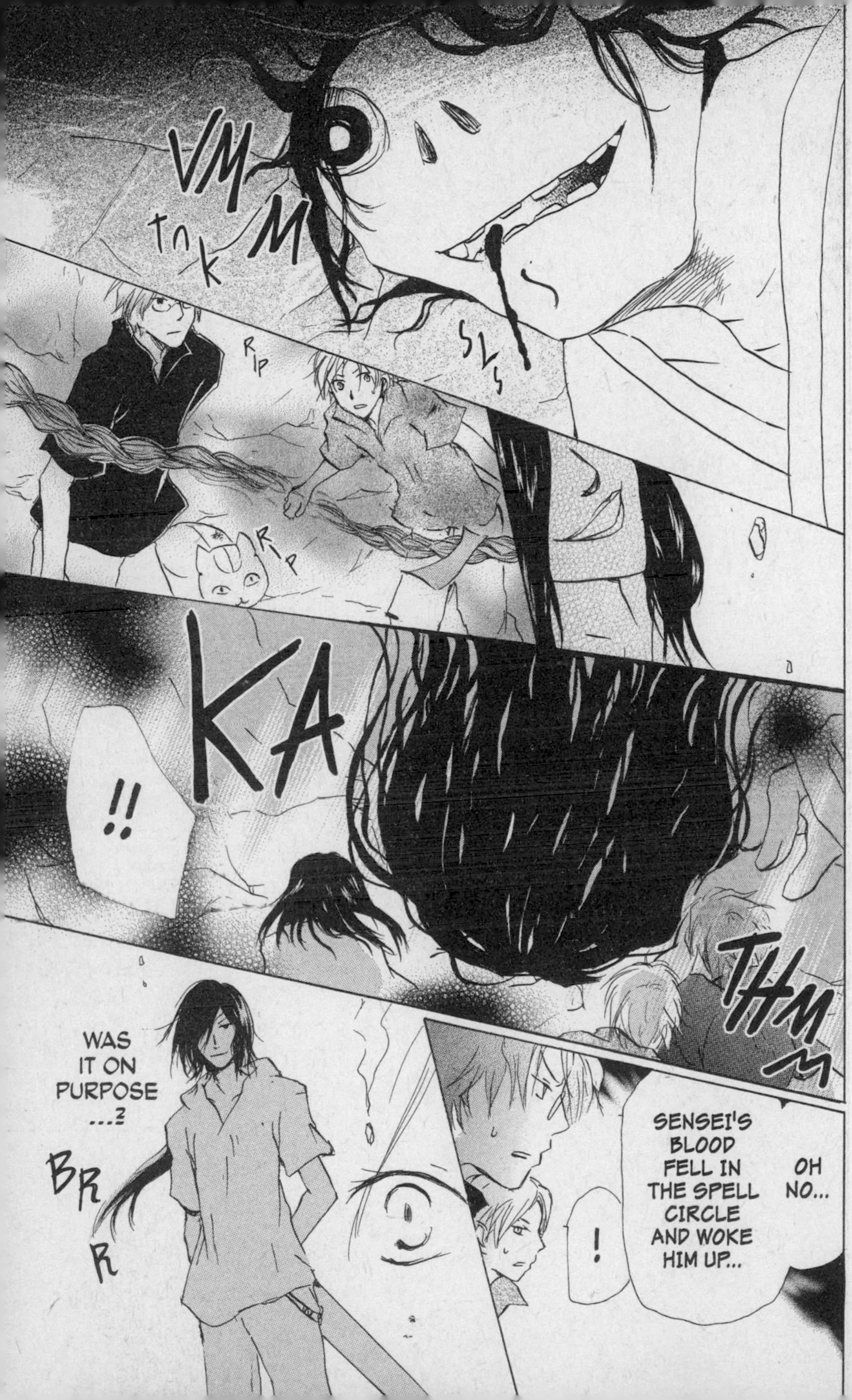

VMM
tnk
sls
Rip
Rip
KA
!!
THUMM
OH NO...
SENSEI'S BLOOD FELL IN THE SPELL CIRCLE AND WOKE HIM UP...
!
WAS IT ON PURPOSE ...?
BRR

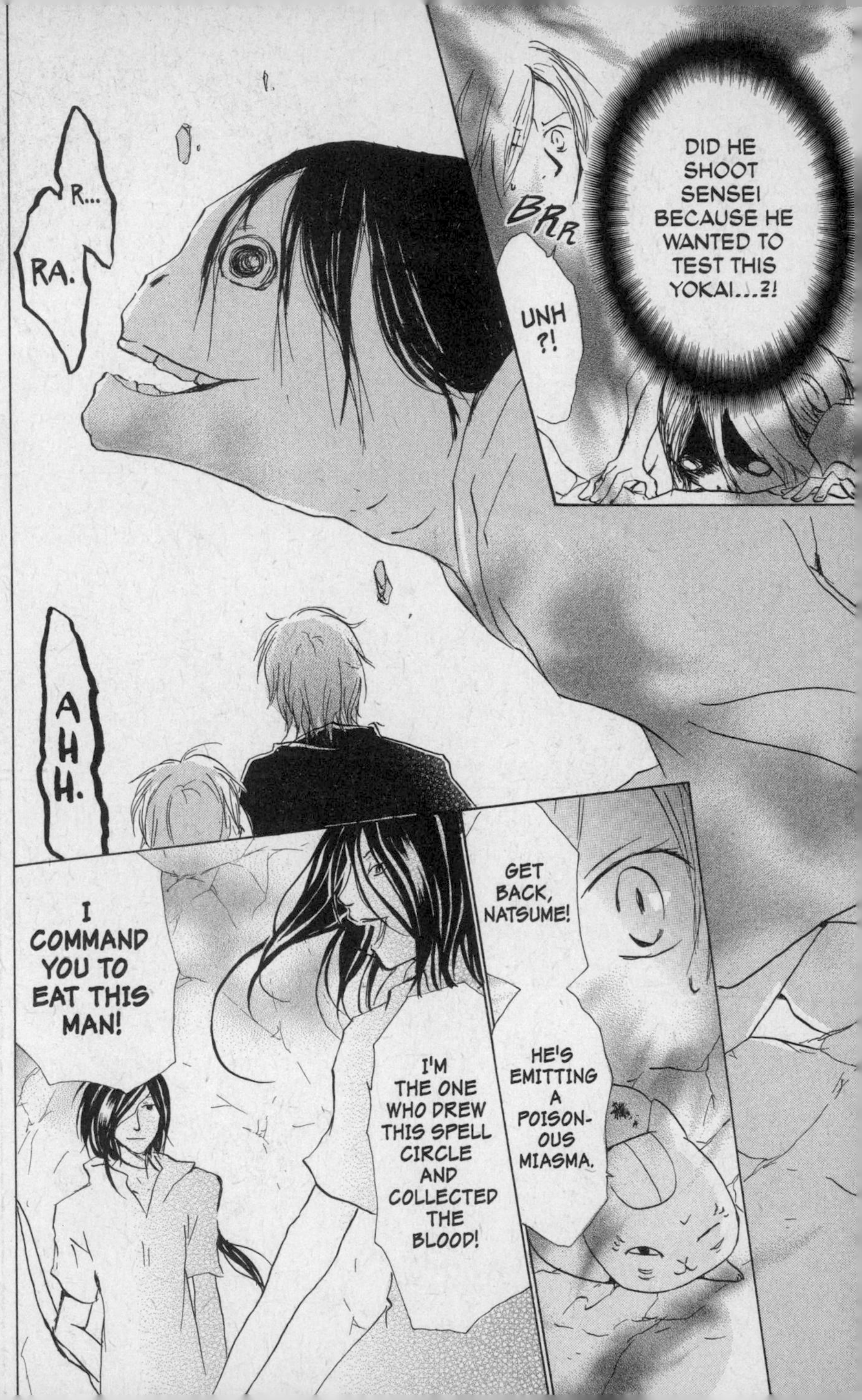
DID HE SHOOT SENSEI BECAUSE HE WANTED TO TEST THIS YOKAI...?!
BRRR
UNH ?!
R...
RA.
AHH.
GET BACK, NATSUME!
HE'S EMITTING A POISON-OUS MIASMA.
I'M THE ONE WHO DREW THIS SPELL CIRCLE AND COLLECTED THE BLOOD!
I COMMAND YOU TO EAT THIS MAN!

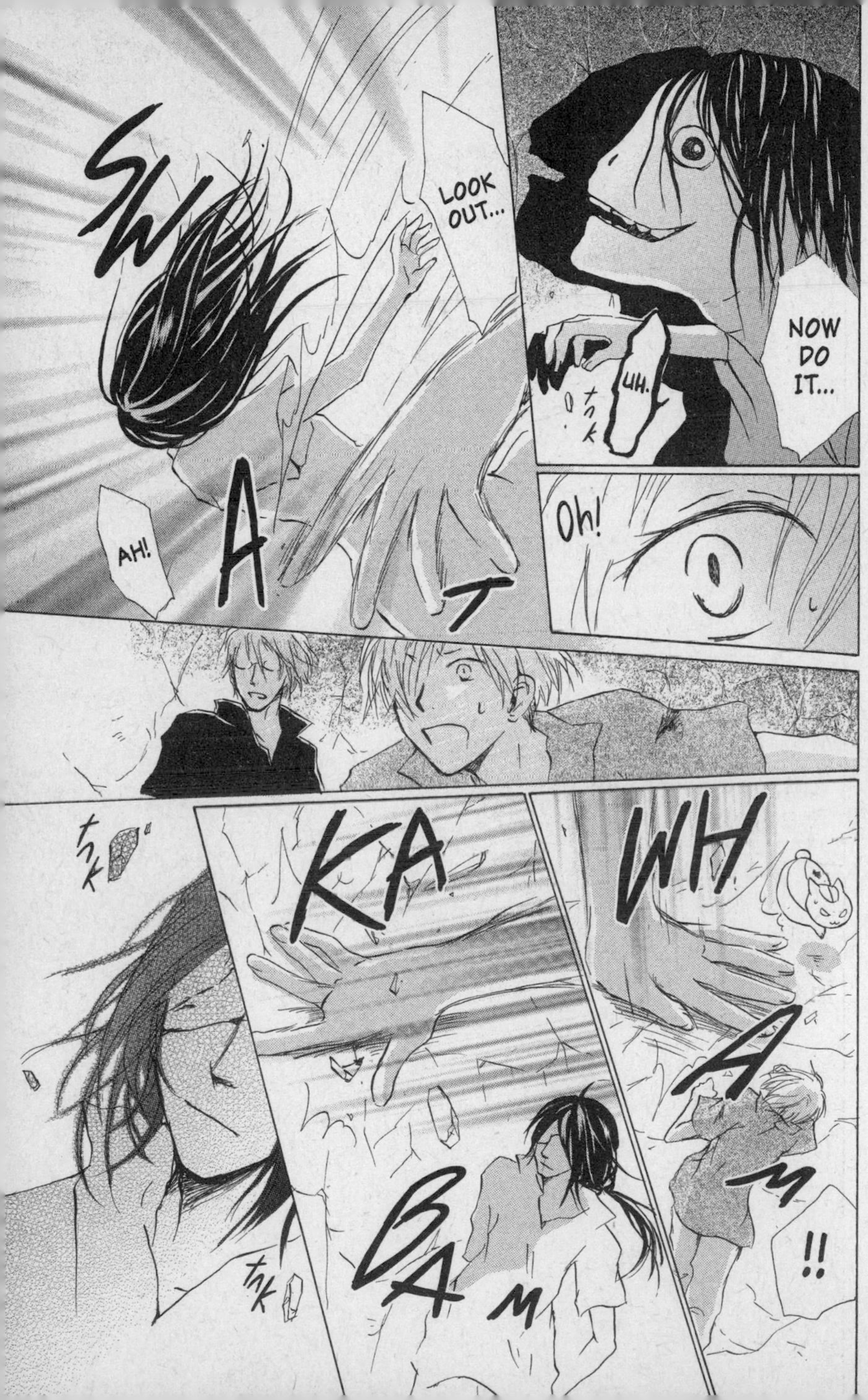
NOW DO IT...
UH.
tnk
Oh!
LOOK OUT...
SWAT
AH!
WHAM
!!
KABAM
tnk
tnk

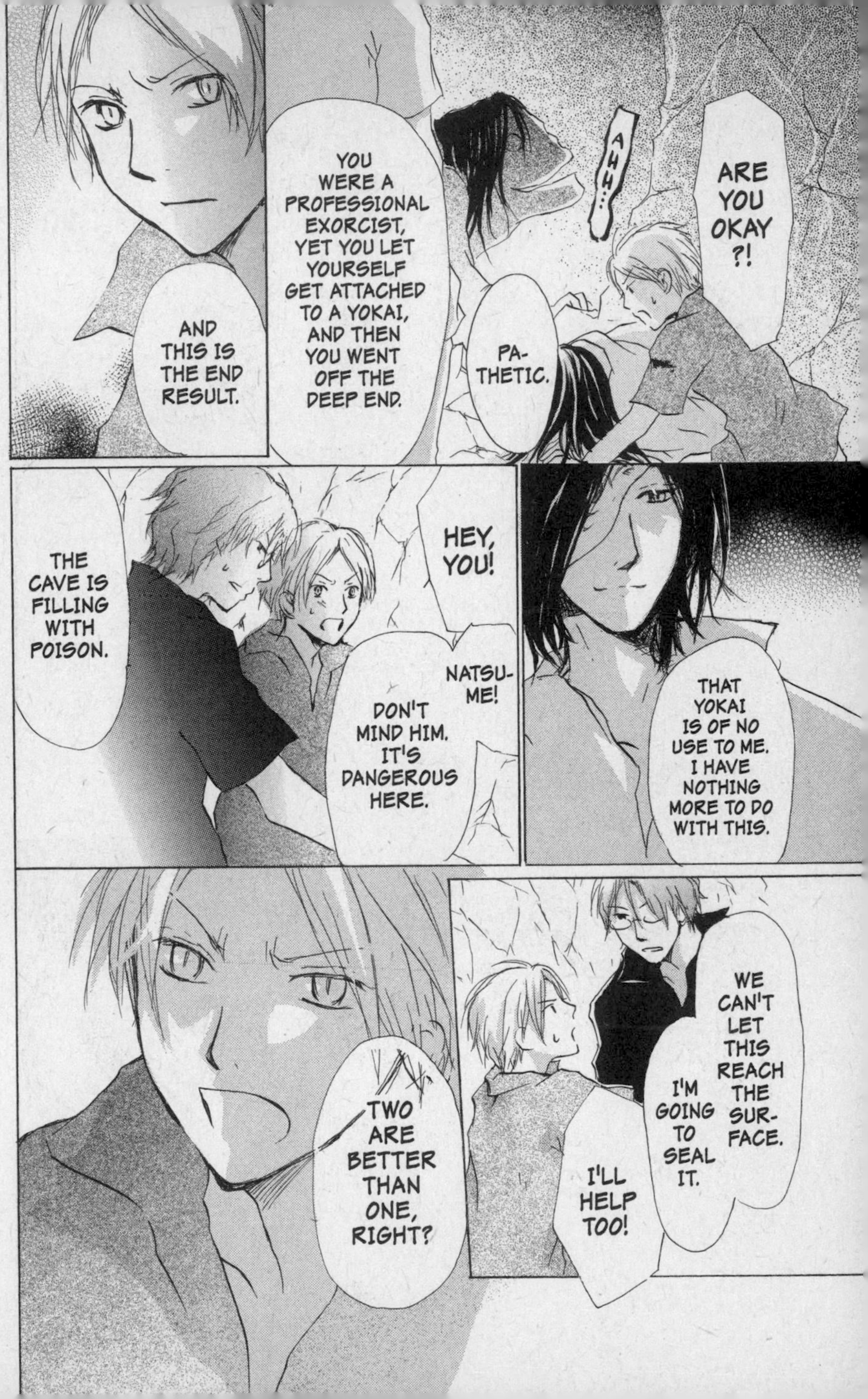
ARE YOU OKAY ?!
AHH...
PA-THETIC.
YOU WERE A PROFESSIONAL EXORCIST, YET YOU LET YOURSELF GET ATTACHED TO A YOKAI, AND THEN YOU WENT OFF THE DEEP END.
AND THIS IS THE END RESULT.
THAT YOKAI IS OF NO USE TO ME. I HAVE NOTHING MORE TO DO WITH THIS.
HEY, YOU!
NATSU-ME!
DON'T MIND HIM. IT'S DANGEROUS HERE.
THE CAVE IS FILLING WITH POISON.
WE CAN'T LET THIS REACH THE SUR-FACE.
I'M GOING TO SEAL IT.
I'LL HELP TOO!
TWO ARE BETTER THAN ONE, RIGHT?

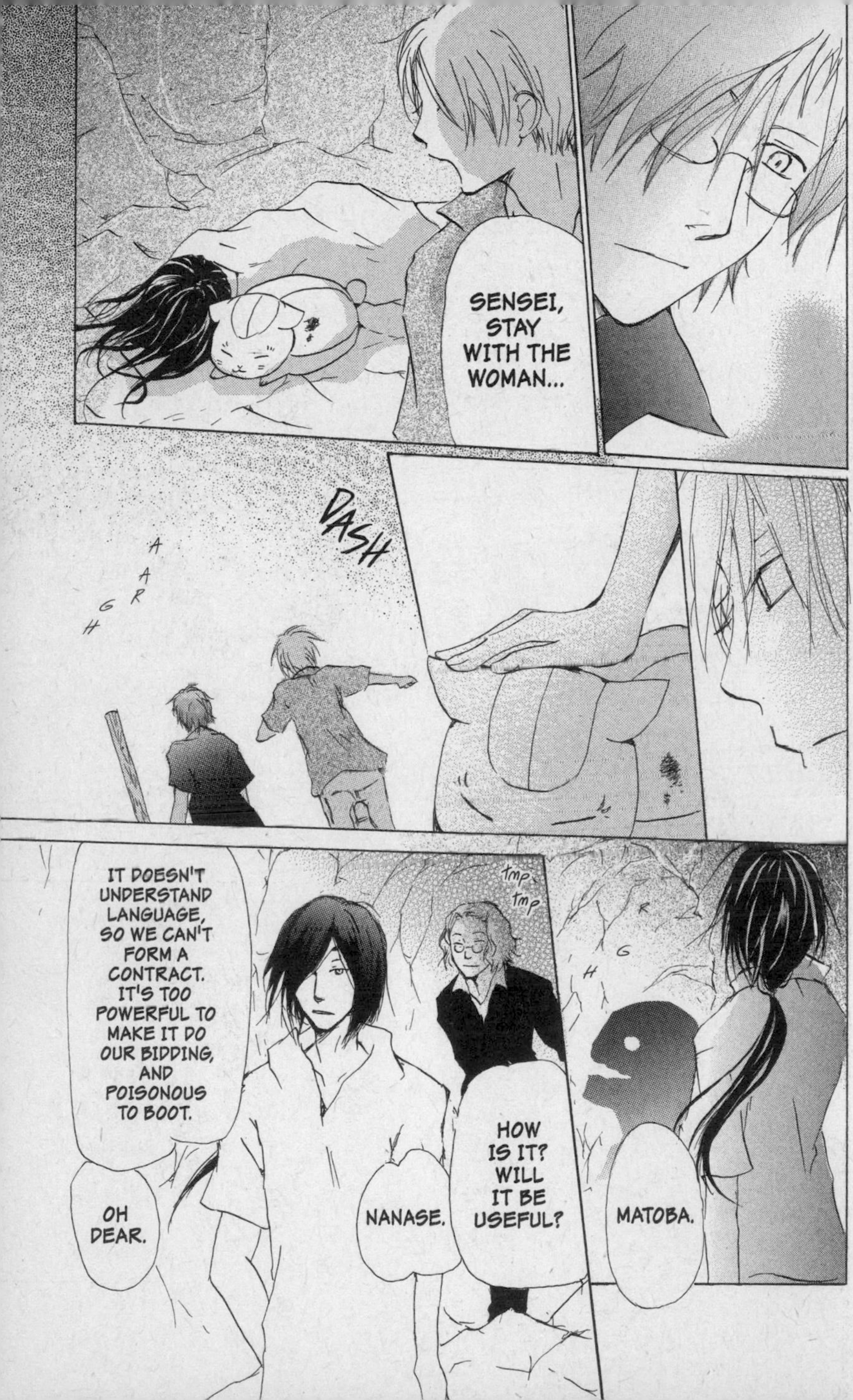

SENSEI, STAY WITH THE WOMAN...
DASH
AARGH
tmp tmp
RGH
MATOBA.
HOW IS IT? WILL IT BE USEFUL?
NANASE.
OH DEAR.
IT DOESN'T UNDERSTAND LANGUAGE, SO WE CAN'T FORM A CONTRACT. IT'S TOO POWERFUL TO MAKE IT DO OUR BIDDING, AND POISONOUS TO BOOT.

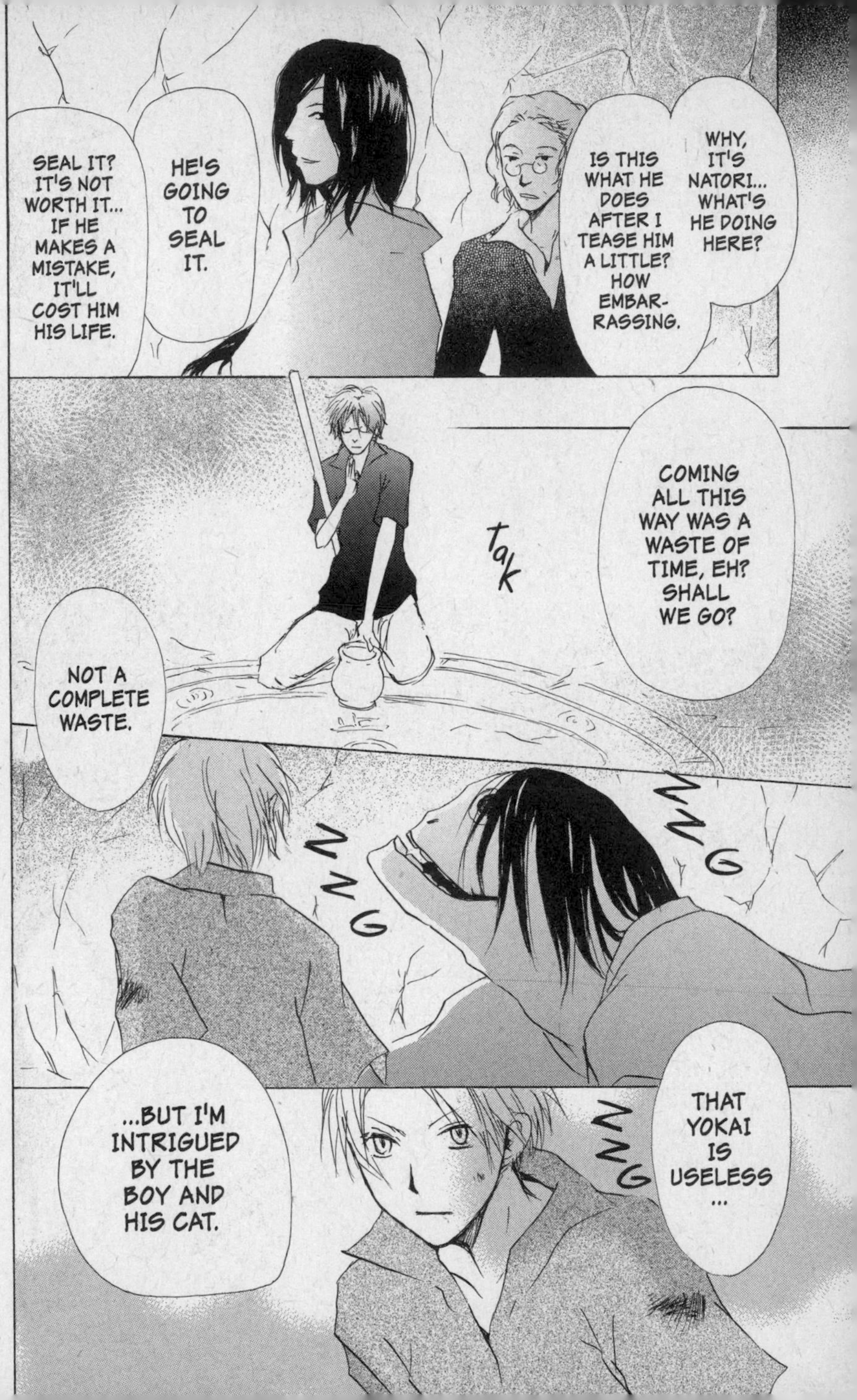
WHY, IT'S NATORI... WHAT'S HE DOING HERE?
IS THIS WHAT HE DOES AFTER I TEASE HIM A LITTLE? HOW EMBAR-RASSING.
HE'S GOING TO SEAL IT.
SEAL IT? IT'S NOT WORTH IT... IF HE MAKES A MISTAKE, IT'LL COST HIM HIS LIFE.
COMING ALL THIS WAY WAS A WASTE OF TIME, EH? SHALL WE GO?
tak
NOT A COMPLETE WASTE.
ZZG
ZZG
THAT YOKAI IS USELESS ...
ZZG
...BUT I'M INTRIGUED BY THE BOY AND HIS CAT.

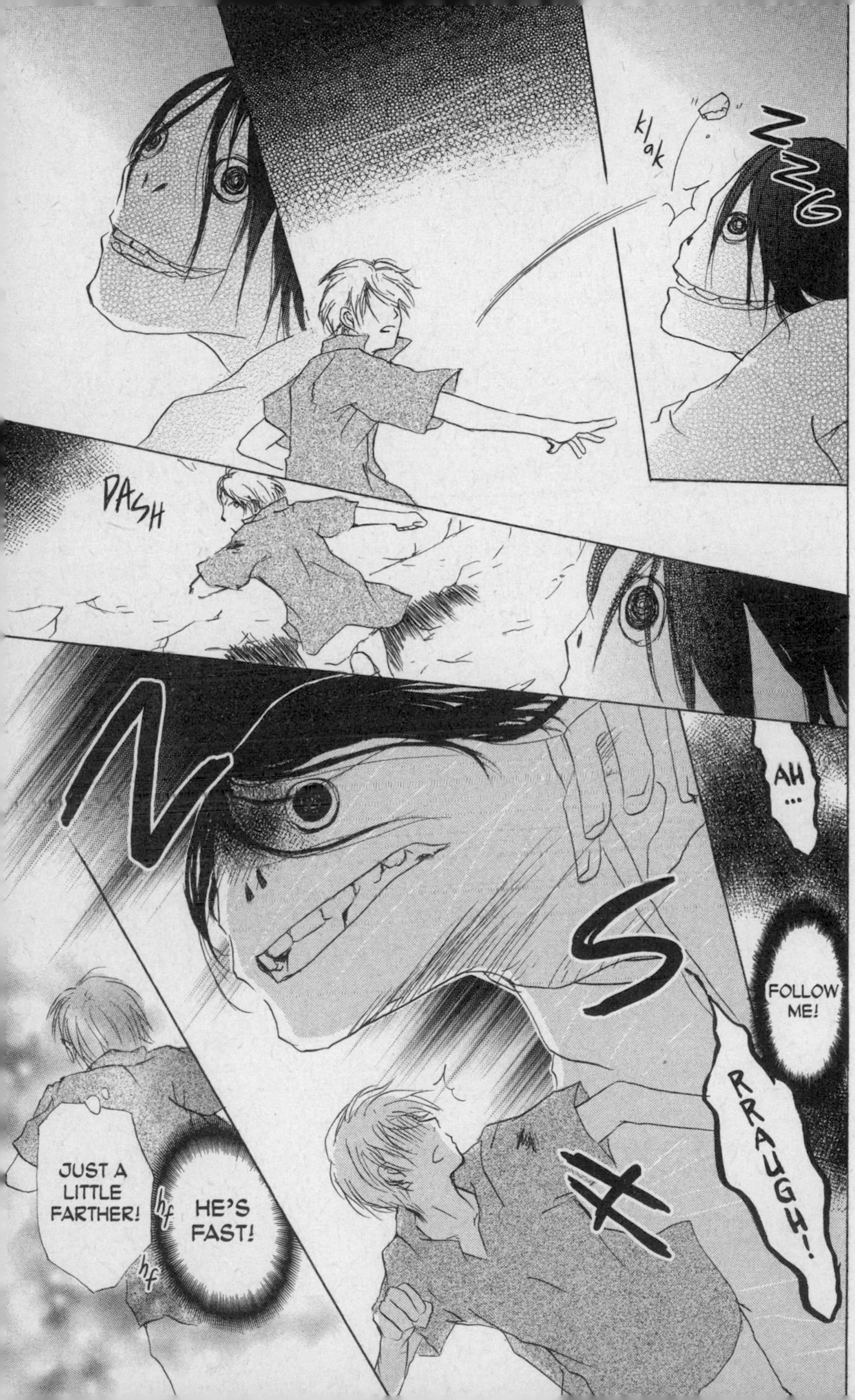
klak
ZZG
DASH
N
AH...
S
FOLLOW ME!
RRAUGH!
HE'S FAST!
hf
hf
JUST A LITTLE FARTHER!

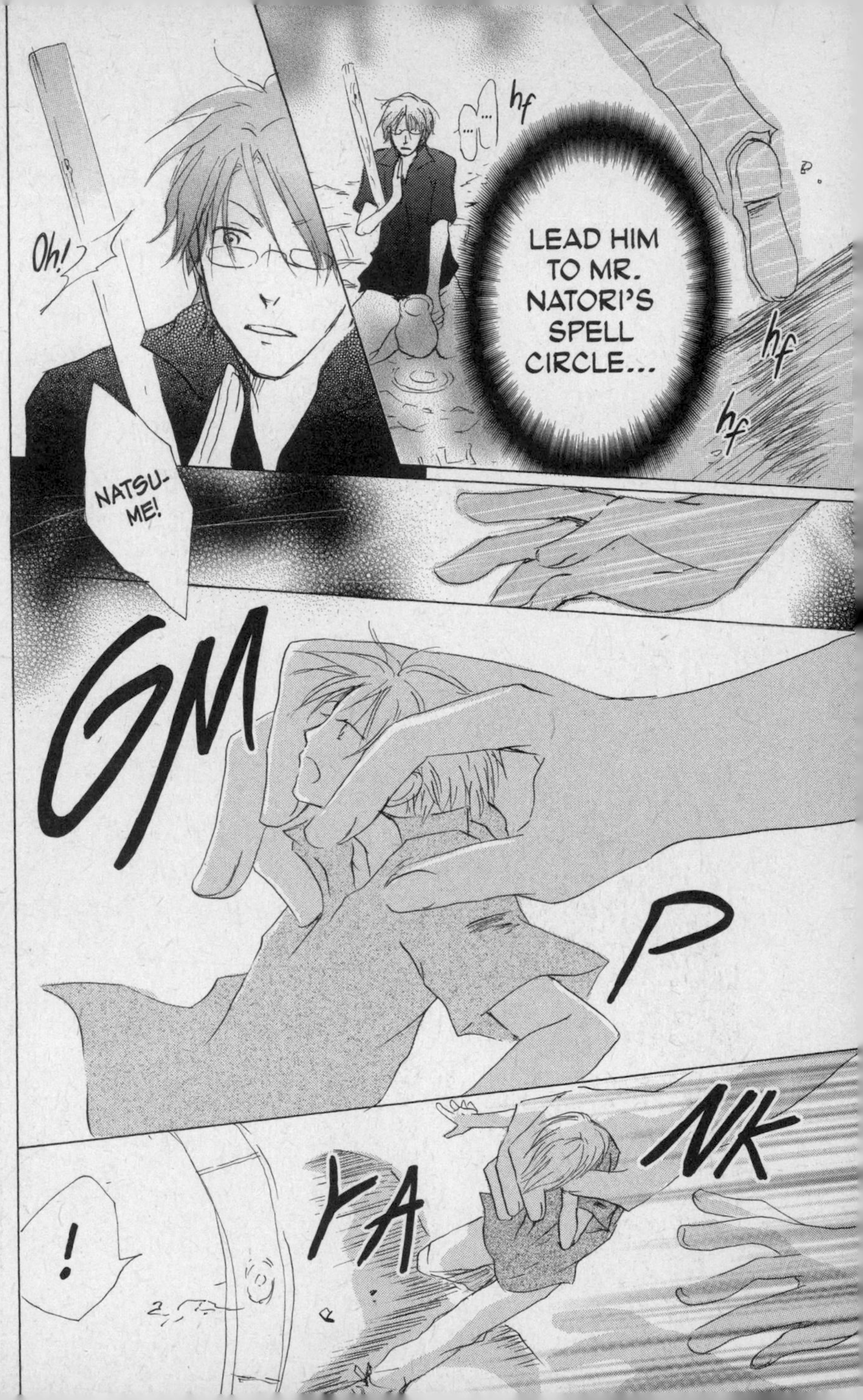
LEAD HIM TO MR. NATORI'S SPELL CIRCLE...
hf
......
hf
hf
Oh!
NATSU-ME!
GMP
YANK
!

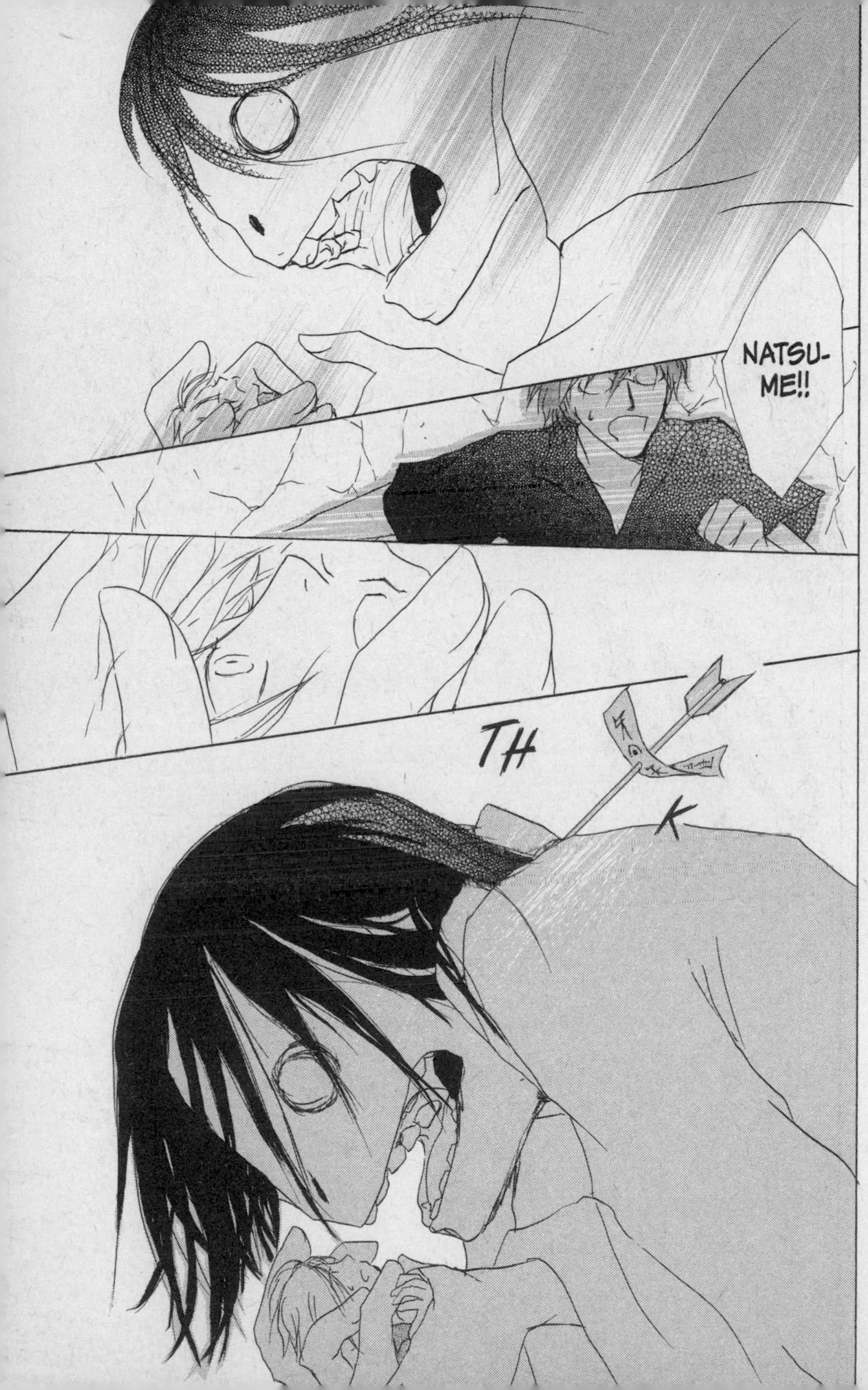
NATSU-
ME!!
TH
K

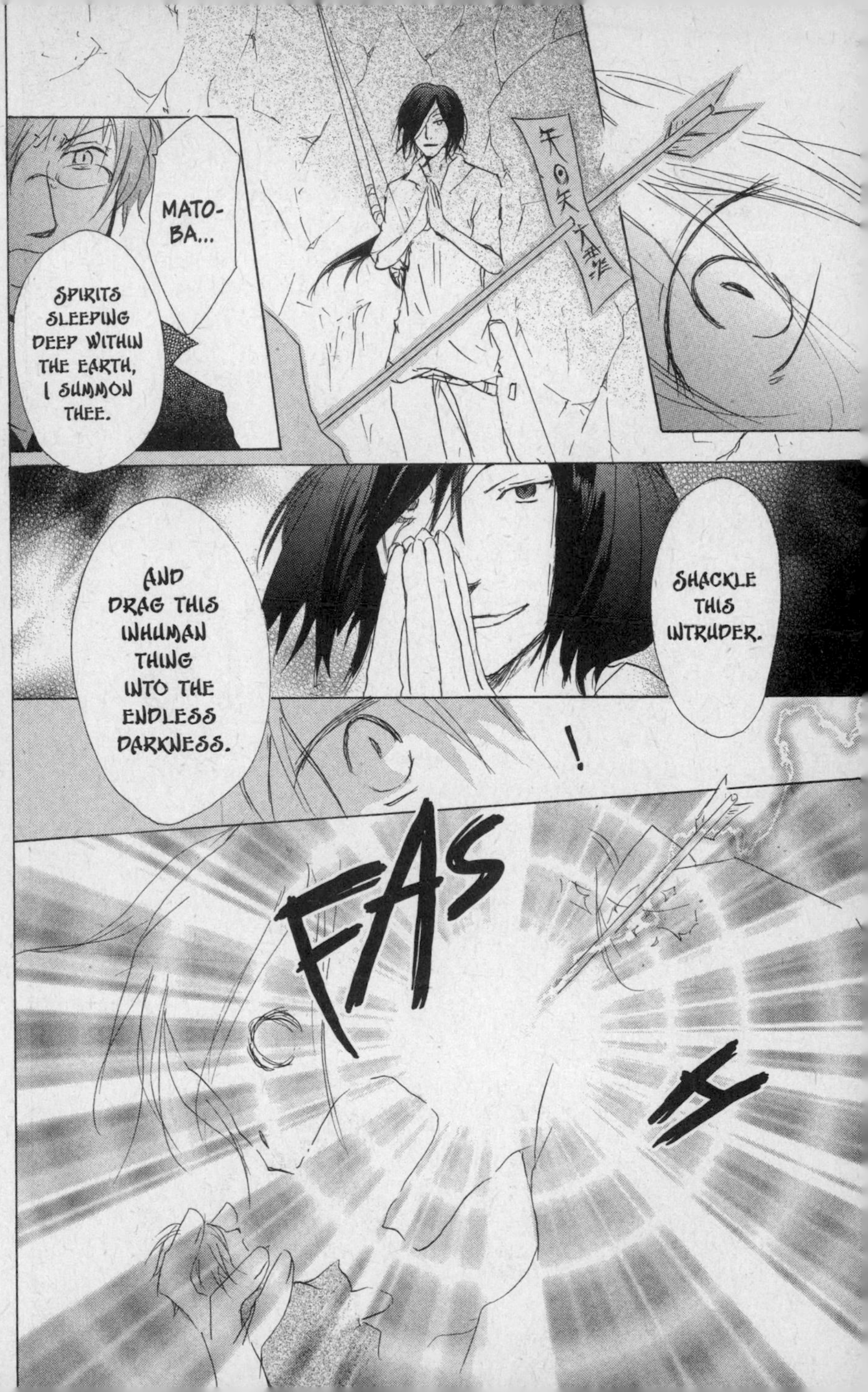
MATO-BA...
SPIRITS SLEEPING DEEP WITHIN THE EARTH, I SUMMON THEE.
SHACKLE THIS INTRUDER.
AND DRAG THIS INHUMAN THING INTO THE ENDLESS DARKNESS.
!
FASH

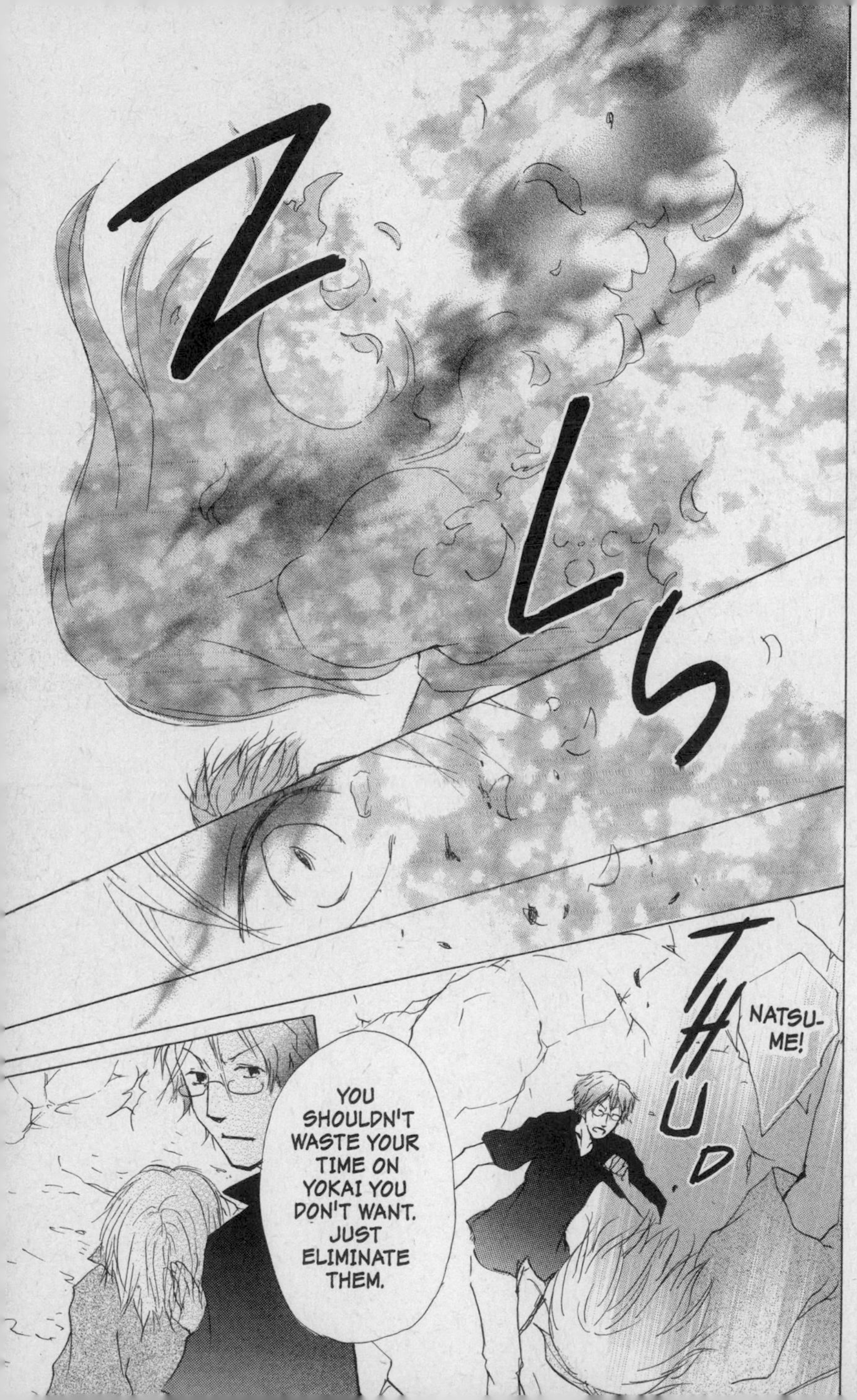
ZLLS
THUD
NATSU-ME!
YOU SHOULDN'T WASTE YOUR TIME ON YOKAI YOU DON'T WANT. JUST ELIMINATE THEM.

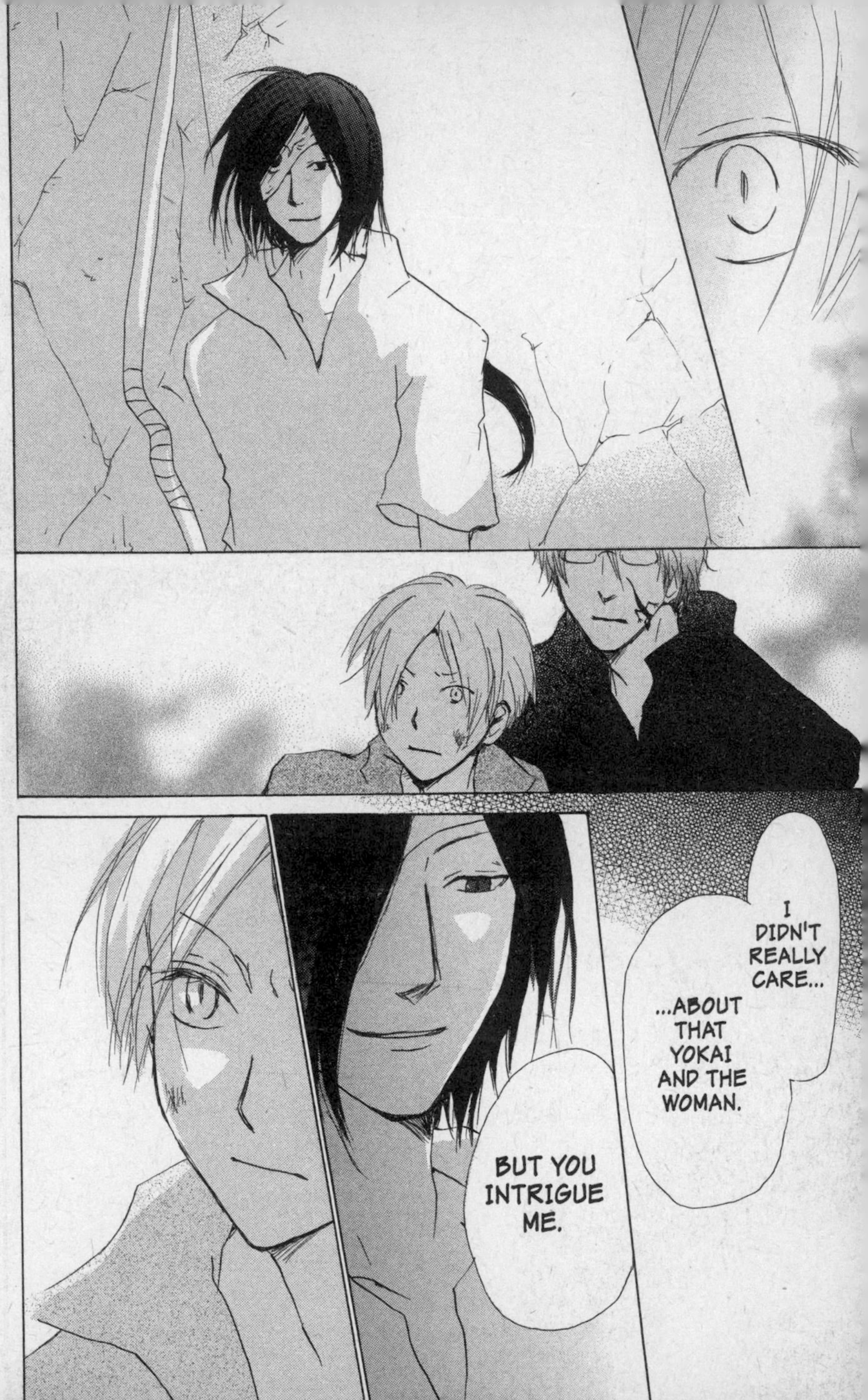
I DIDN'T REALLY CARE...
...ABOUT THAT YOKAI AND THE WOMAN.
BUT YOU INTRIGUE ME.

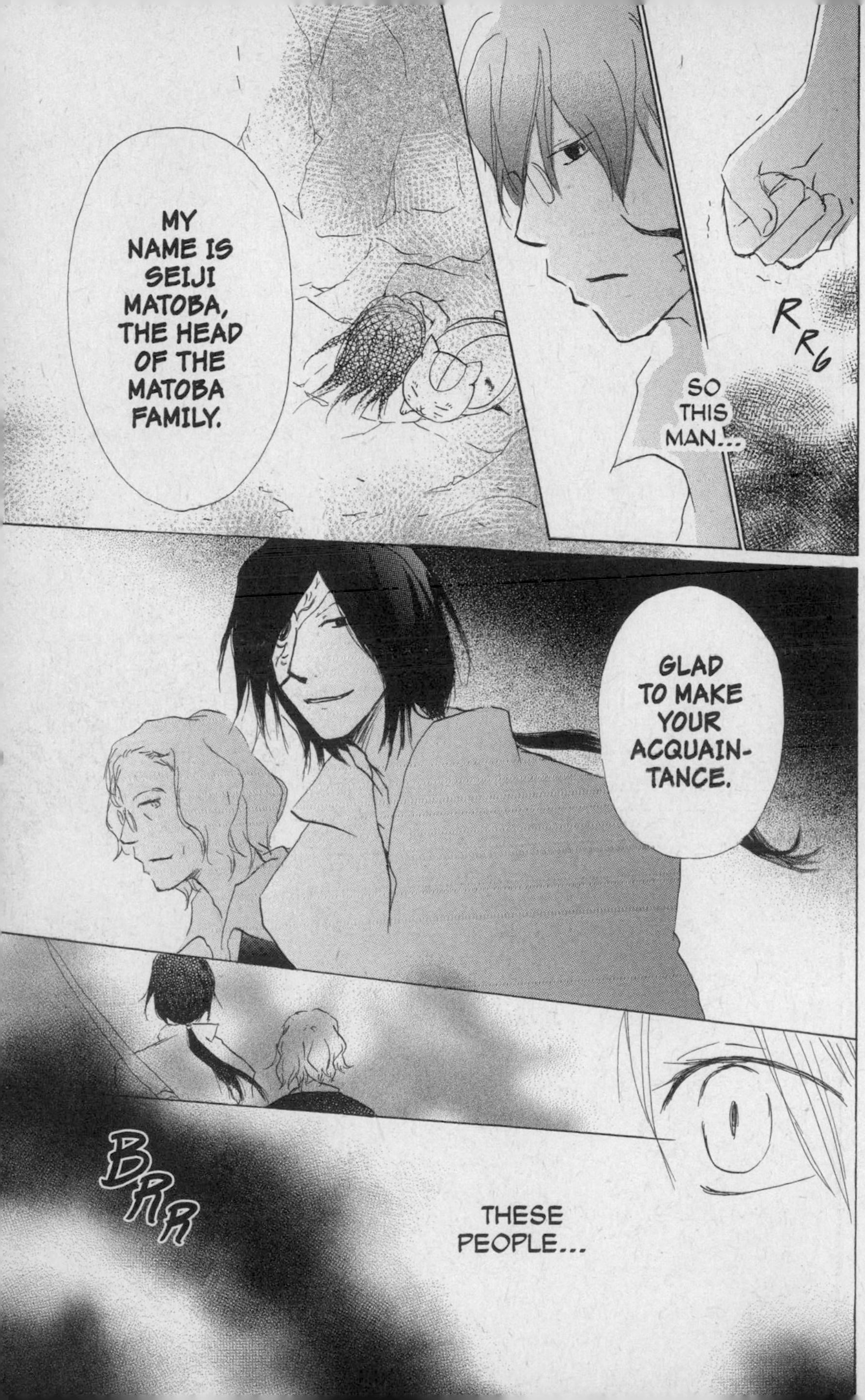
RRG
SO THIS MAN...
MY NAME IS SEIJI MATOBA, THE HEAD OF THE MATOBA FAMILY.
GLAD TO MAKE YOUR ACQUAINTANCE.
THESE PEOPLE...
BRR

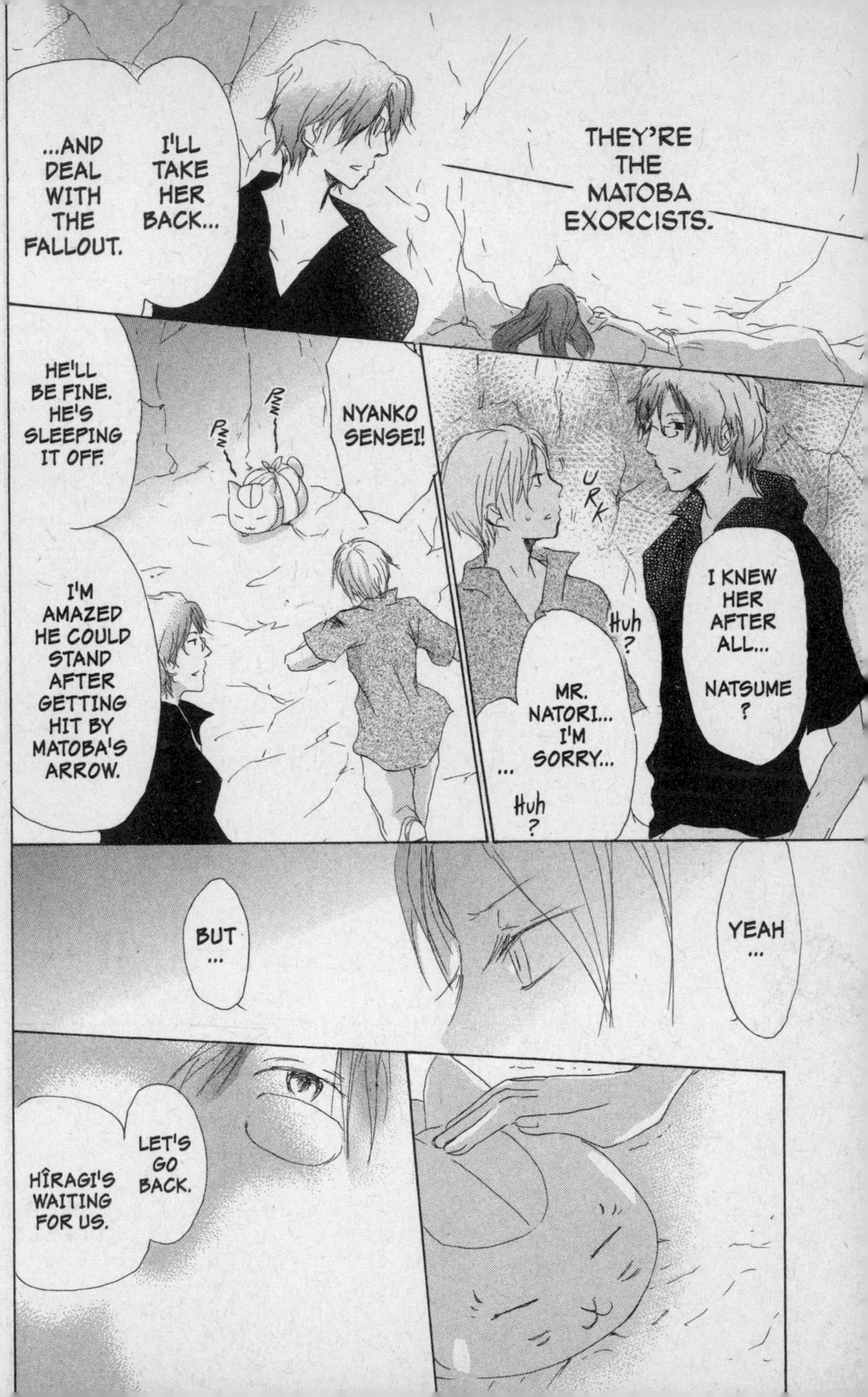
THEY'RE THE MATOBA EXORCISTS.
I'LL TAKE HER BACK...
...AND DEAL WITH THE FALLOUT.
I KNEW HER AFTER ALL... NATSUME?
URK
Huh?
MR. NATORI... I'M SORRY...
...
Huh?
NYANKO SENSEI!
PZZ
PZZ
HE'LL BE FINE. HE'S SLEEPING IT OFF.
I'M AMAZED HE COULD STAND AFTER GETTING HIT BY MATOBA'S ARROW.
YEAH ...
BUT ...
LET'S GO BACK.
HÎRAGI'S WAITING FOR US.

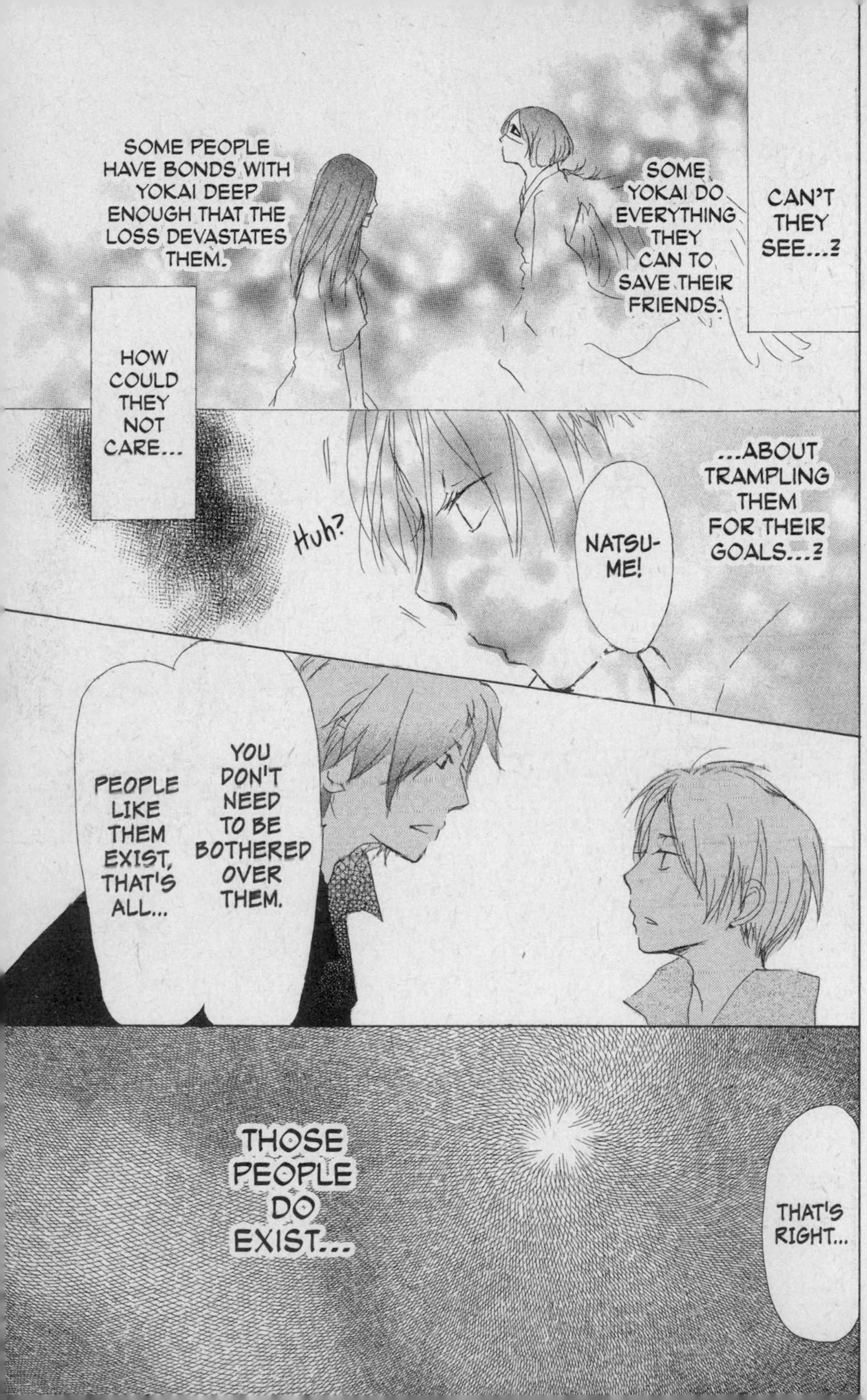
CAN'T THEY SEE...?
SOME YOKAI DO EVERYTHING THEY CAN TO SAVE THEIR FRIENDS.
SOME PEOPLE HAVE BONDS WITH YOKAI DEEP ENOUGH THAT THE LOSS DEVASTATES THEM.
HOW COULD THEY NOT CARE...
...ABOUT TRAMPLING THEM FOR THEIR GOALS...?
NATSU-ME!
Huh?
YOU DON'T NEED TO BE BOTHERED OVER THEM.
PEOPLE LIKE THEM EXIST, THAT'S ALL...
THAT'S RIGHT...
THOSE PEOPLE DO EXIST...

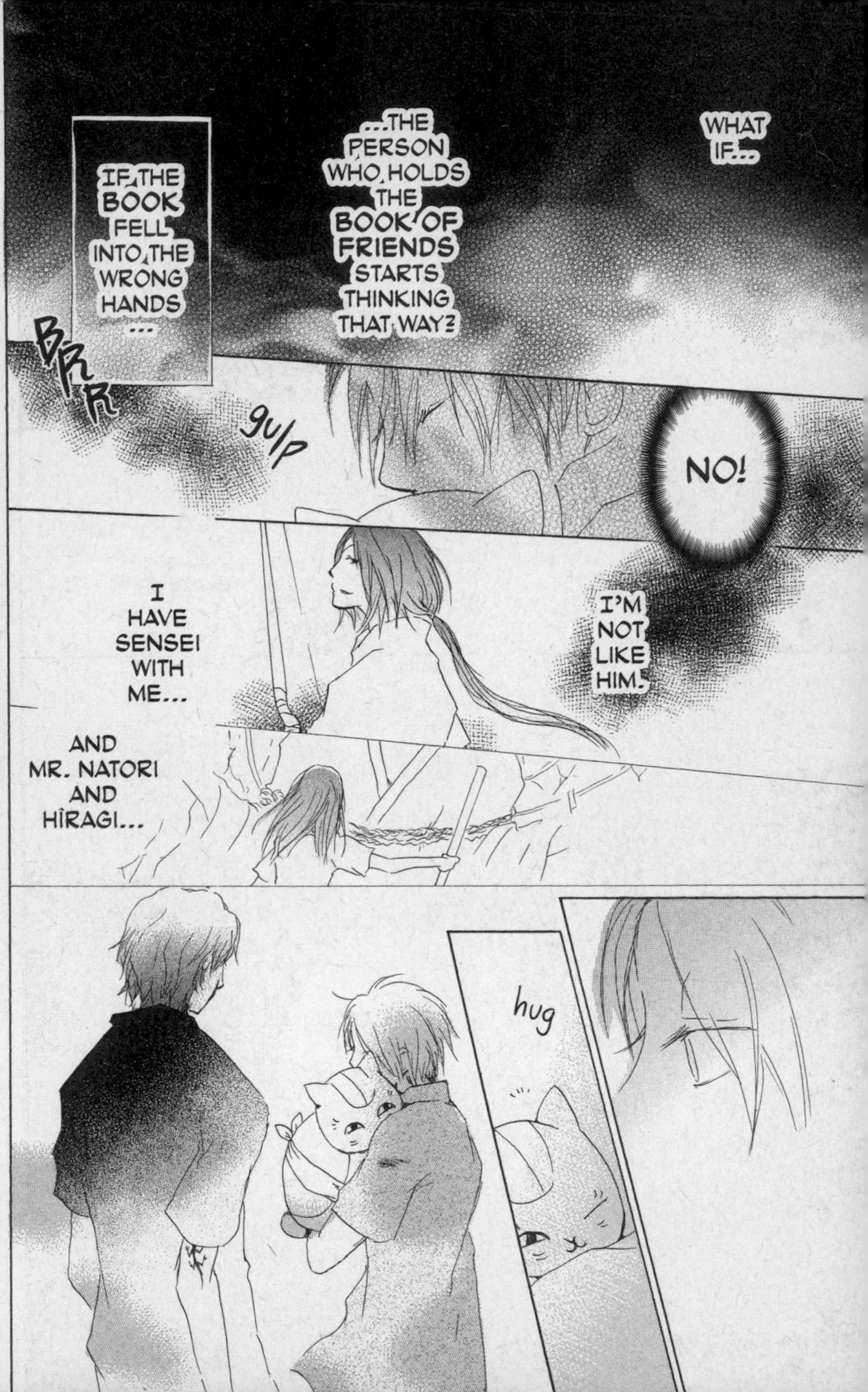
WHAT IF...
...THE PERSON WHO HOLDS THE BOOK OF FRIENDS STARTS THINKING THAT WAY?
IF THE BOOK FELL INTO THE WRONG HANDS...
BRR
NO!
gulp
I'M NOT LIKE HIM.
I HAVE SENSEI WITH ME...
AND MR. NATORI AND HÎRAGI...
hug

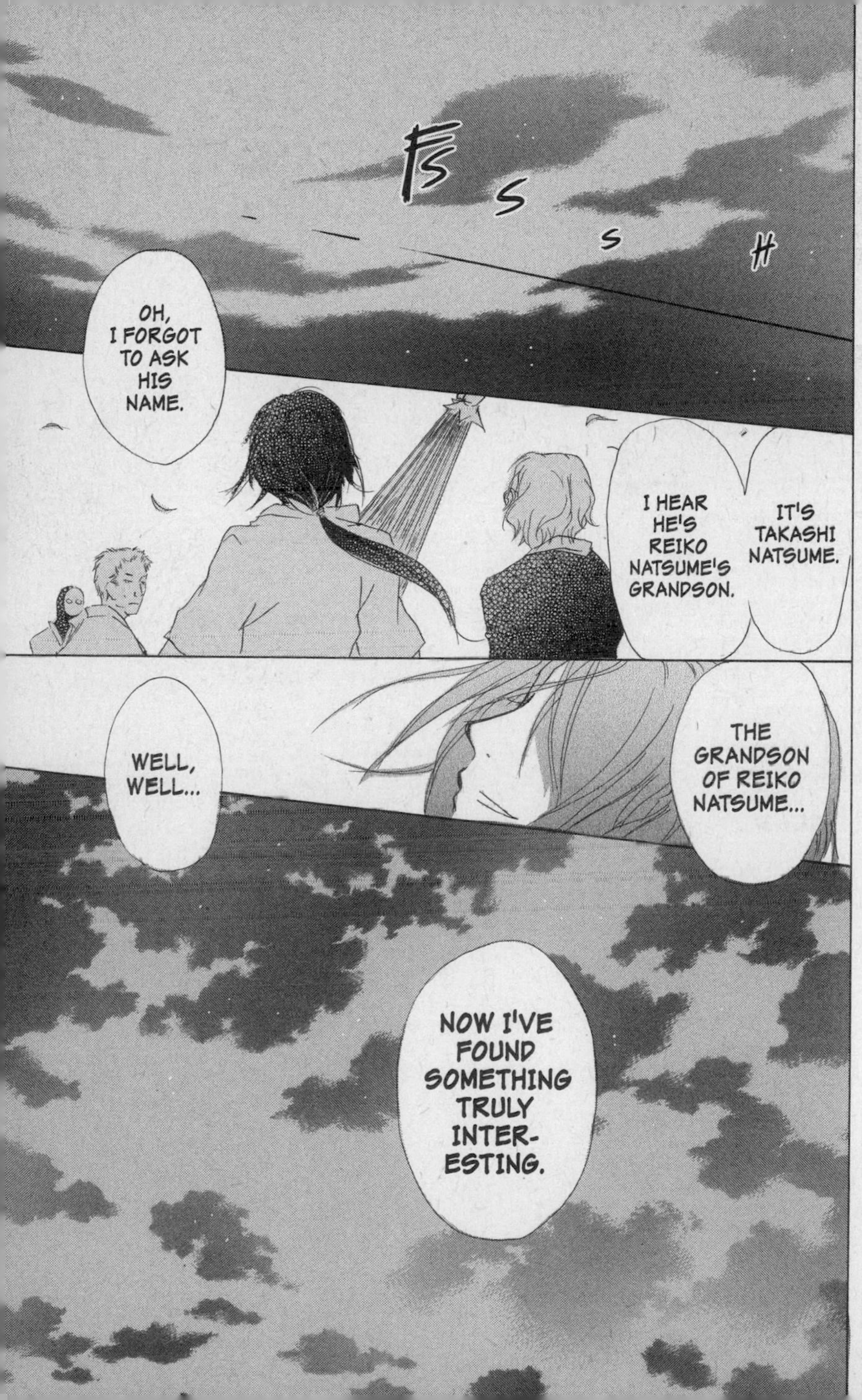
FSSSH
OH, I FORGOT TO ASK HIS NAME.
IT'S TAKASHI NATSUME.
I HEAR HE'S REIKO NATSUME'S GRANDSON.
THE GRANDSON OF REIKO NATSUME...
WELL, WELL...
NOW I'VE FOUND SOMETHING TRULY INTER-ESTING.

## SOMETHING'S WEIRD WITH NYANKO SENSEI!

Can you spot the four differences?

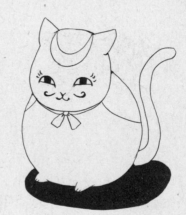

### ANSWERS:

* 1. His Bell is a Bow.
* 2. The pattern on his forehead.
* 3. The length of his tail.
* 4. Chobi moustache.

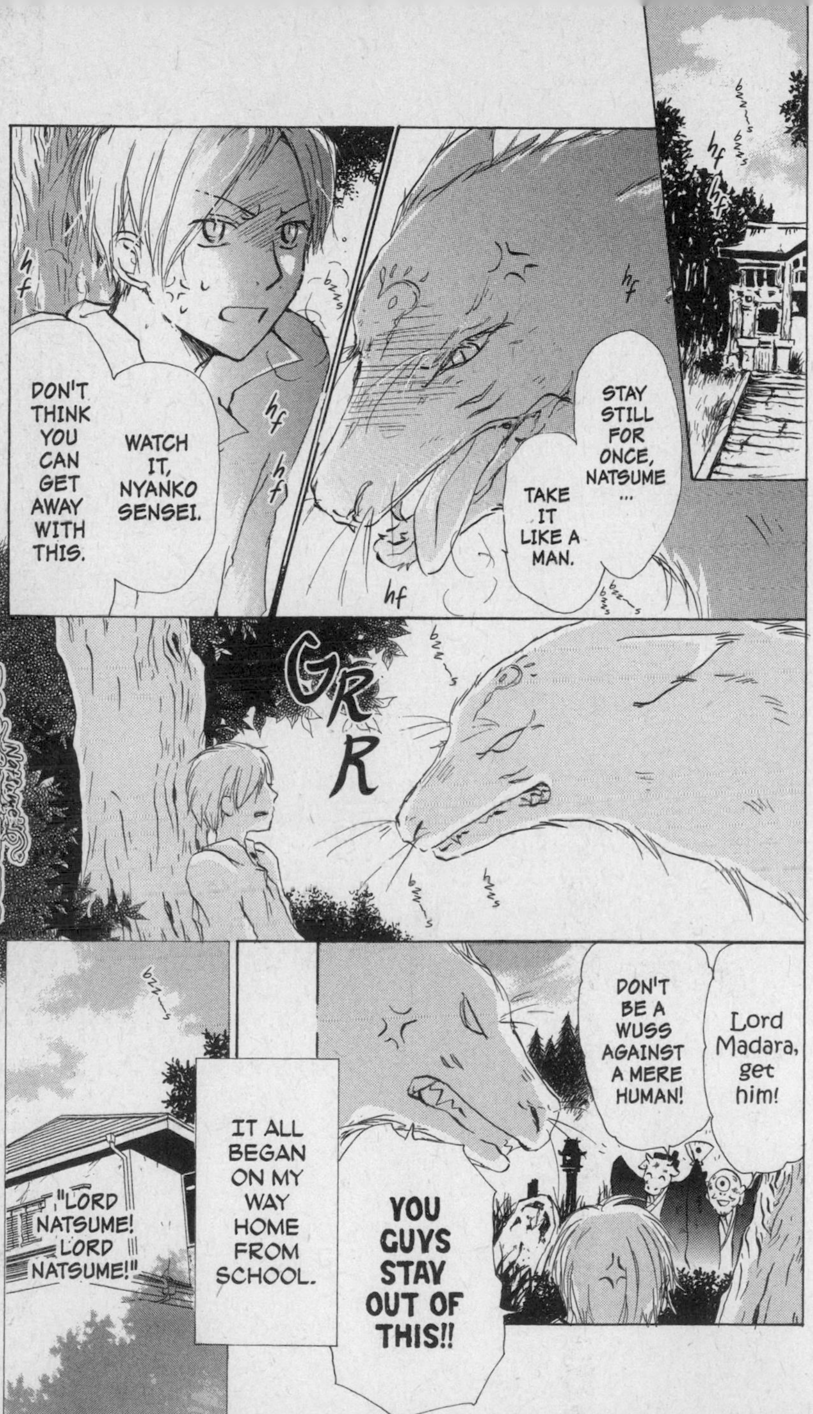

bzz
hf
hf
STAY STILL FOR ONCE, NATSUME...
TAKE IT LIKE A MAN.
hf
WATCH IT, NYANKO SENSEI.
DON'T THINK YOU CAN GET AWAY WITH THIS.
hf
GRR
bzz
Lord Madara, get him!
DON'T BE A WUSS AGAINST A MERE HUMAN!
YOU GUYS STAY OUT OF THIS!!
IT ALL BEGAN ON MY WAY HOME FROM SCHOOL.
"LORD NATSUME! LORD NATSUME!"

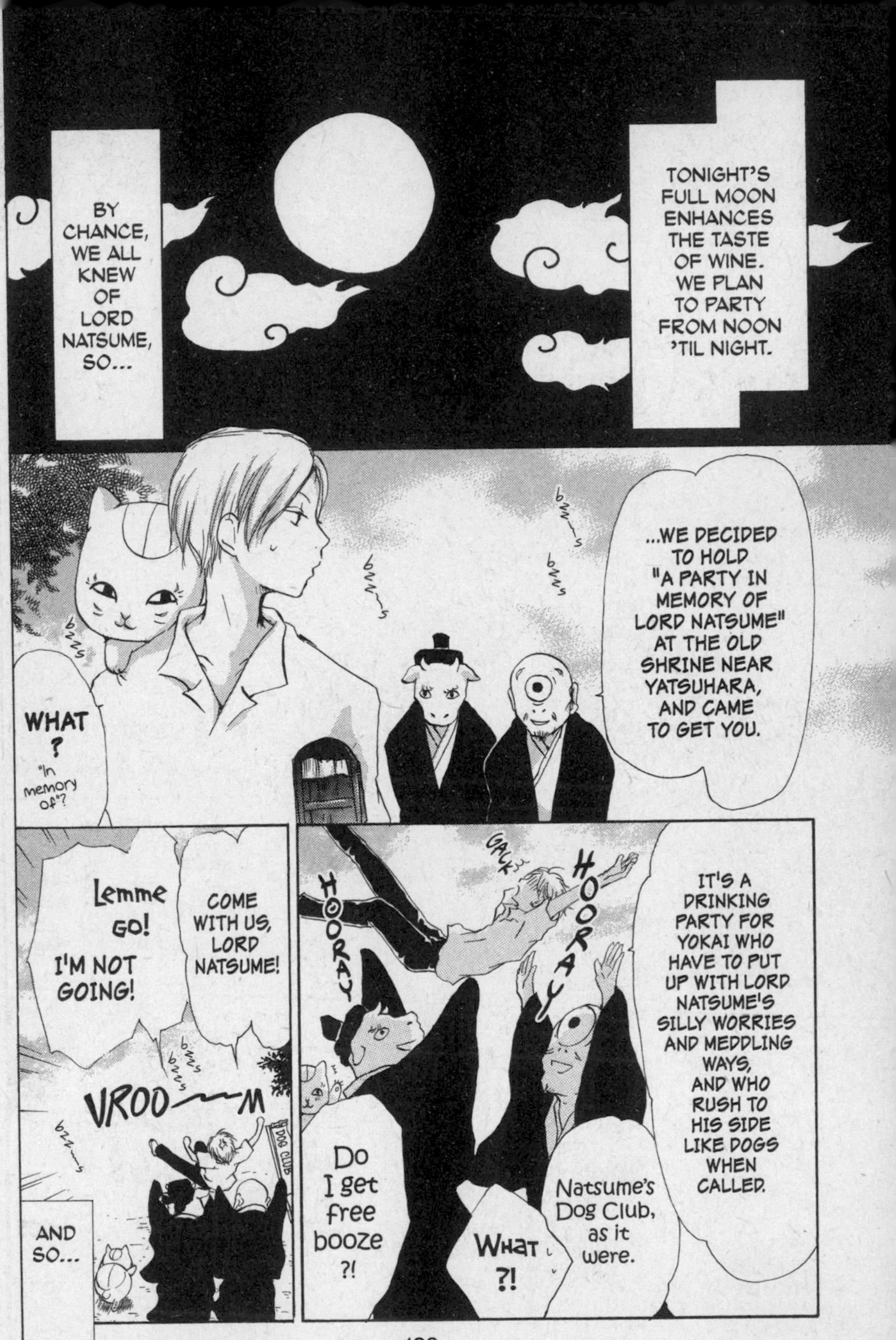
TONIGHT'S FULL MOON ENHANCES THE TASTE OF WINE. WE PLAN TO PARTY FROM NOON 'TIL NIGHT.
BY CHANCE, WE ALL KNEW OF LORD NATSUME, SO...
...WE DECIDED TO HOLD "A PARTY IN MEMORY OF LORD NATSUME" AT THE OLD SHRINE NEAR YATSUHARA, AND CAME TO GET YOU.
WHAT?
"In memory of"?
IT'S A DRINKING PARTY FOR YOKAI WHO HAVE TO PUT UP WITH LORD NATSUME'S SILLY WORRIES AND MEDDLING WAYS, AND WHO RUSH TO HIS SIDE LIKE DOGS WHEN CALLED.
HOORAY
GACK
HOORAY
Natsume's Dog Club, as it were.
WHAT?!
Do I get free booze?!
COME WITH US, LORD NATSUME!
Lemme go!
I'M NOT GOING!
VROO~M
DOG CLUB
AND SO...

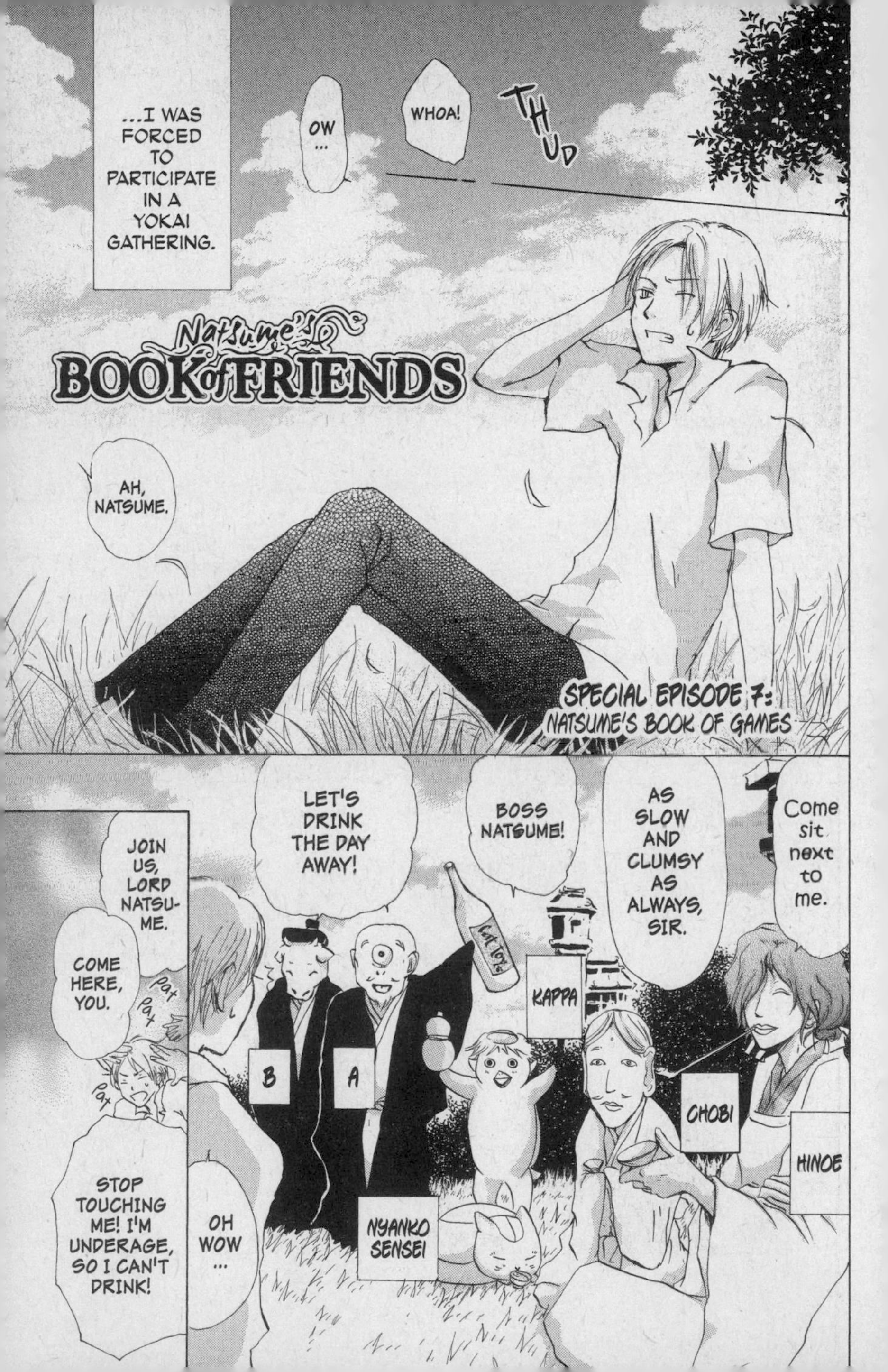
THUD
WHOA!
OW ...
...I WAS FORCED TO PARTICIPATE IN A YOKAI GATHERING.
Natsume's BOOK of FRIENDS
AH, NATSUME.
SPECIAL EPISODE 7: NATSUME'S BOOK OF GAMES
Come sit next to me.
AS SLOW AND CLUMSY AS ALWAYS, SIR.
BOSS NATSUME!
LET'S DRINK THE DAY AWAY!
JOIN US, LORD NATSU-ME.
COME HERE, YOU.
Pat
Pat
Pat
HINOE
CHOBI
KAPPA
A
B
NYANKO SENSEI
OH WOW ...
STOP TOUCHING ME! I'M UNDERAGE, SO I CAN'T DRINK!

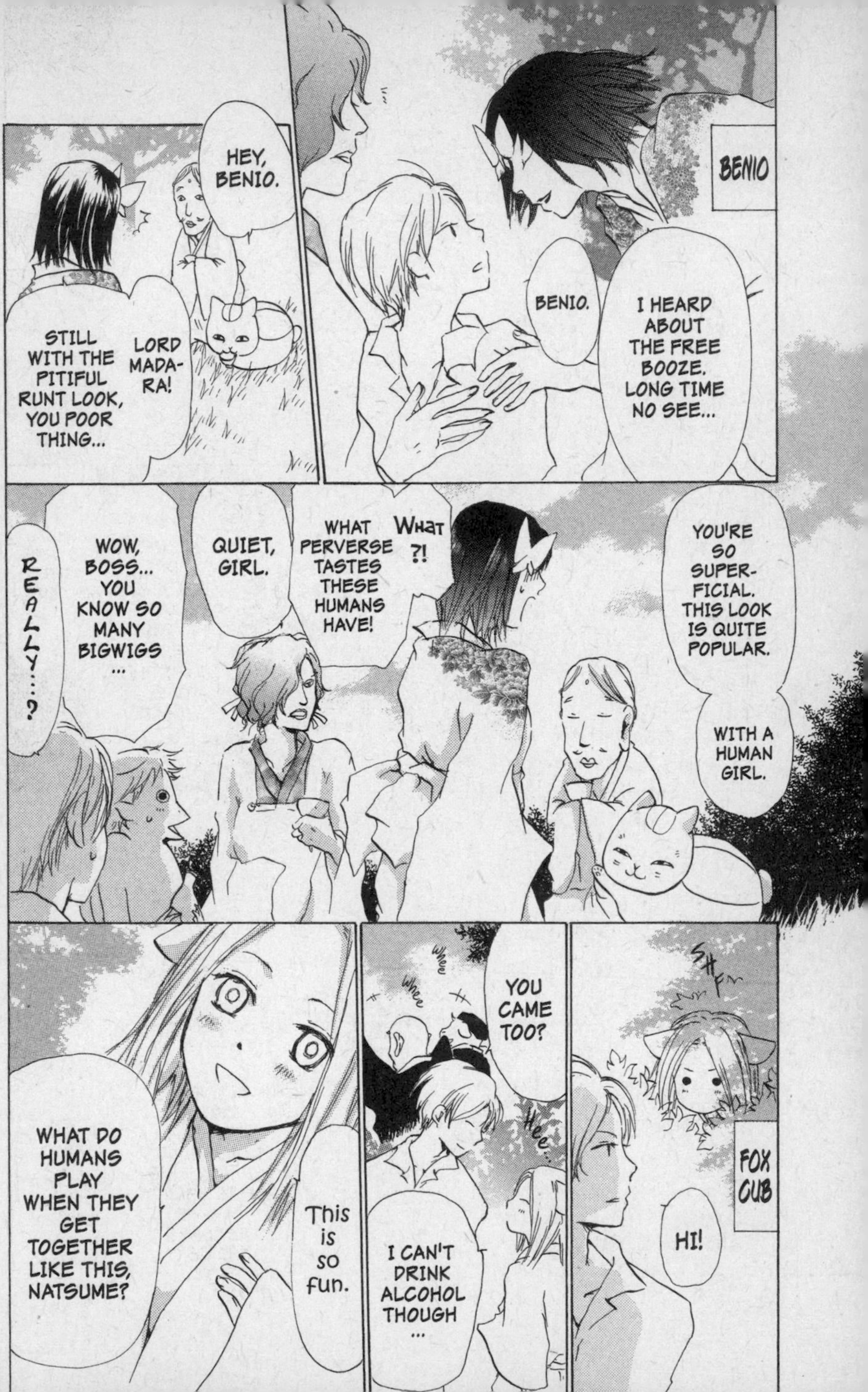
BENIO
I HEARD ABOUT THE FREE BOOZE. LONG TIME NO SEE...
BENIO.
HEY, BENIO.
LORD MADARA!
STILL WITH THE PITIFUL RUNT LOOK, YOU POOR THING...
YOU'RE SO SUPERFICIAL. THIS LOOK IS QUITE POPULAR.
WITH A HUMAN GIRL.
What?!
WHAT PERVERSE TASTES THESE HUMANS HAVE!
QUIET, GIRL.
WOW, BOSS... YOU KNOW SO MANY BIGWIGS...
REALLY...?
SHF
FOX CUB
HI!
YOU CAME TOO?
Whee
Whee
Hee...
I CAN'T DRINK ALCOHOL THOUGH...
This is so fun.
WHAT DO HUMANS PLAY WHEN THEY GET TOGETHER LIKE THIS, NATSUME?

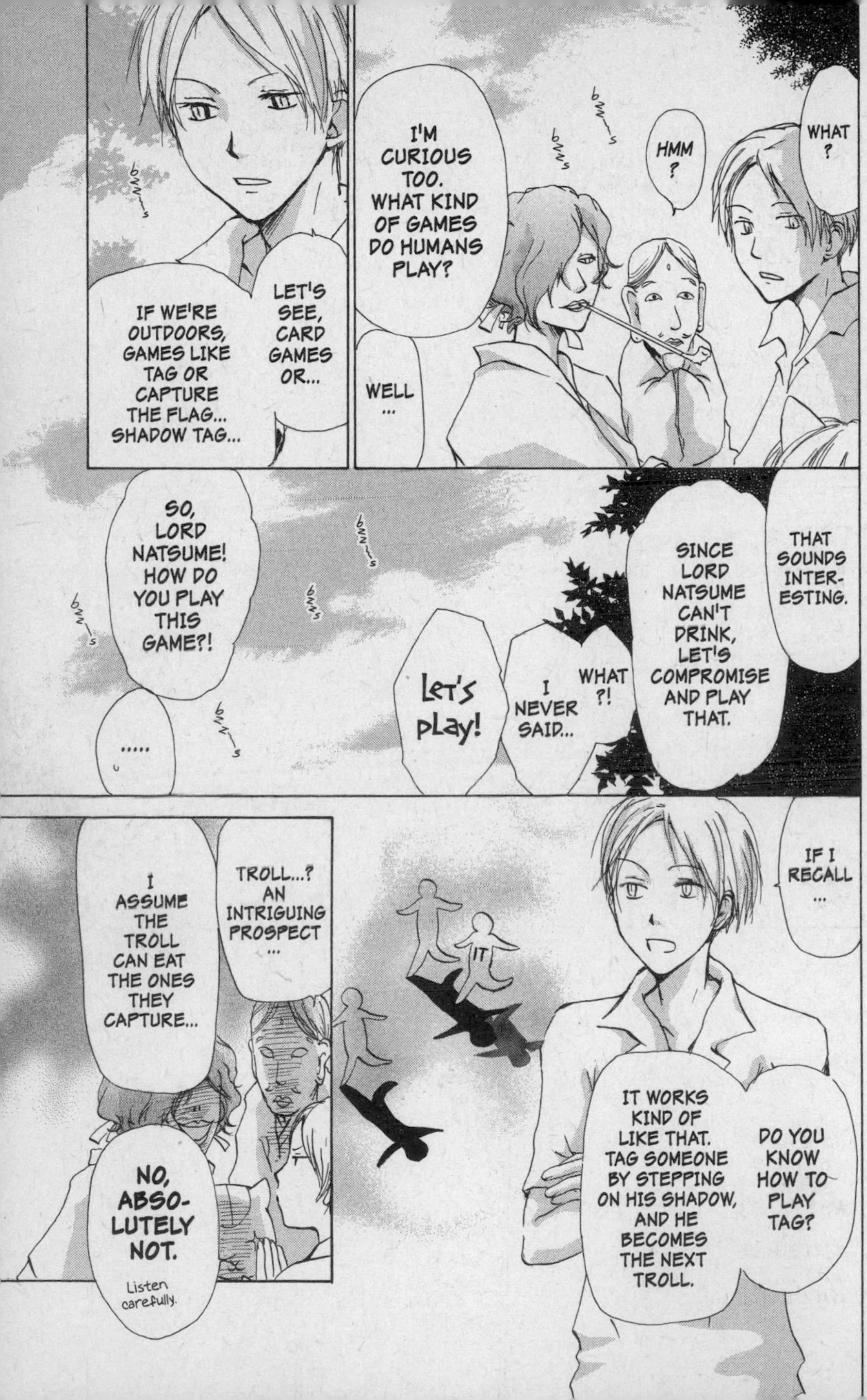
WHAT?
HMM?
I'M CURIOUS TOO. WHAT KIND OF GAMES DO HUMANS PLAY?
WELL ...
LET'S SEE, CARD GAMES OR...
IF WE'RE OUTDOORS, GAMES LIKE TAG OR CAPTURE THE FLAG... SHADOW TAG...
THAT SOUNDS INTERESTING.
SINCE LORD NATSUME CAN'T DRINK, LET'S COMPROMISE AND PLAY THAT.
WHAT?!
I NEVER SAID...
Let's play!
SO, LORD NATSUME! HOW DO YOU PLAY THIS GAME?!
......
IF I RECALL ...
DO YOU KNOW HOW TO PLAY TAG?
IT WORKS KIND OF LIKE THAT. TAG SOMEONE BY STEPPING ON HIS SHADOW, AND HE BECOMES THE NEXT TROLL.
IT
TROLL...? AN INTRIGUING PROSPECT ...
I ASSUME THE TROLL CAN EAT THE ONES THEY CAPTURE...
NO, ABSOLUTELY NOT.
Listen carefully.

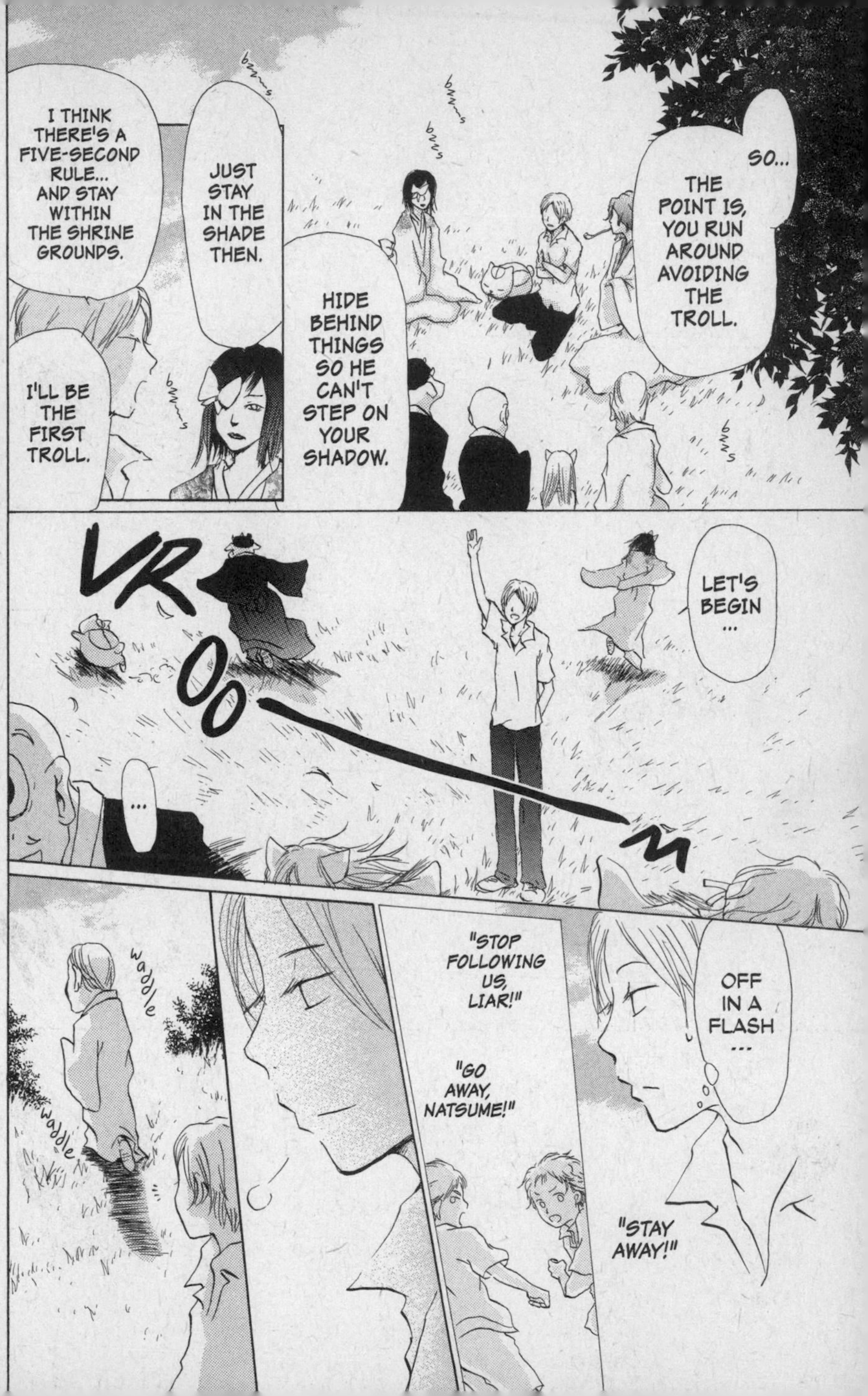
SO... THE POINT IS, YOU RUN AROUND AVOIDING THE TROLL.
HIDE BEHIND THINGS SO HE CAN'T STEP ON YOUR SHADOW.
JUST STAY IN THE SHADE THEN.
I THINK THERE'S A FIVE-SECOND RULE... AND STAY WITHIN THE SHRINE GROUNDS.
I'LL BE THE FIRST TROLL.
LET'S BEGIN ...
VROOOM
...
OFF IN A FLASH ...
"STOP FOLLOWING US, LIAR!"
"GO AWAY, NATSUME!"
"STAY AWAY!"
waddle
waddle

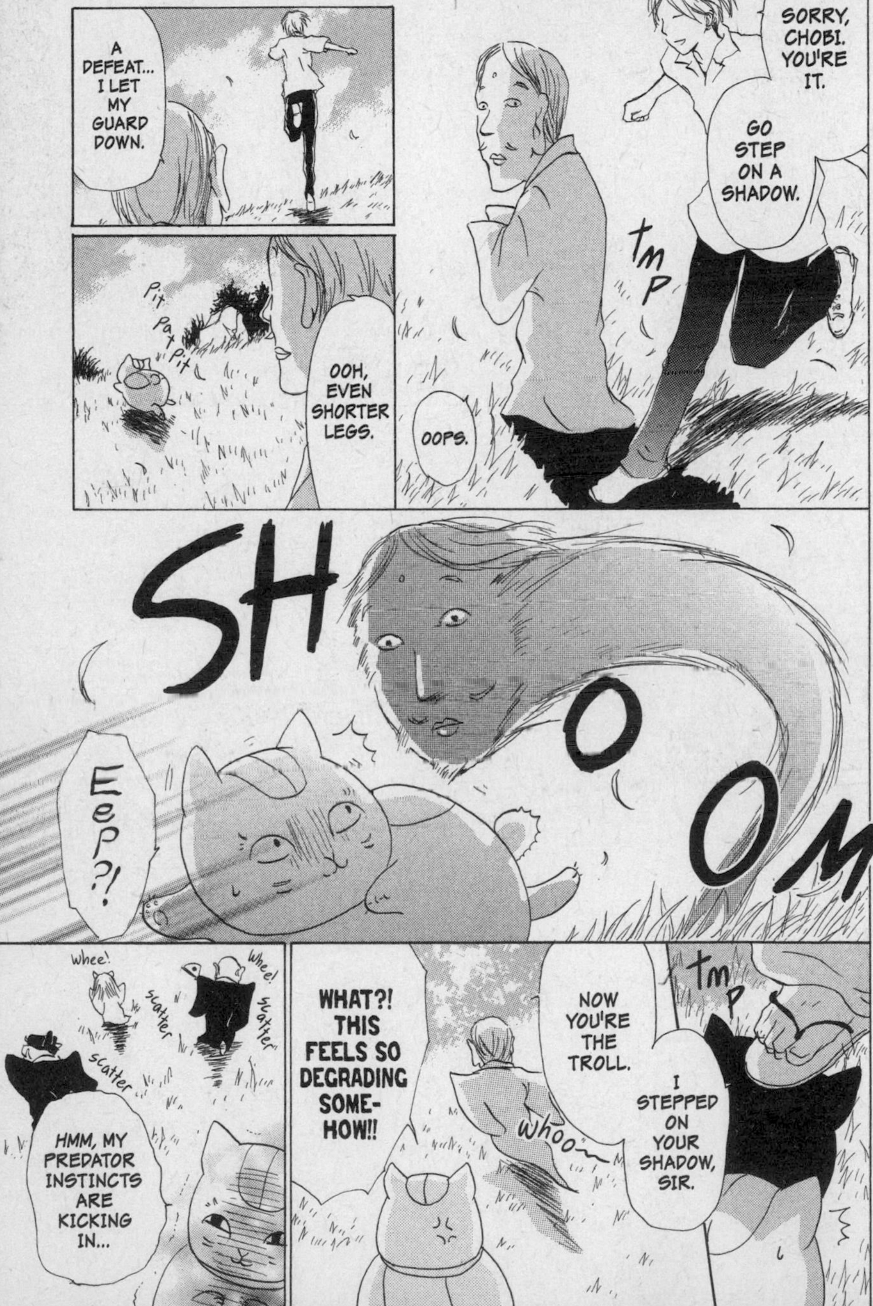
SORRY, CHOBI. YOU'RE IT.
GO STEP ON A SHADOW.
tmp
OOPS.
A DEFEAT... I LET MY GUARD DOWN.
Pit Pat Pit
OOH, EVEN SHORTER LEGS.
SHOOOM
Eep?!
tmp
NOW YOU'RE THE TROLL.
I STEPPED ON YOUR SHADOW, SIR.
whoo~
WHAT?! THIS FEELS SO DEGRADING SOME-HOW!!
whee!
whee!
scatter
scatter
scatter
HMM, MY PREDATOR INSTINCTS ARE KICKING IN...

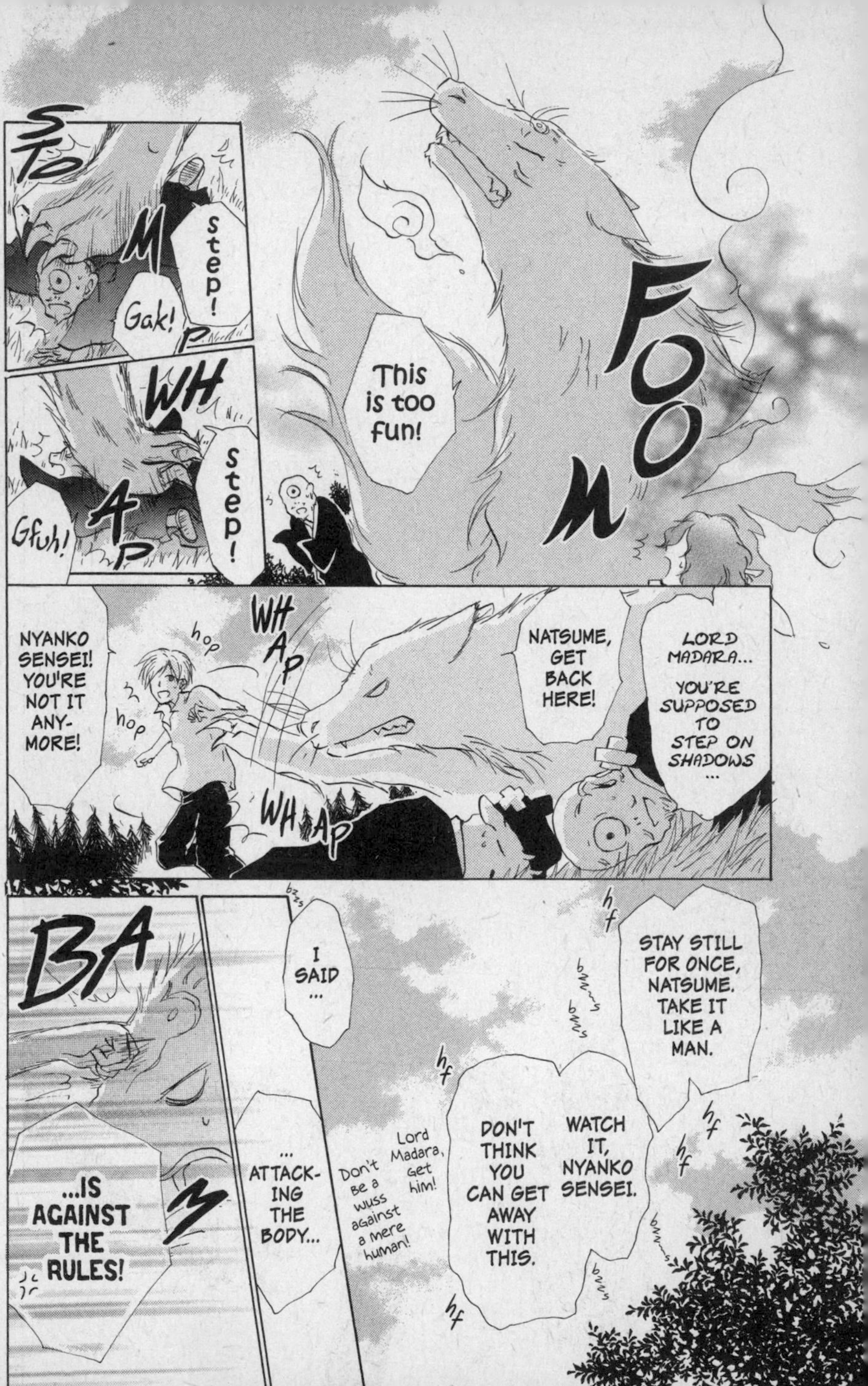
This is too fun!
FOOM
STOMP
step!
Gak!
WHAP
step!
Gfuh!
LORD MADARA... YOU'RE SUPPOSED TO STEP ON SHADOWS...
NATSUME, GET BACK HERE!
WHAP
WHAP
hop
hop
NYANKO SENSEI! YOU'RE NOT IT ANY-MORE!
STAY STILL FOR ONCE, NATSUME. TAKE IT LIKE A MAN.
WATCH IT, NYANKO SENSEI.
DON'T THINK YOU CAN GET AWAY WITH THIS.
Lord Madara, Get him!
Don't be a wuss against a mere human!
I SAID...
...ATTACK-ING THE BODY...
BAM
...IS AGAINST THE RULES!

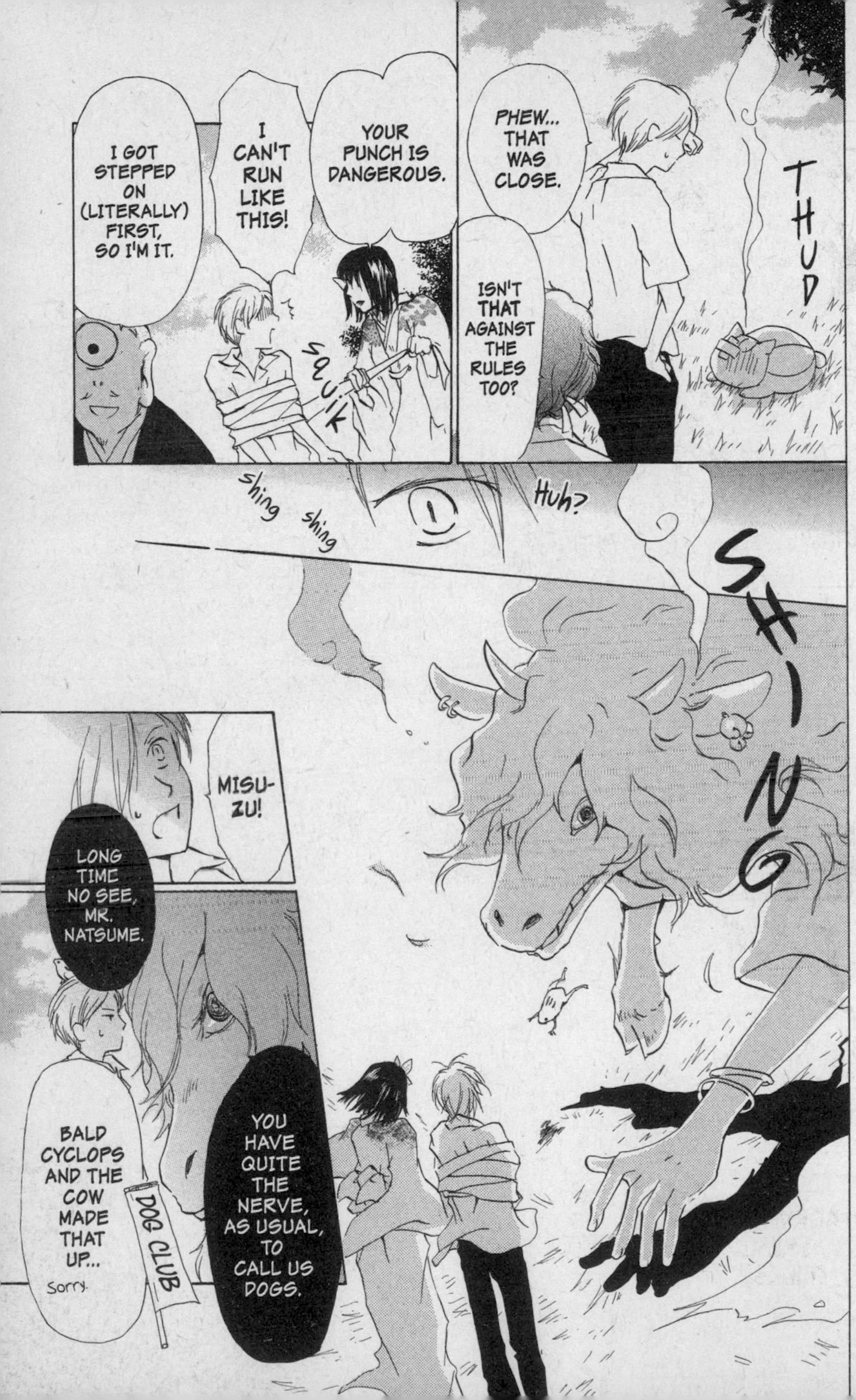
THUD
PHEW... THAT WAS CLOSE.
ISN'T THAT AGAINST THE RULES TOO?
YOUR PUNCH IS DANGEROUS.
I CAN'T RUN LIKE THIS!
I GOT STEPPED ON (LITERALLY) FIRST, SO I'M IT.
SQUIK
Huh?
shing shing
SHING
MISU-ZU!
LONG TIME NO SEE, MR. NATSUME.
YOU HAVE QUITE THE NERVE, AS USUAL, TO CALL US DOGS.
BALD CYCLOPS AND THE COW MADE THAT UP...
Sorry.
DOG CLUB

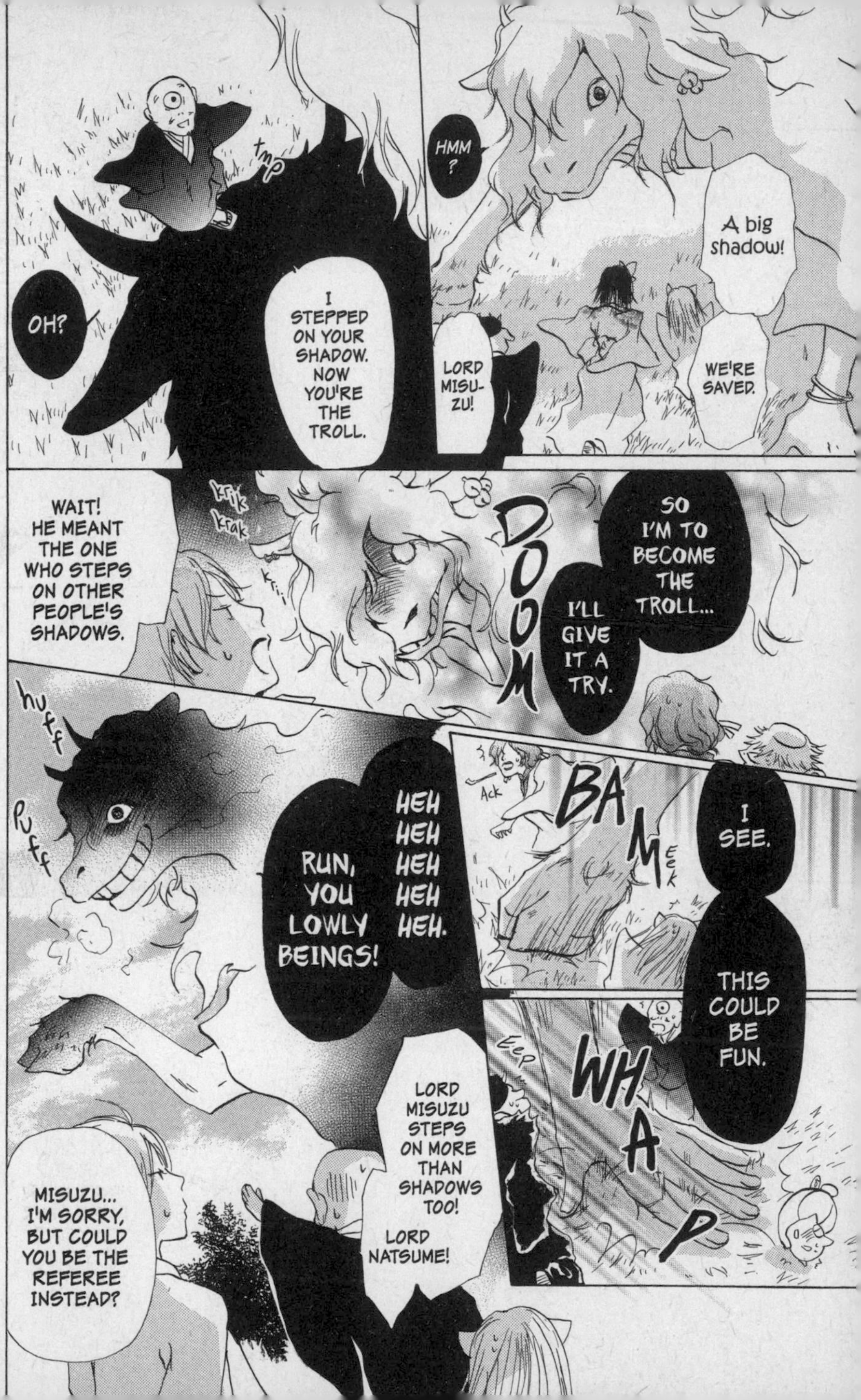
HMM ?
A big shadow!
WE'RE SAVED.
LORD MISU-ZU!
tmp
I STEPPED ON YOUR SHADOW. NOW YOU'RE THE TROLL.
OH?
SO I'M TO BECOME THE TROLL...
I'LL GIVE IT A TRY.
DOOOM
krik krak
kri
WAIT! HE MEANT THE ONE WHO STEPS ON OTHER PEOPLE'S SHADOWS.
BAM
Ack
Eek
I SEE.
THIS COULD BE FUN.
WHAP
Eep
huff
puff
HEH HEH HEH HEH HEH.
RUN, YOU LOWLY BEINGS!
LORD MISUZU STEPS ON MORE THAN SHADOWS TOO!
LORD NATSUME!
MISUZU... I'M SORRY, BUT COULD YOU BE THE REFEREE INSTEAD?

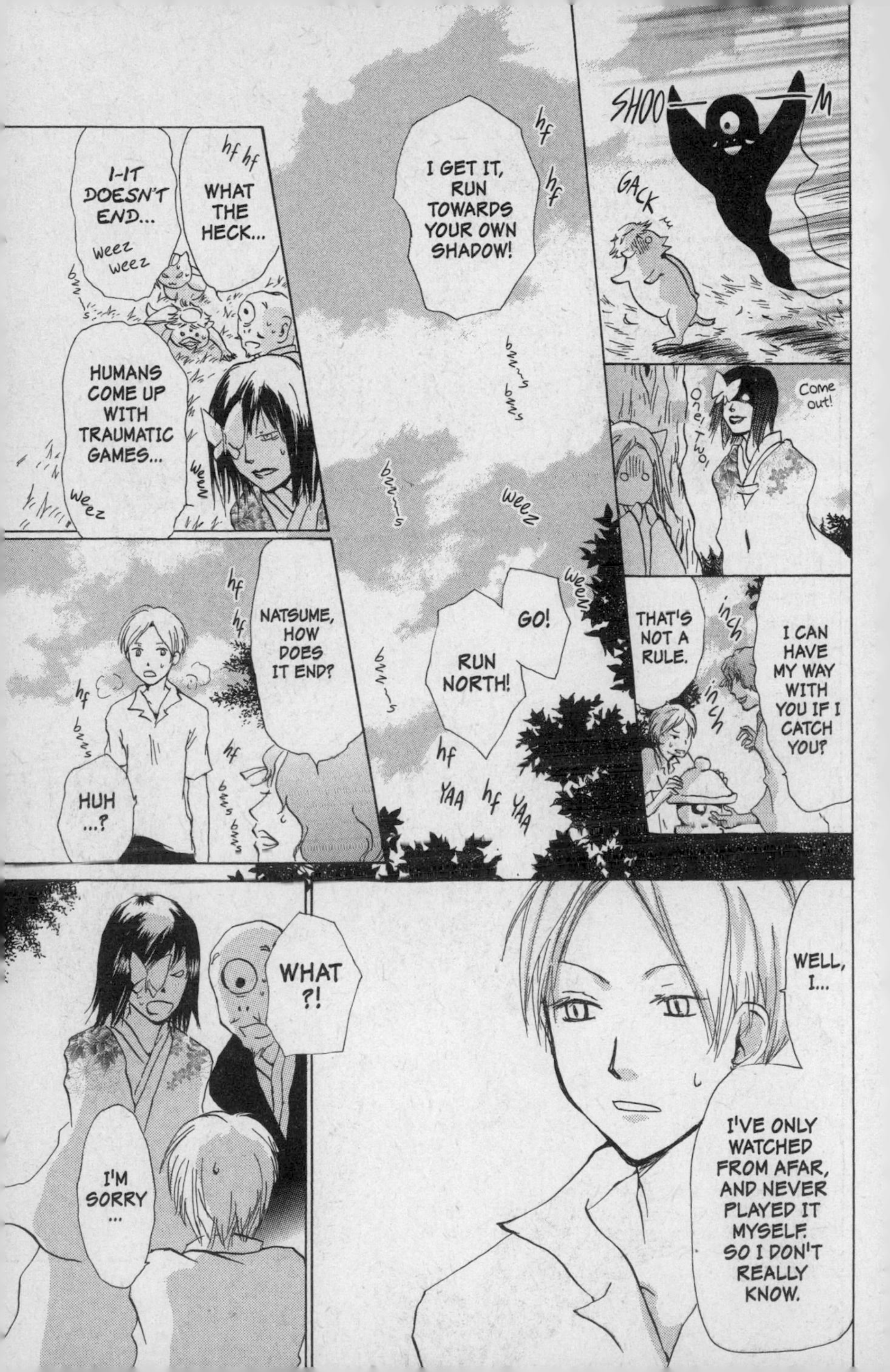
SHOOM
GACK
Come out!
One! Two!
I CAN HAVE MY WAY WITH YOU IF I CATCH YOU?
inch inch
THAT'S NOT A RULE.
hf hf
I GET IT, RUN TOWARDS YOUR OWN SHADOW!
bzzs bzzs
weez
GO!
RUN NORTH!
hf YAA hf YAA
WHAT THE HECK...
hf hf
I-IT DOESN'T END...
weez weez
HUMANS COME UP WITH TRAUMATIC GAMES...
weez
hf hf
NATSUME, HOW DOES IT END?
HUH ...?
WELL, I...
I'VE ONLY WATCHED FROM AFAR, AND NEVER PLAYED IT MYSELF. SO I DON'T REALLY KNOW.
WHAT ?!
I'M SORRY ...

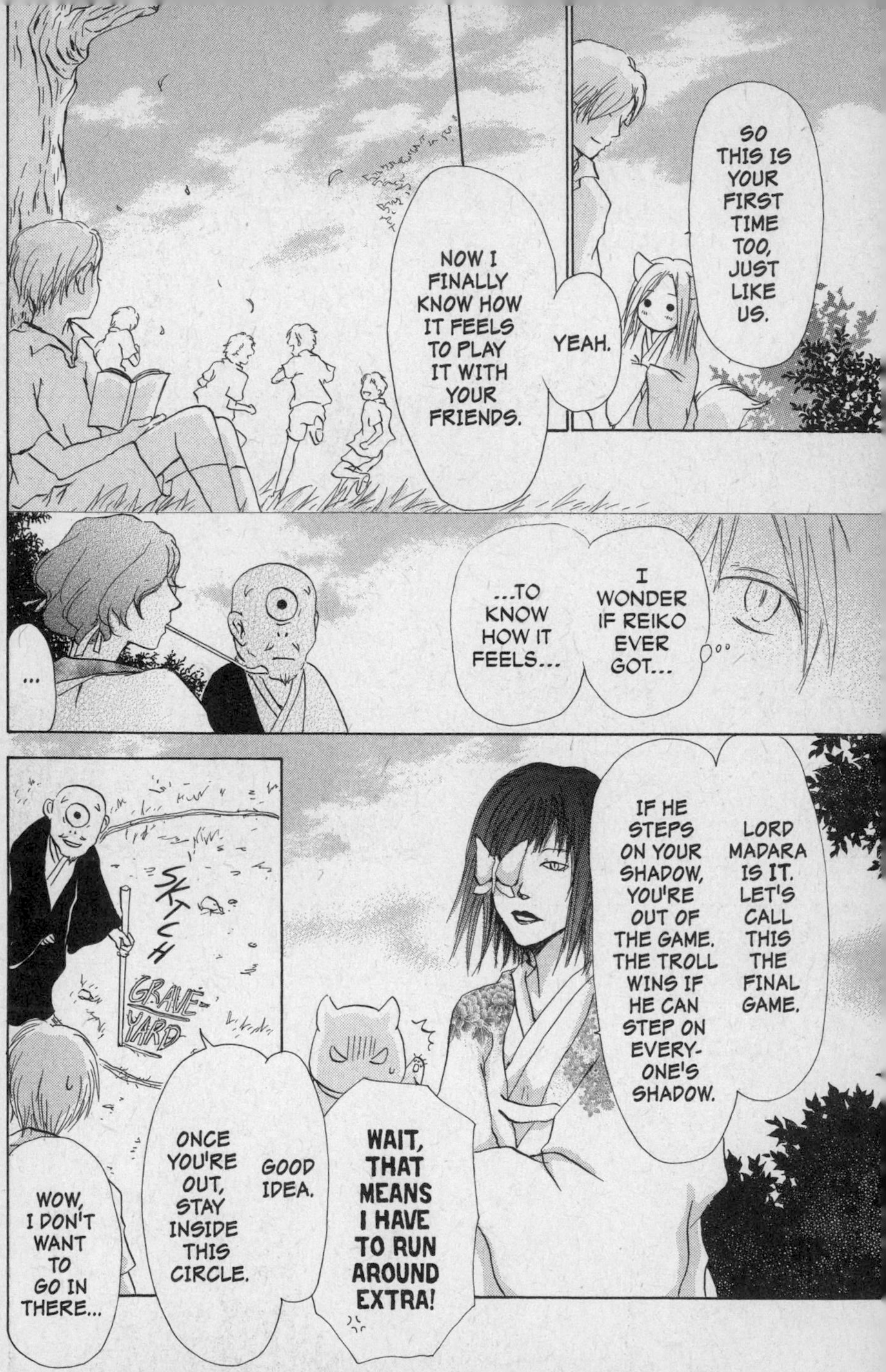
SO THIS IS YOUR FIRST TIME TOO, JUST LIKE US.
YEAH.
NOW I FINALLY KNOW HOW IT FEELS TO PLAY IT WITH YOUR FRIENDS.
I WONDER IF REIKO EVER GOT...
...TO KNOW HOW IT FEELS...
...
LORD MADARA IS IT. LET'S CALL THIS THE FINAL GAME.
IF HE STEPS ON YOUR SHADOW, YOU'RE OUT OF THE GAME. THE TROLL WINS IF HE CAN STEP ON EVERY-ONE'S SHADOW.
WAIT, THAT MEANS I HAVE TO RUN AROUND EXTRA!
GOOD IDEA.
SKTCH
GRAVE-YARD
ONCE YOU'RE OUT, STAY INSIDE THIS CIRCLE.
WOW, I DON'T WANT TO GO IN THERE...

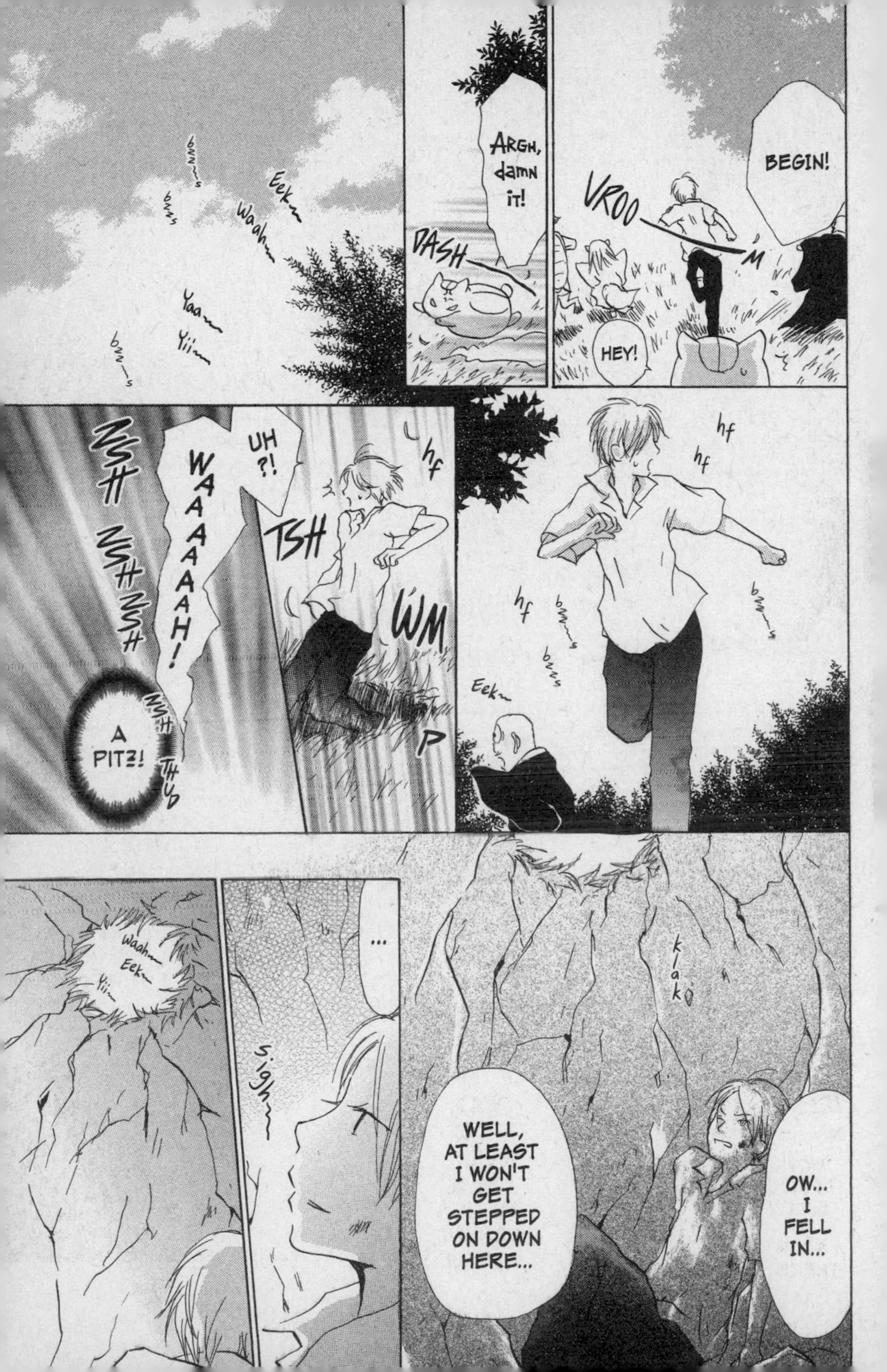
BEGIN!
VROOM
HEY!
Argh, damn it!
DASH
bzz~s
Eek~
bzzs
Waah~
Yaa~
Yii~
bzz~s
hf
hf
hf
bzz~s
bzz~s
bzzs
Eek~
hf
UH?!
TSH
WM
P
WAAAAAAAH!
ZSH ZSH ZSH ZSH
ZSH
A PIT?!
THUD
klak
OW... I FELL IN...
WELL, AT LEAST I WON'T GET STEPPED ON DOWN HERE...
...
sigh~
Waah~
Eek~
Yii~

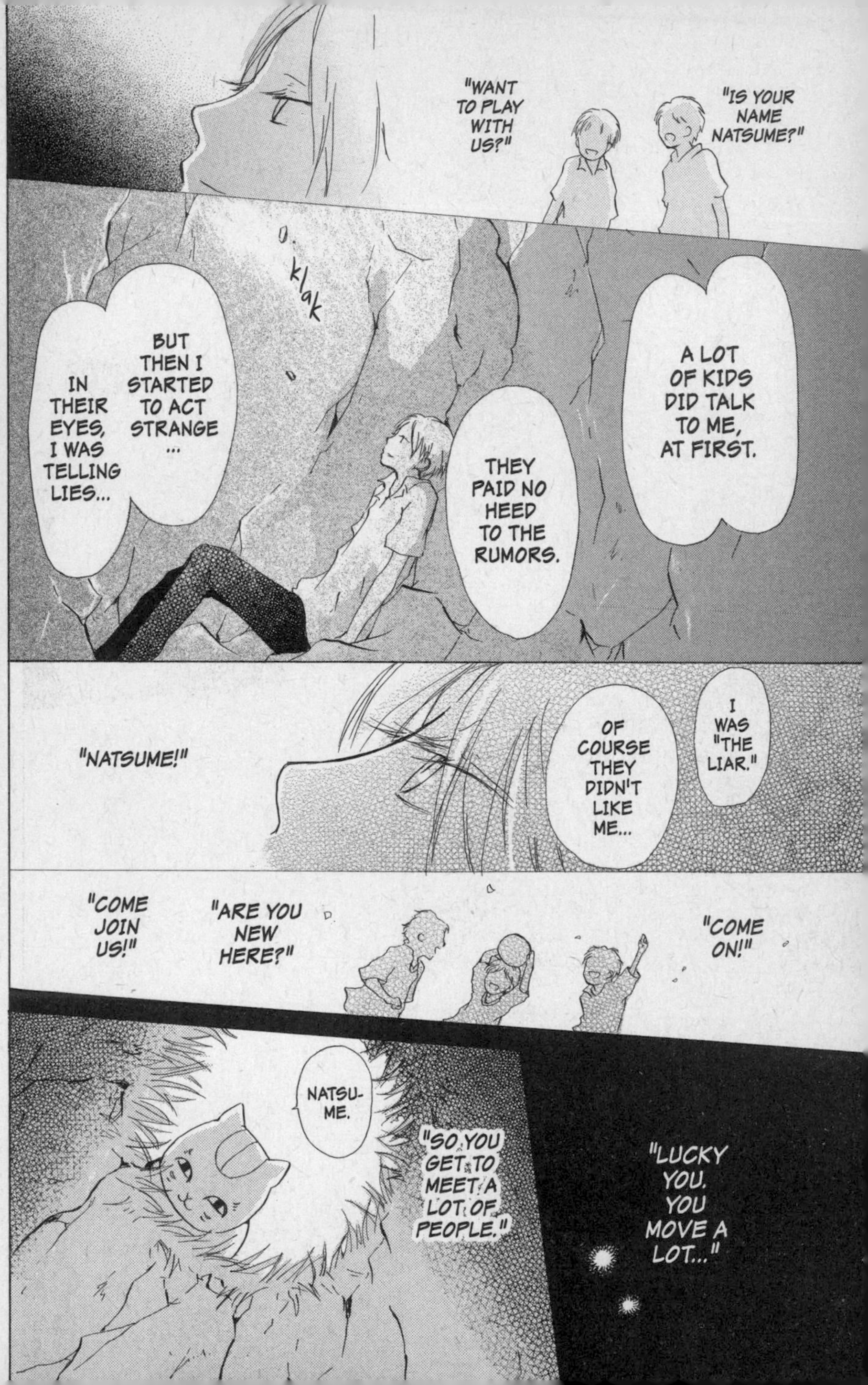
"IS YOUR NAME NATSUME?"
"WANT TO PLAY WITH US?"
A LOT OF KIDS DID TALK TO ME, AT FIRST.
THEY PAID NO HEED TO THE RUMORS.
klak
BUT THEN I STARTED TO ACT STRANGE...
IN THEIR EYES, I WAS TELLING LIES...
I WAS "THE LIAR."
OF COURSE THEY DIDN'T LIKE ME...
"NATSUME!"
"COME ON!"
"ARE YOU NEW HERE?"
"COME JOIN US!"
"LUCKY YOU. YOU MOVE A LOT..."
"SO YOU GET TO MEET A LOT OF PEOPLE."
NATSU-ME.

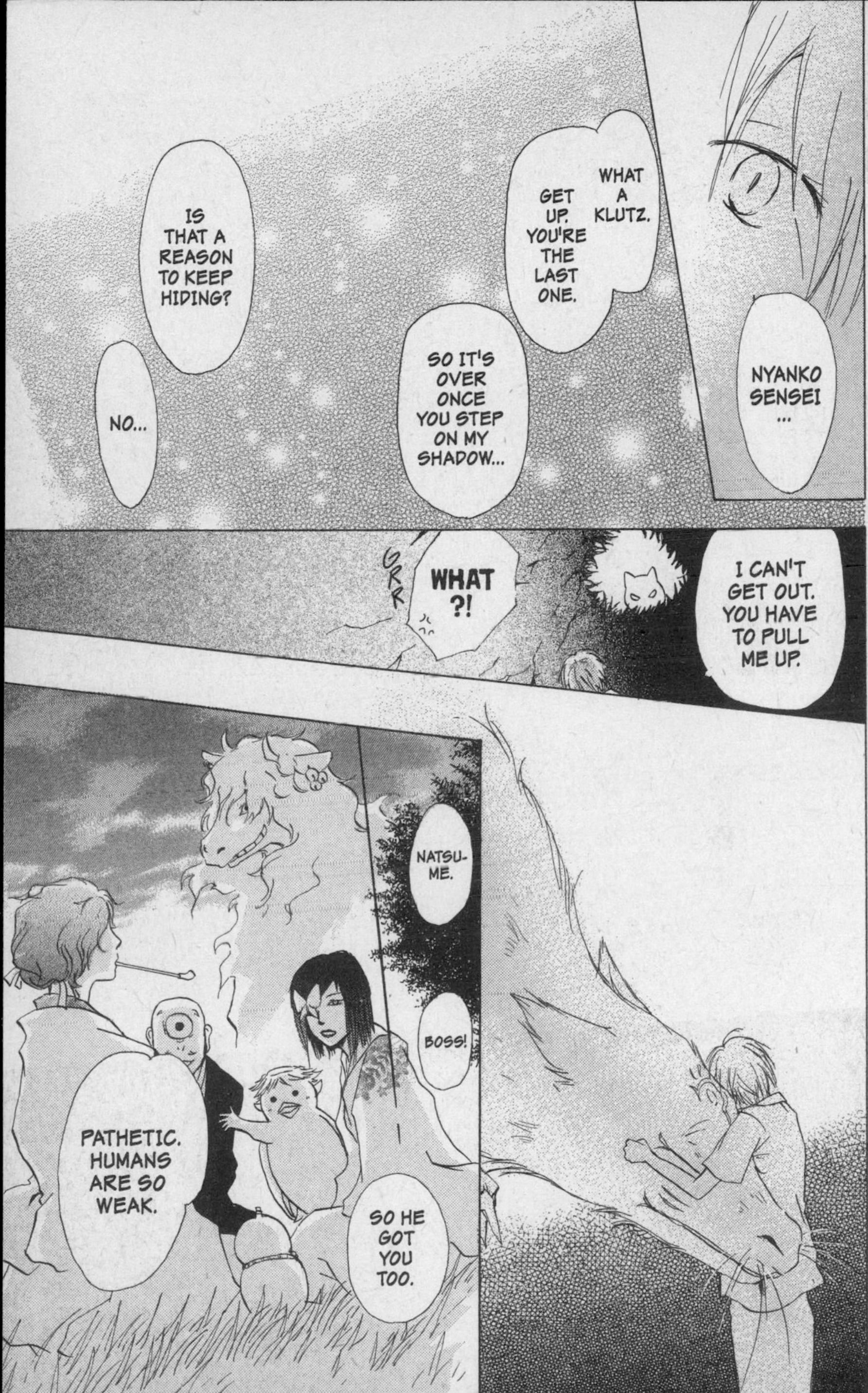
NYANKO SENSEI ...
WHAT A KLUTZ.
GET UP. YOU'RE THE LAST ONE.
SO IT'S OVER ONCE YOU STEP ON MY SHADOW...
IS THAT A REASON TO KEEP HIDING?
NO...
I CAN'T GET OUT. YOU HAVE TO PULL ME UP.
WHAT ?!
GRR
NATSU-ME.
BOSS!
SO HE GOT YOU TOO.
PATHETIC. HUMANS ARE SO WEAK.

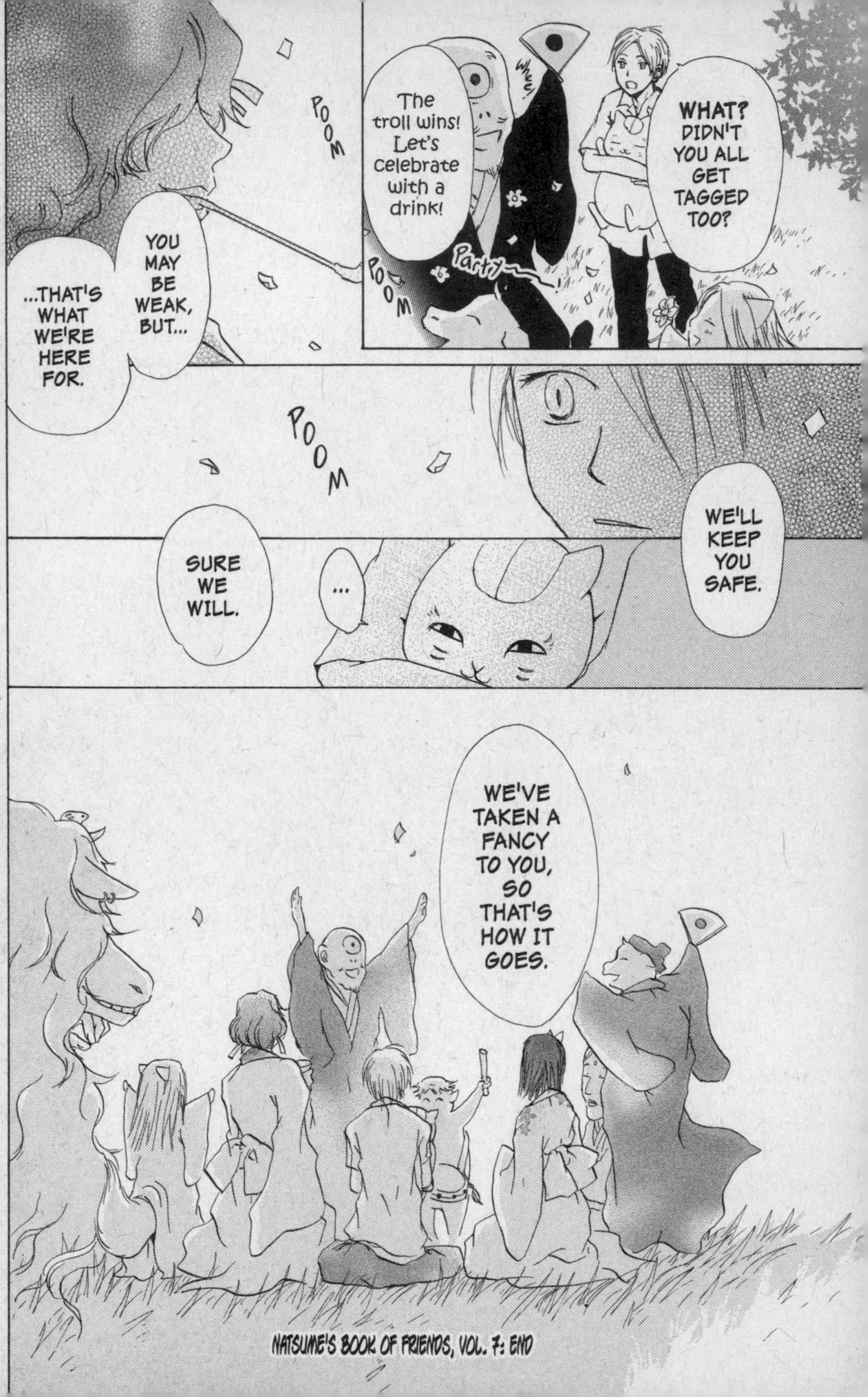
WHAT? DIDN'T YOU ALL GET TAGGED TOO?
Whee!
The troll wins! Let's celebrate with a drink!
Party~!
POOM
POOM
YOU MAY BE WEAK, BUT...
...THAT'S WHAT WE'RE HERE FOR.
WE'LL KEEP YOU SAFE.
POOM
...
SURE WE WILL.
WE'VE TAKEN A FANCY TO YOU, SO THAT'S HOW IT GOES.
NATSUME'S BOOK OF FRIENDS, VOL. 7: END

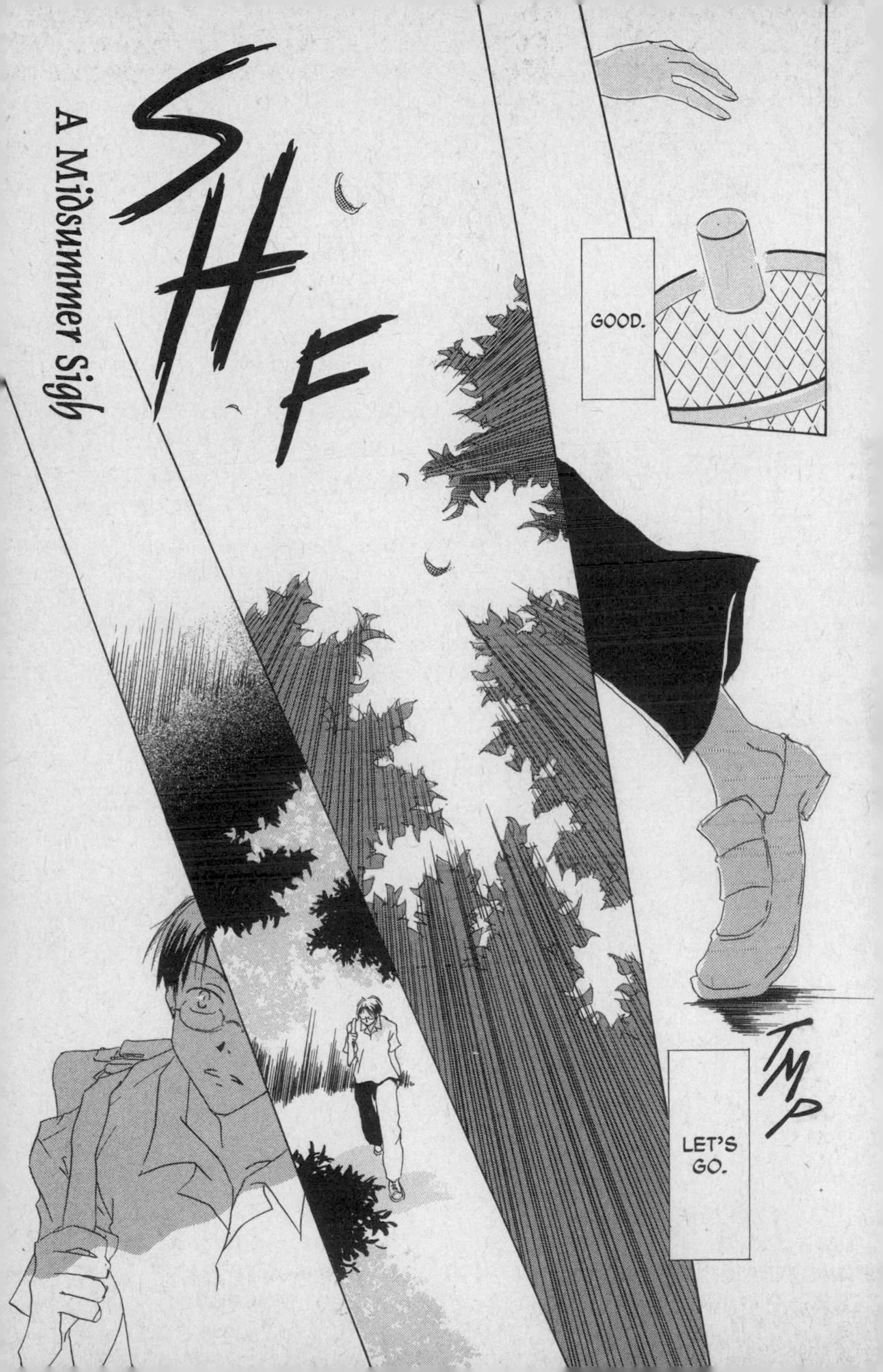
GOOD.
TMP
LET'S GO.
SHF
A Midsummer Sigh

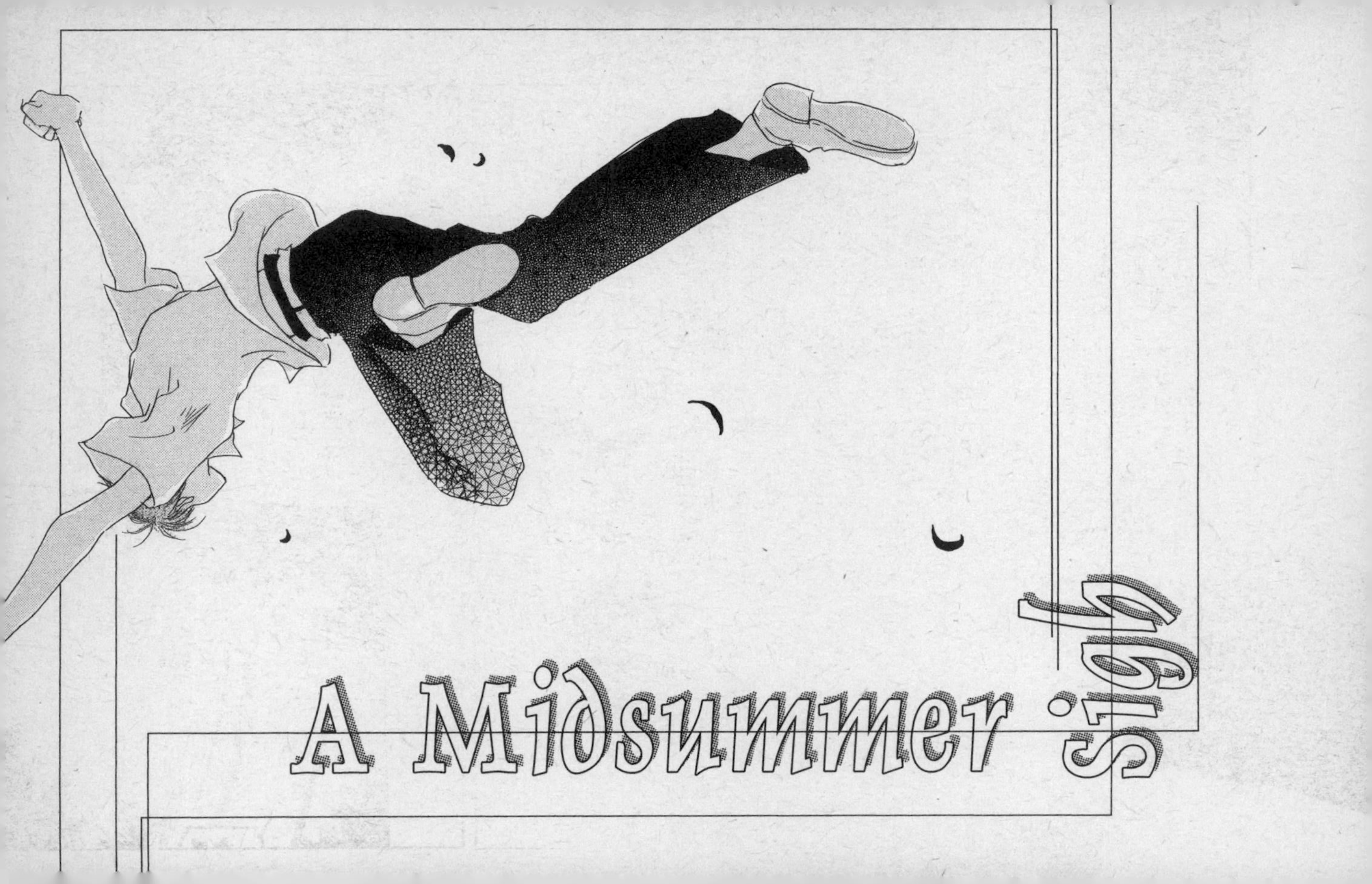
A Midsummer Sigh

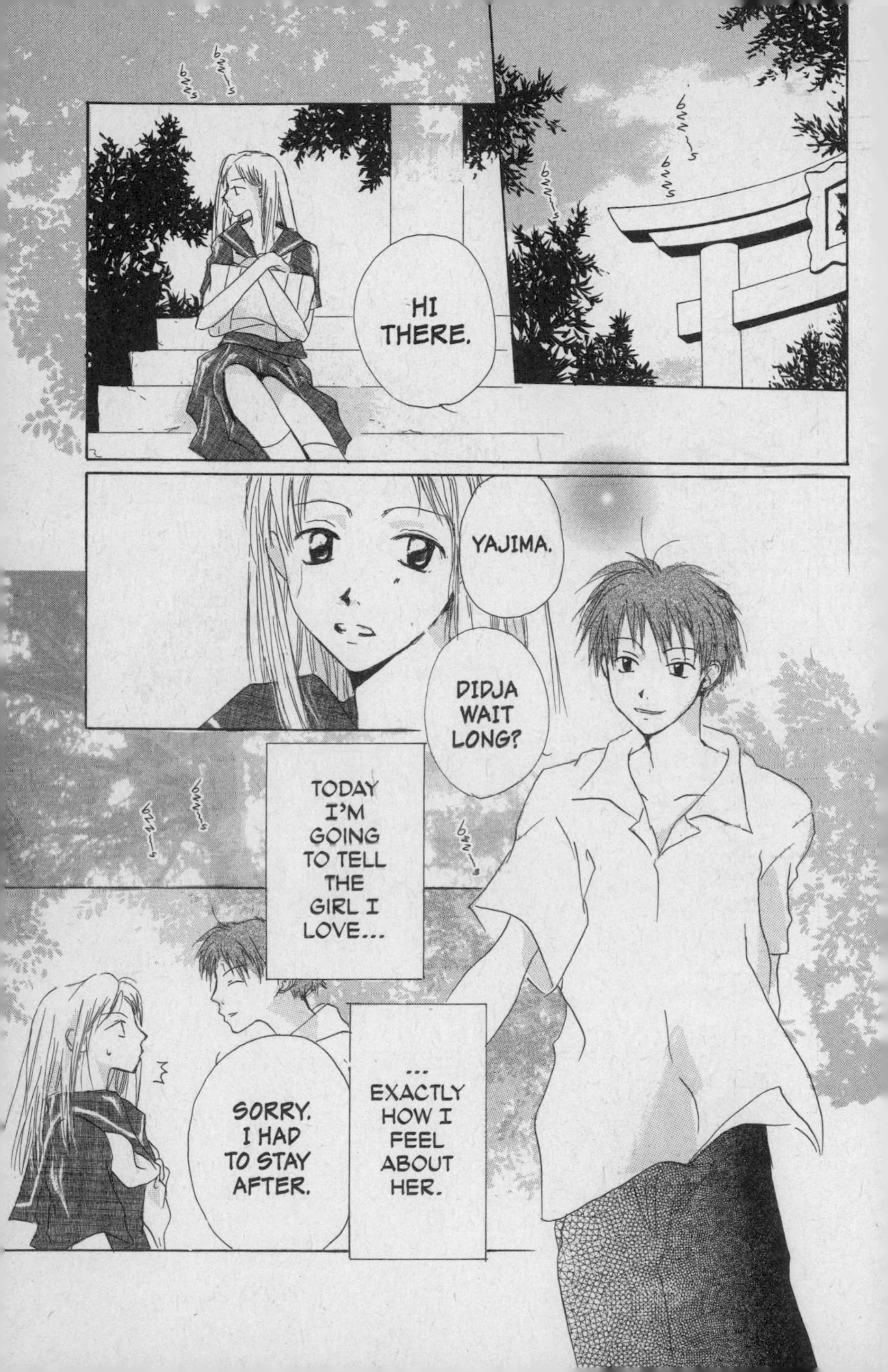
HI THERE.
YAJIMA.
DIDJA WAIT LONG?
TODAY I'M GOING TO TELL THE GIRL I LOVE...
... EXACTLY HOW I FEEL ABOUT HER.
SORRY. I HAD TO STAY AFTER.

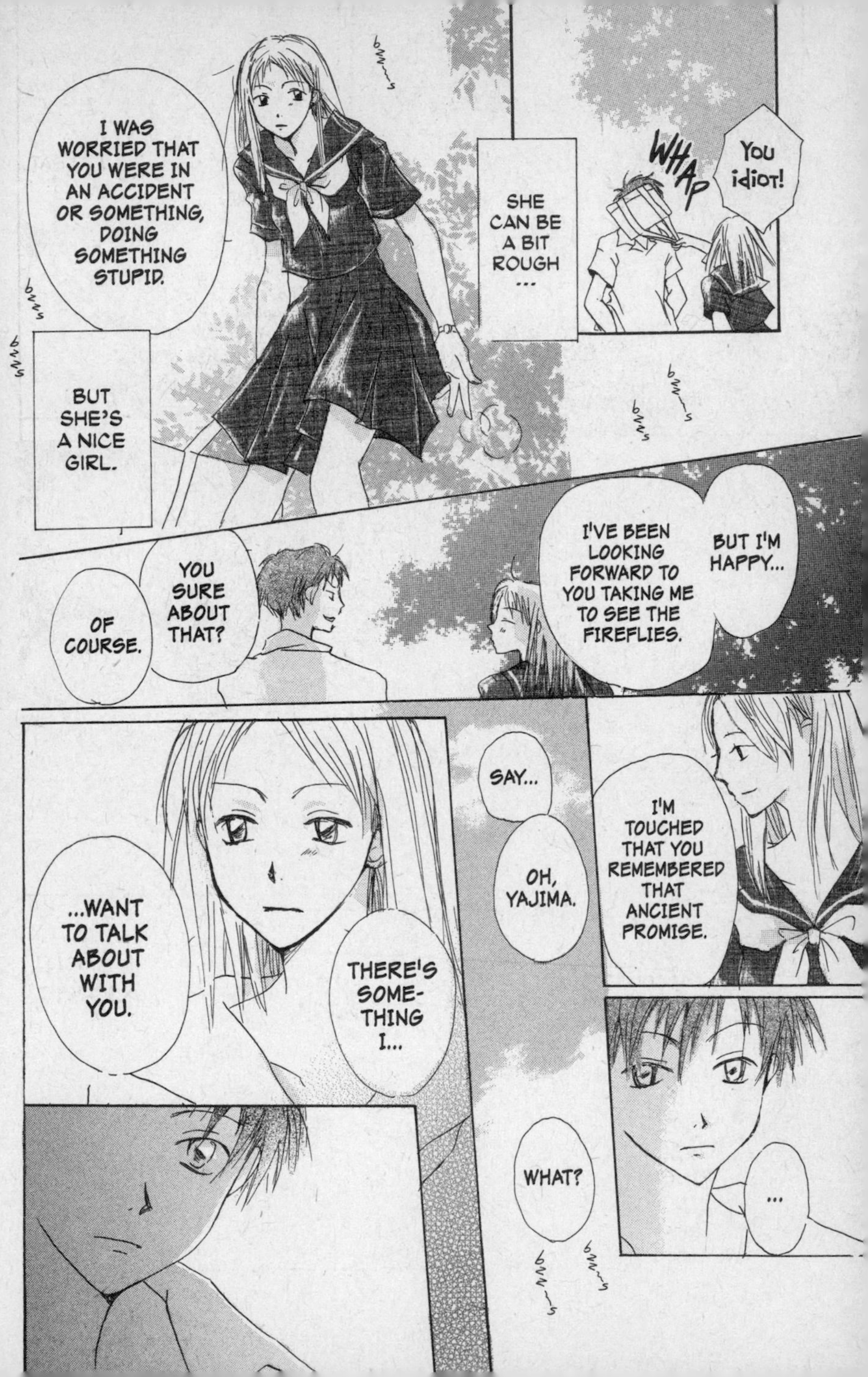
You idiot!
WHAP
SHE CAN BE A BIT ROUGH...
I WAS WORRIED THAT YOU WERE IN AN ACCIDENT OR SOMETHING, DOING SOMETHING STUPID.
BUT SHE'S A NICE GIRL.
BUT I'M HAPPY...
I'VE BEEN LOOKING FORWARD TO YOU TAKING ME TO SEE THE FIREFLIES.
YOU SURE ABOUT THAT?
OF COURSE.
I'M TOUCHED THAT YOU REMEMBERED THAT ANCIENT PROMISE.
SAY...
OH, YAJIMA.
THERE'S SOME-THING I...
...WANT TO TALK ABOUT WITH YOU.
...
WHAT?

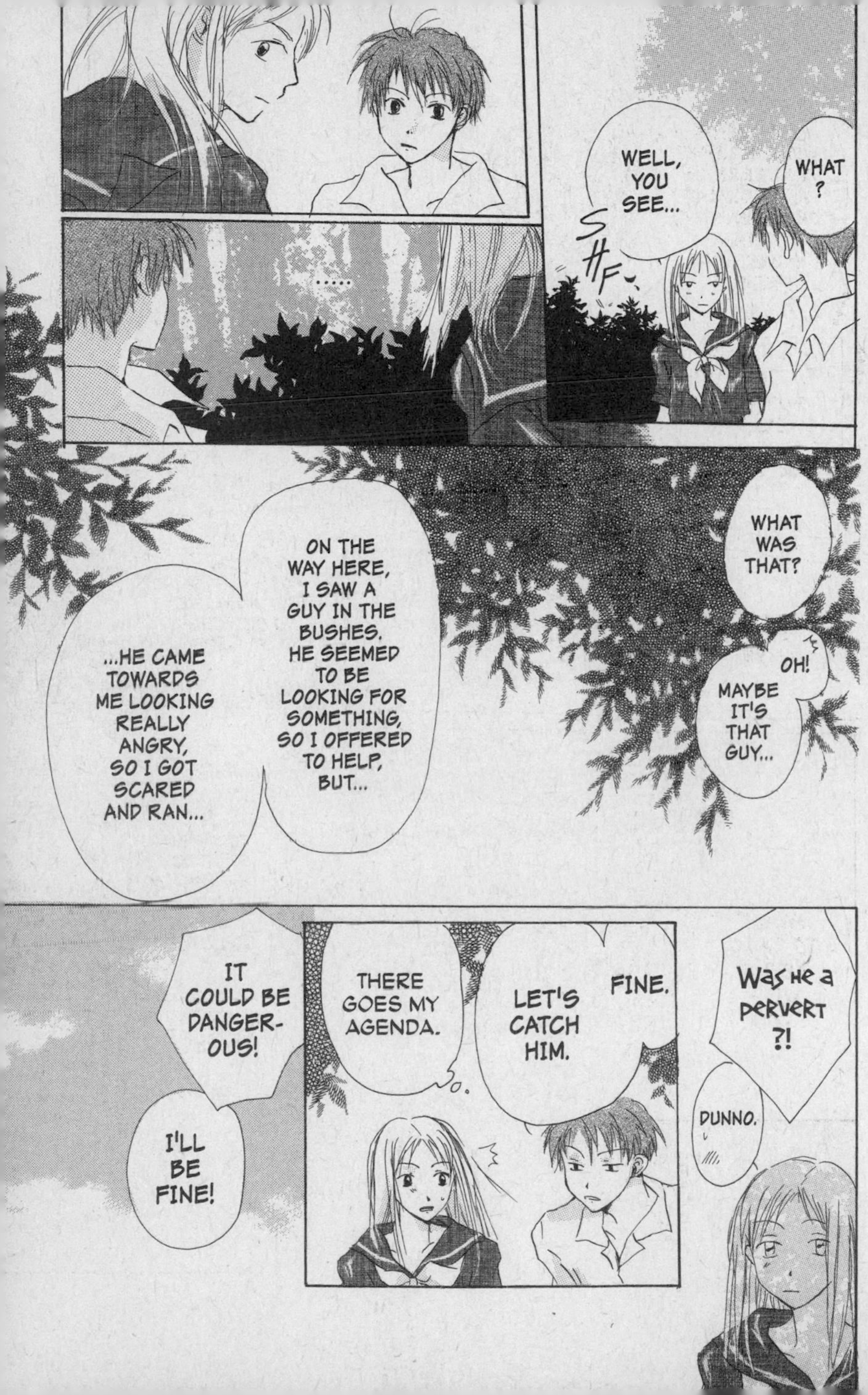
WHAT ?
WELL, YOU SEE...
SHF
.....
WHAT WAS THAT?
OH!
MAYBE IT'S THAT GUY...
ON THE WAY HERE, I SAW A GUY IN THE BUSHES. HE SEEMED TO BE LOOKING FOR SOMETHING, SO I OFFERED TO HELP, BUT...
...HE CAME TOWARDS ME LOOKING REALLY ANGRY, SO I GOT SCARED AND RAN...
Was he a pervert ?!
DUNNO.
FINE. LET'S CATCH HIM.
THERE GOES MY AGENDA.
IT COULD BE DANGER-OUS!
I'LL BE FINE!

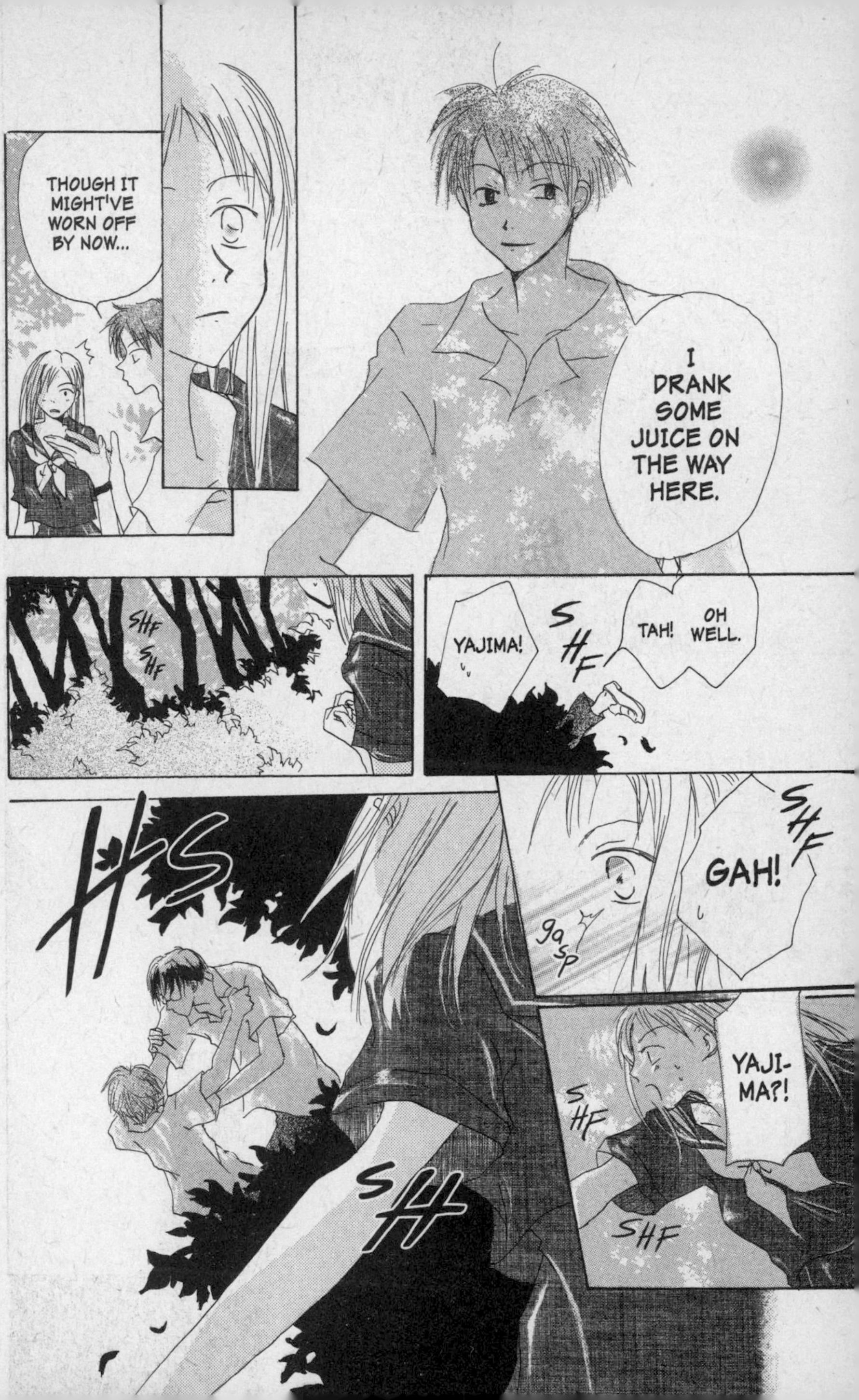
I DRANK SOME JUICE ON THE WAY HERE.
THOUGH IT MIGHT'VE WORN OFF BY NOW...
OH WELL.
TAH!
SHF
YAJIMA!
SHF
SHF
SHF
GAH!
gasp
YAJI-MA?!
SHF
SHF
HS
SH

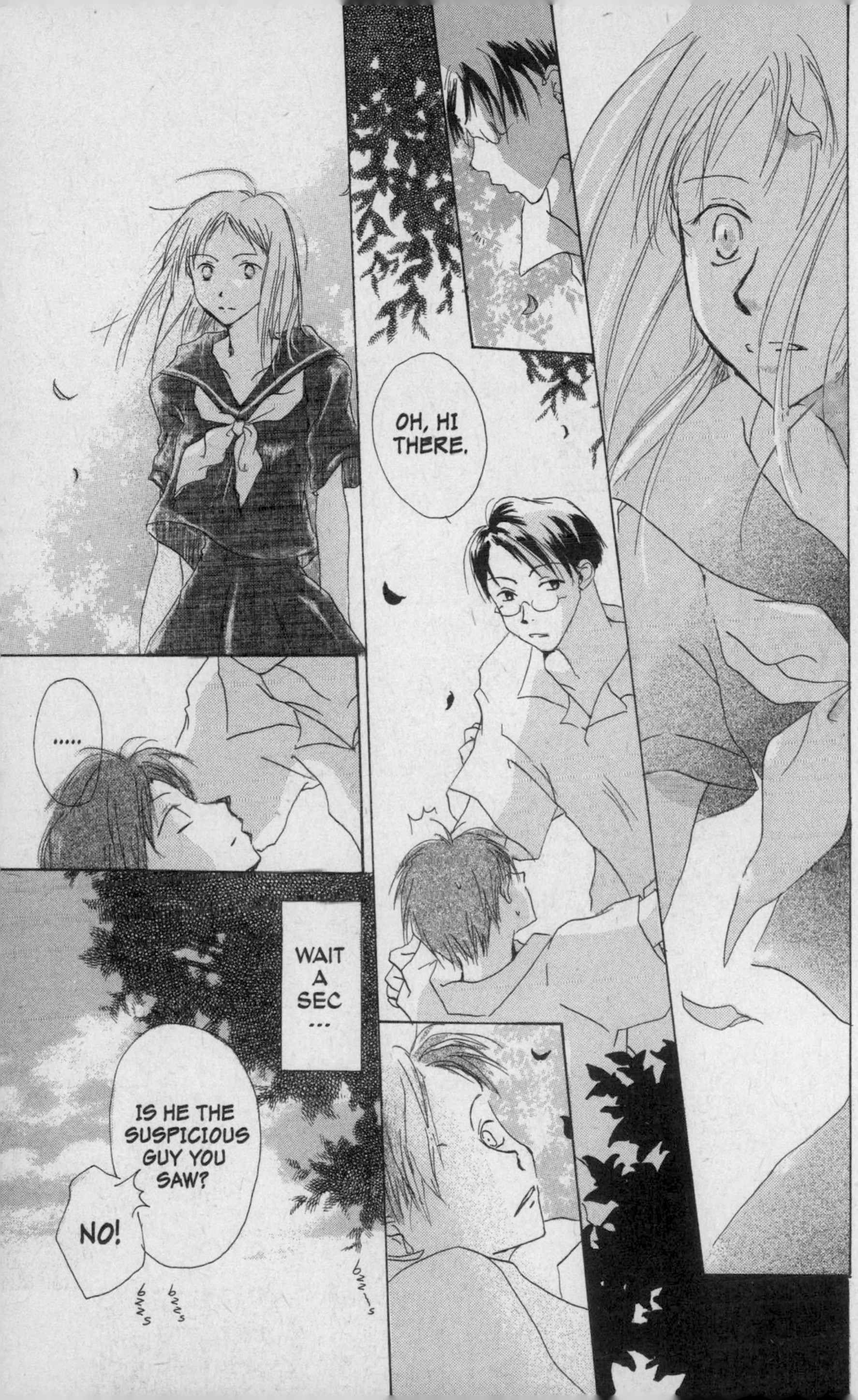
OH, HI THERE.
.....
WAIT A SEC...
IS HE THE SUSPICIOUS GUY YOU SAW?
NO!

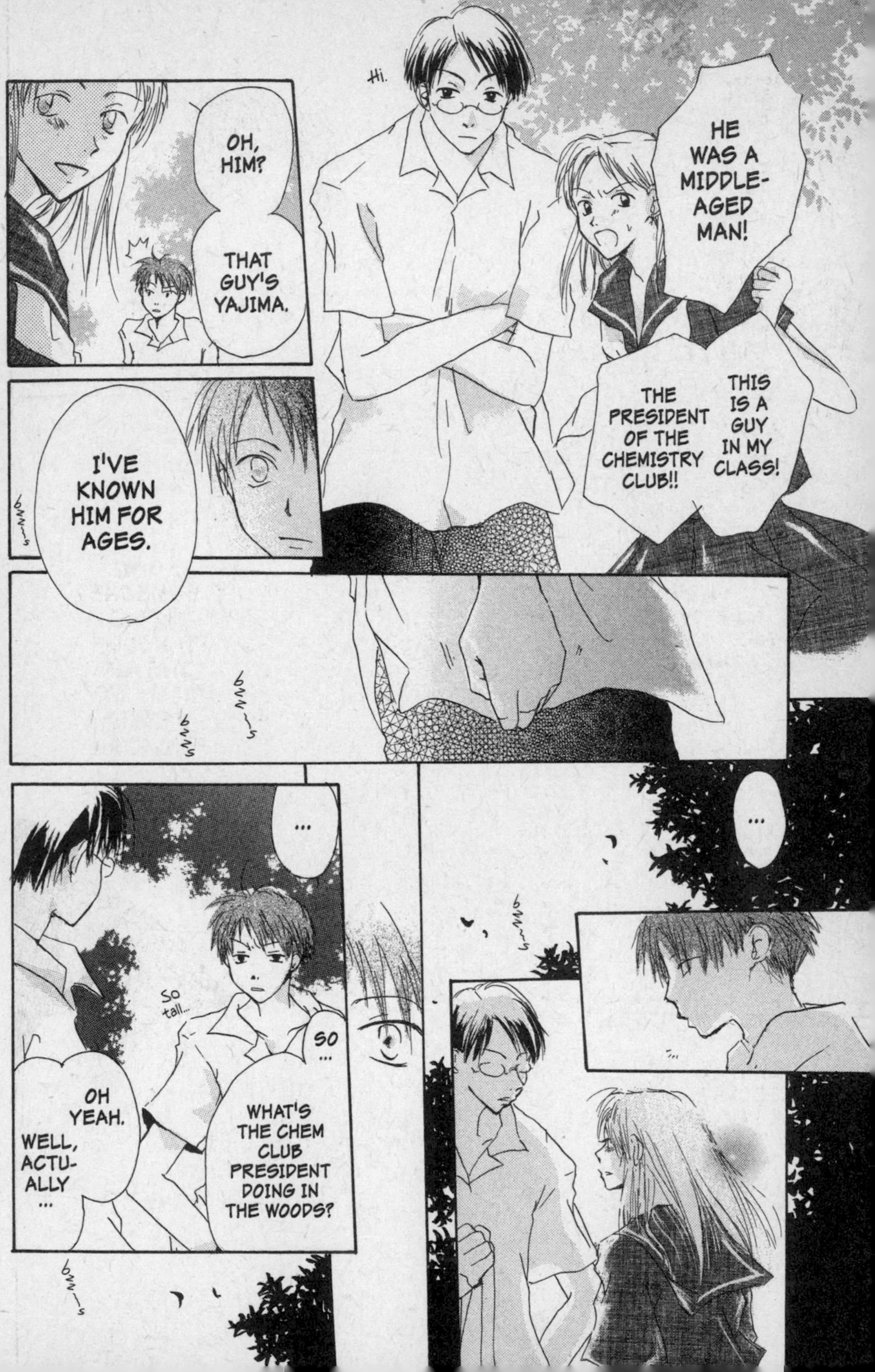
Hi.
HE WAS A MIDDLE-AGED MAN!
THIS IS A GUY IN MY CLASS!
THE PRESIDENT OF THE CHEMISTRY CLUB!!
OH, HIM?
THAT GUY'S YAJIMA.
I'VE KNOWN HIM FOR AGES.
bzzz
bzzz
bzzz
...
bzzz
...
...
So tall...
SO...
WHAT'S THE CHEM CLUB PRESIDENT DOING IN THE WOODS?
OH YEAH.
WELL, ACTUALLY...
bzzz

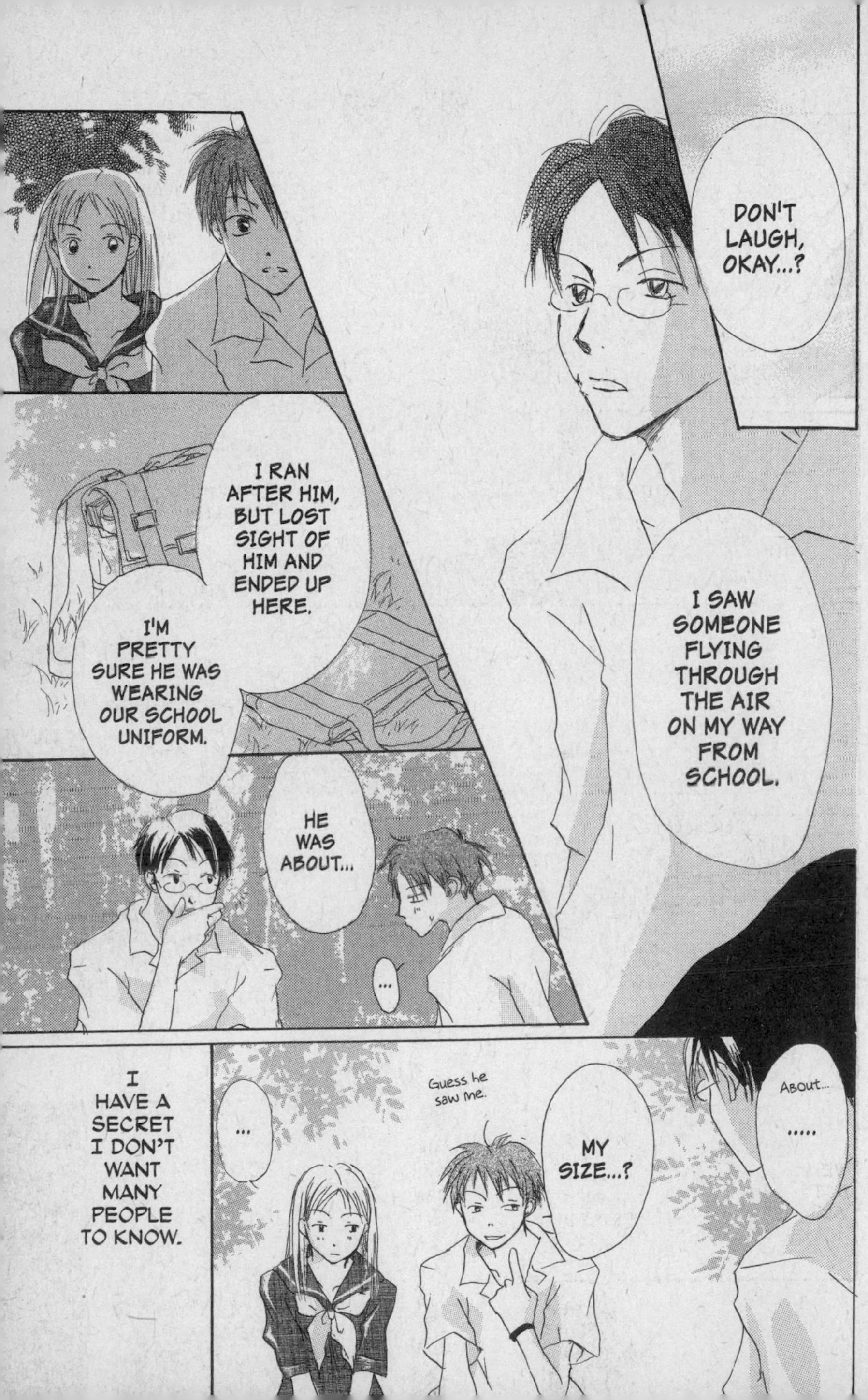
DON'T LAUGH, OKAY...?
I SAW SOMEONE FLYING THROUGH THE AIR ON MY WAY FROM SCHOOL.
I RAN AFTER HIM, BUT LOST SIGHT OF HIM AND ENDED UP HERE.
I'M PRETTY SURE HE WAS WEARING OUR SCHOOL UNIFORM.
HE WAS ABOUT...
...
About...
.....
MY SIZE...?
Guess he saw me.
...
I HAVE A SECRET I DON'T WANT MANY PEOPLE TO KNOW.

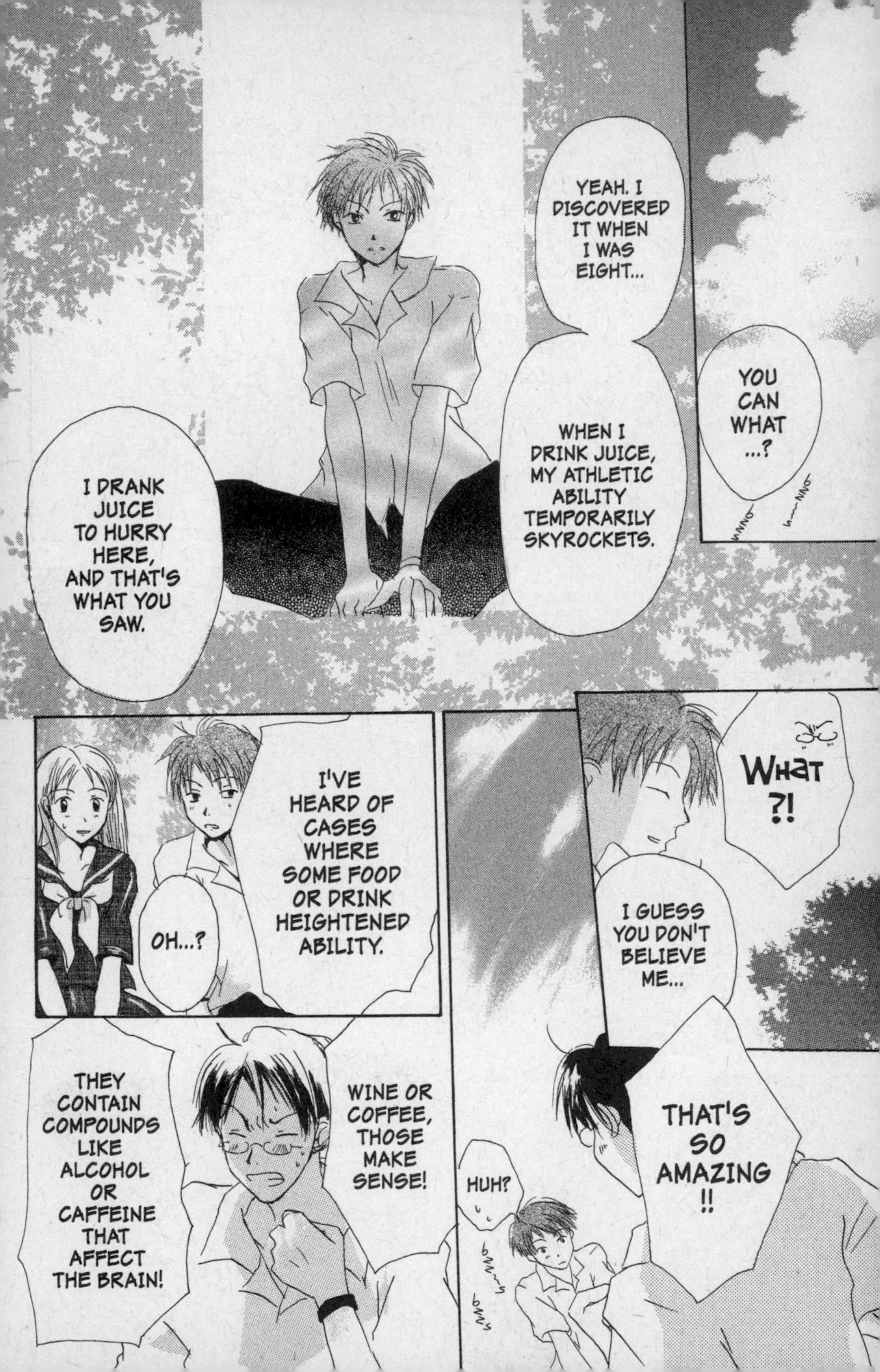
YOU CAN WHAT ...?
YEAH. I DISCOVERED IT WHEN I WAS EIGHT...
WHEN I DRINK JUICE, MY ATHLETIC ABILITY TEMPORARILY SKYROCKETS.
I DRANK JUICE TO HURRY HERE, AND THAT'S WHAT YOU SAW.
WHAT ?!
I GUESS YOU DON'T BELIEVE ME...
I'VE HEARD OF CASES WHERE SOME FOOD OR DRINK HEIGHTENED ABILITY.
OH...?
THAT'S SO AMAZING !!
HUH?
WINE OR COFFEE, THOSE MAKE SENSE!
THEY CONTAIN COMPOUNDS LIKE ALCOHOL OR CAFFEINE THAT AFFECT THE BRAIN!

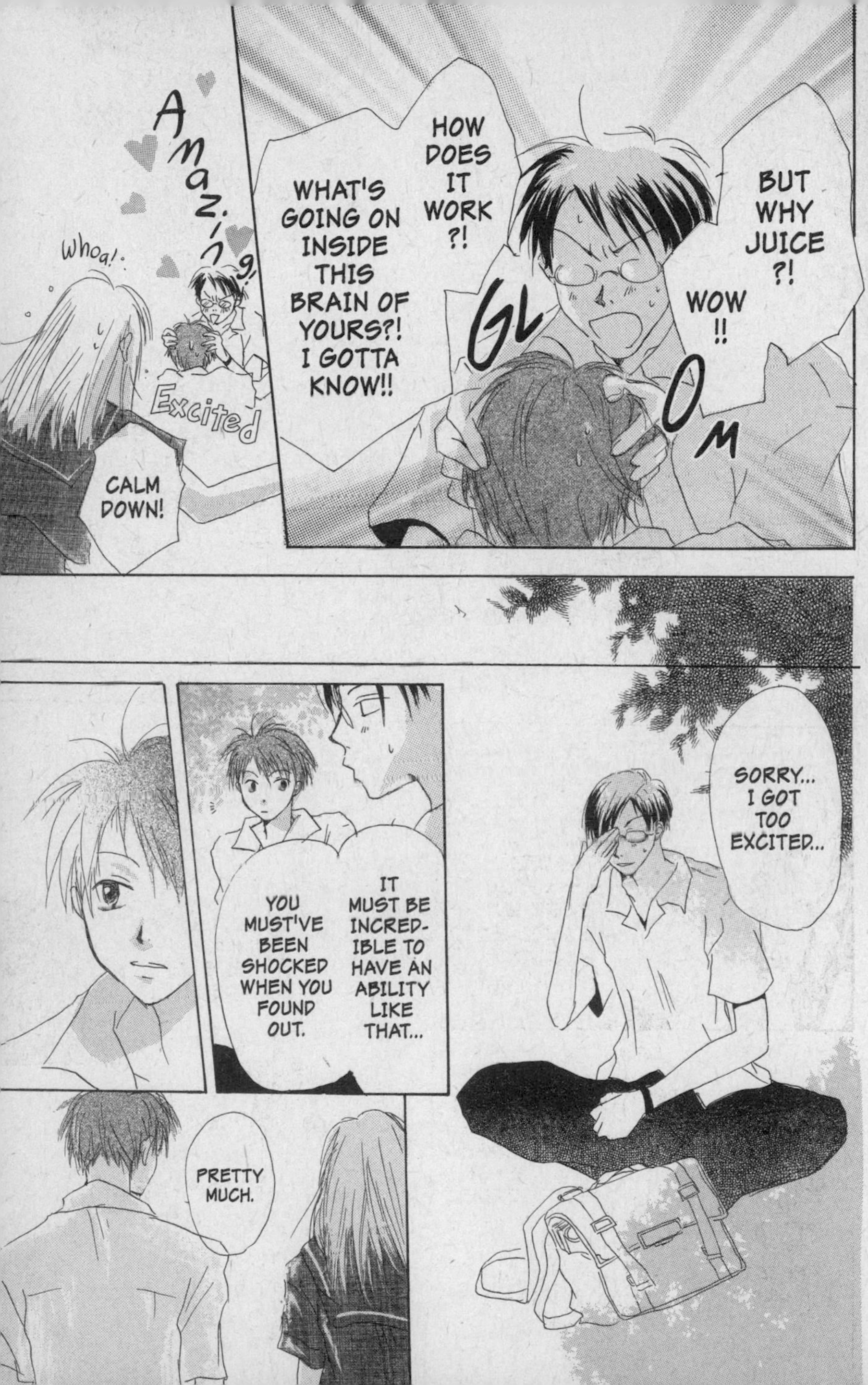
BUT WHY JUICE?!
WOW!!
GLOM
HOW DOES IT WORK?!
WHAT'S GOING ON INSIDE THIS BRAIN OF YOURS?! I GOTTA KNOW!!
Amazing!
Whoa!
Excited
CALM DOWN!
SORRY... I GOT TOO EXCITED...
IT MUST BE INCREDIBLE TO HAVE AN ABILITY LIKE THAT...
YOU MUST'VE BEEN SHOCKED WHEN YOU FOUND OUT.
PRETTY MUCH.

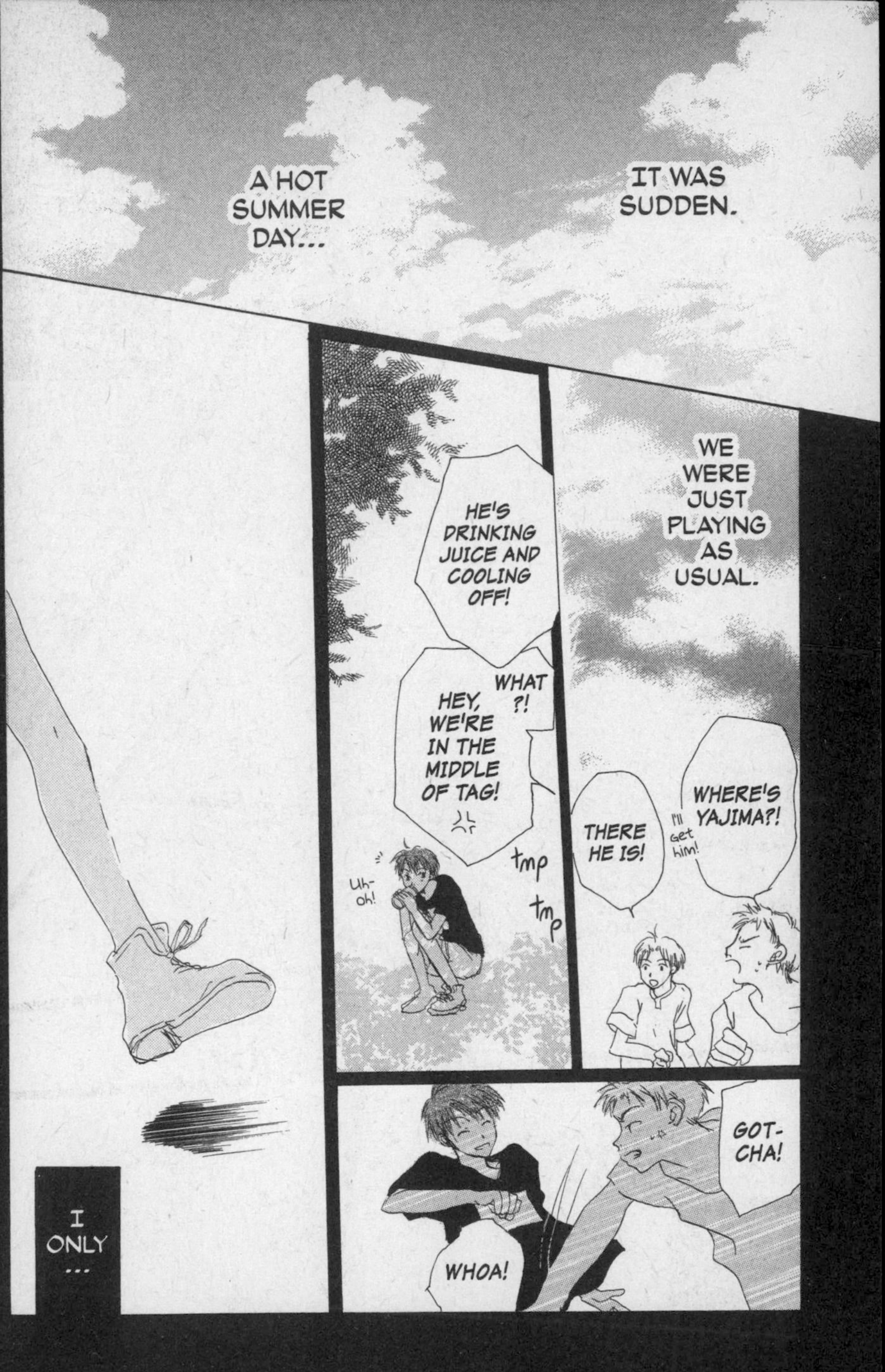
IT WAS SUDDEN.
A HOT SUMMER DAY...
WE WERE JUST PLAYING AS USUAL.
WHERE'S YAJIMA?!
I'll get him!
THERE HE IS!
HE'S DRINKING JUICE AND COOLING OFF!
WHAT?!
HEY, WE'RE IN THE MIDDLE OF TAG!
tmp
tmp
Uh-oh!
GOT-CHA!
WHOA!
I ONLY ...

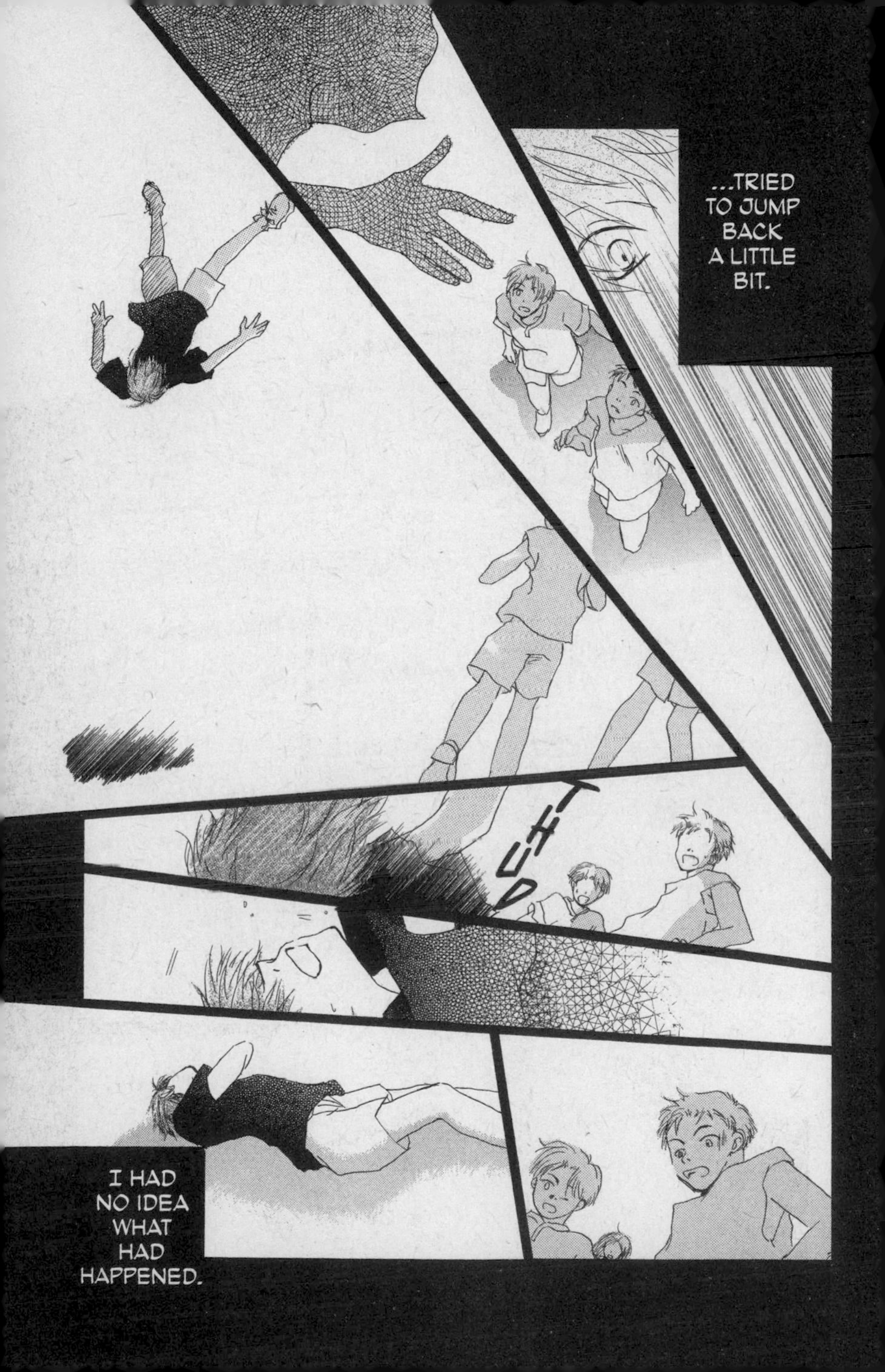
...TRIED TO JUMP BACK A LITTLE BIT.
THUD
I HAD NO IDEA WHAT HAD HAPPENED.

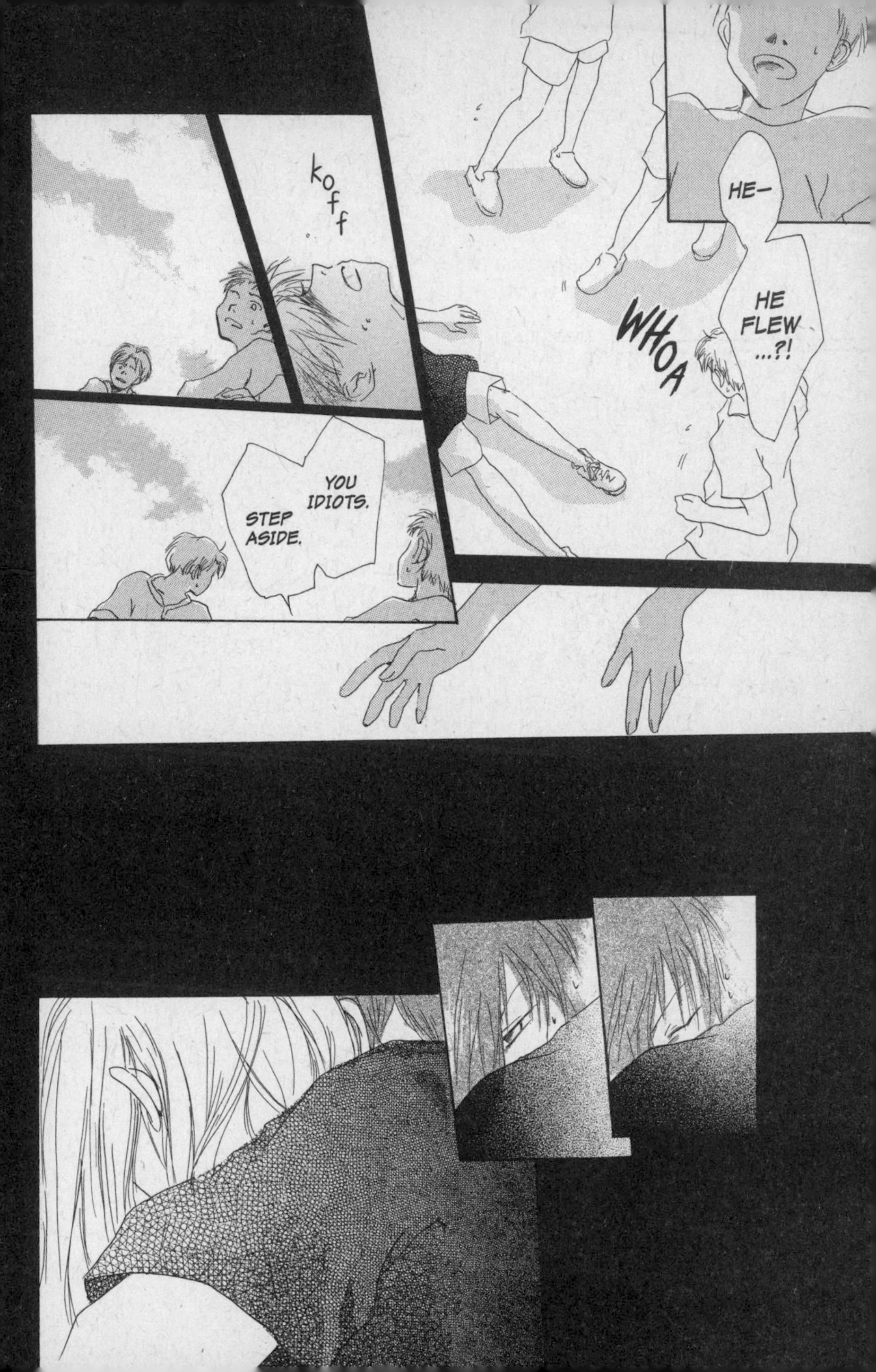
HE—
HE FLEW ...?!
WHOA
koff
YOU IDIOTS. STEP ASIDE.

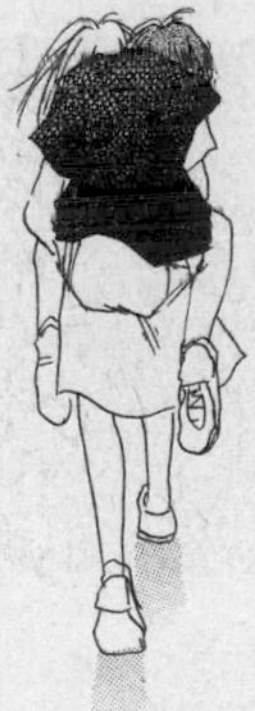

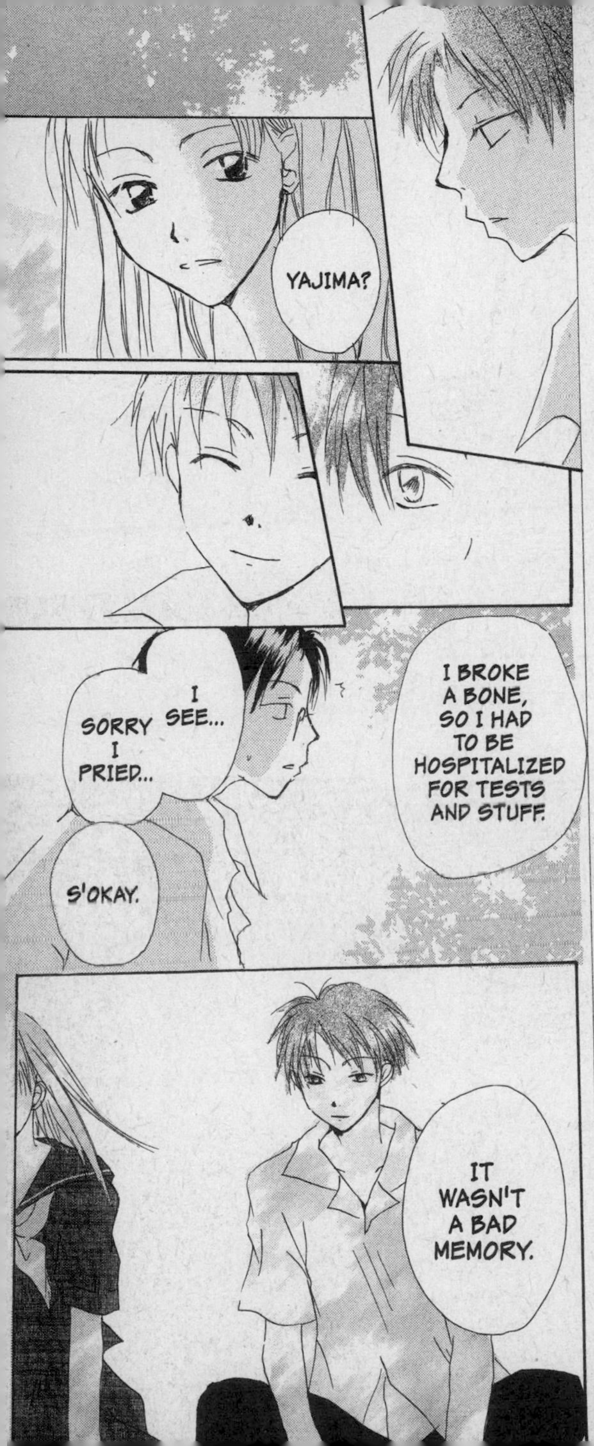
YAJIMA?
I BROKE A BONE, SO I HAD TO BE HOSPITALIZED FOR TESTS AND STUFF.
I SEE...
SORRY I PRIED...
S'OKAY.
IT WASN'T A BAD MEMORY.

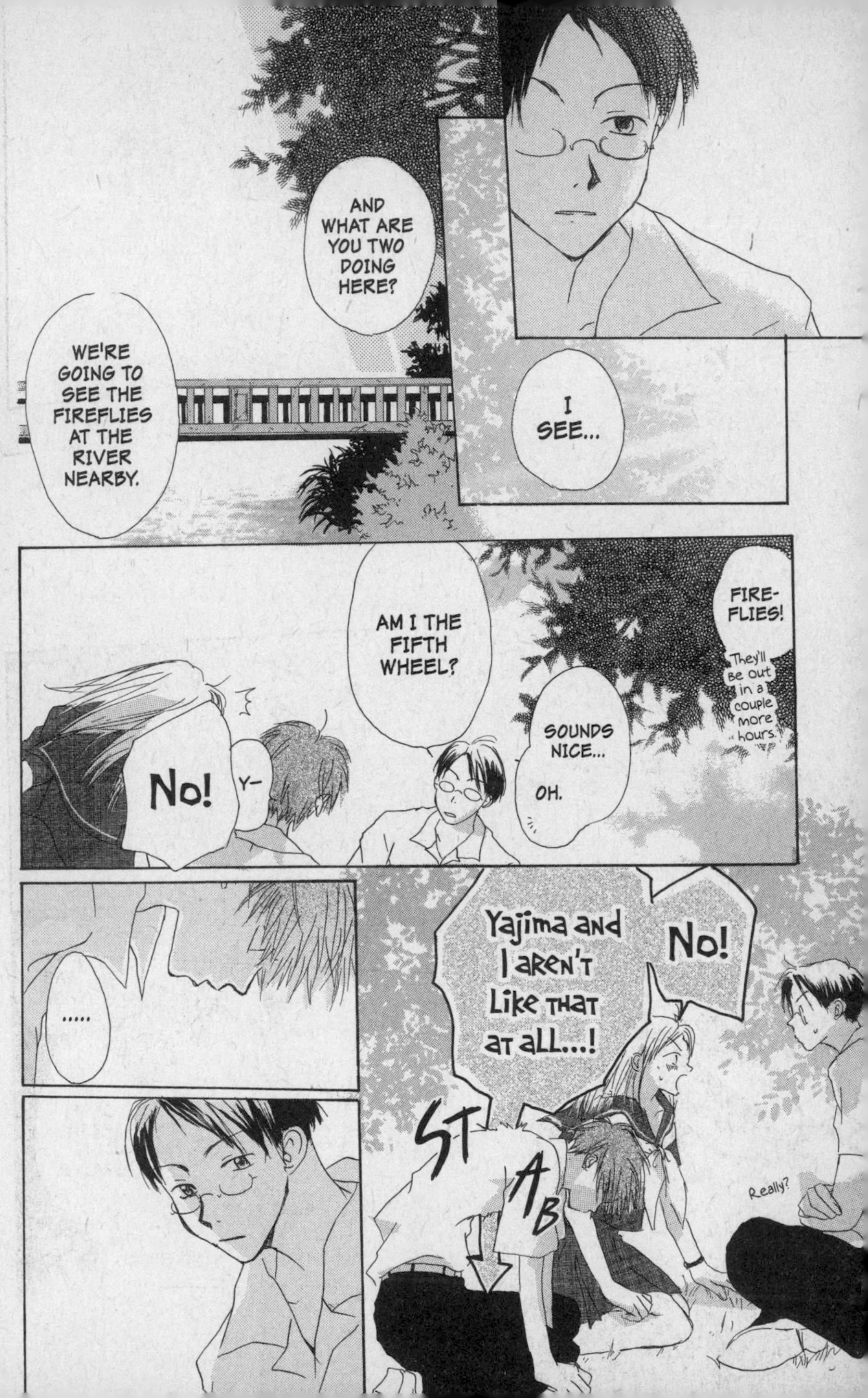
AND WHAT ARE YOU TWO DOING HERE?
WE'RE GOING TO SEE THE FIREFLIES AT THE RIVER NEARBY.
I SEE...
FIRE-FLIES!
They'll be out in a couple more hours.
SOUNDS NICE...
OH.
AM I THE FIFTH WHEEL?
Y-
No!
No!
Yajima and I aren't like that at all...!
STAB
Really?
.....

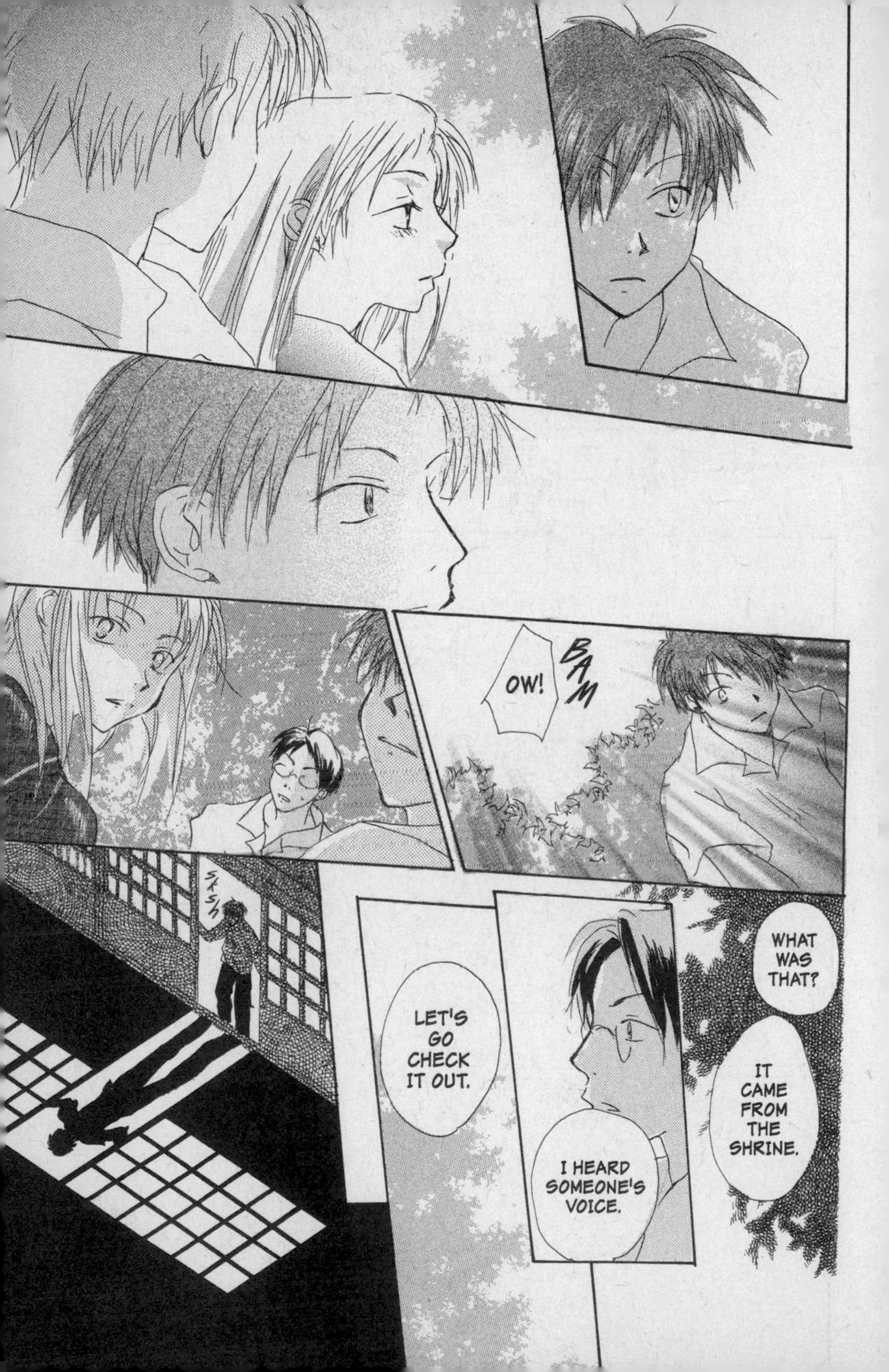
OW!
BAM
WHAT WAS THAT?
IT CAME FROM THE SHRINE.
I HEARD SOMEONE'S VOICE.
LET'S GO CHECK IT OUT.
SASH

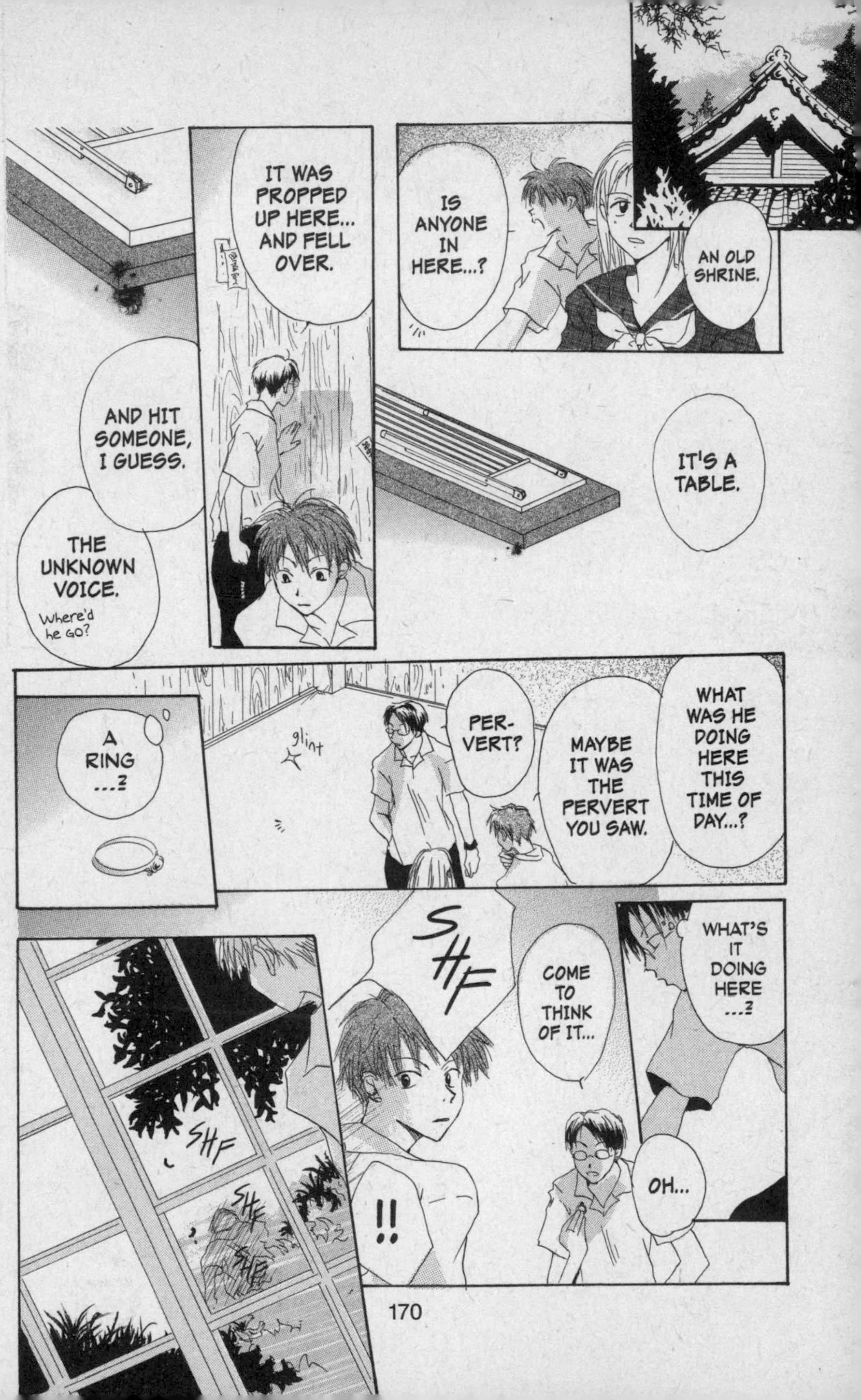
AN OLD SHRINE.
IS ANYONE IN HERE...?
IT'S A TABLE.
IT WAS PROPPED UP HERE... AND FELL OVER.
AND HIT SOMEONE, I GUESS.
THE UNKNOWN VOICE.
Where'd he GO?
WHAT WAS HE DOING HERE THIS TIME OF DAY...?
MAYBE IT WAS THE PERVERT YOU SAW.
PER-VERT?
glint
A RING ...?
WHAT'S IT DOING HERE ...?
COME TO THINK OF IT...
OH...
SHF
!!
SHF
SHF

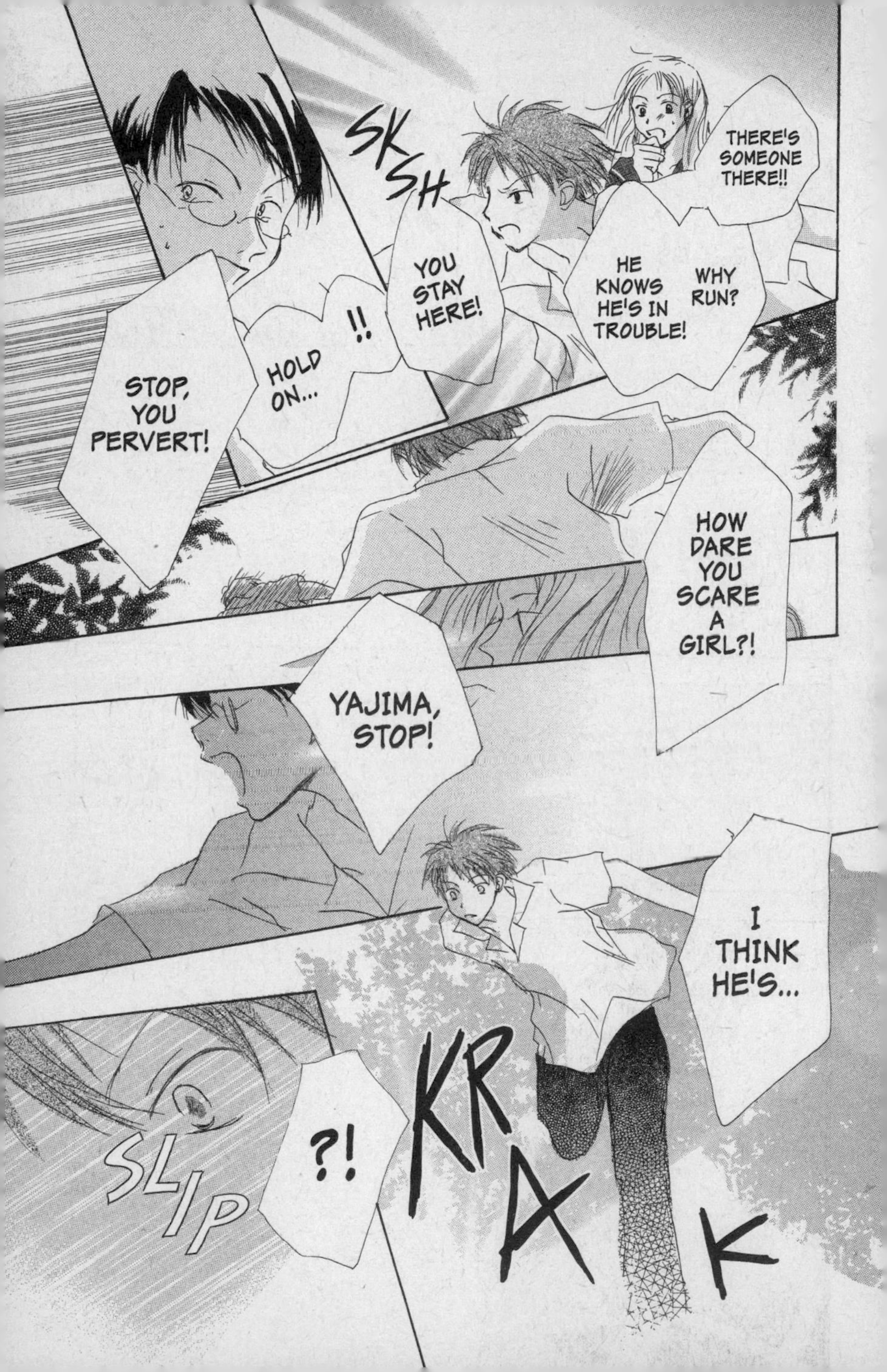
THERE'S SOMEONE THERE!!
WHY RUN?
HE KNOWS HE'S IN TROUBLE!
SKSH
YOU STAY HERE!
!!
HOLD ON...
STOP, YOU PERVERT!
HOW DARE YOU SCARE A GIRL?!
YAJIMA, STOP!
I THINK HE'S...
KRAK
?!
SLIP

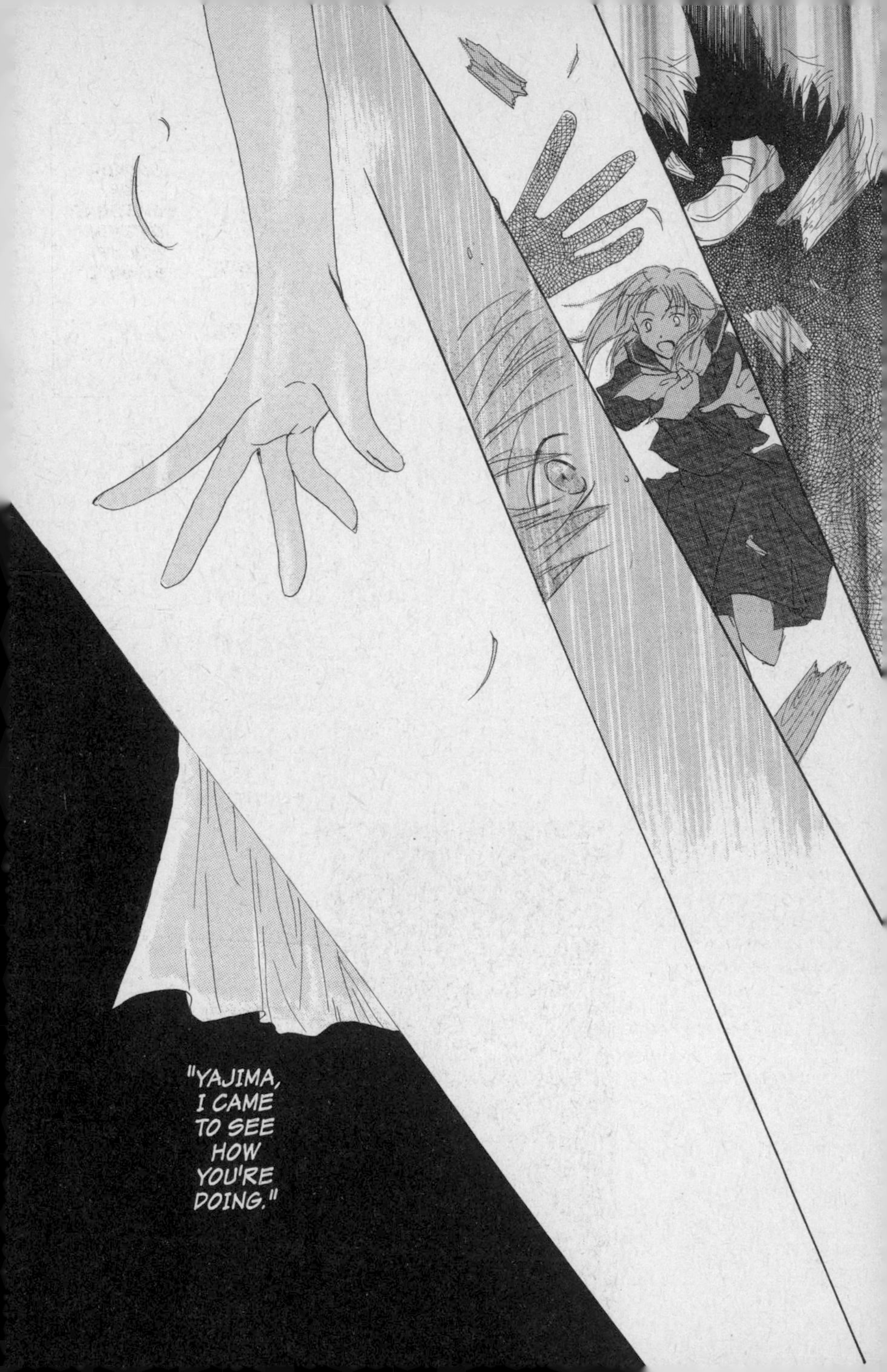
"YAJIMA, I CAME TO SEE HOW YOU'RE DOING."

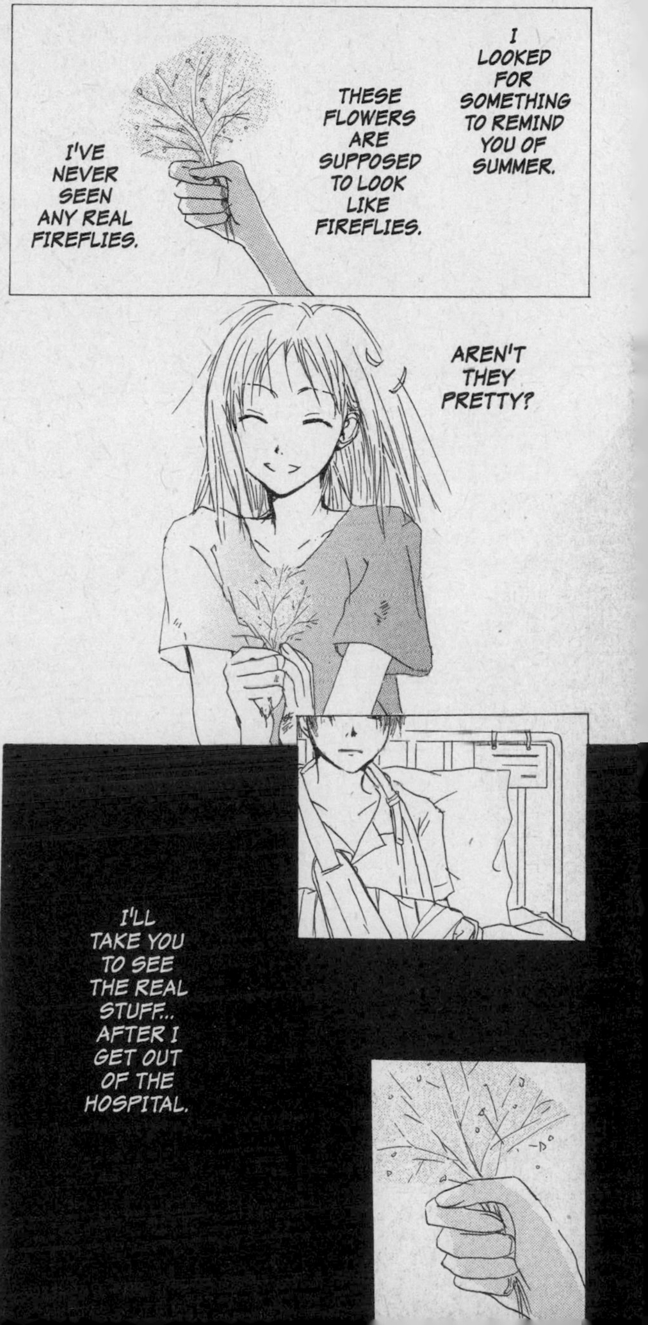

I LOOKED FOR SOMETHING TO REMIND YOU OF SUMMER.
THESE FLOWERS ARE SUPPOSED TO LOOK LIKE FIREFLIES.
I'VE NEVER SEEN ANY REAL FIREFLIES.
AREN'T THEY PRETTY?
I'LL TAKE YOU TO SEE THE REAL STUFF... AFTER I GET OUT OF THE HOSPITAL.


## 05

❋ Anime, second season

The second season of the anime has been announced. I'm really grateful. I must be the biggest fan of Natsume the anime, I love it so much. They made it so fresh. Thank you so much to the producers, actors, the music, opening and ending songs, advertising, Imado Shrine—the shrine of lucky cat statues—everyone who was involved in production, and most of all, the viewers back home who gave their support.

Now I have to work even harder on the manga. I'll do everything I can to keep my dear, precious readers and treat this manga with with tender loving care.

End of $\frac{1}{4}$ columns.

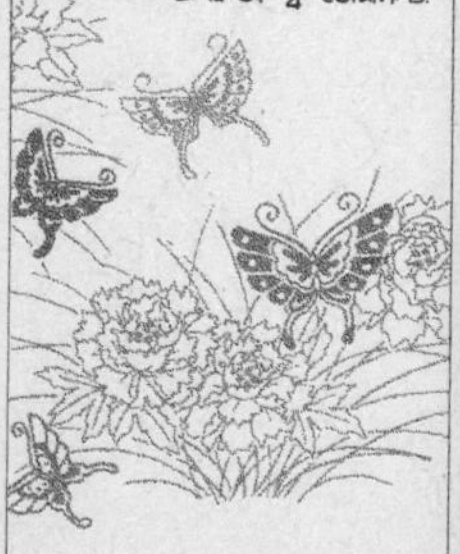

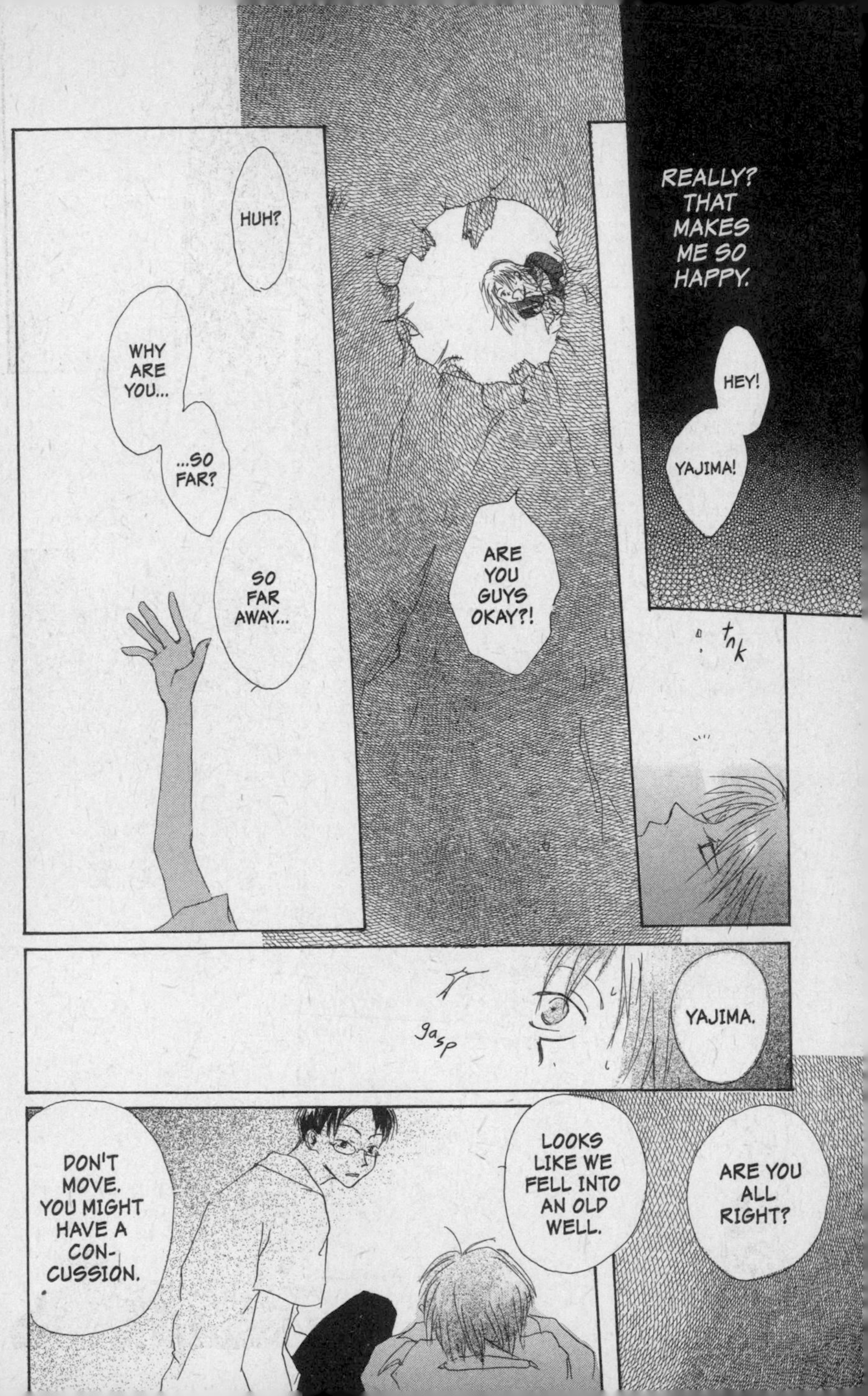
REALLY? THAT MAKES ME SO HAPPY.
HEY!
YAJIMA!
tnk
ARE YOU GUYS OKAY?!
HUH?
WHY ARE YOU...
...SO FAR?
SO FAR AWAY...
YAJIMA.
gasp
ARE YOU ALL RIGHT?
LOOKS LIKE WE FELL INTO AN OLD WELL.
DON'T MOVE. YOU MIGHT HAVE A CON-CUSSION.

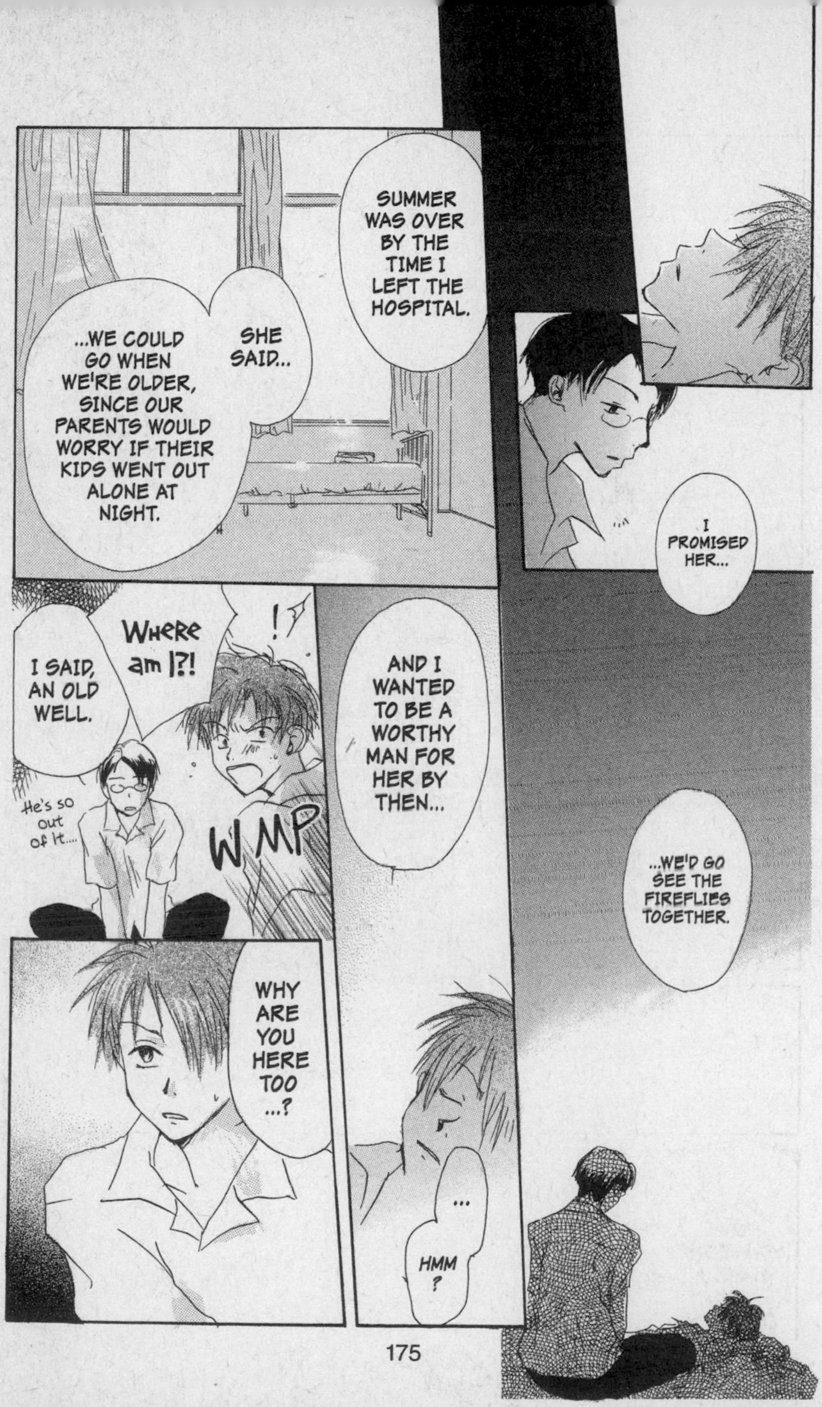
I PROMISED HER...
...WE'D GO SEE THE FIREFLIES TOGETHER.
SUMMER WAS OVER BY THE TIME I LEFT THE HOSPITAL.
SHE SAID...
...WE COULD GO WHEN WE'RE OLDER, SINCE OUR PARENTS WOULD WORRY IF THEIR KIDS WENT OUT ALONE AT NIGHT.
AND I WANTED TO BE A WORTHY MAN FOR HER BY THEN...
!
Where am I?!
WMP
I SAID, AN OLD WELL.
He's so out of it....
...
HMM?
WHY ARE YOU HERE TOO...?

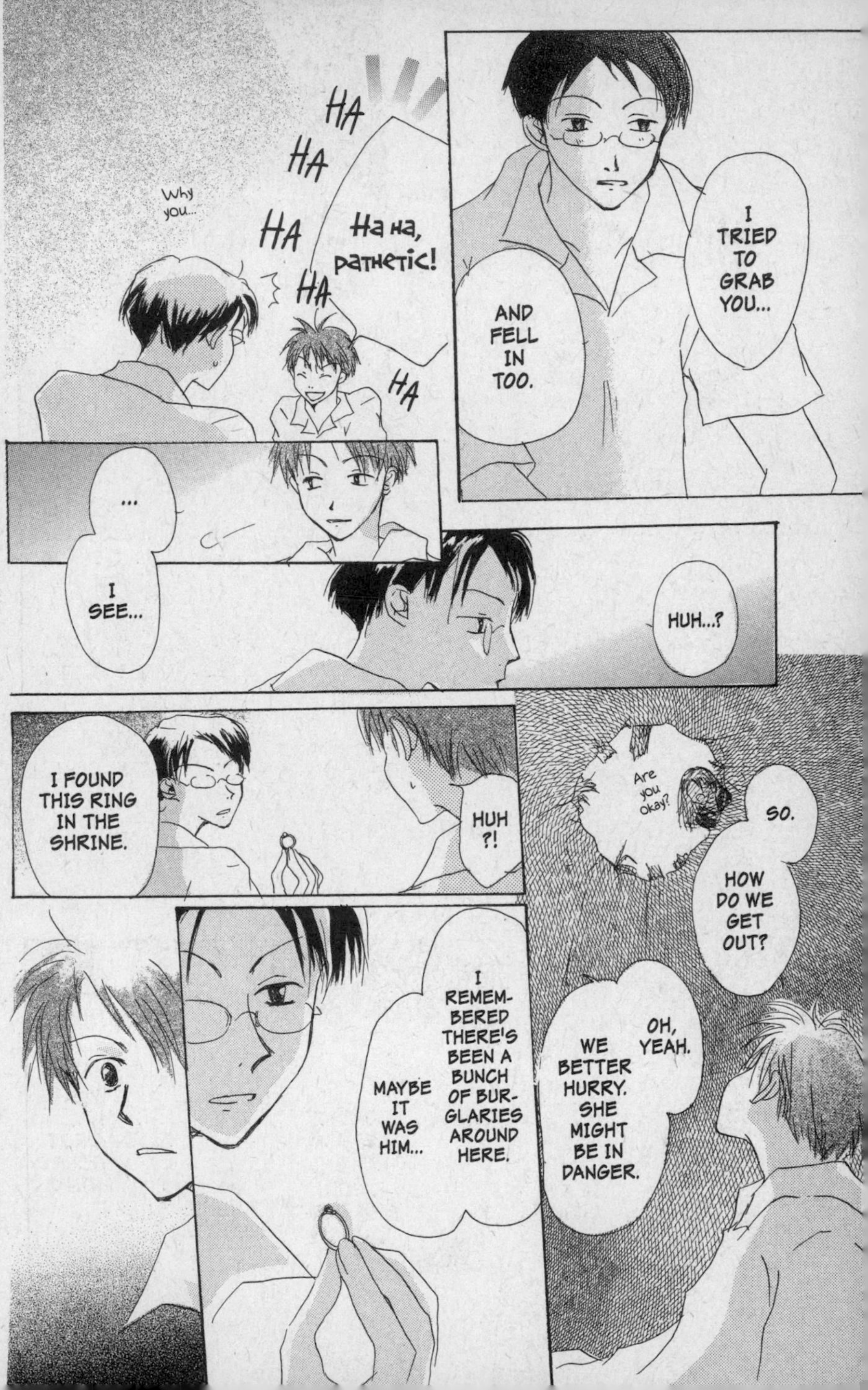
I TRIED TO GRAB YOU...
AND FELL IN TOO.
HA HA HA HA HA
Ha ha, pathetic!
Why you...
...
I SEE...
HUH...?
Are you okay?
SO.
HOW DO WE GET OUT?
OH, YEAH.
WE BETTER HURRY. SHE MIGHT BE IN DANGER.
I FOUND THIS RING IN THE SHRINE.
HUH ?!
I REMEMBERED THERE'S BEEN A BUNCH OF BURGLARIES AROUND HERE.
MAYBE IT WAS HIM...

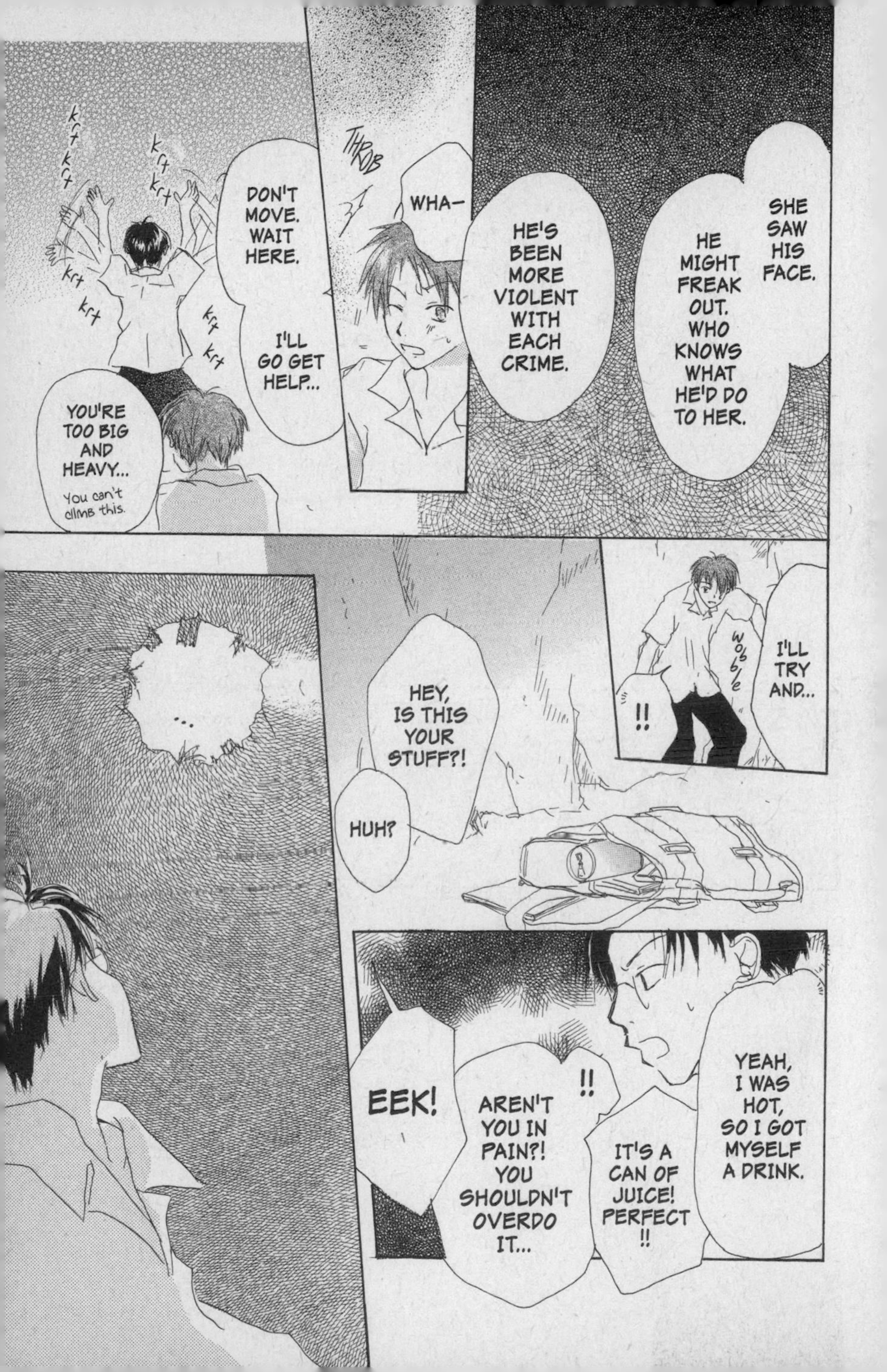
SHE SAW HIS FACE.
HE MIGHT FREAK OUT. WHO KNOWS WHAT HE'D DO TO HER.
HE'S BEEN MORE VIOLENT WITH EACH CRIME.
THROB
WHA-
DON'T MOVE. WAIT HERE.
I'LL GO GET HELP...
krt krt
krt krt
krt krt
krt krt
YOU'RE TOO BIG AND HEAVY...
You can't climb this.
I'LL TRY AND...
wobble
!!
HEY, IS THIS YOUR STUFF?!
HUH?
YEAH, I WAS HOT, SO I GOT MYSELF A DRINK.
IT'S A CAN OF JUICE! PERFECT!!
!!
AREN'T YOU IN PAIN?! YOU SHOULDN'T OVERDO IT...
EEK!
...

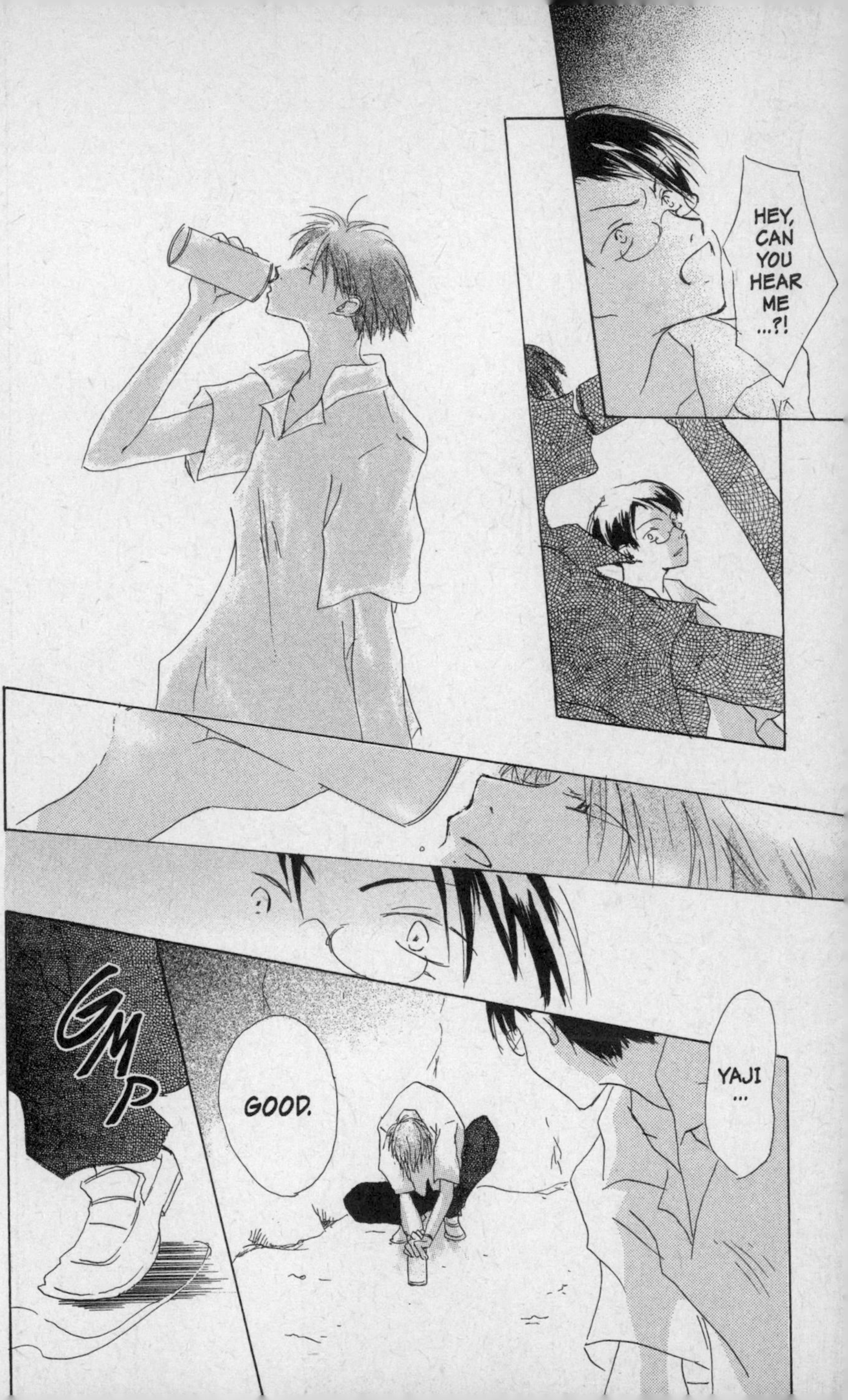
HEY, CAN YOU HEAR ME ...?!
YAJI ...
GOOD.
GMP

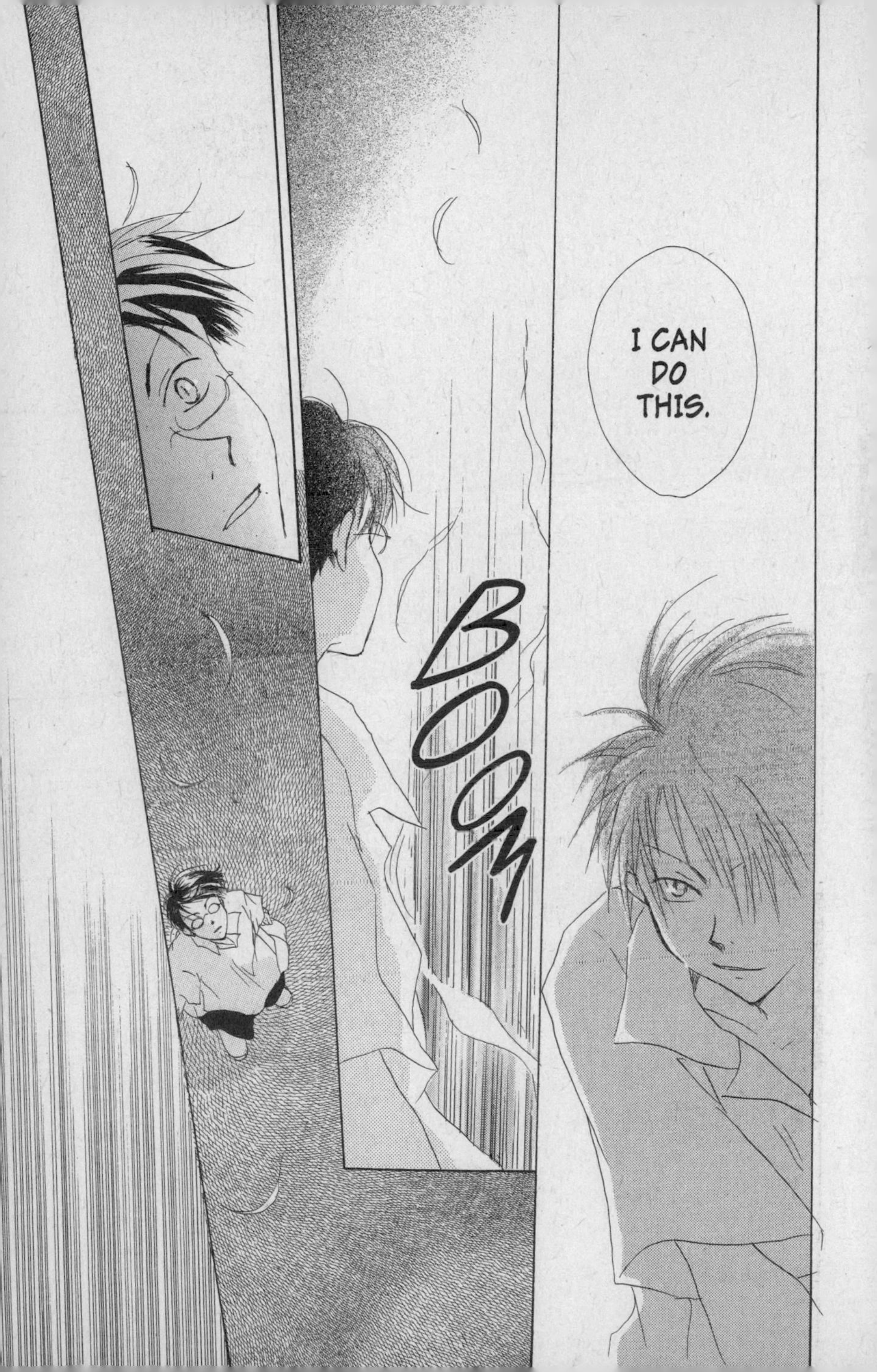
I CAN DO THIS.
BOOM

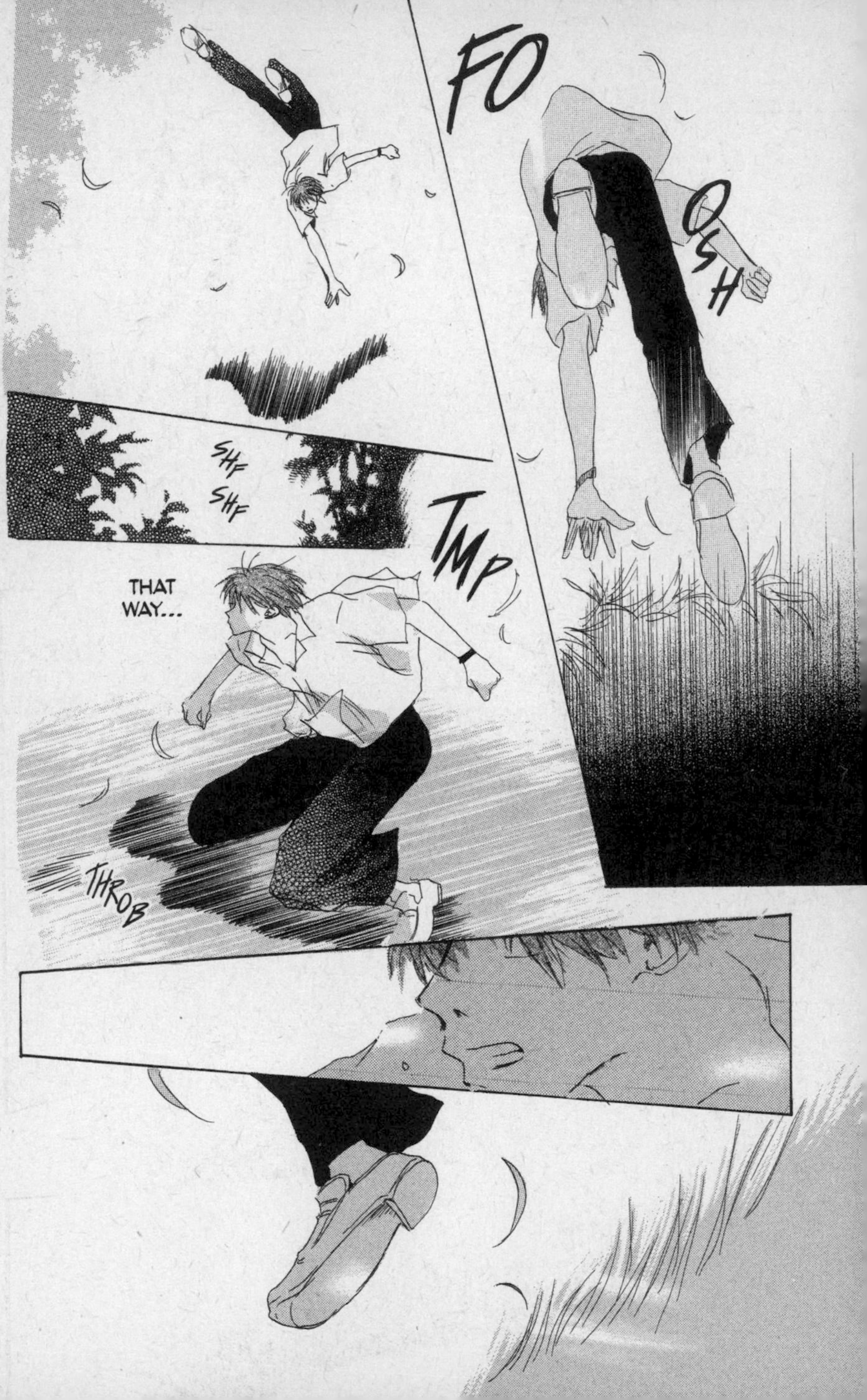
FOOSH
SHF SHF
TMP
THAT WAY...
THROB

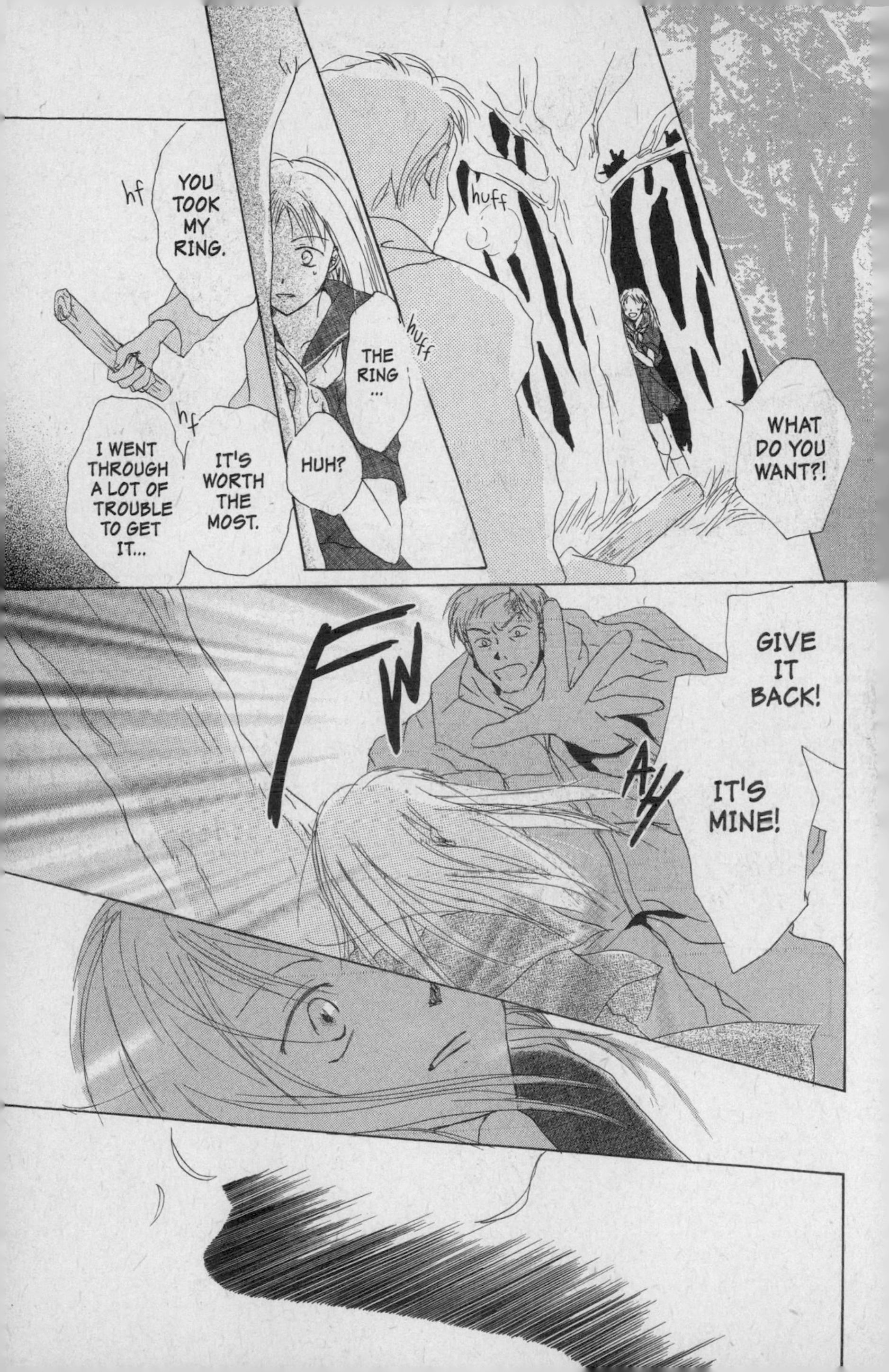
WHAT DO YOU WANT?!
huff
huff
THE RING ...
HUH?
hf
YOU TOOK MY RING.
hf
IT'S WORTH THE MOST.
I WENT THROUGH A LOT OF TROUBLE TO GET IT...
GIVE IT BACK!
IT'S MINE!
FWAH

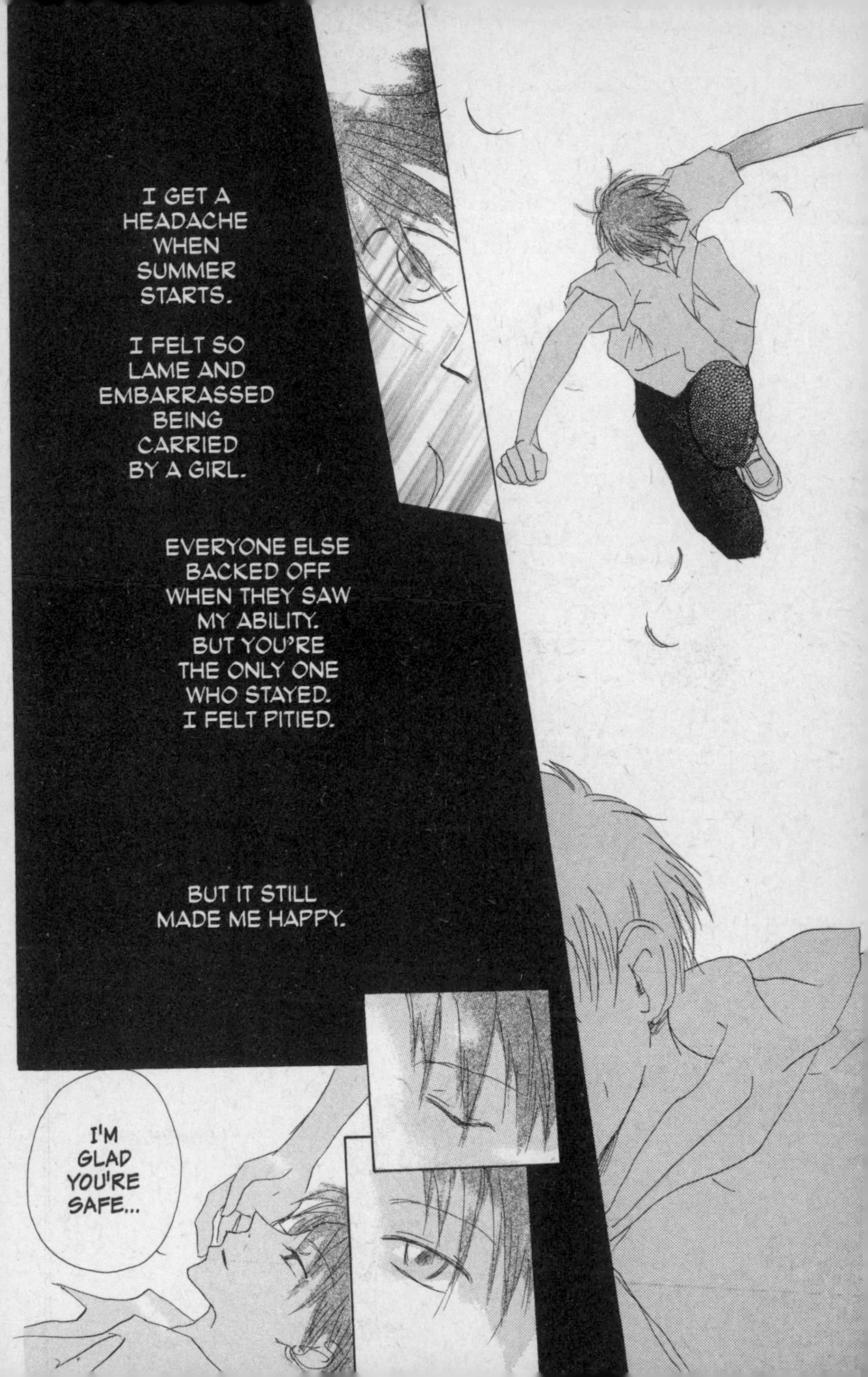
I GET A HEADACHE WHEN SUMMER STARTS.
I FELT SO LAME AND EMBARRASSED BEING CARRIED BY A GIRL.
EVERYONE ELSE BACKED OFF WHEN THEY SAW MY ABILITY. BUT YOU'RE THE ONLY ONE WHO STAYED. I FELT PITIED.
BUT IT STILL MADE ME HAPPY.
I'M GLAD YOU'RE SAFE...

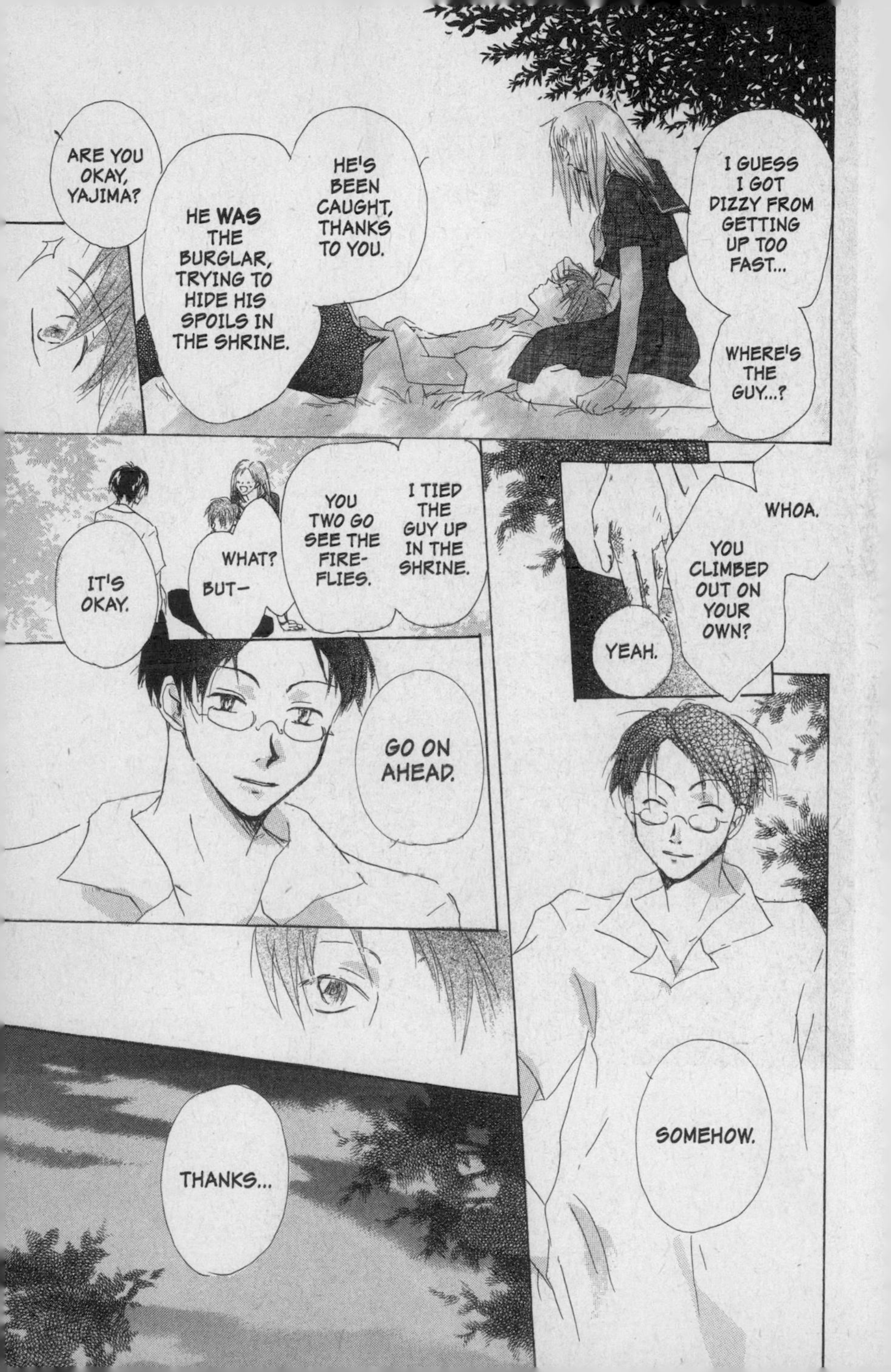
I GUESS I GOT DIZZY FROM GETTING UP TOO FAST...
WHERE'S THE GUY...?
HE'S BEEN CAUGHT, THANKS TO YOU.
HE WAS THE BURGLAR, TRYING TO HIDE HIS SPOILS IN THE SHRINE.
ARE YOU OKAY, YAJIMA?
WHOA.
YOU CLIMBED OUT ON YOUR OWN?
YEAH.
SOMEHOW.
I TIED THE GUY UP IN THE SHRINE.
YOU TWO GO SEE THE FIRE-FLIES.
WHAT? BUT—
IT'S OKAY.
GO ON AHEAD.
THANKS...

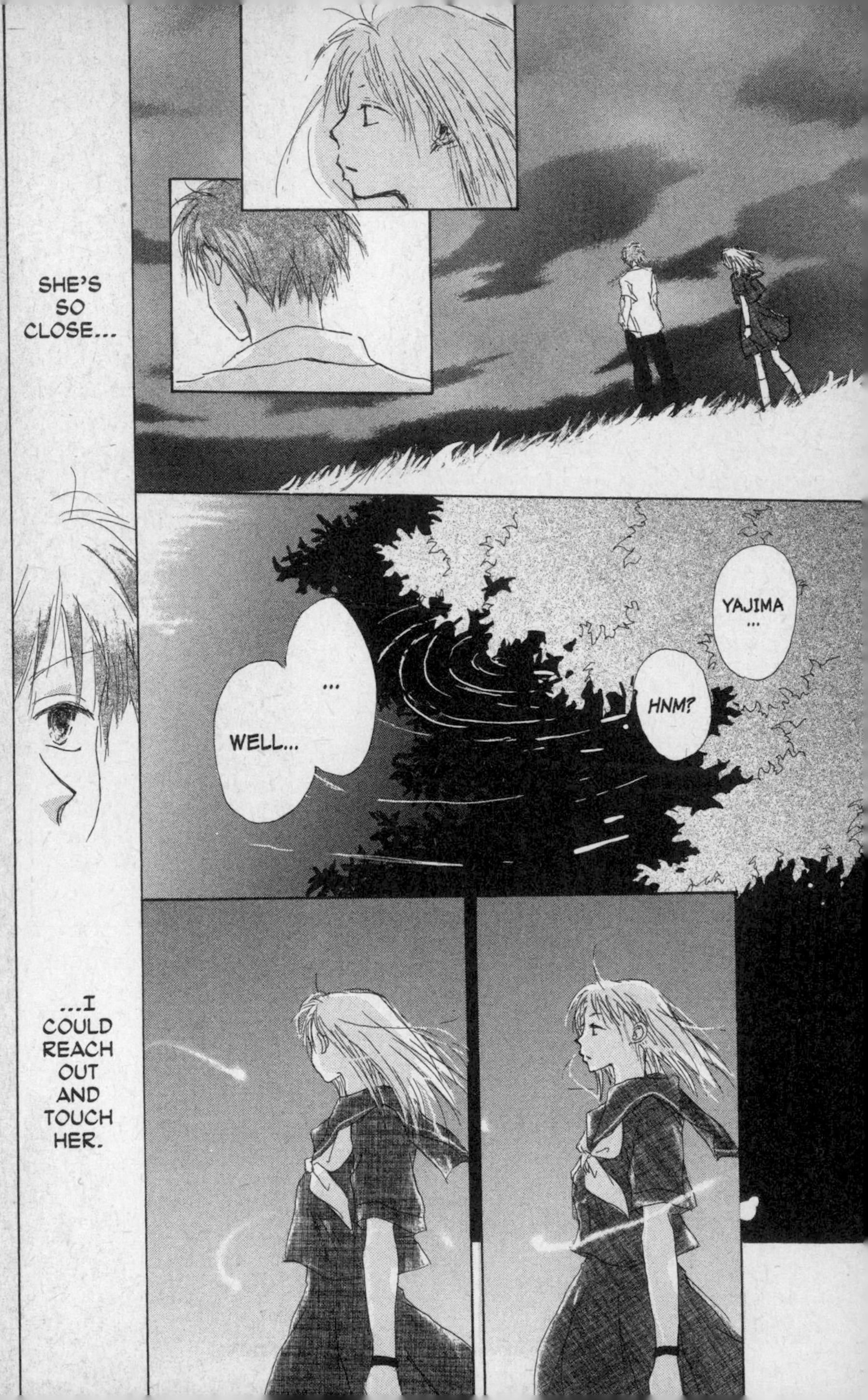
YAJIMA ...
HNM?
... WELL...
SHE'S SO CLOSE...
...I COULD REACH OUT AND TOUCH HER.

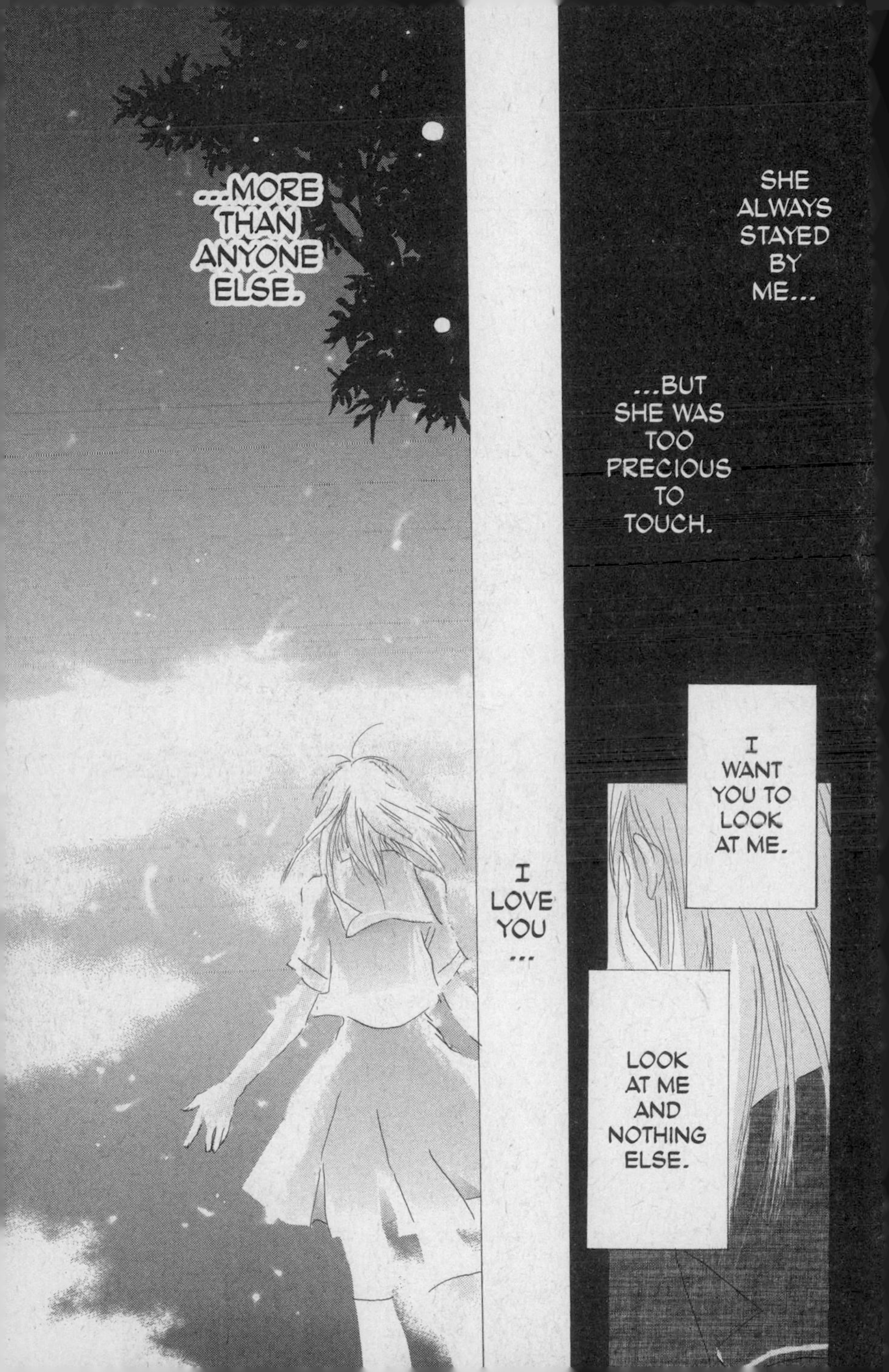
SHE ALWAYS STAYED BY ME...
...BUT SHE WAS TOO PRECIOUS TO TOUCH.
I WANT YOU TO LOOK AT ME.
LOOK AT ME AND NOTHING ELSE.
I LOVE YOU...
...MORE THAN ANYONE ELSE.

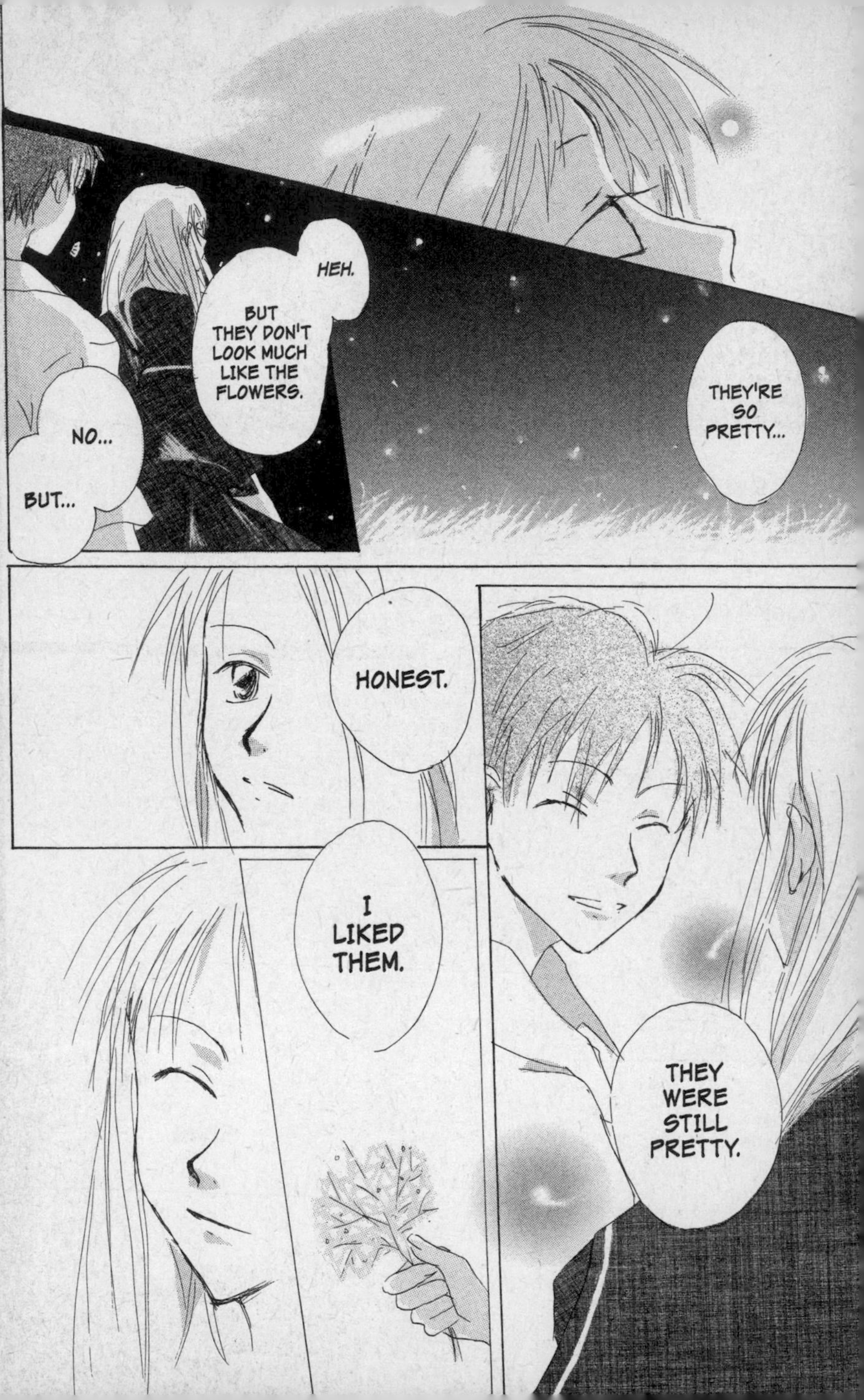
THEY'RE SO PRETTY...
HEH.
BUT THEY DON'T LOOK MUCH LIKE THE FLOWERS.
NO...
BUT...
THEY WERE STILL PRETTY.
HONEST.
I LIKED THEM.

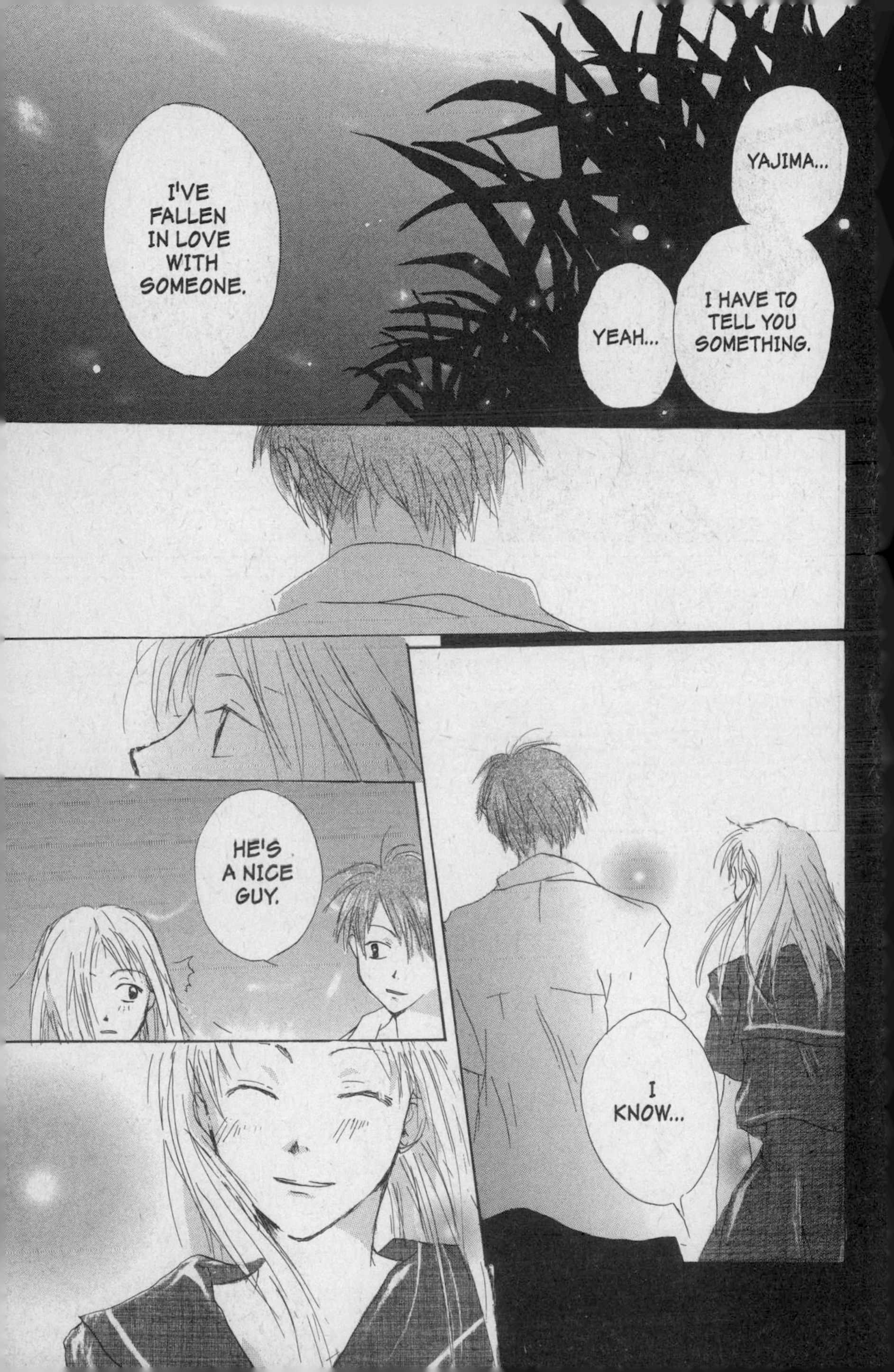
YAJIMA...
I HAVE TO TELL YOU SOMETHING.
YEAH...
I'VE FALLEN IN LOVE WITH SOMEONE.
I KNOW...
HE'S A NICE GUY.

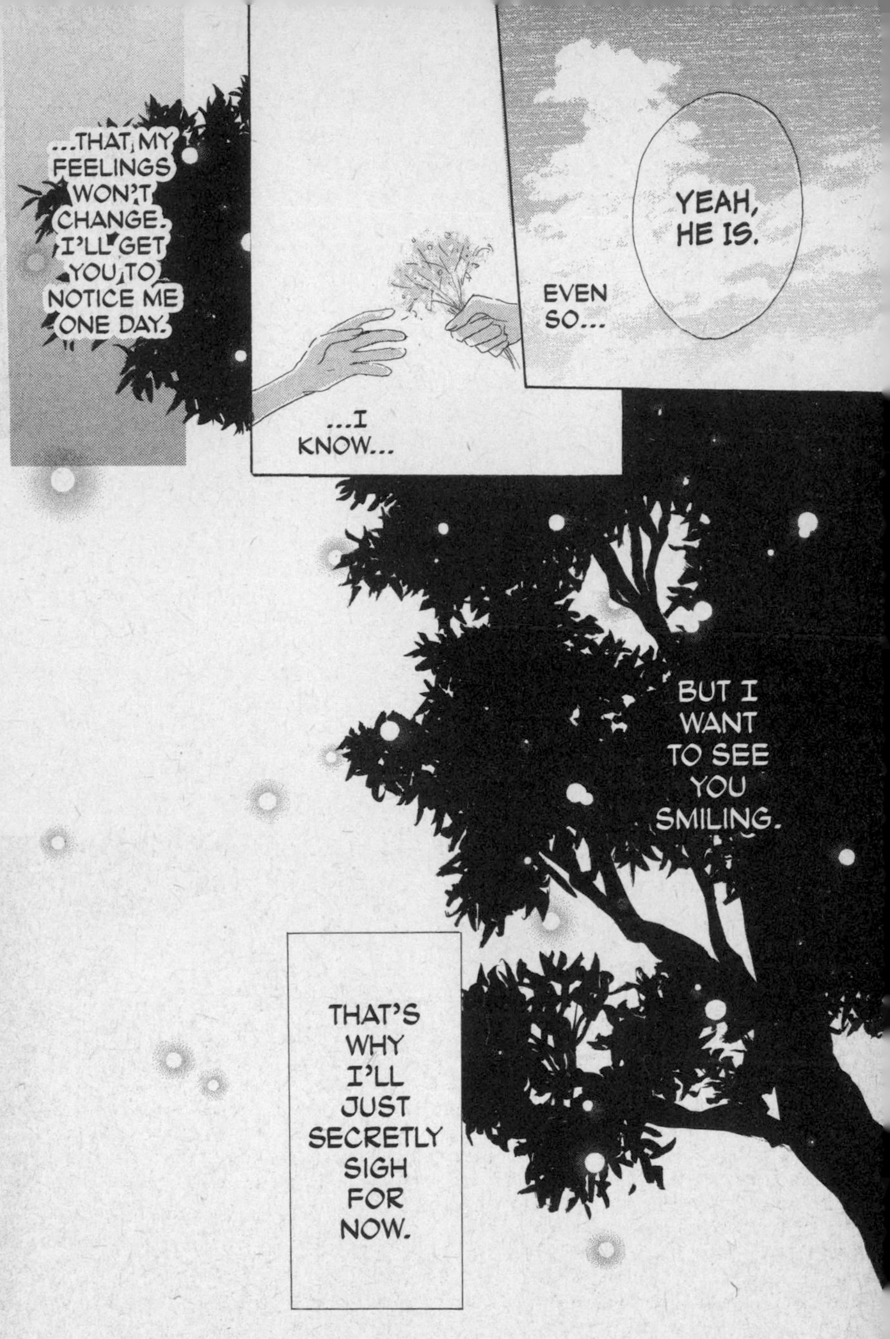
YEAH, HE IS.
EVEN SO...
...I KNOW...
...THAT MY FEELINGS WON'T CHANGE. I'LL GET YOU TO NOTICE ME ONE DAY.
BUT I WANT TO SEE YOU SMILING.
THAT'S WHY I'LL JUST SECRETLY SIGH FOR NOW.

A *Midsummer Sigh*: END.

# AFTER-WORD

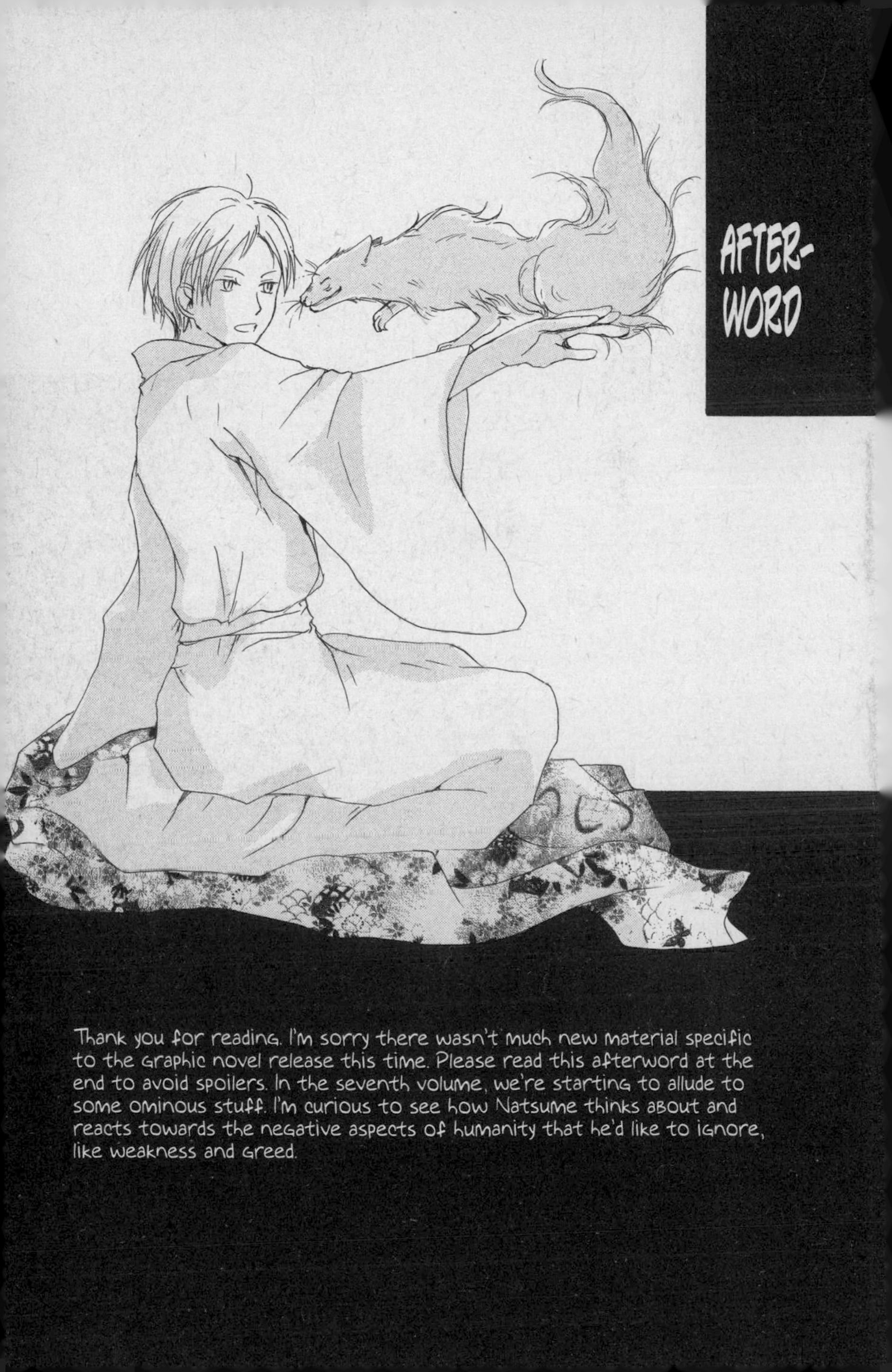

Thank you for reading. I'm sorry there wasn't much new material specific to the graphic novel release this time. Please read this afterword at the end to avoid spoilers. In the seventh volume, we're starting to allude to some ominous stuff. I'm curious to see how Natsume thinks about and reacts towards the negative aspects of humanity that he'd like to ignore, like weakness and greed.

## A MIDSUMMER SIGH

This is one of my early works, so I'm a little embarrassed. This was my first stab at a romantic story back when I didn't have much experience with it. It's a little messy, but its energy is so nostalgic.

I was assigned to do this story out of the blue, and I was at a loss at first. But I do remember that the story was a labor of love. While I was drawing about going to see the fireflies, I felt that I wanted to draw stories about yokai, too. This story contained many of the prototypes of my future manga.

## CHAPTERS 23, 24, 25
### Inhuman Thing

I didn't have a chance to write a story about Matoba until now due to page constraints or manga cycling issues in the magazine. I had fun when I finally got around to it. Matoba's appearance means Natori's hardships become more obvious. Natori settled upon his current philosophy after a lot of reflection. But then he sees Natsume wrestling with the same choices and slogging through the same place he used to be, and it's both amusing and frustrating at the same time for him. Natsume might realize this and not be able to presume so much on his kindness. Natsume and Natori are left with a problem, so I hope to take my time drawing them dealing with it.

## SPECIAL EPISODE 7
### Natsume's Book of Games

I wanted to let Natsume enjoy himself for the first time. And I think the yokai also enjoy playing the game of humbling themselves to the young "Lord Natsume." It's similar to a rookie being thrown into a drinking party with the company's top managers. Both sides roll their eyes at each other, but I hoped they could have some fun.

**Yuki Midorikawa
c/o Shojo Beat
P.O. Box 77010
San Francicso, CA 94107**

Special thanks to:
Tamao Ohki
Chika
Mr. Sato
My sister     Thank you so much.

Thank you for reading.
Yuki Midorikawa
緑川 ゆき   Nov. 2008

AFTERWORD: END

# Natsume's BOOK of FRIENDS

## VOLUME 7 END NOTES

### PAGE 7 PANEL 2: Summer Festival
Local celebrations that are similar to carnivals and have fair food like cotton candy and yakisoba, as wells as toys and games.

### PAGE 10, PANEL 1: Umbrella
Traditional Japanese umbrellas (*bangasa*) were made by covering bamboo frames with oil paper.

### PAGE 59, PANEL 1: Udon, soba
Thick wheat noodles, usually served in hot or cold broth with various toppings. *Soba* are thin buckwheat noodles, served hot or cold.

### PAGE 62, PANEL 7: Jelly noodles
*Tokoroten* are gelatinous strips made from *agar*, a kind of seaweed that can be used in place of gelatin.

**Yuki Midorikawa**
is the creator of *Natsume's Book of Friends*, which was nominated for the Manga Taisho (Cartoon Grand Prize). Her other titles published in Japan include *Hotarubi no Mori e* (Into the Forest of Fireflies), *Hiiro no Isu* (The Scarlet Chair) and *Akaku Saku Koe* (The Voice That Blooms Red).

# NATSUME'S BOOK OF FRIENDS

*Vol. 7*
Shojo Beat Edition

STORY AND ART BY *Yuki Midorikawa*

Translation & Adaptation *Lillian Olsen*
Touch-up Art & Lettering *Sabrina Heep*
Design *Fawn Lau*
Editor *Pancha Diaz*

Natsume Yujincho by Yuki Midorikawa
© Yuki Midorikawa 2009
All rights reserved.
First published in Japan in 2009 by HAKUSENSHA, Inc., Tokyo.
English language translation rights arranged with HAKUSENSHA, Inc., Tokyo.

The stories, characters and incidents mentioned in this publication are entirely fictional.

Printed in Canada

Published by VIZ Media, LLC
P.O. Box 77010
San Francisco, CA 94107

10 9 8 7 6 5 4
First printing, June 2011
Fourth printing, November 2019

viz.com

PARENTAL ADVISORY
NATSUME'S BOOK OF FRIENDS is rated T for Teen and is recommended for ages 13 and up. This volume contains fantasy violence.

shojobeat.com

Escape to the World of the

# Young, Rich & Sexy

Ouran *High School*

# Host Club

## By Bisco Hatori

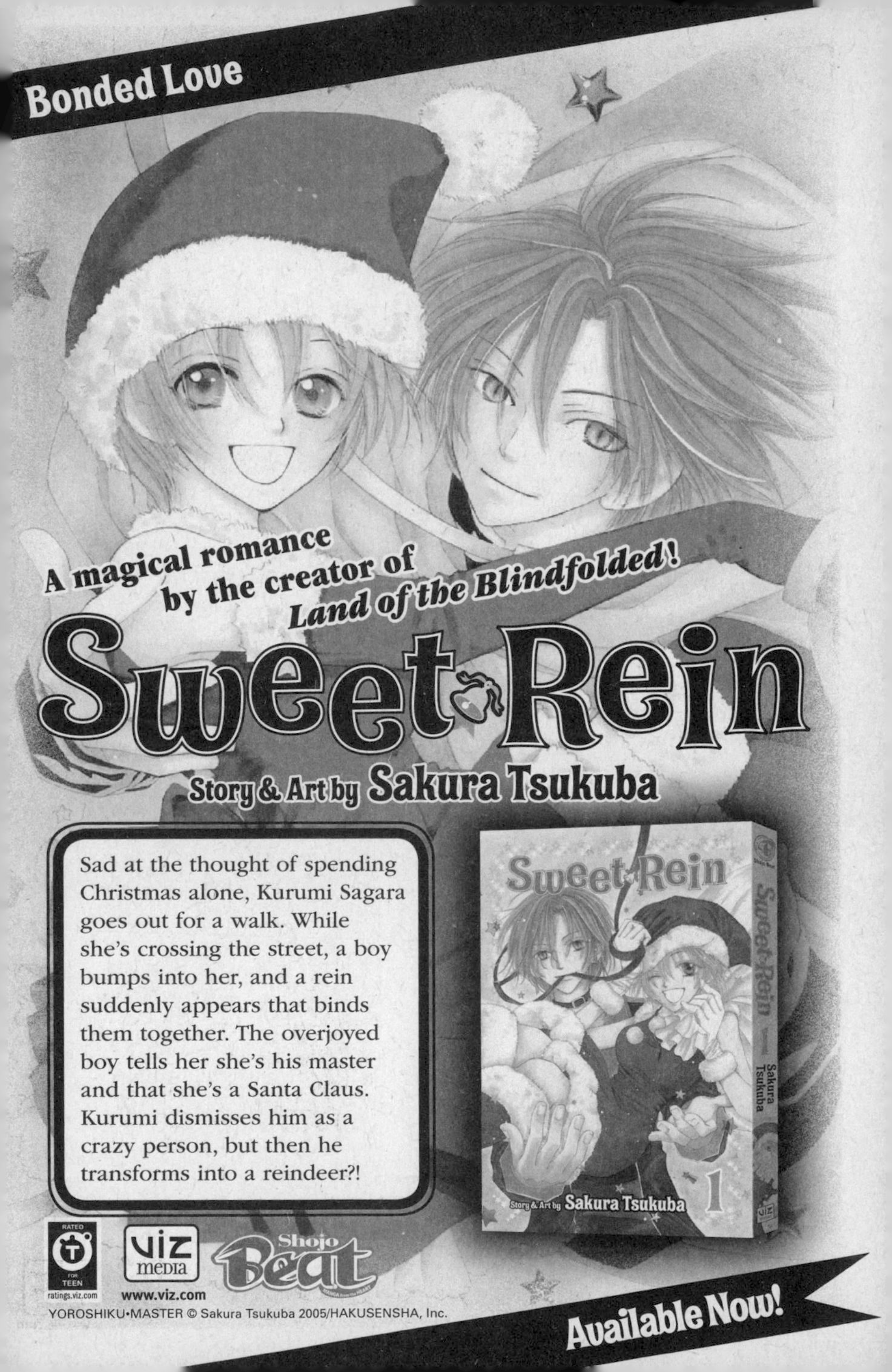
Bonded Love
A magical romance by the creator of Land of the Blindfolded!
Sweet Rein
Story & Art by Sakura Tsukuba
Sad at the thought of spending Christmas alone, Kurumi Sagara goes out for a walk. While she's crossing the street, a boy bumps into her, and a rein suddenly appears that binds them together. The overjoyed boy tells her she's his master and that she's a Santa Claus. Kurumi dismisses him as a crazy person, but then he transforms into a reindeer?!
Sweet Rein
Story & Art by Sakura Tsukuba
1
Sweet Rein
Sakura Tsukuba
RATED T FOR TEEN
ratings.viz.com
VIZ media
www.viz.com
Shojo Beat
YOROSHIKU•MASTER © Sakura Tsukuba 2005/HAKUSENSHA, Inc.
Available Now!

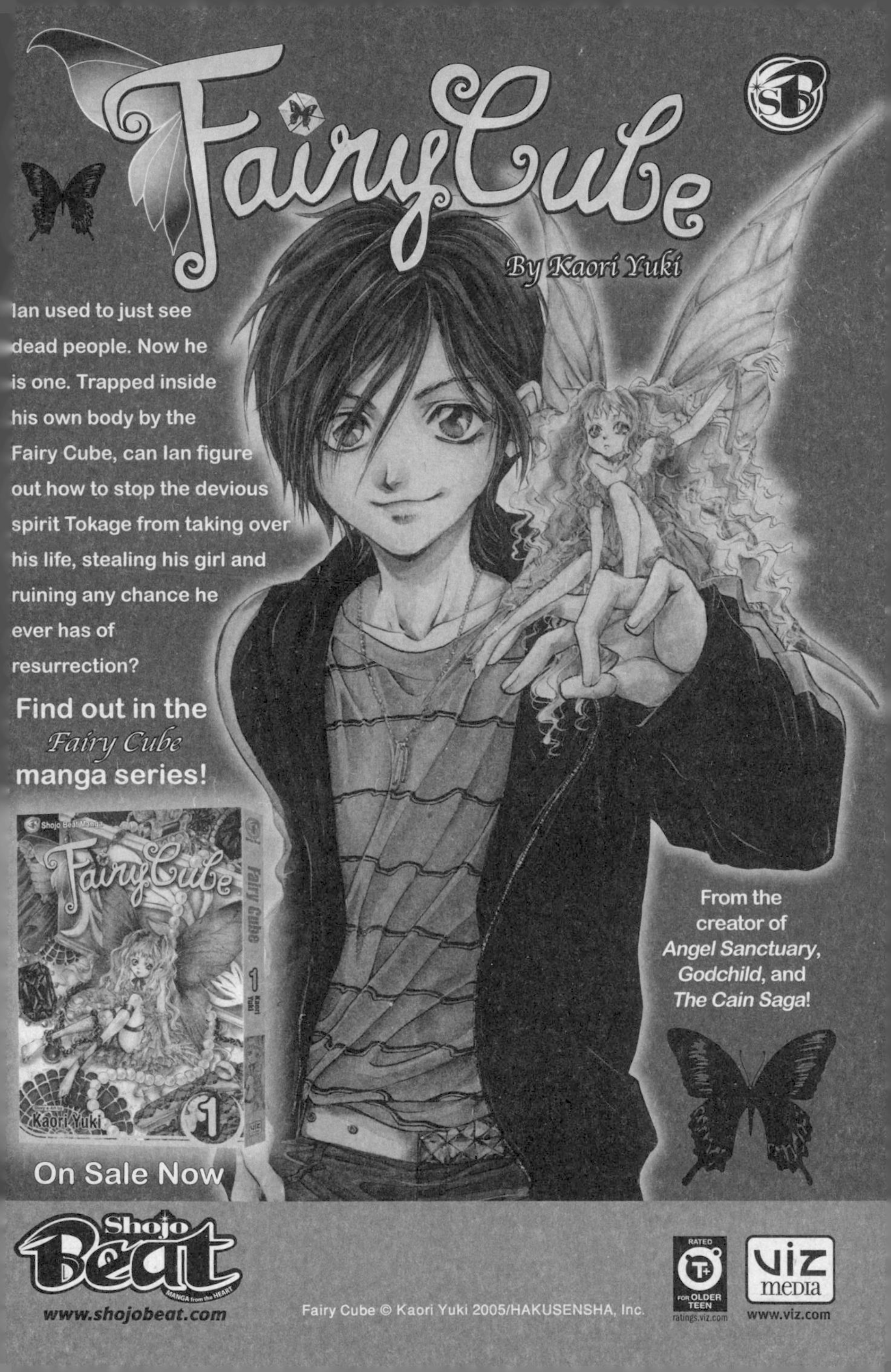

Fairy Cube
By Kaori Yuki
Ian used to just see dead people. Now he is one. Trapped inside his own body by the Fairy Cube, can Ian figure out how to stop the devious spirit Tokage from taking over his life, stealing his girl and ruining any chance he ever has of resurrection?
Find out in the *Fairy Cube* manga series!
Shojo Beat Manga
Fairy Cube
Fairy Cube
1
Kaori Yuki
Kaori Yuki
On Sale Now
From the creator of *Angel Sanctuary*, *Godchild*, and *The Cain Saga*!
Shojo Beat
MANGA from the HEART
www.shojobeat.com
Fairy Cube © Kaori Yuki 2005/HAKUSENSHA, Inc.
RATED
T+
FOR OLDER TEEN
ratings.viz.com
VIZ media
www.viz.com

# SURPRISE!

## You may be reading the wrong way!

It's true: In keeping with the original Japanese comic format, this book reads from right to left— so action, sound effects, and word balloons are completely reversed. This preserves the orientation of the original artwork—plus, it's fun! Check out the diagram shown here to get the hang of things, and then turn to the other side of the book to get started!

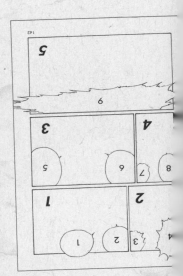

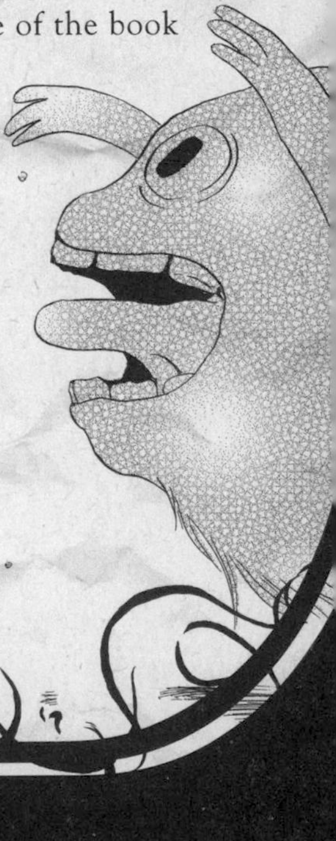